'This volume takes the course of addressing separately domestic arbitration, international arbitration, investment arbitration, and mediation. Each is addressed in scholarly but manageable chapters written by prominent experts in the field. The chapters are well referenced not only to Indian authority but to wider international materials.'

David Joseph QC,
Essex Court Chambers, London

'It is to be commended that Shashank Garg chose to devote a large section to mediation, in which mediation in general and mediation in the Indian legal and cultural contexts are presented in depth. The chapters on mediation in India explain the process and its legal settings, and they offer pragmatic tips for users, advocates, and mediators. This is a timely and optimistic plea to advance mediation culture in India and across the world.'

Greg Bond, University of Applied Sciences Wildau,
Bond and Bond Mediation, Germany

'This volume is a compilation of topical articles authored by leading practitioners of alternative dispute resolution in India, including members of the judiciary, private practitioners, and in-house counsel. Spanning domestic and international arbitration as well as mediation, it provides insightful commentary on subjects such as the appointment of emergency arbitrators and expert witnesses, the Commercial Courts Act 2015, the allocation of costs in international arbitrations, institutional arbitration in India, and the rise of commercial mediation.'

Brooks Daly, Deputy Secretary General,
Permanent Court of Arbitration, The Hague, The Netherlands

'This volume is a rich and ready resource of important issues and challenges that exist in the current system, as well as a commentary on the evolving legal and judicial outlook. The contributors are accomplished judges and lawyers—stalwarts of the profession, their writings reflecting their intellectual zeal and insightfulness. The topics explore the classical as well as current aspects of India's legal framework for alternative dispute resolution with rigorous jurisprudence.'

S.A. Bobde,
Judge, Supreme Court of India

'With contributions from luminaries in the field of ADR, the volume has been strategically divided into three segments, which pave way through the myriad complexities in the fields of arbitration and meditation, with a simple, yet elaborate insight. The grass-root level approach of the book, into understanding arbitration and mediation has the ability to engage a wide array of readers from students, academicians, scholars, to professionals.'

R.K. Agrawal,
Judge, Supreme Court of India

'A large canvas of issues involved have been dealt with in respect of both domestic and international arbitration, investment arbitration, and the amicable resolution method of mediation. Opinions have been expressed by judges, arbitrators, counsels, solicitors, and in-house counsels through the lucid chapters published in this volume specially taking into consideration the amendments to the law and the international trends and practices.'

Sanjay Kishan Kaul,
Judge, Supreme Court of India

'A very timely and original addition in a critically important field.'

Gary Born,
President, Singapore International Arbitration Centre Court

'This volume is an in-depth study of the growth and progress in the said field of arbitration and mediation. The chapters are written by eminent experts who have a varied experience in the field. They are informative and have dealt with a number of issues extensively, such as interim measures, independence of arbitration tribunal, seat of international arbitration, commercial mediation, and so on.'

Jayant Nath,
Judge, High Court of Delhi

'*Alternate Dispute Resolution* will be immensely useful to young lawyers in charting their path to academic excellence and professional success. This coveted compilation provides the readers with a comprehensive resource which succinctly encapsulates the relevant legal concepts in the field of ADR. It will undoubtedly be a crucial addition to the law libraries, illuminating the readers across the country and beyond.'

Dilip B. Bhosale,
Chief Justice, High Court of Allahabad

'The volume is an all-encompassing compilation of essays by authors who exhibit a deep understanding of the underlying theme that is the importance of ADR practices as means of resolving disputes in India. A product of Shashank Garg's tireless efforts, it is a comprehensive volume which addresses a diverse audience comprising not only the conventional players in our field, such as lawyers, judges, academicians, and law students but may also be of interest to general public.'

Gita Mittal,
Acting Chief Justice, High Court of Delhi

'*Alternative Dispute Resolution: The Indian Perspective* is a book one of its kind, seldom found but desperately sought. It deals with the diverse nuances of the subject making an inimitable contribution to the field especially for those who have an interest in arbitration, want to familiarize themselves with the basics and even those who are on a hunt for a comprehensive conception.'

A.K. Sikri,
Judge, Supreme Court of India

'This volume is avowedly distinct from other books on the same subject and is a must-in-hand for every user of alternative dispute resolution practices as it is written in a language that is lucid and explains the subject in a notional manner instead of the classic method of provision-wise study by memorization. A sweeping coverage of the Indian law and the amplitude of the subject matter are the essence of this volume, but it is indeed the reconnaissance of best practices that forms the silver lining. The arrangement of the book as conceived and adopted by Shashank Garg and maintained by the contributors is exactly what makes it a remarkable beneficence to the domain of ADR and an opulent resource for both Indian practitioners and those seeking to resolve their disputes with the aid of ADR.'

Martin Hunter,
International Arbitration Expert, Essex Court Chambers, London

Alternative Dispute Resolution

Alternative Dispute Resolution
The Indian Perspective

Edited by
SHASHANK GARG

Guest Editor
JUSTICE AJIT PRAKASH SHAH

OXFORD
UNIVERSITY PRESS

OXFORD

UNIVERSITY PRESS

Oxford University Press is a department of the University of Oxford.
It furthers the University's objective of excellence in research, scholarship,
and education by publishing worldwide. Oxford is a registered trademark of
Oxford University Press in the UK and in certain other countries.

Published in India by
Oxford University Press
2/11 Ground Floor, Ansari Road, Daryaganj, New Delhi 110 002, India

ISBN-13: 978-0-19-948361-7
ISBN-10: 0-19-948361-2

Typeset in Adobe Garamond Pro 11/13
by Tranistics Data Technologies, New Delhi 110 044
Printed in India by Replika Press Pvt. Ltd

Contents

Foreword by Alexis Mourre   xiii

Preface   xv

Guest Editor's Note by Justice Ajit Prakash Shah   xvii

Introduction: Experts on ADR in India by Justice D.Y. Chandrachud   xxi

List of Abbreviations   xxvii

PART I   DOMESTIC ARBITRATION

1. Alternative Dispute Resolution: Is It an Alternative
   Mechanism?   3
   Arijit Pasayat

2. Interim Measures under the Indian Arbitration
   and Conciliation Act, 1996   10
   Atmaram N.S. Nadkarni

3. Impartiality and Independence of the Arbitral Tribunal   20
   R.C. Lahoti and *Divyakant Lahoti*

4. The Doctrine of *Kompetenz–Kompetenz*: An Indian Perspective   38
   Suresh C. Gupte

5. Grounds for Challenging an Arbitral Award in India   63
   Tushar Mehta

6. Rectification of Jurisdiction to Entertain Arbitration Applications in the Commercial Courts Act 2015: Pending Practical Re-alignment to Restore the Statutory Right to Appeal? 80
Ajay Bhargava

7. Institutional Arbitration in India: The Way Forward 92
Deepto Roy and *Madhukeshwar Desai*

8. Emergency Arbitrator in the Indian Context 120
Tejas Karia

9. Rise of the Expert Witness in Alternative Dispute Resolution 135
Gagan Puri, Geetu Singh, and *Deepankar Sanwalka*

10. Med-Arb 146
Rajiv Shakhder

11. Limits of Arbitrability: Some Jurisdictional Issues in the Context of Public Law Remedies 154
Parag P. Tripathi

12. Arbitration: An In-house Counsel's Perspective 172
Sanjeev Gemawat

PART II INTERNATIONAL ARBITRATION

13. The Concept of Seat in International Arbitration: Developments in India 187
Vikramjit Sen and *Satyajit Gupta*

14. Introduction to Investment Arbitration: A Perspective from India 206
Shreyas Jayasimha and *Radha Raghavan*

15. Allocation of Costs in International Arbitration 233
Sonal Kr. Singh and *Manish Lamba*

16. International Arbitration with an Indian Connection 249
Sheila Ahuja

PART III   MEDIATION

17. Commercial Mediation: An Evolving Frontier of
    Alternative Dispute Resolution in India   319
    Allison M. Malkin and *D. Gracious Timothy*

18. Mediation in India: Practical Tips and Techniques   389
    Thomas P. Valenti and *Tanima Tandon*

    Annexure I: Resources   423

    Annexure II: References   427

    Index   429

    About the Editor and Contributors   443

Foreword

I have been invited to contribute a foreword to this volume and I am delighted to have been given this opportunity. The development of arbitration in Asia, especially India, has been spectacular as I have keenly observed over the years. The number of arbitrations in India is rapidly increasing, and it is my sincere belief that India is on the way to develop itself as a centre for dispute resolution services, apart from becoming an economic superpower.

There are several books on Alternative Dispute Resolution (ADR) which are available as authoritative texts for practitioners of international arbitration. What distinguishes this volume from the others is the diverse Indian perspective that it provides. Several eminent jurists, senior advocates, partners of various law firms, and individual practitioners, among others, have all examined a number of topics in a conceptual manner. They have all, through their experiences and plethora of knowledge gathered over the years, successfully illustrated the principal features of ADR, mainly arbitration, in India.

The volume has been thoughtfully divided into three parts: the first part of the volume presents a panorama of domestic arbitration and discusses essential topics like impartiality and independence of the arbitral tribunal, grounds for challenging an award, institutional arbitration, and emergency arbitrator. The second part explores the classic aspects of international arbitration, the concept of seat, and provides a perspective on investment arbitration, all in the context of India. Lastly, the third part offers an insight into the development of mediation in India culminating with practical tips and techniques for mediation, which will prove beneficial to the practitioner.

Each writer has tried to cover the topic in easy-to-understand language and eliminated unnecessary details which make simplicity and clarity the hallmarks of this volume.

I want to congratulate Shashank Garg, for putting this excellent volume together with its unique focus on India. This volume is an extremely remarkable contribution to the world of arbitration proving valuable to arbitration practitioners, academics, scholars, and students of arbitration interested in arbitration in India.

ALEXIS MOURRE
ICC International Court of Arbitration
Paris

Preface

This volume is not a commentary on the subject, although it covers a range of critical aspects of ADR practice in India. Seasoned practitioners, arbitrators, mediators, and third-party experts from India and abroad have come together and contributed to this volume. It would not be an exaggeration if the last five years are called the renaissance of ADR in India: we not only saw a dramatic rise in interest amongst parties but also saw how Indian courts started dealing with the concept of justice in commercial issues. The Supreme Court of India uplifted the country's image worldwide through judgments like BALCO and Associated Builders. Interestingly, Indian laymen have always found it difficult to come to terms with drastic changes brought out in law, either by legislature or by courts; thus, end users of this process are least informed of most crucial concepts or they end up making incorrect choices. Through this publication, we have tried to fill the gap of information by providing conceptual understanding of frequently asked questions. Divided into three sections beginning with domestic arbitration followed by international arbitration and lastly mediation, this volume through its eighteen chapters goes into the process of deciphering both law and practice. This is not an exhaustive text for all the raging issues India is facing in the practise of ADR, but this is certainly a humble beginning in providing answers.

An effort has been made to simplify controversies and twisted conceptual paradoxes that are cropping up each day. Contributors have used simple and lucid presentation skills while keeping the in-depth analysis of their topic intact. Illustrious arbitrators from Indian judiciary, who have come on board for this project, have carefully chosen their subjects and have successfully busted the myth about retired Indian judges lacking the skill set to take the centre stage of international arbitration. I would therefore begin with thanking Justice R.C. Lahoti, Justice Arijit Pasayat, and Justice Vikramjit Sen for their equable contribution. This volume also has the rare privilege of having contributions from sitting judges, namely, Justice Shakdher and Justice Gupte, who have taken out time from their extremely busy schedule and have raised the standards of academic excellence and contribution a judge can make. I am grateful to the senior advocates who readily believed in this publication and made excellent contributions on some of the most important questions in domestic arbitration practice. Contributions from other experts, namely, Atmaram N.S. Nadkarni, Tushar Mehta, Parag P. Tripathi, Divyakant Lahoti, Ajay Bhargava, Deepto Roy, Madhukeshwar Desai, Tejas Karia, Gagan Puri, Geetu Singh, Deepankar Sanwalka, Sanjeev Gemawat, Satyajit Gupta, Shreyas Jayasimha, Radha Raghavan, Sonal Kr. Singh, Manish Lamba, Sheila Ahuja, Allison M. Malkin, D. Gracious Timothy, Thomas P. Valenti, and Tanima Tandon, have made this project a reality by setting a new standard in knowledge-sharing domain for Indian legal fraternity.

I cannot thank enough for the support and encouragement provided by Justice Ajit Prakash Shah as the guest editor of this volume, it would not be out of place to mark special appreciation for Namit Oberoi who assisted me in the project end-to-end and Samridhi Hota for her able assistance. I am greatly indebted to Justice D.Y. Chandrachud for writing the most insightful introduction and Alexis Mourre for writing the foreword. I would fail in my duty if I do not thank Justice A.K. Sikri, Justice S.A. Bobde, Justice R.K. Agrawal, Justice Sanjay Kishan Kaul, Justice Geeta Mittal, Justice Jayant Nath, Justice Sanjeev Sachdeva, Justice Vibhu Bakhru, David Joseph QC, Brooks Daly, Greg Bond, and Gary Born for sparing time to review this publication and for providing critical inputs.

SHASHANK GARG

Guest Editor's Note

This volume is a practitioner's guide and ready-reckoner aimed to provide an account of the evolving practice and procedure of ADR in India through the perspectives of highly regarded and expert practitioners in the field. Noted national and international experts with various practice focuses within the domain of dispute resolution have come together to answer complex legal issues relating to ADR and have addressed common usages and best practices of dispute resolution in India. The guide is not a commentary on ADR processes nor does it seek to be exhaustive or comprehensive. Instead, it attempts to provide the necessary navigational correction to in-house counsel and corporates, while also providing insight into legal, practical, and strategic considerations during the resolution process, keeping in view the evolving legal environment and the judicial outlook in India.

We commence with the chapter 'Alternative Dispute Resolution: Is It an Alternative Mechanism?' by Hon'ble Justice (Retd.) Arijit Pasayat, Supreme Court of India, which sets out the principles for using ADR mechanisms in a large developing country like India. It carefully analyses the potential of the ADR machinery in giving impetus to the constitutional and administrative goal of creating an effective, inexpensive, and speedy justice delivery framework. It also lays the groundwork for the subsequent articles which delve into specific legal and practical issues around the Indian Arbitration and Conciliation Act, 1996.

Atmaram N.S. Nadkarni and Tushar Mehta, both Additional Solicitors General of India, review, in their respective contributions, the law and practice of the grant of interim measures in Indian arbitrations and challenges against arbitral awards in Indian courts. A succinct comment by the former Chief Justice (Retd.) of India R.C. Lahoti and Divyakant Lahoti, Advocate-on-Record, Supreme Court of India, deals with the statutory and judicial safeguards for ensuring the impartiality and independence of arbitrators towards the arbitral process, the contesting parties, and the outcome of the dispute, followed by a discussion around the doctrine of *Kompetenz-Kompetenz*, steering through the doctrine's development and its legal and practical considerations.

Deepto Roy and Madhukeshwar Desai's chapter addresses the malignant problems of ad hoc arbitrations and argues for promoting the use of arbitral institutions in India to ensure a predictable, friendly, and transparent environment for parties. Individual sections are then devoted to select practices which are relatively new to Indian arbitration: the concept of emergency arbitrators, the role and utility of expert witnesses and claim consultants, and the idea of 'Med-Arb'—a form of arbitration which starts with a mediation but in the event of its failure, proceeds like an arbitration (with a binding adjudication on the contesting parties).

Another fascinating read is Senior Advocate Parag P. Tripathi's contribution on the interplay between arbitration and public law, cases such as laws of fraud, oppression, and mismanagement, competition law and policy. It analyses issues of compatibility of arbitration with disputes involving interests above and beyond those of the parties. The last chapter in Part I is by Sanjeev Gemawat who provides an interesting perspective towards arbitration as an in-house counsel.

Part II of the volume focuses on international arbitration. The fast-evolving realm of 'investment arbitration law' is the subject of discussion by Shreyas Jayasimha and Radha Raghavan, who probe into the (typical) bundles of rights and responsibilities tied with investors and state parties in such arbitrations and revisit the various (unfortunate) encounters the Indian sovereign had to face in the domain of international arbitration law. The part ends with 'International Arbitration with an Indian Connection' by Sheila Ahuja of Allen & Overy, which provides a comprehensive commentary on aspects of international arbitration which are closely tied with issues of Indian arbitral law and practice.

The last part of the volume is devoted to mediation, an effective ADR tool gaining immense popularity the world over. Various jurisdictions are increasingly embracing comprehensive mediation frameworks and encouraging problem-solving mediation advocacy through statutory and institutional mechanisms. The acute shortage of local material available on the subject of commercial mediation highlights the unrealized potential of mediation in the Indian legal market. In this regard, a detailed analysis of the concept of mediation and its unique potential in transforming commercial dispute resolution eradicating the prevailing roadblocks in efficient justice delivery in India is provided by Allison M. Malkin and D. Gracious Timothy in the first of the two chapters of the last part.

The volume ends with a chapter by Thomas P. Valenti and Tanima Tandon providing useful practical insights and techniques in making the best use of the rather underused mechanism of mediation.

JUSTICE AJIT PRAKASH SHAH
Former Chief Justice of Delhi High Court

Introduction

Experts on ADR in India

The diversity of human needs, interests, and goals have led to conflicts becoming an inevitable part of our lives. While some of these conflicts are resolved through communication and cooperation, some require the assistance of a third party for their resolution. Thomas Crum, who wrote *The Magic of Conflict* and taught people to resolve conflicts creatively, said, 'Our lives are not dependent on whether or not we have conflict. It is what we do with conflict that makes the difference. Resolving conflict is rarely about who is right. It is about acknowledgment and appreciation of differences.'

In India, the settlement of disputes without court intervention dates back to ancient times. Our ancient texts tell us about systems of arbitration and mediation that were practised to resolve various kinds of disputes that arose within the community. In the last several decades, alternative dispute resolution (ADR) methods, such as arbitration and mediation, are being increasingly resorted, particularly, to resolve commercial disputes. Globalization and a rapidly changing landscape of business and commerce have led to a demand for efficient and time-bound methods of dispute resolution, which are comparable to international standards. The growing relevance of alternative forms of dispute resolution marks a significant departure from a traditional adversarial legal set-up. However, the popularity of ADR is not limited solely to commercial disputes. Legal practitioners are increasingly encouraging the resolution of non-commercial disputes such as matrimony, family, and employment through ADR methods like mediation. Indeed, mediation can be adopted to resolve almost all kinds of non-criminal disputes. Mediation expert Joseph Grynbaum has famously remarked on the benefits of ADR that, 'An ounce of mediation is worth a pound of arbitration and a ton of litigation!'

American philosopher and psychologist William James said, 'Whenever two people meet, there are really six people present. There is each man as he sees himself, each man as the other person sees him, and each man as he really is.' An effective dispute resolution process must comprehend all these perspectives.

This volume is an endeavour by various experts in ADR to explore contemporary aspects of the law and practice of ADR in India. Kenneth Kaye, a leading expert in resolution of family business conflicts, said, 'If necessity is the mother of invention, conflict is its father'. Conflicts have led to the innovation of alternate forms of dispute resolution which are best suited to the needs and priorities of the parties involved in the dispute. ADR grew out of a desire to empower and better meet the needs of disputants, as well as an alternative adversarial court system and its associated costs and delays. Consequently, ADR is now referred to as 'appropriate dispute resolution', as the emphasis is shifting towards finding the best or most appropriate way of resolving a particular dispute.

The initial chapters of the volume analyse diverse issues related to domestic arbitration in India. Justice Arijit Pasayat sheds light on the meaning of ADR, India's constitutional commitment to securing access to justice for its citizens, different methods of ADR practised in India, and the rationale behind adopting ADR. Atmaram N.S. Nadkarni delves into the scope of interim measures under Indian arbitration law and related judicial developments. Justice R.C. Lahoti and Divyakant Lahoti highlight the importance of independence and impartiality as 'indispensable prerequisites' of the arbitration process. Justice Suresh C. Gupte traces the genesis and historical development of the *Kompetenz-Kompetenz* doctrine (the power of the arbitral tribunal to rule on its own jurisdiction), the position under Indian arbitration law, current problems, and the road ahead. Tushar Mehta looks at the various grounds on which arbitral awards can be challenged in an Indian court, especially the ground of 'public policy'.

The Commercial Courts, Commercial Division, and Commercial Appellate Division of the High Courts Act, 2015, was enacted on 31 December 2015, replacing an earlier ordinance. The Act had retrospective effect from the date on which the 2015 ordinance came into force (23 October 2015). This has led to some complexities and ambiguities which have been addressed by Ajay Bhargava. Deepto Roy and Madhukeshwar Desai identify the slow growth of institutional arbitration in India as one of the significant impediments to arbitration not being able to achieve its full potential in India. They explore the disadvantages of the current culture of ad hoc arbitration and the advantages of institutional arbitration and conclude that the strict procedure to be followed under the 2015 Amendment Act is likely to favour the growth of institutional arbitration. Tejas Karia has analysed the concept of emergency arbitration and the legal framework governing it under Indian law and institutional rules. Gagan Puri, Geetu Singh, and Deepankar Sanwalka highlight the role and functions of an expert witness. The chapter contemplates the forms of disputes where expert witnesses can be crucial and the practices that ought to be adopted by such witnesses. Rajiv Shakhder comments on the shortcomings of arbitration practice in India and dwells upon the intricacies of mediation-arbitration and its potential benefits in the Indian scenario. He thus analyses the less popular arbitration-mediation process.

Parag P. Tripathi examines the limits of arbitrability in the context of public law remedies and concludes that in private law, arbitration is the chosen forum of dispute resolution even where concurrent court and arbitration proceedings are likely to result in conflicting judgments. However, when there are specific statutory provisions in the realm of public law as in the case of competition law, or like the statutory remedies of oppression and mismanagement under the Companies Act, 'the private forum of arbitration may have to yield to the larger public interest'. Sanjeev Gemawat provides a perspective about the 'evolution of the role of in-house counsel in the present business environment and the difficulty the in-house counsel faces in framing a dispute resolution policy in the backdrop of present arbitration system in India'.

The second segment of the volume explores various topics of relevance in international arbitration from an India-centric lens. Vikramjit Sen and Satyajit Gupta analyse the development of precedent in India with regard to the concept of the seat in international arbitration and the profound consequences of the seat on the arbitration process. Shreyas Jayasimha and Radha Raghavan write about the genesis of investment arbitration, watershed events in India's history of investment treaty arbitration, and the rights of parties under bilateral investment treaties. International commercial arbitration having become an increasingly expensive affair, Sonal Kr. Singh looks at the existing practices and factors that influence allocation of funds for international arbitration in India. Sheila Ahuja distinguishes between different types of arbitration proceedings with an Indian connection and addresses some of the issues that arise in the context of international arbitration proceedings related to India.

The final segment of the volume provides an insight into mediation, the next most popular method of dispute resolution which is useful to resolve various kinds of disputes. Allison M. Malkin and D. Gracious Timothy explore the potential for mediation as a dispute resolution method for commercial disputes in the rapidly changing economic and business environment of India. They shed light upon the existing legal and regulatory framework for mediation in India, the stages of mediation, the role of the mediator, and the suitability of mediation for different kinds of disputes. Thomas P. Valenti and Tanima Tandon, in their chapter on 'Practical Tips and Techniques', analyse the historical evolution of mediation in India, the role of every stakeholder in mediation, specific mediation advocacy tools, and the enforceability of mediated settlements.

Appropriate dispute resolution necessitates an awareness of the range of dispute resolution processes that are available and weighing the advantages and disadvantages of each process for the specific dispute, before the most suitable method of dispute resolution can be chosen for a particular dispute. As French moralist Joseph Joubert has said, 'The aim of argument, or of discussion, should not be victory, but progress', parties must not make winning their sole priority in a dispute, at the expense of time, money, and other resources that are expended in prolonged disputes. This is particularly relevant in India where the judicial system is overburdened. Dispute resolution methods such as mediation emphasize on the interests of the parties and enable them to arrive at a win-win solution for both, which make it more successful in the long run. Additionally, there are various advantages such as party autonomy, confidentiality, and flexibility that address the interests of the concerned, better than an adversarial system.

The ADR experiment has been largely successful in Western countries with advanced legal systems. Countries such as the United Kingdom have made it mandatory to refer certain kinds of family disputes to mediation, before approaching courts. Sandra Day O'Connor, a former US Supreme Court judge, said that 'The courts of this country should not be the places where resolution of disputes begins. They should be the places where the disputes end after alternative methods of resolving disputes have been considered and tried.'

India is making strides in embracing ADR. Some of the recent steps include the Arbitration Amendment Act of 2015 which has provisions that seek to make arbitration in India a time-bound and efficient process of dispute resolution, with minimum court interference. Courts across the country are also increasingly supporting mediation and referring several species of disputes that come before them to mediation. In a country such as India where dispute resolution mechanisms are dynamic and will continue to develop to meet India's rapidly changing needs, there are myriad opportunities for practitioners of ADR. The extent to which ADR will be successful in India will depend largely on the fostering of an ADR culture within the bar, bench, law schools, and society.

The expertise of practitioners of ADR in India is reflected in the essays authored by them and will enrich existing literature and scholarship in a constantly evolving area of law. The efforts of the authors and editors in creating this comprehensive volume of essays exploring the nuances of ADR in India are commendable. The diversity of topics covered is sure to stimulate readers' minds and broaden their horizons and perspectives. The language of the text makes it accessible to a wide range of readers (not limited to lawyers) who may be interested in exploring this field. With the rapid pace of developments in the field of ADR, it is of critical importance that practitioners as well as law students are kept abreast of these developments. The volume is a laudable effort in this regard.

JUSTICE D.Y. CHANDRACHUD
Judge, Supreme Court of India

Abbreviations

APEC	Asia Pacific Economic Cooperation
BATNA	Best Alternative to a Negotiated Agreement
BIPA	Bilateral Investment Protection Agreement
BIT	Bilateral Investment Treaty
CAMP	Centre for Advanced Mediation Practice
CECA	Comprehensive Economic Cooperation Agreements
CEPA	Comprehensive Economic Partnership Agreements
CETA	Comprehensive Economic and Trade Agreement
CETAC	China International Economic and Trade Arbitration Commission
CIC	Central Information Commission
CPC	Civil Procedure Code
CRCICA	Cairo Regional Centre for International Commercial Arbitration
DIS	German Institution of Arbitration
DPC	Dabhol Power Corporation
DRB	Dispute Review Board
ECT	Energy Charter Treaty
FCN	Friendship, Commerce, and Navigation
FET	Fair and Equitable Treatment
FRAND	Fair, Reasonable, and Non-discriminatory Terms
FTA	Free Trade Agreement
GATS	General Agreement on Trade in Services
GE	General Electric
HKIAC	Hong Kong International Arbitration Centre
IACA	Indian Arbitration and Conciliation Act
ICA	International Court of Arbitration

ICC	International Chamber of Commerce
ICD	Inter Corporate Deposits
ICDR	International Centre for Dispute Resolution
ICSID	International Centre for Settlement of Investment Disputes
IIA	International Investment Agreement
IIAM	Indian Institute of Arbitration and Mediation
ILC	International Law Commission
IMI	International Mediation Institute
IP	Intellectual Property
ISDS	Investor State Dispute Settlement
LCIA	London Court of International Arbitration
MAI	Multilateral Agreement on Investment
MCCI	Moscow Chamber of Commerce and Industry
MCPC	Mediation and Conciliation Project Committee
MFN	Most Favoured Nation
MSEB	Maharashtra State Electricity Board
NAFTA	North American Free Trade Agreement
ODR	Online Dispute Resolution
OECD	Organisation for Economic Co-operation and Development
ONGC	Oil and Natural Gas Corporation
PCA	Permanent Court of Arbitration
PPA	Power Purchase Agreement
PSU	Public Sector Undertaking
SCC	Stockholm Chamber of Commerce
SIAC	Singapore International Arbitration Centre
SIMC	Singapore International Mediation Centre
TPP	Trans-Pacific Partnership
TRIMs	Trade-Related Investment Measures
TTIP	Transatlantic Trade and Investment Partnership
UNCTAD	United Nations Conference on Trade and Development
WTO	World Trade Organization

PART I

DOMESTIC ARBITRATION

1

Alternative Dispute Resolution

Is It an Alternative Mechanism?

Arijit Pasayat

The goal of the Constitution is to render justice—social, economic, and political. Access to fast, inexpensive, and expeditious justice is a basic human right. Equal access to justice for all segments of society is important to engender respect for law and the judicial system. Article 39A of the Constitution of India, 1950 (in short, Constitution), 'Equal Justice and Free Legal Aid', is a mandate in this regard, which reads as follows: 'The State shall secure that the operation of the legal system promotes justice, on a basis of equal opportunity, and shall provide free legal aid, by suitable legislation or schemes or in any other way, to ensure that opportunities for securing justice are not denied to any citizen by reason of economic or other disabilities.'

Methods of ADR in India

Arbitration and Conciliation

Marketplace has lengthened the process of judicial dispute resolution in the courts. The delays inherent in judicial proceedings are often unacceptable to those involved in modern commercial transactions, and a simpler, faster method of dispute resolution is required. Commercial arbitration is becoming the most widely utilized alternative. In conciliation, a neutral third party helps in resolving disputes by improving communications, lowering tensions, and identifying issues and potential solutions by shuttling information between the disputing parties.

Mediation

Mediation can be thought of as an assisted negotiation aimed at arriving at an outcome agreeable to the parties. This is done by involvement of an independent third party—a mediator—who helps the parties to arrive at an agreement. The mediator is responsible for facilitating effective communication and building consensus between the parties.

Summary Trial

A summary trial means determination of a case which is capable of being tried and disposed of at once and is intended for matters which are not contentious and complicated and do not merit a lengthy inquiry and fact finding. In summary trials, detailed evidence of the claims of the parties is not led, and determinations are based on a record which is sufficient to provide justice in a given case.

Other Methods or Techniques of ADR Adopted in India

The other methods or techniques of alternative dispute resolution (ADR) adopted in India are: private mediation, judicial settlement, case management, and plea bargaining.

While focussing on the ills of avoidable litigations, the views of legendary visionaries and intellectuals need to be noted.

I realized that the true function of a lawyer was to unite the parties riven asunder. The lesson was so indelibly burnt into that the large part of my time during the twenty years of my practice [as] a lawyer was occupied in bringing about private compromises of hundreds of cases. I lost nothing thereby. [Not] even money, certainly not my soul.

—Mahatma Gandhi

Discourage litigation. Persuade your neighbours to compromise whenever you can. Point out to them how the nominal winner is often a real loser—in fees, expenses, and waste of time.

—Abraham Lincoln, a noted trial lawyer himself who is estimated to have pleaded around 5,000 cases

To go to law is for two persons to kindle a fire, at their own cost, to warm others and singe themselves to cinders.

—Owen Felltham

A system of justice which a very substantial section of its own citizens cannot afford is a system which contains a fundamental law and leaves them vulnerable to exploitation.

—Lord Woolf

Justice is the first virtue of social institutions. With India's independence, a system of advertorial adjudication of various types of disputes, which is still in vogue, has been inherited. The Law Commission of India observed that the appropriate ways and means to ensure that justice is dispensed should be simple, speedy, cheap, effective, and substantial.[1] With the passage of time, the adequacies of the system have been increasingly felt inherent in the system. The docket explosion and heavy pendency of cases, both at the trial and appellate stages, have been a matter of global concern for all associated with the administration of justice. Establishment of a number of courts, raising the strength of the judges, and so on, by itself may not solve the problem unless some alternatives are found. Time has come to recognize an alternative in the form of ADR procedures. An awakening has come to reduce both institution and pendency of cases in the courts by finding recourse in ADR. The lead has come from the US later followed by the UK, India, and so on.

All lawyers are patently aware of the time-worn cliché 'justice delayed is justice denied', but the economic consequence of it is a reality check to both consumers and people involved in businesses when disputes arise. Any delay invariably has financial implications for the commercial community. The delays and expenses historically associated with the law, compound the financial consequences of such disputes. The proposal to establish commercial courts to expeditiously dispose of corporate disputes has become a recent reality. The different non-court methods available to assist in the dispute resolution process are grouped under the general heading ADR. The proponents of the ADR methods suggest that greater use of such alternative methods as opposed to the traditional court system would unburden the judiciary of a part of its workload, streamline the judicial process, and ultimately preserve the quality of the judicial system.

What Is ADR?

ADR is an alternative way to settle disputes. But alternative to what? One needs to understand what is meant by 'dispute' and what can appropriately be termed as 'resolution'. ADR is an alternative mechanism to solve a problem or dispute through means other than approaching regular courts, instituted by the state machinery, through less expensive means, on the one hand, and reducing the burden of courts, on the other. Thus, in other words, it is a supplement rather than a replacement to the regular courts.

ADR is a process which is different from the traditional litigation before a court of law and is qualitatively different in terms of the end result. It is not intended to supplant altogether the traditional means of resolving disputes by means of litigation, but it offers only alternative options to dispute resolution. A better meaning which can be attributed to the system is dispute resolution mechanism without the intervention of a formal procedure of state laws. Just as a democratic country like India refers to its government as one which is of the people, by the people, and for the people, the procedure of ADR may be termed as a machinery to sort dispute by the participation of the people and for the people.

Objectives of ADR

ADR represents only a change in forum, not in the substantive rights of the parties. The primary object of ADR system is avoidance of vexation, expenses and delay, and promotion of the idea of 'access to justice'. ADR techniques can be used at any time even when a case is pending before a court of law. If recourse is made to ADR as soon as the dispute arises, it may confer maximum advantages on the parties, it can be used to reduce the number of contentious issues between the parties. It can provide a better solution to disputes more expeditiously at lesser cost than litigation. The disputes are kept as a private matter and promote creative and realistic business solutions. ADR programme is flexible and not afflicted with rigorous rules of procedure and evidence. The freedom of parties to litigation is not affected by this proceeding. ADR procedure helps in reducing the work load of judiciary thereby helping them to decide the cases which are more importantly to be decided by the courts.

The parties to arbitration have added advantage of exercising control over the seat of arbitration along with the substantive and the procedural rules to be made applicable to the resolution of a dispute. Unlike the traditional system of courts, parties to an arbitration may choose to decide the appropriate decision makers, the applicable law, and language of the proceedings. The increasingly technical and complex nature of disputes brought by the advent of innovation and development in science and technology, and sophistication in commercial dealings has necessitated appointment of experts who are well equipped and qualified to appreciate the various technicalities in the given field as the adjudicating authority in the realm of dispute resolution mechanisms. The process of arbitration goes a long way in providing the parties the opportunity to appoint arbitrators of their own choice, by nomination or agreement. Increased autonomy of this nature also provides parties the freedom to devise a resolution procedure that best suits their needs and goals, such as saving of cost and time.

Another aspect is that of confidentiality. Arbitration proceedings, being private and confidential, the details of the claims of the parties and which way the arbitral award goes are all kept confidential giving parties an added incentive, since the public impact, business reputation, and disclosure of trade secrets, a major cause of concern in a traditional court litigation, become non-issues.

ADR in India

The method of settlement of disputes by reference to a third person was known and has been followed in India since ancient times. The words 'panch' (arbitrator) and 'panchayat' (arbitration) are as old as Indian history. But there is no comprehensive enactment on the system of ADR unlike in the US. In India, the situation is appalling. It is easily accessible for the rich, be they individual or corporations, who can afford to litigate. The poor can afford to litigate to some extent as we have legal aid boards, which provide legal assistance to the lower class. However, these techniques are scattered in different enactments. The techniques, that is, negotiation, conciliation, mediation, and arbitration, are widely used in India. They have been employed with very encouraging results in several categories of disputes, especially civil, commercial, industrial, and family disputes.

Development of ADR

ADR is not a revolutionary development or a legal process threatening law practitioners. It is no more than the stage of art of settlement techniques used by lawyers to resolve disputes of their clients. It is based on the adversary system, which is a key to the common law system. It is truly an alternative and not a replacement for traditional dispute resolution in the courts. In the United States, ADR was fostered by the crises in judicial administration caused by the explosion in litigation and by the increasing burden of legal expenses imposed on commercial enterprises out of the litigation. Alternate dispute resolution, or ADR, as it has become known in the US became quite popular in the law profession in the past decades.

Why Use ADR?

ADR has become popular in recent years because it is timely, more efficient, and more cost-effective than the traditional, formal redressal mechanisms. The use of conflict prevention also tends to mend or improve the overall relationship between the parties, because the focus is largely on the community or disputants' interests, while litigation focuses on positions. In addition, the parties can draft the agreement or solution themselves and they are generally more committed to the agreement compared to a judge or hearing officer imposing a solution. ADR process also can allow the parties to develop a more flexible or creative solution than is generally possible in courts or formal hearings and appeals.

In India, the legislators thought it fit to amend the Civil Procedure Code, 1908, taking into consideration the implementation of various recommendations made by the Law Commission to reduce decade-long pending litigations. The Parliament amended the Civil Procedure Code, 1908, by the Civil Procedure Code (Amendment) Act 46 of 1999.

The Supreme Court of India has also encouraged the ADR process by directing the parties in the litigation or the lawyers representing the parties to settle the dispute amicably out of the court. The court, specifically in matrimonial disputes, has tried to encourage litigating spouses to settle their differences out of court. Long-disputed matters, which are prolonged by family members over partition of property are also given an opportunity to sort out their differences. The general policy adopted by the court in the aforesaid cases has encouraged the bar to help the litigating parties to resolve their disputes amicably. The disputes of fact, such as family (divorce, property, etc.), contract (commercial and private contracts), sale of goods or specific reliefs, and so on, can be solved by mediation and by encouraging lawyers' participation so that the courts can concentrate on other important legal matters, where the attention or intervention of court is mandatory.

Reference

1. Law Commission of India, 77th Report (Delay and Arrears in Trial Courts), 1979.

2

Interim Measures under the Indian Arbitration and Conciliation Act, 1996

Atmaram N.S. Nadkarni

The Indian Arbitration and Conciliation Act, 1996, was introduced to bring the Indian legislation in line with the Model Arbitration Law brought about by the United Nations Commission on International Trade Law (UNCITRAL) in 1985 and to replace the earlier Arbitration Act of 1940. The UNCITRAL Model Law was introduced to inculcate an arbitration-friendly legal system in its member-countries and assist them in reforming and modernizing their pre-existing laws dealing with commercial arbitration. The goal was to achieve a uniform domestic and international arbitration legal regime so as to facilitate the enforceability of international arbitral awards in cross-border jurisdictions.

The Arbitration and Conciliation Act, 1996, in the Indian context, thus, attempts to serve its purpose by introducing a system in which the involved parties consider arbitration as a feasible and efficient mode of resolution of commercial disputes. The other two objectives are to minimize court interference in arbitral awards and to implement, as far as possible, an arbitration law in conformity with international standards. This assumes special significance in the Indian jurisdiction, given the proverbial delays associated with civil court functions, making traditional litigation a costly and time-consuming option.

During the course of an arbitration, it may become necessary for the arbitral tribunal or a national court to issue orders intended to preserve evidence, to protect assets, or in some other way to maintain the status quo, pending the outcome of the arbitration proceedings themselves. Such orders are known as 'interim measures' under the Indian Arbitration and Conciliation Act, 1996. They are intended, in principle, to operate as mandatory orders to maintain the status quo pending disposal of the arbitral process.

Sections 9 and 17 of the Arbitration and Conciliation Act, 1996, deal with the award of interim measures during the arbitration process either by the courts or the arbitrators or both the parties involved in the process. Section 9 empowers the court to order a party to take an interim measure for protection when an application is made, while Section 17 gives power to the arbitral tribunal to order interim measures unless the agreement expressly prohibits such power. Interim measures thus take on the role of providing relief on a temporary basis to the parties while the arbitration process is ongoing. The right of a party to apply to the court for interim measures of protection exists until the arbitral award in question is enforced in accordance with Section 36 of the Act.

Orders of the court under Section 9 of the Indian Arbitration and Conciliation Act and orders of the tribunal under Section 17 granting or refusing to grant an interim measure are appealable under Section 37 of the Act. Providing appeals against interim relief does not necessarily advance the stated objective of the Act for curtailment of judicial intervention, but reasonable justifications lie behind the institution of such appeals. It would not be appropriate to deprive the aggrieved party of all measures of challenge against 'interim order', which does not culminate into an award until the conclusion of the arbitration. Since the nature of reliefs requested by the parties would often be urgent and pressing, this may be too late and render the parties' prayer infructuous.

In many cases where interim measures of protection are required, the arbitral tribunal itself has the power to issue them. Article 17 of the UNCITRAL Model Law states:

1. Unless otherwise agreed by the parties, the arbitral tribunal may, at the request of a party, grant interim measures.
2. An interim measure is any temporary measure, whether in the form of an award or in another form, by which, at any time prior to the issuance of the award by which the dispute is finally decided, the arbitral tribunal orders a party to:
    i.   maintain or restore the status quo pending determination of the dispute;
    ii. take action that would prevent, or refrain from taking action that is likely to cause, current or imminent harm or prejudice to the arbitral process itself;
    iii. provide a means of preserving assets out of which a subsequent award may be satisfied; or
    iv. preserve evidence that may be relevant and material to the resolution of the dispute.

Until the recent amendments in the Indian Arbitration and Conciliation Act, 1996, India had incorporated a much watered-down version of this provision in its Arbitration Act. The UNCITRAL Rules and the Model Law both provide for interim measures to be awarded by the arbitral tribunal in a much more extensive manner than the Arbitration and Conciliation Act, 1996. The powers given to the arbitral tribunal under the Model Law are wider ranging than those given in the 1996 Act. Whilst most arbitration rules and arbitration laws permit interim measures to be granted at the tribunal's discretion, very little guidance was given as to how the said discretion is to be exercised.

The Model Law was amended in 2006 to include conditions for granting these interim measures. Under the old provisions, the Model Law seemed to proceed with the dangerous assumption that an interim order of the tribunal would be voluntarily accepted by the parties and did not contemplate an enforcement procedure. With the introduction of Article 17H, the Model Law now provided recognition and enforcement of interim orders of the tribunal and recognized them as binding. The amended Article 17 empowered the tribunal, as seen earlier, to maintain or restore the status quo pending determination, direct a party to refrain from taking actions that would prejudicially affect the arbitral process, provide a means for preserving assets for satisfaction of the award, or preserve evidence that may be material for resolution of the dispute. The amendments comprehensively captured the concept of ex-parte ad-interim orders which are essentially aimed at maintaining the status quo.

Subsequently, the relevant provision for interim measures to be awarded by the arbitral tribunal, that is, Section 17 of the Indian Arbitration and Conciliation Act, 1996, has also been overhauled by the Arbitration (Amendment) Act, 2015. The interim measures that can be applied before the court under Section 9, and now also before the tribunal under Section 17, are:

1. Appointment of a guardian for a minor or person of unsound mind;
2. Preservation or interim custody or sale of goods, if goods are of perishable nature;
3. Securing the amount of claims;
4. Allowing inspection or interim injunction or appointment of receiver; and
5. Any other relief as the court or arbitral tribunal may in its discretion deem proper considering the circumstances of the case.

The arbitral tribunal can order the parties to take such interim measures of protection as it may deem necessary in respect of the subject matter of the dispute. In the process, it can order for providing appropriate security in exercise of this power. All of this, however, must be within the scope of the arbitration agreement between the two parties.

Once the arbitral process has begun and the baton has been passed to the arbitrators, it is essential to ensure that the involvement of the courts is kept to a minimum. That is the driving force behind Section 17 of the Arbitration and Conciliation Act, 1996, which vests the power of taking interim measures on the arbitral tribunal. This power is necessary to ensure a smooth arbitral process while retaining its autonomy and not having to involve the courts repeatedly.

A factor limiting the powers of the arbitral tribunal when it comes to interim measures is that the tribunal orders can only be against the parties involved in the arbitration. The tribunal cannot order interim measures against any third party who is not involved in the arbitration process or is not party to the arbitration agreement. This serves as a limitation in the extent of authority that is given to the arbitral tribunal in comparison to the courts.

Perhaps the most important aspect which had been overlooked in India in the original Arbitration and Conciliation Act, 1996, was the tribunal's power to enforce interim measures awarded by it. Prior to the 2015 amendment, in India, even the courts did not have the power to enforce an interim measure awarded by a tribunal, which had the effect of undermining the significance and utility of the 'award'. The Delhi High Court tried to find a solution to the problem of enforceability of an interim award by the arbitral tribunal in *Sri Krishan v. Anand*.[1] The court held that any person failing to comply with the order of the arbitral tribunal under Section 17 would be deemed to be 'making any other default' or 'guilty of any contempt to the arbitral tribunal during the conduct of the proceedings' under Section 27 (5) of Act. The remedy of the aggrieved party would then be to apply to the arbitral tribunal for making a representation to the court to mete out appropriate punishment. Once such a representation is received by the court from the arbitral tribunal, the court would be competent to deal with such party in default as if it is in contempt of an order of the court, that is, either under the provisions of the Contempt of Courts Act or under the provisions of Order 39, Rule 2A of Code of Civil Procedure, 1908.

The Law Commission in its 246th report (August 2014) felt that the judgment of the Delhi High Court in *Sri Krishan v. Anand* is not a complete solution and recommended amendments to Section 17 of the Act which would make orders of the arbitral tribunal enforceable in the same manner as the orders of a court. The amendment has the effect of bringing an interim award of the tribunal at par with a decree of a court. Section 17 (2) now provides, 'Subject to any orders passed in an appeal under Section 37, any order issued by the arbitral tribunal under this section shall be deemed to be an order of the Court for all purposes and shall be enforceable under the Code of Civil Procedure, 1908, in the same manner as if it were an order of the Court'.

The amended section thus extends the powers of the arbitral tribunal in terms of the interim measures that can be granted in line with the powers of the court. Orders of the arbitral tribunal are now enforceable as if they were a decree of the court, which has the effect of attaching the same standard of legitimacy to interim measures as is provided to arbitral awards.

However, in a recent judgment passed by the Kerala High Court,[2] the learned single judge has taken a view that under the Amendment Act, the arbitral tribunal cannot pass an order to enforce its own orders and the parties will have to approach the courts for seeking such enforcement. The arbitral tribunal acting under the new Section 17 had granted the claimant possession of a vehicle (secured asset) against a loan, appointed an advocate commissioner to ensure the same and further ruled that the claimant is entitled to seek assistance of state house officer of the concerned police station in case there is any threat posed to the claimant's person or life while taking this repossession. The court ordered that the repossession of the vehicles by enforcing the order of the arbitral tribunal without the intervention of the civil court has to be treated as violation of Article 21 of the Constitution of India. In the colour of statutory backing, the tribunal's order has been allowed to be enforced without any statutory authority. The encroachment into a public law field in a private law remedy is nothing but a sheer abuse of process of law. It will be interesting to see how the other courts interpret this judgment and if it stands the test of further judicial scrutiny.

Two major changes made by way of the amendment are to Sections 2 and 17 of the Act. Section 2 (2) has been amended to read as:

This Part shall apply where the place of arbitration is in India:
[Provided that subject to an agreement to the contrary, the provisions of sections 9, 27, and clause (a) of sub-section (1) and sub-section (3) of section 37 shall also apply to international commercial arbitration, even if the place of arbitration is outside India, and an arbitral award made or to be made in such place is enforceable and recognised under the provisions of Part II of this Act.]

This amendment was needed to neutralize the judgment in *Bharat Aluminium and Co. v. Kaiser Aluminium and Co.*[3] (BALCO) due to which the Indian courts had no jurisdiction to intervene in arbitrations which were seated outside India. Post BALCO, if the assets of a party were located in India, and there was a likelihood of the dissipation of the assets, the other party could not approach the Indian courts for interim orders. Since the interim orders made by arbitral tribunals outside India could not be enforced in India, it created major hurdles for parties who had chosen to arbitrate outside India.

Section 2 (2) now states that Part I of the Act would apply if the place of arbitration is in India, but Sections 9 and 27 and some parts of Section 37 would be applicable to international commercial arbitration, even if the seat of arbitration is outside India. Thus, we observe a return to the principle laid down in *Bhatia International*[4] which also said that Part I of the Act would be applicable to the International Commercial Arbitrations whose seat was outside India unless there was an agreement between the parties to the contrary.

There may be a few concerns on this issue even after this amendment. As this option is only applicable to parties to an International Commercial Arbitration with a seat outside India, it is unclear whether two Indian parties who choose a foreign seat of arbitration would be entitled to such interim protections under Section 9 when the impugned assets are situated in India. *M/s Addhar Mercantile Private Limited v. Shree Jagdamba Agrico Exports Private Limited*[5] is the latest in the line of decisions which holds that two Indian parties cannot choose to arbitrate outside India whereby they apply foreign law as the substantive law of contract, since this would be a practice in derogation of public policy of India, for which heavy reliance was placed on the Supreme Court's decision in *TDM Infrastructure*.[6] However, the Madhya Pradesh High Court arrived at an opposite conclusion by holding that Indian parties are free to choose a foreign seat.[7] Most noticeably, this decision considered a larger bench decision[8] than *TDM Infrastructure* to arrive at a contrary finding. This decision of Madhya Pradesh High Court was affirmed in an appeal on 24 August 2016.[9]

Another crucial aspect relating to the award of interim measures by an arbitral tribunal is the time period in which these measures can be awarded. The law in India is that these can only be awarded during the arbitral process, which is when the arbitration tribunal retains all its authority. There can be situations where there is an urgent requirement for such an interim measure before the process has been initiated. An arbitral tribunal which is not yet in existence can clearly not offer any relief at this stage. Therefore, the interim measure at this stage can be provided by the courts, who have this power and no such restriction in terms of time period, under Section 9 of the Arbitration and Conciliation Act, 1996. As per the Apex Court, the court has jurisdiction to pass interim orders even before the arbitral proceedings commence and before an arbitrator is appointed.

The issue of whether relief under Section 9 of the Act can be granted even before the commencement of the arbitration process was dealt with by the Supreme Court in *M/s. Sundaram Finance Limited v. M/s. NEPC India Limited.*[10] It was held that the court has the jurisdiction to pass interim orders even before arbitral proceedings commence and before an arbitrator is appointed. The Supreme Court held that it is not necessary that arbitral proceedings must be pending or at least a notice invoking arbitration clause must have been issued before an application under Section 9 is filed.

A limitation has now been introduced in terms of the time period within which the arbitration proceedings must commence after the passing of an order for any interim measure by the courts. The reasoning behind this amendment is to ensure that parties to the future arbitration do not abuse the relief they have in terms of interim measures and delay the initiation of the arbitration proceedings at their whim. This amendment has been added to make sure that any party approaching the court to apply for an interim measure, and obtaining that measure, has to participate in arbitral proceedings which will commence within ninety days of the passing of the order for interim relief.

The legislators have also attempted to enhance the authority provided to the arbitral tribunal in terms of interim measures under Section 17. The addition of Sub-section (3) to Section 9 of the Act removes the overlap of authority that existed between the courts and the arbitral tribunal when it comes to interim measures during the arbitral proceedings. Under the original Act, both the courts and the arbitral tribunal had the power to award interim measures while the arbitral proceedings were ongoing, which meant that the concerned party could approach either of the two to obtain this relief. Distinguishing Sections 9 and 17, the Supreme Court in *Firm*

Ashok Traders v. Gurumukhdas Saluja[11] held that the difference was in relation to the time period in which the court could award interim measures under Section 9, and the arbitral tribunal's corresponding power under Section 17. It was stated that the powers of the court were wider in this sense as well, as the courts could award interim relief even before and after the arbitral proceedings. The arbitral tribunal could only exercise this power during the proceedings, when the powers of the two may overlap. Thus, there was an overlap of authority between the courts and the arbitral tribunal.

With this amendment, there has been an attempt to clearly define the boundaries between the power that has been given to the courts and the arbitral tribunal, respectively. Only the arbitral tribunal would now have this power during the proceedings, while the courts would have this power at all other times. The one exception is that the courts can intervene in terms of interim measures when it is deemed that circumstances exist which may not render the remedy provided under Section 17 efficacious. Thus, a further demarcation in this respect is now laid out between the courts and the arbitral tribunal.

To conclude, law relating to interim protection in India with regard to conduct of arbitral proceedings were not the most refined of laws, but the recent amendments will undoubtedly refurbish the law and practice of conduct of arbitral proceedings in India and bring it at par with international best practices and developed arbitral laws in cross-border jurisdictions. Courts' interpretation of these amendments though is dubious in certain contexts as reflected in the comments made in this chapter and will be settled only upon a further judicial scrutiny by the Apex Court; it would not be incorrect to say that arbitral tribunals' powers in India have never been this authoritative.

Notes and References

1. *Sri Krishan v. Anand* (2009) 3 Arb LR 447 (Del).
2. *Pradeep K.N. v. The Station House Officer, Perumbavoor Police Station & Ors* (2015) in W. P. (Civil) No. 38725 of 2015.
3. *Bharat Aluminum Co. v. Kaiser Aluminum Technical Services Inc* (2012) 9 SCC 552.

4. *Bhatia International v. Bulk Trading S.A.* (2002) 4 SCC 105.
5. *M/s Addhar Mercantile Private Limited v. Shree Jagdamba Agrico Exports Pvt Limited* (2014) Bombay High Court in Arbitration Application No. 197 of 2014 along with A.P. No. 910 of 2013.
6. *TDM Infrastructure Private Limited v. UE Development India Private Limited* (2008)14 SCC 271.
7. *Sasan Power Limited v. North America Coal Corporation India Private Limited* (2015) First Appeal 310 of 2015.
8. *Atlas Exports Industries v. Kotak & Company* (1999) 7 SCC 61.
9. Civil Appeal No. 8299 of 2016, decided on 24 August 2016.
10. *M/s. Sundaram Finance Limited v. M/s. NEPC India Limited*, AIR (1999) SC 565.
11. *Firm Ashok Traders v. Gurumukhdas Saluja*, AIR (2004) SC 1433.

3

Impartiality and Independence of the Arbitral Tribunal

R.C. Lahoti and *Divyakant Lahoti*

Dedicating the Constitution to the citizens of India, B.R. Ambedkar had said, 'However good a constitution may be, if those who are implementing it are not good, it will prove to be bad. However bad a constitution may be, if those implementing it are good, it will prove to be good.'[1] These words of constitutional prophecy have unbound applications. Howsoever good a law governing arbitration may be attempted to be drafted, at the end its success would depend on the quality of those who would be implementing it.

Lord Hewart CJ's idiomatic words[2] provide a touchstone for testing the purity of not only the traditional justice delivery system (through the process of the courts), but also to any judicial and quasi-judicial method of justice dispensation. He said, 'it is of fundamental importance that justice [should] not only be done but should manifestly and undoubtedly be seen to be done'. This is true of arbitral process, as it is an accepted system of delivering justice, which serves as an alternate to the courts.

Independence and impartiality of the person entrusted with the task of decision-making are indispensable prerequisites of his qualification. As sacred is the task, so must be its traits. 'Independent' is one who can act on his own and does not depend on, much less be guided or influenced by, anyone except his own volition and conscience. 'Independence' is keeping away from any external influence.

> According to the definition of our standard lexicographers, a man who is impartial is one who is not biased in favour of one party more than another; who is indifferent, unprejudiced, disinterested; as an impartial judge or arbitrator. The primary idea contained in this definition is freedom from personal bias, indifference between the parties as persons; nor prejudiced against one or the other; disinterested as between them.[3]

Simplistically put, 'impartial' means not partial, free from bias, indifferent between the parties. Significance of judicial independence and impartiality lies not so much in its legal sanction as in its propriety, indispensability, and ethics in any justice dispensation process. This trait owes its origin more to culture rather than in law. Independence and impartiality are constituents of integrity. The two are ideal means to achieving an ideal end.

An arbitrator is not one who performs his functions by virtue of his holding an office. Arbitral authority is conferred by voluntary act of parties or, may be, by assignment from an arbitral institution having power to do so and at times also by legislation. However, an arbitrator does not take an oath or make an affirmation referable to discharge of his incoming duty. This is in contradistinction to the performance of duty by a judge, who takes an oath or makes an affirmation while entering upon his office. 'An oath is a religious asseveration, by which a person renounces the mercy and imprecates the vengeance of Heaven if he do not speak the truth.'[4] An oath is 'an appeal to the Supreme Being for the truth of what the party declares'.[5] 'An oath is a solemn adjuration to God to punish the affiant if he swears falsely'.[6] An affirmation is a solemn declaration without taking oath, but it is a confirmation, ratification, that what has been affirmed shall be done. Often such declaration is made before an authority. In a wider sense, affirmation is included in oath. The fact remains that oath or affirmation provides a basic assurance that the person shall stand by a particular code of conduct or standards as professed. A host of literature has developed around the sanctity of oath or affirmation by judges.

Every arbitrator, whether nominated by a party or appointed independently, must carry out his duty independently, honestly, and with integrity. Indeed, it is essential to the success of any arbitration that both parties are able to have confidence and trust in the tribunal's ability to act with independence and impartiality, both 'independence' and 'impartiality' are interrelated concepts. An arbitrator may fail to act impartially by favouring one of the parties or by having preconceived prejudices about the issues in dispute. An arbitrator may fail to be independent because of a relationship with one of the parties, be it financial, professional, or social, which gives the appearance of a personal interest or bias in the result or process of the arbitration. An arbitrator must not only act impartially but he must also be completely independent of any relationship with any of the parties, else it may cast a doubt, at least a reasonable doubt as to his independence and impartiality. The thought 'Justice should not only be done but seem to be done' applies to arbitral justice too.

Appropriate disclosure made by the arbitrator, before or during the arbitral proceedings to the parties, may or may not have a real bearing on the proceedings, but such a disclosure is suggestive of the honesty and integrity of the arbitrator on his part. Such disclosure may also give rise to justifiable doubts as to his/her impartiality and/ or independence in the mind of those who are associated or concerned. The arbitrators, in general, may be trusted to recuse or resign from the arbitral tribunal in the event of genuine conflict of interest, either personal, professional, or referable to the subject matter of a dispute. Notes on Rule 8 of the International Centre for Settlement of Investment Disputes (ICSID) Arbitration Rules authoritatively states that:

> [A]n arbitrator is to [resign] if, for instance, he may have an interest in the result of the dispute. In fact, in view of the qualities he is required to possess, a candidate is unlikely to accept an appointment as arbitrator where his personal interest is involved and, if he realises such involvement after the appointment, he may be trusted to resign. The experience of other international arbitration bodies has, in this respect, apparently been reassuring; it therefore seems unnecessary to particularise grounds for resignation.

A prospective arbitrator should not accept an appointment if there is reason(s) to believe that either party will genuinely feel that the person concerned is not independent, or not capable of approaching the issues.[7] It is often embarrassing for the parties, and arbitrator in particular, if the challenge is made after his appointment. As a matter of principle and propriety, the arbitrator should resign if both the parties determinatively agree that the arbitrator ought to resign. Moreover, the arbitrator should also resign if it seems, on reflection, that the objection is or appears to be well founded and supported by judicial precedence.

Independence is a notional concept; however, it has to be objectively evaluated in case there is a challenge to the arbitrator in respect of his appointment and continuance. Undoubtedly, in an arbitration, the parties may come from different jurisdictions having different cultural and commercial backgrounds. In such a scenario, more so in international arbitrations, it is imperative that parties repose their confidence and trust in the tribunal's ability to act fairly, impartially, and independently. The requirement for independence allows parties to exclude, in the early stages of the arbitration, those prospective arbitrators whose impartiality could reasonably be called into question, rather than allow the proceedings to continue and run the risk of a challenge arising at a later stage when the bias becomes apparent. In the case of *Szilard v. Szasz* (1955) SCR 3, it was held that:

> From its inception arbitration has been held to be of the nature of judicial determination and to entail incidents appropriate to that fact. The arbitrators are to exercise their function not as the advocates of the parties nominating them, and a fortiori of one party when they are agreed upon by all but with as free, independent and impartial minds as the circumstances permit. In particular, they must be untrammelled by such influences as to a fair-minded person would raise a doubt of that impersonal attitude which each party is entitled to.

Since the cardinal principles of neutrality, impartiality, and independence cannot be sidelined, at any stage of the proceedings, there must be minimum level of qualitative independence and neutrality of the arbitral tribunal, irrespective of parties' apparent agreement. The concept of party autonomy cannot be extended to subdue the basic notion of impartial and independent arbitrators. The Law Commission of India in its 246th Report has considered the issue of party autonomy to appoint their own employees as arbitrators especially in the cases where state is a party. The report states:

> In fact, when the party appointing an adjudicator is the State, the duty to appoint an impartial and independent adjudicator is that much more onerous—and the right to natural justice cannot be said to have been waived only on the basis of a 'prior' agreement between the parties at the time of the contract and before arising of the disputes.

The grounds for challenge and the procedure for challenging the appointment of the Arbitrator are codified under Sections 12 and 13 of the Arbitration and Conciliation Act, 1996.

Guidelines on Independence and Impartiality of Arbitrators

Various international organizations have developed guidelines relevant to the conduct of the arbitrator(s) in international arbitrations. Among them, the International Bar Association (IBA) adopted its guidelines on conflicts of interests in international arbitration in May 2004. The IBA guidelines focus on the ethical obligations of arbitrators and use a two-part approach to address the issue. The first sets forth general standards and explanations of those standards and the second provides examples of a variety of situations that arbitrators might face, and categorizes those situations as Green, Orange, or Red.

The green list includes situations that *should not be considered* to give rise to an appearance of a lack of impartiality or independence; the orange list enumerates situations that may, in the eyes of the parties, give rise to *justifiable doubts* as to an arbitrator's impartiality or independence; and the red list contains situations that give rise to *objectively justifiable doubts* as to an arbitrator's impartiality and independence. The red list is further divided into 'waivable' and 'non-waivable' situations.

The Law Commission of India has also proposed in its 246th report, the requirement of having specific disclosures by the arbitrator, at the stage of his possible appointment, regarding existence of any relationship or interest of any kind which is likely to give rise to justifiable doubts. The Law Commission has proposed the incorporation of the Fourth Schedule, which has drawn from the red and orange lists of the IBA guidelines on conflicts of interest in international arbitration, and which would be treated as a 'guide' to determine whether circumstances exist which give rise to such justifiable doubts. Therefore, while the disclosure is required with respect to a broader list of categories (as set out in the Fourth Schedule, and as based on the red and orange lists of the IBA Guidelines), the ineligibility to be appointed as an arbitrator (and the consequent de jure inability to so act) follows from a smaller and more serious subset of situations (as set out in the Fifth Schedule, and as based on the red list of the IBA Guidelines).

It was felt that real and genuine party autonomy should be considered, and in certain cases, the parties should be allowed to waive even the categories of ineligibility of the arbitrator. To deal with such situation, the Commission had proposed a proviso to Section 12(5), where parties may, subsequent to disputes having arisen between them, waive the applicability of the proposed Section 12(5) by an express agreement in writing. In all other cases, the general rule in the proposed Section 12(5) must be followed. Further, it has been recommended that the high court must seek the disclosure in terms of Section 12(1) and give 'due regard' to the contents of such disclosure before appointing the proposed arbitrator.

The requirement of impartiality and independence of the arbitrator(s) is imperative to both the process of selecting arbitrator(s) and the subsequent process(es) of their challenge and/or seeking to annul or enforce the arbitral award. Keeping this in view, Section 12 of the Act has been extensively amended to incorporate the recommendations of the Law Commission by the Arbitration and Conciliation (Amendment) Act, 2015. The amendment in Section 12 is intended to augment and achieve independence and impartiality in arbitration substantively. The newly inserted Fifth Schedule shall guide in determining whether circumstance exists which gives rise to justifiable doubts as to the independence or impartiality of the arbitrator. Pristine Section 12(5) specifically states that any person whose relationship, with the party or with counsel or the subject matter of the dispute, falls under any of the categories specified in the Seventh Schedule shall be ineligible to be appointed as an arbitrator. However, the parties may waive the applicability of such condition by an express agreement, in writing. Such amendment brings Indian

Arbitration Law in conformity with international best practices and would contribute to improving the clarity and consistent application of standards listed in various arbitration rules and laws.

The scheme of the Arbitration and Conciliation Act clearly contemplates non-permissibility of interference with the arbitral proceedings except as specified under the Act. Section 13 of the Act provides the procedure for challenging the arbitrator. In terms of Section 13(3) of the Act, unless an arbitrator withdraws from his office or the other party agrees to the challenge, the arbitral tribunal is required to decide the same. If the challenge fails, in terms of Section 13(4) of the Act, the arbitrator is required to continue with the arbitral proceedings and make an award.[8] Section 13(5) of the Act excludes interference by the court of law in the challenge procedure, though in terms of Section 13(5) of the Act, a party challenging the arbitrator is at liberty to make an application for setting aside the arbitral award, which may be rendered after the arbitral tribunal rejects the challenge. It is clear from the said scheme that the stage of challenging the impartiality or independence of the arbitrator is in the first instance before the arbitrator, then the tribunal and if the said challenge is not successful then under Section 34 of the Act after the award has been made and published. Given the specific provisions of Section 13, recourse to Section 14 of the Act is not available to challenge the decision of the arbitrator rejecting the challenge under Section 12 of the Act and to continue with the arbitral proceedings.[9]

Looking at the scheme of Section 13, and generally speaking, the adjudication by the arbitrator, rejecting the challenge application under Section 12, cannot be assailed by resorting to Section 14 of the Act. A resort to Section 14 can be availed in case the arbitrator is de jure or de facto unable to act as an arbitrator and/or he fails to act without undue delay. The distinction is this: Section 13 deals with disqualification of a person to act as an arbitrator; Section 14 deals with physical or mental capability or competence to function as arbitrator though not suffering from any disqualification. It can also be said that inability to perform arbitral functions, under Section 14, is based on the circumstances post appointment as arbitrator.

Disqualification envisaged by this provision is personal to the arbitrator and emerges because of his own voluntary or involuntary participation in the facts constituting it. It contemplates a situation in which the arbitrator enters a state that renders him incapable of adjudicating the dispute within the four corners of the law either generally or qua that particular dispute. His mandate is terminated because the dispute between the parties still survives and requires appointment of another arbitrator for its resolution.[10] Any other interpretation to this section will defeat the very purpose of the Act and would open the gates of the court for litigation.

In some decisions, courts have interpreted de jure rather widely to include cases of bias, partiality, and lack of independence by the arbitrator(s) that justify interference under Section 14 of the Act in order to terminate the mandate of an arbitral tribunal.[11] Section 5 of the 1996 Act recognizes and emphasizes the need for minimal court intervention in arbitral process. This provision gives rise to an apparent conflict between Section 14(2) and Section 34 of the Act as to the appropriate stage when the court can be requested to step in on the ground of bias or disqualification imputed to arbitrator, that is, midway the proceedings or post award. Two decisions of Delhi High Court need to be noted.

In *NHAI v. K.K. Sarin & Ors*,[12] the court held that de jure or de facto inability to perform the functions by an arbitrator can be brought to the notice of the court both under Sections 14 and 34, and once established, it would necessarily result in terminating the mandate of the arbitrator. The test for determining which of the two alternative remedies to avail is this: If the challenge laid is capable of summary decision, resort to Section 14 is permissible. If the allegation made raises complicated questions requiring inquiry or appreciation of evidence, it should be left to be determined by Section 34. However, an application under Section 14 must be preceded by Section 13(2) procedure having been followed, that is, the party intending to challenge an arbitrator should have, within 15 days after becoming aware of the constitution of the arbitral tribunal or after becoming aware of such circumstances, communicated to the arbitral tribunal a written statement of the reasons for the challenge.

In *Alcove Industries Limited*,[13] one party was entitled to nominate the sole arbitrator. The nominated arbitrator had, prior to commencement of arbitration, chaired the Dispute Resolution Board and formulated an opinion on the issues likely to arise in arbitration. This fact was consciously suppressed by the party and the arbitrator, both, but came to the fore during arbitration from the course of correspondence exchanged between the parties. This gave rise to de jure inability or at least a justifiable apprehension of bias in the arbitrator in relation to disputes arising out of the contracts between the parties. The court held that the obligation to disclose on the part of the arbitrator continues throughout the arbitral proceedings. A limitation on the right of a party raising the challenge, if he has participated in the appointment of the arbitrator, is that the party should have become aware of the grounds of challenge *after* the appointment of the arbitrator. An application under Section 14(2) would lie and the party need not wait for the stage of invoking Section 34; else, the provision would become counterproductive. As to the inability arising out of formulation of an earlier opinion on the facts or law of the points at issue in the case, a distinction has to be drawn between the situation where the arbitrator has already expressed himself on this very issue which is in dispute at an earlier stage of this very proceeding though not necessarily as an arbitrator; and a situation where the arbitrator has decided the same issue of fact or law in the course of an arbitration between different parties. In the former case, the inability is undoubtedly attracted as giving rise to a justifiable doubt of bias; in the latter situation, the disqualification is not attracted as the arbitrator can always be reminded that it is his duty to approach the issue afresh in the light of evidence and argument addressed to him on each occasion.

Grounds of Challenge

Russell unequivocally states that:

> [T]he first principle is that the arbitrator must act fairly to both parties, and in the proceedings throughout the reference he must not favour one party more than another, or do anything for one party which he does not do or offer to do for the other. He must observe in this the ordinary well understood rules of the administration of justice.[14]

The dawn of year 2016 has witnessed the enactment of the Arbitration and Conciliation (Amendment) Act, 2015, amending the Indian Arbitration and Conciliation Act, 1996. India had earlier promulgated an Ordinance on 23 October 2015, which substantially culminated into the aforesaid amended Act. Taking assistance from the recommendations of the 246th Report of the Law Commission of India, the amendment endeavours to curtail intervention of courts in arbitral process, accelerate the arbitration, introduce safeguards to warrant fairness in the arbitral process, and align the Indian Arbitration Act with international best practices. The amendment proposes to enhance arbitral efficacy and efficiency. To augment fairness in the arbitral process, the Amendment Act has introduced welcome changes in Section 12 of the Act. Indeed, a statutory requirement of specific disclosures by an arbitrator at the initiation of his possible appointment has been enacted which requires revelation of any relationship or interest that is likely to create justifiable doubts regarding his neutrality. Section 12(1) refers to the newly added Fifth Schedule which enumerates 34 grounds which may give rise to justifiable doubts as to the independence or impartiality of the arbitrator(s). These grounds have further been classified into seven categories.[15]

Relationship between the Arbitrator and the Parties or Its Counsel

Relationship with a party may be a disqualification of the arbitrator if the relationship is likely to bias him.[16] De Smith, Woolf, and Jowell have observed:

> [R]eal danger of bias may arise from the fact that an adjudicator is the employer or employee of one of the parties, if their personal relationship is a close one or if their respective interests are directly involved in the subject-matter of the proceedings. The special position of an arbitrator who is the employee of one of the parties to a contract has already been noted. It is not open to the other party to complain that the arbitrator, to whose appointment he agreed, has certain preconceived views on the issue and is not wholly impartial but he is entitled to require that the arbitrator shall act fairly and shall not wholly commit himself beforehand or act in collusion with his employer.[17]

The First Clause of Fifth Schedule read with Section 12(l)(b) addresses the aforesaid issue and states that in case the arbitrator is an employee, consultant, advisor, or has had any other past or present business relationship with a party, may give rise to justifiable doubt as to his independence or impartiality. Similarly, the Seventh Schedule read with Section 12(5) mandates that there shall not be any arbitrator relationship with the parties or counsel and the arbitrator must not be an employee, consultant, advisor, or have had any other past or present business relationship with a party. If such a relationship does exist, the person should not be appointed as arbitrator in the said matter.[18]

A financial or business or commercial relationship between an arbitrator and one of the parties to an arbitration is an apparent challenge on the grounds of lack of independence or partiality. However, in such cases, a more pragmatic and objective view may be adopted which satisfactorily answers the question of arbitrator's impartiality. The fact that the arbitrator was indebted to one of the parties at the time of the reference and that fact was not known to the other party (also not disclosed by the arbitrator) amounts to misconduct.[19] Importantly, a challenge on the ground of past relationship is less capable of being successful than the one based on a subsisting financial or commercial or professional relationship. Needless to say, each challenge must be evaluated on its own merits, based on facts of each case.

It is quite common for lawyers to be nominated as arbitrators. If an arbitrator is a former lawyer of a party, and that fact was not known to the other party, it amounts to misconduct on the part of the arbitrator.[20] A mere allegation, unsubstantiated by any proof, that the arbitrator was regularly appearing for one of the parties and assisting him/her in preparation of cases cannot be countenanced.[21] For seeking revocation of the authority of the appointed arbitrator, such grounds which would cast reasonable doubt in the mind of a reasonable person, has to be shown when seeking removal of an arbitrator.[22]

Article 7(2) of the International Chamber of Commerce (ICC) Rules states that any circumstance which may 'call into question the arbitrator's independence in the eyes of the parties' must be disclosed. It is impossible to lay down any principle more precise than the test of what a reasonable man would think for ascertaining whether the relationship is close enough to be objectionable.[23] Where the arbitrator, umpire, and appointer were joint purchasers of an apartment block, it was held that it is the probability or the reasonable suspicion of biased appraisal and judgment, unintended though it may be, that defeats the adjudication at its threshold.[24] Similarly, the fact that the arbitrator was the respondent's brother was held sufficient to disqualify him.[25]

As an abundant caution, it must be understood that the arbitrators who justifiably take for granted the probity of themselves and their colleagues sometimes forget that those who do not know either them or the system so well may not make the same assumptions. The arbitrators must therefore be alert to see that a friendly and informal way of conducting the reference does not lead an uninformed party to the mistaken conclusion that the arbitrator is not maintaining a truly judicial approach.[26] It occasionally happens that party nominated arbitrators make little or no secret of their sympathy with the party who nominated them, both at hearings and in the private deliberations of the arbitral tribunal. There are two remedies if this occurs. The first, which is extreme and in any event rarely successful, is for the aggrieved party to make a formal challenge of the offending arbitrator. The second, which is usually followed in practise and is generally more constructive, is to rely on the other members of the arbitral tribunal, and in particular, on the presiding arbitrator, to deal with the situation in a diplomatic manner.[27]

Relationship of the Arbitrator to the Dispute

The rule in *Dimes v. Grand Junction Canal*[28] that bias is presumed where a judge has a direct pecuniary or financial interest in the subject matter is the only special case where it is unnecessary to inquire whether there was a real danger of bias.[29] Interest in the subject matter of litigation,[30] and other pecuniary interest,[31] disqualifies the arbitrator, but the objection would become waived if the other party appoints his own arbitrator with full knowledge of the disqualification.[32] There is an automatic disqualification for an arbitrator who has a direct pecuniary interest in one of the parties.[33] It is well-settled that there must be purity in the administration of justice as well as in the administration of quasi-justice as are involved in the adjudicatory process before the arbitrators.[34]

One of the clearest basis for finding a lack of independence and impartiality is the arbitrator's material or financial interest in the outcome of the arbitration[35] as, then, the arbitrator is 'acting as a judge in his or her own cause'. All cases where the arbitrator would profit financially from his own decision or had an ownership interest in a party to the arbitration[36] disqualify the arbitrator. Another clear presumptive basis is an arbitrator's prior involvement in the parties' dispute, either as a corporate officer, other decision maker, lawyer, witness, or expert.[37] An arbitrator's appointment or service in any related proceedings are usually not grounds of challenge. As a general rule, the impartiality of an arbitrator should not be doubted because of the fact that he is called to decide a dispute based on the same facts on which he was previously called to arbitrate as a member of a different arbitral tribunal.[38] A mind willing to accept and entrusted with performance of duty to decide, judicially or quasi-judicially, ought to be trusted with having openness to reconsider his opinion in new set of facts and circumstances though similar.

Rightly, the 'investment and even commercial arbitration would become unworkable if an arbitrator were automatically disqualified on the ground only that he or she was exposed to similar legal or factual issues in concurrent or consecutive arbitrations'.[39] There is no impediment for the same arbitrator to come to the later arbitration with an open mind. That in itself should not preclude him from making an impartial award placed with the facts and applicable law presented in newer and, may be, different perspectives and dimensions. However, repeated nominations of the same arbitrator by a particular party must be avoided lest it should be a reasonable ground for challenge.

In 'Med-Arb' or 'Arb-Med' or 'Arb-Med-Arb' cases, an arbitrator may be requested to serve as a mediator (or vice versa) of the same dispute in which he or she acts as an arbitrator or mediator, as the case may be. The dual roles of this nature can raise issues concerning the arbitrator's independence and impartiality.[40]

Other Grounds

Connections between one arbitrator and other arbitrators on the tribunal may be considered as relevant to the arbitrator's independence.

Courts have rejected challenges where an arbitrator and counsel for one party were sitting as arbitrators in an unrelated case.[41] The relationship between arbitrators may be strained during the course of arbitration, and this could be a sufficient ground for challenge. For example, two arbitrators appointed by Iran to the Iran–US. Claims Tribunal physically assaulted a third (presiding) arbitrator who they believed was biased against Iran. This in turn led the US to challenge these two arbitrators as biased. Iran had replaced the two arbitrators before the challenge could be decided.[42]

An arbitrator's significant business or personal relationship with a material witness for one party can create ground for questioning his impartiality.[43] The fact that an arbitrator has previously sat in an arbitration which considered the evidence from a fact or expert witness should not be a ground for disqualification or a subject of disclosure. Similarly, the fact that an arbitrator or his law firm has previously retained an expert witness, or is presently retaining that witness, should not be a ground for disqualification.[44]

It is sometimes contended that the failure to make a required disclosure, even if the non-disclosed matter would not independently be disqualifying, can itself become grounds for challenging an arbitrator.[45] Certain facts or circumstances are of such a magnitude that failure to disclose them would, thereby in and of itself indicate a manifest lack of reliability of a person to exercise independent and impartial judgment.[46] Neutral arbitrator selected by the parties or their representatives exhibits evident partiality if he does not disclose facts that might, to an objective observer, create a reasonable impression of the arbitrator's partiality.[47]

Duty of Disclosure

Disclosure is imperative to the process of constitution of arbitral tribunal. Disclosure(s) are sine qua non to the parties or appointing institutions by prospective arbitrator(s) of their relationship or other circumstances which might raise justifiable grounds regarding their impartiality and independence. Timely and complete performance of disclosure obligation is vital to the integrity of the arbitral process.[48] The importance of the duty of disclosure becomes quite clear as it is the backbone that holds together the foundation of the arbitration, that is, the arbitral tribunal.[49] The disclosure requirement mandates the arbitrator to make disclosures, both prior to accepting the appointment and in the event of the new development, during the course of arbitration.

The rationale behind the mandatory requirement of disclosure(s) by arbitrator(s) has been explained succinctly by a court thus:

> [I]t is important that courts enforce rules of ethics for arbitrators in order to encourage businesses to have confidence in the integrity of the arbitration process, secure in the knowledge that arbitrators will adhere to these standards. In the years since Justice Black's decision, international arbitrations have taken on an extremely important role in facilitating international commercial transactions among businesses located in all parts of the world. Businesses in many countries are wary of the courts favouring the party resident within their jurisdiction and favour an independent arbitral panel for the prompt resolution of any commercial dispute. Confidence in the arbitral panel to render fair and impartial decisions is important to this country's international trade, and full disclosure is integral to the integrity of the panel's decision. Because of the increase in international transactions and the corresponding increase in disputes it is crucial that there exists a requirement of an appearance of impartiality in arbitrators conducted in this jurisdiction, and that courts take actions designed to assure foreign entities that arbitrations in the United States are free from suggestion of partiality.[50]

***

Arbitral fora, as dispute resolution institutions, are the future of litigation because of the informality, simplicity, quickness, and possibly cost efficacy inherent in them. As compared with justice administration by courts, the arbitral institution is still in its infancy. Conventions and traditions take time to develop. They have a history of trial and errors and lessons learnt therefrom, tested on the touchstone of times. Efficacy and acceptability are acquired by being handed over from generation to generation. There is need to develop an arbitration bar consisting of such law professionals dedicated exclusively to practicing arbitration. The practitioners of arbitration need to have a mindset grinded differently. Equally important is to lay down a code of conduct for arbitrators and subject their performance to constant vigil. Institutionalization of arbitration can go a long way in securing such ideals. Needless to say, the watchman and the institutions too shall have to be equally impartial and independent.

Notes and References

1. Excerpt from Constituent Assembly Speech by B.R. Ambedkar on Friday, 25 November 1949.
2. *R. v. Sussex Justices*, (1924) 1 K.B. 256 at 259.
3. P. Ramanatha Aiyar, *Advanced Law Lexicon*, 3rd ed. (LexisNexis, 2017), p. 2212.
4. *R. v. White, Leach*, 430, 431.
5. *Butts vs. Swartwood* (2 Cow, 431).
6. Aiyar, *Advanced Law Lexicon*, p. 3269.
7. Alan Redfern, Martin Hunter, and Nigel Blackaby, *Law and Practice of International Commercial Arbitration*, 4th ed. (Thomson Sweet & Maxwell, 2004), p. 247.
8. *Gangotri Enterprises Limited v. NTPC Tamil Nadu Energy Company Limited*, (2017) SCC Online Del 6560.
9. *Progressive Career Academy Private Limited v. FIITJEE Limited*, 180 (2011) DLT 714.
10. *Vilas v. Ganesh Builders*, (2005) 2 MAH LJ 912: 2005 SUPP ARB LR 364.
11. *National Highways Authority of India v. K.K. Sarin*, (2009) 159 DLT 314; *Alcove Industries Limited v. Oriental Structural Engineers Limited*, 2008 (1) Arb LR 393 (Del).
12. (2009) 159 DLT 314.
13. *Alcove Industries Limited v. Oriental Structural Engineers Limited*, (2008) 1 Arb LR 393.
14. *Russell on Arbitration*, 20th ed. (Thomson), pp. 213–14.
15. Arbitrator's relationship with the parties or counsel; relationship of the arbitrator to the dispute; arbitrator's direct or indirect interest in the dispute; previous services for one of the parties or other involvement in the case; relationship between an arbitrator and another arbitrator or counsel; relationship between arbitrator and party and others involved in the arbitration; and other circumstances.
16. *Motharam Dowlatram v. Mayadas Dowlatram*, AIR 1925 Sind 150; *Ghulam Mohammad Khan v. Gopaldas Lal Singh*, AIR 1933 Sind 68.
17. Lord Woolf, S.A. De Smith, and Jeffrey L. Jowell, *Judicial Review of Administrative Action*, 5th ed. (London: Sweet & Maxwell, 1995), p. 538.

18. *Assignia-VIL JV v. Rail Vikas Nigam Limited*, (2016) 230 DLT 235.
19. *Jagrup Ram v. Kashi Prasad*, AIR 1934 All 586; *Mohammad Wahiuddin v. Hakiman*, ILR (1902) 29 Cal 278.
20. *Murlidhar Roongta v. S. Jagannath Tibrewala*, (2005) (1) Arb LR 103 (Bom).
21. *State of Rajasthan v. Navbharat Construction Company*, (2006) 1 SCC 86.
22. P.C. Markanda, *Law Relating to Arbitration and Conciliation*, 9th ed. (LexisNexis, 2016), p. 593.
23. *Morgan v. Morgan*, (1832) 2 LJ Ex 56.
24. *Szilard v. Szasz*, (1955) 1 DLR 370, at 373–4.
25. *Turnbul v. Rural Municipality of Pipestone*, (1915) 24 DLR 281.
26. Lord Mustill and Stewart C. Boyd, *Commercial Arbitration*, 2nd ed. (LexisNexis, 1995), p. 255.
27. Redfern, Hunter, and Blackaby, *Law and Practice of International Commercial Arbitration*, p. 240.
28. (1852) 3 HL Cas 759.
29. *R. v. Gough*, (1993) AC 646.
30. *Earl v. Stocker*, (1691) 2 Vern. 251; *Blanchord v. Sun Fire Office*, (1890) 6 TLR 365; *Yusuf Khan v. Riyasat Ali*, AIR 1926 Oudh 307.
31. *Karumuthu Thiagarajan Chettiar v. Thos Smith & Co.*, AIR 1935 Bom 155.
32. *Elliot & South Devon Ry. Re*, (1848) 12 Jur. (OS) 445.
33. *AT&T Corp v. Saudi Cable*, (2000) 2 All ER (Comm) 625.
34. *International Airports Authority v. K. D. Bali*, (1988) 2 SCC 360, at 367.
35. Gary B. Born, *International Commercial Arbitration*, vol. II, 2nd ed. (Wolters Kluwer, 1989), p. 1867.
36. *Middlesex Mut. Ins. Co. v. Levine*, 675 F.2d 1197 (11th Circuit 1982); *Hyman v. Pottberg's Executors*, 101 F.2d 262 (2nd Circuit 1939); *Rand v. Readington*, 13 N.H. 72 (N.H. Super. Ct. 1842).
37. *Veritas Shipping Corp. v. Anglo-Canadian Cement Ltd.*, (1966) 1 Lloyd's Rep. 76 (QB).
38. Van Houtte, 'The Right of Defense in Multi-Party Arbitration', *International Construction Law Review* (1989), p. 397.
39. *Tidewater v. Venezuela*, Decision on the proposal to disqualify Professor Brigitte Stern, Arbitrator in ICSID Case No. ARB/10/5 of 23 December 2010.
40. Jacob Rosoff, 'Hybrid Efficiency in Arbitration: Waiving Potential Conflicts for Dual Role Arbitrations in Med–Arb and Arb–Med Proceedings', *Journal of International Arbitration*, 26 (1, 2009), p. 89.
41. *In re Andros Compania Maritima, SA*, 579 F.2d 691 (2d Cir. 1978).

42. C.N. Brower and J.D. Brueschke, *The Iran–United States Claim Tribunal* (Martinus Nijhoff Publishers, 1998), pp. 169–71.
43. D. Caron and L. Caplan, *The UNCITRAL Arbitration Rules: A Commentary*, 2nd ed. (Oxford University Press, 2013), pp. 215–16.
44. Born, *International Commercial Arbitration*, p. 1888.
45. Born, *International Commercial Arbitration*, p. 1891.
46. *Alpha Projektholding GmbH v. Ukraine*, Decision on Respondent's Proposal to Disqualify Arbitrator Dr. Yoram Turbowicz in ICSID Case No. ARB/07/16 of 19 March 2010.
47. *Karlseng v. Cooke*, 346 S.W. 3d 85, 94 (Tex. App. 2011).
48. Catherine A. Rogers, 'Regulating International Arbitrators: A Function Approach to Developing Standards of Conduct', *Stanford Journal of International Law*, 41 (53, 2005), p. 118.
49. Fatima-Zahra Slaoui, 'The Rising Issue of "Repeat Arbitrators": A Call for Clarification', *Arbitration International*, 25 (1, 2009), p. 118.
50. *Applied Indus. Material Corp. v. Ovalar Makine Ticaret Ve Sanayi*, AS 2006 U.S. Dist. LEXIS 44789, at *27–8 (S.D.N.Y.).

4

The Doctrine of *Kompetenz-Kompetenz*

An Indian Perspective

Suresh C. Gupte

The doctrine of *Kompetenz-Kompetenz* along with its allied principle of separability of the arbitration agreement is amongst the most significant doctrines in modern-day arbitration. The concept implies, to put it simply, the arbitral tribunal's power to comprehensively rule on its own jurisdiction. One may ask why, in the first place, is it important to confer such power specifically on the arbitrator. After all, every adjudicating authority, before embarking on the exercise of adjudication, is expected to first inquire into its own jurisdiction and rule on it. Then, is it not natural and a matter of elementary principle that the arbitral tribunal should have such power? The answer lies in the arbitrator's unique position and distinction, as an adjudicator, from other adjudicating authorities, all of which derive their power to adjudicate from the state's sovereign power to administer justice or statutes designating them as adjudicators for deciding questions arising thereunder. The arbitrator, on the other hand, is a privately chosen forum, owing its power and authority to an agreement entered into by the parties, which is usually a part of an underlying contract, to decide disputes under which the parties seek to resort to such forum. What if the contract containing the arbitration agreement is itself invalid or ceases to exist? What happens then to the arbitration agreement? Is it not rendered invalid or non-existent? How can a forum, which owes its very existence to such agreement, then continue to operate? Throughout the history of arbitration law, the courts have tried to grapple with these conceptually tricky issues, till the arrival of the present-day doctrines of *Kompetenz-Kompetenz* and separability. The purpose of this essay is to trace the development of these doctrines and find their exact place in Indian law to ascertain their reach and content under Indian arbitration law, the problem areas that continue to dog us even today, and finally, the road ahead.

Under the principle of *Kompetenz-Kompetenz*, the arbitral tribunal, whilst exercising the power to rule on its own jurisdiction, decides any objections with respect to the existence or validity of the arbitration agreement. Apart from providing the theoretical basis for the arbitrator's jurisdiction and authority, unaffected by the existence or validity of the agreement from which such jurisdiction and authority are sourced, it works on a practical level as well. Every time an issue arises concerning the existence or validity of the arbitration agreement, it allows the arbitrator to decide such issue, at least in the first instance, without the parties having to go to the national courts for such decision. The emphasis, after all, of the modern-day arbitration law is to retain party autonomy to the fullest measure possible and keep the interference of the ordinary courts, correspondingly, to the minimum.

Almost as a logical corollary to the doctrine of *Kompetenz-Kompetenz*, the law had to invent the principle of separability of the arbitration agreement from the 'main' or 'underlying' contract. The doctrine goes hand-in-hand with the power of the arbitral tribunal to determine its own jurisdiction, in that it requires treating the arbitration clause as an agreement independent of the other terms of the contract. 'The doctrine of separability establishes that the arbitration agreement has a separate life from the contract for which it provides the means of resolving disputes. This enables the arbitration agreement to survive breach of the contract of which it is a clause.'[1] Even if the 'main' or 'underlying' contract is regarded as invalid, non-existent, or ineffective, the arbitration clause, which is but a part of such contract, survives as a distinct and separate agreement so as to enable the arbitrator appointed under it to determine the very invalidity, non-existence, and inefficacy. Every decision of the arbitrator on his own jurisdiction is, of course, subject to the final ruling of a competent court, if and when the matter is brought before it, but that still does not prevent the arbitrator from assuming such jurisdiction and upon a finding in favour of such jurisdiction, even completing the arbitration proceedings and rendering an award. The matter goes to the national courts only after the award is rendered, in a challenge to the award.

The two principles, thus, together form the bedrock of the arbitrator's jurisdiction. The principle of separability, by affirming the separate existence of the arbitration agreement, allows the arbitrator to decide the disputes under the main contract even if the latter is null and void. But this is on the footing that such invalidity does not affect the arbitration agreement itself. If and to the extent, however, such invalidity affects the agreement itself, it is the principle of *Kompetenz-Kompetenz*, rather than the separability principle, which allows the arbitrator to rule on his jurisdiction. The separability principle, essential as it is to provide the theoretical basis of the arbitrator's jurisdiction, is still insufficient in a fundamental sense to enable the arbitration agreement to survive any invalidity which goes to the very root of the contract or to the making of it. It is inconceivable that when signing of the main contract is itself under a cloud, say when the signature is claimed as a forgery, the resultant invalidity would not affect the arbitration clause which is a part of that very contract, even if it is to be treated as distinct from it. The difficulty is then gotten over through the statutory interdict of the principle of *Kompetenz-Kompetenz*, giving the arbitrator the power to rule nevertheless on his jurisdiction.

The Early Roots of the Doctrine and Its Development up to the Case of *Heyman v. Darwins Limited*

The early decisions of English Courts seem to restrict the application of arbitration clause where the 'underlying' contract, for some reason or the other, has come to an end. The House of Lords, in the case of *Johannesburg Municipal Council v. Stewart*,[2] dealt with an action for damages brought by a municipal council, averring repudiation of the contract for supply of a plant by the defendant. The contract had an arbitration clause. The question was whether the clause was applied. One of the grounds of the decision, formulated by Lord Loreburn L.C. was, 'If the course of action which is established be that there has been repudiation or a breaking of contract in the sense that the contract has been frustrated by the breach, then it would not be within the arbitration clause'.

In *Jureidini v. National British and Irish Millers Insurance Company Limited*,[3] Viscount Haldane, L.C. made the following observations: 'Now, my Lords, speaking for myself, when there is a repudiation which goes to the substance of the whole contract I do not see how the person setting up the repudiation can be entitled to insist on a subordinate term of the contract still being enforced.'

Then came the decision of the Judicial Committee in *Hirji Mulji v. Cheong Yue Steamship Company Limited*.[4] In this case, a ship on a time charter was requisitioned on behalf of His Majesty's Government before the date at which she was to have entered upon the performance of the charter. The dispute was whether such requisition frustrated the performance of the charter party. The conclusion of the Judicial Committee was that such dispute was not 'a dispute arising under this charter'. The arbitration clause under the charter party was, thus, held to be inapplicable. Lord Sumner, who delivered the judgment for the court, held that the execution of the contract had not begun and that the dispute first arose when the charter no longer existed.

This, then, was the law when the House of Lords delivered its judgment in the celebrated case of *Heyman v. Darwins Limited*.[5] That was a case arising under a sole selling agency agreement. The appellants, who were sole selling agents of the respondents, claimed that the respondents 'have repudiated and/or evinced an intention not to perform' the agreement (an allegation which the respondents denied). A writ was issued, directing the court to make a declaration that the defendants have repudiated or evinced an intention and also claiming damages. The defendants opposed the action, citing the arbitration clause forming part of the agreement. The clause ran in the following terms, 'If any dispute shall arise between the parties hereto in respect of this agreement or any of the provisions herein contained or anything arising hereout the same shall be referred for arbitration in accordance with the provisions of the Arbitration Act, 1889, or any then subsisting statutory modification thereof'.

The House of Lords treated this clause as a widely drawn arbitration agreement. Viscount Simon, L.C. observed as follows, 'Ordinarily speaking, there seems no reason at all why a widely drawn arbitration clause should not embrace a dispute as to whether a party is discharged from future performance by frustration, whether the time for performance has already arrived or not'.

The learned Lord Chancellor proceeded to lay down the law in the following words:

> An arbitration clause is a written submission, agreed to by the parties to the contract, and, like other written submissions to arbitration, must be construed according to its language and in the light of the circumstances in which it is made. If the dispute is as to whether the contract which contains the clause has ever been entered into at all, that issue cannot go to arbitration under the clause, for the party who denies that he has ever entered into the contract is thereby denying that he has ever joined in the submission. Similarly, if one party to the alleged contract is contending that it is void *ab initio* (because, for example, the making of such a contract is illegal), the arbitration clause cannot operate, for on this view the clause itself also is void.
>
> If, however, the parties are at one in asserting that they entered into a binding contract, but a difference has arisen between them as to whether there has been a breach by one side or the other, or whether circumstances have arisen which have discharged one or both parties from further performance, such differences should be regarded as differences which have arisen 'in respect of' or 'with regard to', or 'under' the contract, and an arbitration clause which uses these, or similar, expressions should be construed accordingly. By the law of England (though not, as I understand, by the law of Scotland), such an arbitration clause would also confer authority to assess damages for breach, even though it does not confer upon the arbitral body express power to do so.
>
> I do not agree that an arbitration clause expressed in such terms as above ceases to have any possible application merely because the contract has 'come to an end', as, for example, by frustration. In such

cases, it is the performance of the contract that has come to an end. The doctrine of discharge from liability by frustration has often been explained as flowing from the inference of an implied term, and, in giving my opinion on the occasion of the recent decision of this House in *Joseph Constantine S.S. Line Ltd. v. Imperial Smelting Corp. Ltd.* (11) at p. 171, I expressed the view that the most satisfactory basis upon which the doctrine can be put is 'that it depends on an implied term in the contract of the parties'. If, therefore, when parties have entered into a contract, circumstances arise before the performance of the contract is completed which, in the view of one party, bring the contract to an end by frustration, and, therefore, discharge both parties from further performance, but the other party does not agree, this is a difference about the applicability of the implied term and is just as much within the arbitration clause as if it were a difference about an express term of the contract.

The rationale of this statement of law was succinctly put by Lord Macmillan in these words:

I venture to think that not enough attention has been directed to the true nature and function of an arbitration clause in a contract. It is quite distinct from the other clauses. The other clauses set out the obligations which the parties undertake towards each other *hinc inde*; but the arbitration clause does not impose on one of the parties an obligation in favour of the other. It embodies the agreement of both parties that, if any dispute arises with regard to the obligations which the one party has undertaken to the other, such dispute shall be settled by a tribunal of their own constitution. Moreover, there is this very material difference, that whereas in an ordinary contract the obligations of the parties to each other cannot in general be specifically enforced and breach of them results only in damages, the arbitration clause can be specifically enforced by the machinery of the Arbitration Acts. The appropriate remedy for breach of the agreement to arbitrate is not damages, but its enforcement. Moreover, there is the further significant difference that the courts in England have a discretionary power of dispensation as regards arbitration clauses which they do not possess as regards the other clauses of contracts.

The principle of separability was, thus, taking a firm shape. The case of *Heyman v. Darwins Limited* was the first authoritative statement of the principle and paved the way for further developments in this behalf. It was this case which guided Indian Courts in construing arbitration clauses under the framework of the Arbitration Act, 1940.

The Arbitration Act, 1940

The Arbitration Act, 1940, did not per se recognize the separability of the arbitration clause contained in a contract from the substantive stipulations of the contract. In all cases, where the contract (which inter alia contained the arbitration agreement) was either void or being voidable was avoided by a party or discharged or substituted, the arbitration agreement contained in it was also said not to survive. 'The arbitration clause, which is contained in the original contract, perishes with it', was the original dictum. Indian Courts, however, started recognizing the principle of law laid down in *Heyman v. Darwins Limited*. In *Union of India v. Kishanlal Gupta & Bros.*,[6] one of the early cases under the Arbitration Act of 1940, Calcutta High Court (per Justice R.S. Bachawat), relying on the observations in *Heyman's* case, held that total breach of the substantive stipulations, even when it is accepted by the other party, does not abrogate the arbitration clause, and even the party in default may invoke that clause. The learned judge, however, proceeded to observe that the parties are not bound to have recourse to arbitration; that they may settle their disputes directly and agree not to invoke the arbitration clause for that purpose, and that in reference to the disputes which are thus settled the arbitration clause ceases to exist. They may also enter into a substituted contract in complete supersession of the original contract and thereby abrogate the original contract and with it the arbitration clause contained in it. In another important judgment of the time, *Tolaram Nathmull v. Birla Jute Manufacturing Company Ltd.*,[7] after taking a review of all English cases on the point right up to *Heyman's* case, Das J (as he then was) laid down the principles deducible from the authorities reviewed. Finally, the Supreme Court in *Union of India v. Kishorilal Gupta and Bros.*[8] affirmed, after an extensive analysis of all English and Indian cases on the point, the following principles:

> The following principles relevant to the present case emerge from the aforesaid discussion: (1) An arbitration clause is a collateral term of a contract as distinguished from its substantive terms; but none the

less it is an integral part of it; (2) however comprehensive the terms of an arbitration clause may be, the existence of the contract is a necessary condition for its operation; it perishes with the contract; (3) the contract may be non est in the sense that it never came legally into existence or it was void ab initio; (4) though the contract was validly executed, the parties may put an end to it as if it had never existed and substitute a new contract for it solely governing their rights and liabilities thereunder; (5) in the former case, if the original contract has no legal existence, the arbitration clause also cannot operate, for along with the original contract, it is also void; in the latter case, as the original contract is extinguished by the substituted one, the arbitration clause of the original contract perishes with it; and (6) between the two falls many categories of disputes in connection with a contract, such as the question of repudiation, frustration, breach etc. In those cases it is the performance of the contract that has come to an end, but the contract is still in existence for certain purposes in respect of disputes arising under it or in connection with it. As the contract subsists for certain purposes, the arbitration clause operates in respect of these purposes.

This position broadly continued to obtain till we come upon the Arbitration and Conciliation Act, 1996. A broad arbitration clause, though held to be of sufficient amplitude to take in a dispute as to the validity of the agreement when disputes raised pertained to 'repudiation, frustration, breach, etc.', all of which related to the performance of the contract and thus survived such repudiation, frustration, breach, and so on, was not good enough to decide disputes under an agreement found to be bad or invalid. 'On principle therefore it must be held that when an agreement is invalid every part of it including the clause as to arbitration contained therein must also be invalid.' That was the dictum of the Supreme Court in *Khardah Company Ltd. v. Raymon & Co. (India) Private Ltd.*[9] The dictum was followed in later judgments of the Supreme Court.

In keeping with this position, the Arbitration Act, 1940, allowed the parties to contest the arbitration agreement before a court of law even before a reference was invoked under the agreement or after such invocation but before conclusion of the reference, by an application to the court (Section 33), though a suit contesting an arbitration agreement on any such ground was barred (Section 32). Any party to an arbitration agreement or any person claiming under him could challenge the existence or validity of an arbitration agreement or have its effect determined through such challenge. The courts decided such application on affidavits usually, though it was permissible to admit other evidence also. As held by the Supreme Court in *Khardah Co.*'s case, Section 33 represented 'the law on the subject as understood in England at the time of that legislation and as declared later by the House of Lords' in *Heyman*'s case.

Further Strides: The Case of *Harbour Assurance Co.*

The case of *Harbour Assurance Co. (UK) Ltd. v. Kansa General International Assurance Co. Ltd.*[10] posed the following question directly: whether in English law, under the principle of separability or autonomy of the agreement expressed in an arbitration clause, which clause is contained in a written contract, the clause can give jurisdiction to the arbitrators under that clause to determine a dispute over the initial *validity* or *invalidity* of the written contract on the assumptions that upon its true construction the arbitration clause covers such a dispute and that the nature of the invalidity alleged does not attack the validity of the agreement expressed in the arbitration clause itself?

At the outset, the judgment of the appeal court acknowledges[11] the orthodox view in English law that 'if the contract in which the arbitration clause is contained is void ab initio, and therefore nothing, so also must the arbitration clause in the contract. That is the proposition that nothing can come of nothing, *ex nihil nil fit*'. That view was put to test in the facts of *Harbour Assurance Co.*'s case, where the plaintiffs claimed that certain reinsurance policies were void and did not give rise to any liability on the part of the plaintiffs. The allegations were that the defendants were guilty of non-disclosure of material facts and misrepresentation, by reason of which the plaintiffs were entitled to, and did, avoid the reinsurances. In addition, the plaintiffs claimed that the defendants were not registered or approved to effect or carry on insurance or reinsurance business in Great Britain, and as a result, the reinsurances were void for illegality. The latter contention, it was claimed, undermined the whole contract. The trial court felt 'compelled by authority' to hold that the principle of separability could not extend so as to enable the arbitrator to determine whether or not the contract, in which the arbitration clause is contained, is in fact void ab initio for illegality and dismissed the application for stay of the proceedings. The Court of Appeal noted the developments of law in other jurisdictions, Leggatt, L.J. observed as follows:

> In my judgment this court is not obliged by authority to prevent the arbitrator from determining the issue of initial illegality. The tide is flowing in favour of permitting the arbitrator to do so, and it is no more necessary on grounds of public policy for the courts to retain exclusive control over the determination of the initial legality of agreements than over their subsequent legality. In particular, it would ill become the courts of this country, by setting their face against this jurisdiction, to deprive those engaged in international commerce of the opportunity of entrusting such disputes to English commercial arbitrators without the need for arbitration clauses containing elaborate self-fulfilling formulae.

Lord Hoffman rejected the sweeping proposition that the separability doctrine cannot apply to any rule which prevents the contract from coming into existence or makes it void ab initio, in the following words:

> It seems to me impossible to accept so sweeping a proposition. There will obviously be cases in which a claim that no contract came into existence necessarily entails a denial that there was any agreement to arbitrate. Cases of non est factum or denial that there was a concluded agreement, or mistake as to the identity of the other contracting party suggest themselves as examples. But there is no reason why every case of initial invalidity should have this consequence. A curious contrary example is the decision of the Court of Appeal of Bermuda in *Sojuznefteexport v. Joc Oil Ltd.* (1990) 15 YBCA 384, in which the signatory to an agreement containing an arbitration clause had no authority to bind the plaintiff to the substantive obligations but was authorized to sign an arbitration agreement. The court held that the arbitration clause was separable and binding. The decision was reached under Soviet law as the proper law of the contract, but I think that the answer in English law would have been the same.
>
> In every case it seems to me that the logical question is not whether the issue goes to the validity of the contract but whether it goes to the validity of the arbitration clause. The one may entail the other but, as

we have seen, it may not. When one comes to voidness for illegality, it is particularly necessary to have regard to the purpose and policy of the rule which invalidates the contract and to ask, as the House of Lords did in *Heyman v. Darwins Ltd.*, whether the rule strikes down the arbitration clause as well. There may be cases in which the policy of the rule is such that it would be liable to be defeated by allowing the issue to be determined by a tribunal chosen by the parties. This may be especially true of *contrats d'adhesion* in which the arbitrator is in practice the choice of the dominant party. Thus saying that arbitration clauses, because separable, are never affected by the illegality of the principal contract is as much a case of false logic as saying that they must be.

Through these words, the English law took one further important step towards the fullest effect to the separability principle. Short of the initial illegality striking at the very validity of the arbitration clause, the Appeal Court in *Harbour Assurance Co.* in effect declared that disputes as to the initial illegality or ab initio voidness of the underlying or containing contract could very well be gone into by the arbitrators, provided of course the arbitration clause was wide enough to cover such disputes. There was nothing in principle to require the courts to hold otherwise.

With these dicta, the separability principle received its fullest content. It was firmly entrenched in English law as the basis of the arbitrator's jurisdiction. It was now left to the advent of the principle of *Kompetenz-Kompetenz* to overcome the last barrier, namely, unworkability of the arbitration clause where the initial illegality struck at its very root. The law had to await the formation of the UNCITRAL Model Arbitration Law, which was followed up by various jurisdictions by amending their respective domestic laws.

UNCITRAL Model Law

This model law is probably the single-most important contribution by the United Nations to international arbitrations. It is this law which has greatly influenced the making of the new Act of 1996 in India, namely, the Arbitration and Conciliation Act, 1996. The Model Law took the separability principle one notch above and combined with it the principle of *Kompetenz-Kompetenz*. Paragraph (1) of Article 16, which in substance formulates the amalgam, is in the following terms:

> The arbitral tribunal may rule on its own jurisdiction, including any objection with respect to the existence or validity of the arbitration agreement. For that purpose, an arbitration clause which forms part of a contract shall be treated as an agreement independent of the other terms of the contract. A decision by the arbitral tribunal that the contract is null and void shall not entail *ipso jure* the invalidity of the arbitration clause.

Paragraph (1), apart from affirming that the arbitration clause forming part of the contract shall have a separate existence from the other terms of the contract, grants the arbitral tribunal the power to rule on its own jurisdiction, including any objections with respect to the *existence or validity of the arbitration agreement.* That is precisely the principle of *Kompetenz-Kompetenz.* The separation of the arbitration clause is not only complete and pervasive but the arbitrator appointed under it has, by a statutory fiction, the authority to rule on it even if the initial illegality of the contract undermines the very arbitration clause. When the power of the arbitral tribunal was expressed in such widest terms, a concern was expressed in the UN that,

> [T]he provision would not be acceptable to certain States which did not grant such power to arbitrators or to those parties who did not want the arbitrators to rule on their own jurisdiction. It was stated in reply that the principle embedded in the paragraph was an important one for the functioning of international commercial arbitration; nonetheless, it was ultimately for each State, when adopting the Model Law, to decide whether it wished to accept the principle and, if so, possibly to express in the text that parties could exclude or limit that power.[12]

Each contracting state had a different response to this Article. The US has traditionally been rather reluctant to acknowledge the principle of *Kompetenz-Kompetenz.* The Federal Arbitration Act makes no mention of the principle. On the other hand, Section 3 of the Act empowers the courts to decide all arbitrability issues.[13] The U.S. Supreme Court and most commentators acknowledged the fullest jurisdiction in this behalf to the federal court till the landmark decision of the U.S. Supreme Court in the case of *First Options of Chicago, Inc. v. Kaplan*.[14] In *First Options*' case, the court held that arbitrability is an issue that has to be decided in courts 'unless the parties clearly and unmistakably provide otherwise'. The courts, ruled the *First Options*' case, would respect the parties' choice to unambiguously contract for *Kompetenz-Kompetenz*. The question, to be asked, is: Whether the parties unambiguously agreed to submit the arbitrability question itself to arbitration? The French view the matter in an entirely different manner. The rule of *Kompetenz-Kompetenz*, codified in Art. 1465 and 1448 of the French Code of Civil Procedure, provides for an *exclusive* jurisdiction of the arbitral tribunal to rule on objections to its jurisdiction and an intervention of the court only when the arbitration agreement is manifestly void or manifestly not applicable, though even in that case, the review of the court is possible only if the arbitral tribunal is not seized of the dispute. Once the arbitral tribunal is constituted, it is for the tribunal to exclusively resolve challenges to its own jurisdiction, whatever the basis of the objections. Once the award is rendered, however, all inquiries into the arbitral jurisdiction are open to French Courts. The English Arbitration Act, 1996, modeled on UNCITRAL Law, whilst accepting in the fullest measure the principle of Article 16(1), leaves it to the parties to apply for stay of proceedings before the arbitral tribunal,[15] 'whilst an application is made to the Court under Section 32 (determination of preliminary point of jurisdiction)'. Section 32, in turn, provides for the power of the court to determine questions 'as to the substantive jurisdiction of the tribunal' on an application made by a party to arbitral proceedings with the agreement in writing of all the other parties to the proceedings or made with the permission of the tribunal and the court is satisfied, (a) that the determination of the question is likely to produce substantial savings in costs, (b) that the application was made without delay, and (c) that there is good reason why the matter should be decided by the court. Indian law, on the other hand, has no such reservation. It states the principle on exactly the same terms as Article 16(1).[16] However, as we shall see in the following section, judicial inroads still continued to be made under the Indian Arbitration Act of 1996, particularly under powers reserved to the courts under Sections 8, 11, and 45 of that Act.

The Arbitration and Conciliation Act, 1996

The Arbitration and Conciliation Act, 1996, which notes in its preamble the significant contribution made by the Model Law and Rules of UNCITRAL to the 'establishment of a unified legal framework for the fair and efficient settlement of disputes arising in international commercial relations' and acknowledges the expediency of making a law 'respecting arbitration and conciliation, taking into account the aforesaid Model Law and Rules', fully adopts the principles of separability and *Kompetenz-Kompetenz* in UNCITRAL Model Law and Rules. These are contained in Section 16 of the act, *Competence of Arbitral Tribunal to Rule on its Jurisdiction*. The pivotal provision, sub-section (1) of that section, is in the following terms:

(1) The arbitral tribunal may rule on its own jurisdiction, including ruling on any objections with respect to the existence or validity of the arbitration agreement, and for that purpose,

    (a) an arbitration clause which forms part of a contract shall be treated as an agreement independent of the other terms of the contract; and

    (b) a decision by the arbitral tribunal that the contract is null and void shall not entail ipso jure the invalidity of the arbitration clause.

The provision is cast in exactly the same terms as Article 16(1) of the Model Law. Complementing the power and authority of the arbitrator to rule on his own jurisdiction is the lack of power in any judicial authority to rule on such jurisdiction at any time before the arbitrator ruling on it. This is achieved by Section 16(5) and (6) read with Section 34 and Section 5. Under Section 16(5) and (6), the arbitrator has to decide the plea that he either lacks the jurisdiction or is exceeding it and where he takes a decision rejecting the plea, continue with the arbitral proceedings and make an award. Such award can be challenged only under Section 34. (Acceptance of the plea calls for an appeal under Section 37) Section 5 prohibits any intervention by a judicial authority in a matter governed by Part I except where so provided in the Part. [Sections 16(1), (5), and (6), 34, and 37 come within Part I.]

The Supreme Court noted in *Wellington Associates Ltd. v. Kirit Mehta*[17] that the disability resulting from Section 33 of the Old Act of 1940, namely, that any question as to the 'existence' of the arbitration agreement was to be decided only by application to the court, and not by the arbitrator, was now removed by Section 16 of the new Act. Section 16, corresponding to Article 16 of the UNCITRAL Model Law and Article 21 of the UNCITRAL Arbitration Rules, provides for the power of the arbitral tribunal to decide whether there is in 'existence' an arbitration clause. Though the power of the arbitral tribunal to decide issues of arbitrability was, thus, fully recognized in the arbitration law of India, by means of the provisions of the new Act of 1996, the exclusive power of the arbitral tribunal to rule on its jurisdiction in the first instance was not recognized. In *Wellington Associates*' case itself, the Supreme Court observed that the language of Section 16 of the new Act showed that it was only an 'enabling' provision; the section permits the arbitral tribunal to rule on the 'existence' of the arbitration clause, but does not declare that except the arbitral tribunal none else could do so. In particular, the court held that Section 16 did not take away the jurisdiction of the Chief Justice or his designate to decide the question of 'existence' of the arbitration agreement whilst considering an application for appointment of the arbitral tribunal under Section 11.

The immediate question which arose out of this position, particularly in the context of Section 11 of the new Act, was what really is the nature of the jurisdiction exercised by the Chief Justice or his designate under that provision: is it really adjudicatory or is it something akin to an administrative function. In *Konkan Railway Corporation Ltd. v. Rani Construction P. Ltd.*,[18] the Supreme Court held that the order of the Chief Justice or his designate under Section 11 nominating an arbitrator is neither an adjudicatory order nor those functionaries could be held to be a tribunal to make such a decision the subject matter of an appeal under Article 136 of the Constitution of India. Adverting to Section 16 of the 1996 Act, the Constitution Bench held that the questions relating to improper constitution of an arbitral tribunal or its want of jurisdiction or objections with respect to the existence or validity of the arbitration agreement are matters which should be canvassed before the arbitral tribunal itself which has been specifically empowered to rule on such issues and on its own jurisdiction, as well. The decision in *Konkan Railway Corporation Ltd. v. Mehul Construction Co.*,[19] rendered sometime before *Rani Construction*'s case, also proceeded on the basis that at a time when the matter comes before the Chief Justice or his nominee under Section 11, it would not be appropriate for them to entertain any contentious issues between the parties and decide the same; their decision is merely an administrative order. Based on these two decisions, the Supreme Court in *Food Corporation of India v. Indian Council of Arbitration*[20] struck down a Delhi High Court order where the High Court had adopted an adjudicatory role and 'returned a verdict recording reasons as to the very existence or otherwise of the agreement as well as the tenability and legality or otherwise of making a reference to an arbitrator'. The court held that even if there be any infirmity in the arbitration clause which goes to the root of the arbitrator's jurisdiction, it had to be adjudicated by the arbitral tribunal itself, under Section 16.

This position was, however, overturned by the momentous decision of a Seven Judge Constitution Bench in the case of *S.B.P. & Co. v. Patel Engineering Ltd.*[21] In that case, after surveying all previous authorities on the subject, the Supreme Court held that the exercise of the power by the Chief Justice or his designate under Section 11 was a 'Judicial' act. The net result of the decision was that the Chief Justice or his designate, whilst considering the question of appointment of an arbitrator, was required to go into the questions of existence and validity of the arbitration agreement, all of which are jurisdictional matters covered by Section 16.

This position further gave rise to a distinction between three types of issues: (a) issues which *have to be decided* under Section 11, which included the question of 'existence' of an arbitration agreement, (b) issues which *may be decided* by the Chief Justice or his designate, which included issues as to limitation, and accord and satisfaction, and (c) issues which *have to be left to the arbitral tribunal* to decide, such as arbitrability of a claim (whether it falls within the arbitration clause) and merits of a claim. This was recognized in a lucid judgment of the Supreme Court in *National Insurance Co. Ltd. v. Boghara Polyfab Pvt.Ltd.*[22]

That was the ruling position in respect of Section 11, but even under Section 8, the court or judicial authority, as the case may be, it was held, had to decide the questions of existence and validity of the arbitration agreement under the new Act. Though unlike Article 8 of the UNCITRAL Model Law, the power of a judicial authority under the Act of 1996, to refer the parties to arbitration, when a matter covered by an arbitration agreement was brought before it, was not circumscribed by the qualification 'unless it finds that the said agreement is null and void, inoperative, or incapable of being performed', there was a divergence of authority in India relating to the scope and nature of powers under Section 8, in this behalf. Some courts took a view that these decisions of a judicial authority would be binding on the arbitral tribunal, and to that extent, excluded the power of the arbitral tribunal under Section 16.[23] The other view was that these jurisdictional issues must be left to be determined by the arbitral tribunal.[24]

Yet another provision of the new Act, which retained the power of judicial authorities to rule on the arbitrator's jurisdiction before he did so, was Section 45 of the Act which came under Part II dealing with 'enforcement of certain foreign awards'. Section 45 required a judicial authority, when seized of an action in a matter covered by an international commercial arbitration agreement to which the New York Convention applied, to refer the parties, at the request of one of them, to arbitration, 'unless it finds that the said agreement is null and void, inoperative, or incapable of being performed'. Thus, in order to relegate the parties to arbitration, the court had to be satisfied that the agreement is valid, operative, and capable of being performed. This section was interpreted by the Supreme Court in *Shin-Etsu Chemical Co. Ltd. v. Aksh Optifibre Ltd.*[25] to the effect that the review by the court to determine the validity of the arbitration agreement has to be on a prima facie basis. The court's view was that any other interpretation would defeat the basic principle of the new Act, namely, enabling expeditious arbitration with limited court interference. In case of an affirmative finding with respect to the existence of an arbitration agreement, the party challenging it could still argue otherwise before the arbitral tribunal, since it was competent to rule on its jurisdiction under Section 16. The issue could be raised, once again, under Section 48(a) whilst opposing the enforcement of the award. In case of a negative finding, on the other hand, there was a right to appeal under Section 50. Dharmadhikari J., in a concurring judgment, explained the matter in the following words:

The main issue is regarding the scope of power of any judicial authority including a regular civil court under Section 45 of the Act in making or refusing a reference of dispute arising from an international
arbitration agreement governed by the provisions contained in Part
III [*sic*: Part II] Chapter I of the Act of 1996. I respectfully agree with
learned Brother Srikrishna, J. only to the extent that if on a prima
facie examination of the documents and material on record including
the arbitration agreement on which request for reference is made by
one of the parties, the judicial authority or the court decides to make
a reference, it may merely mention the submissions and contentions
of the parties and summarily decide the objection if any raised on
the alleged nullity, voidness, inoperativeness, or incapability of the
arbitration agreement. In case, however, on a prima facie view of
the matter, which is required to be objectively taken on the basis of
material and evidence produced by the parties on the record of the
case, the judicial authority including a regular civil court, is inclined
to reject the request for reference on the ground that the agreement
is 'null and void' or 'inoperative' or 'incapable of being performed'
within the meaning of Section 45 of the Act, the judicial authority or the court must afford full opportunities to the parties to lead
whatever documentary or oral evidence they want to lead and then
decide the question like trial of a preliminary issue on jurisdiction or
limitation in regular civil suit *and* pass an elaborate reasoned order.
Where a judicial authority or the court refuses to make a reference on
the grounds available under Section 45 of the Act, it is necessary for
the judicial authority or the court which is seized of the matter to pass
a reasoned order as the same is subject to appeal to the appellate court
under Section 50(1)(a) of the Act and further appeal to this Court
under sub-section (2) of the said section.[26]

Once again, the position was overturned by the three judge bench
ruling of the Supreme Court in the case of *Chloro Controls India
Private Limited v. Severn Trent Water Purification Inc.*[27] The Supreme
Court appears to have based its decision on two grounds. First, it
applied the law laid down by the Supreme Court in *S.B.P. & Co.*'s
case on Section 11 to an application under Section 45 of the 1996
Act. Just as the decision of the Chief Justice or his designate on the
issue of jurisdiction and the existence of a valid arbitration agreement
would be binding on the parties when the matter goes to the arbitral tribunal, it would be so in the case of a decision of the judicial

authority under Sections 8 and 45. 'The underlining [*sic*: underlying] principle of finality in Section 11(7) would be applicable with equal force while dealing with the interpretation of Sections 8 and 45'.[28] Secondly, the court observed that there was an absence in Chapter I Part II of the 1996 Act of any provision like Section 16 appearing in Part I of the same Act, suggestive of the requirement for the court to determine the question referred to in Section 45, namely, the nullity, voidness, inoperability, or incapability of performance of the arbitration agreement, at the threshold itself. As for the rule of *Kompetenz-Kompetenz*, this is what the court had to say:

> We are not oblivious of the principle 'kompetenz kompetenz'. It requires the Arbitral Tribunal to rule on its own jurisdiction and at the first instance. One school of thought propagates that it has duly the positive effect as it enables the arbitrator to rule on its own jurisdiction as it widely recognized international arbitration. However, the negative effect is equally important, that the courts are deprived of their jurisdiction. The arbitrators are to be not the sole judge but first judge, of their jurisdiction. In other words, it is to allow them to come to a decision on their own jurisdiction prior to any court or other judicial authority and thereby limit the jurisdiction of the national courts to review the award. The kompetenz kompetenz rule, thus, concerned not only is the positive but also the negative effect of the arbitration agreement.[29]

The resulting position presented a peculiar picture. Though the arbitral tribunal had unbridled power to rule on its jurisdiction and whilst doing so, determine the existence, validity, and effect of the arbitration agreement under Section 16 of the Act, the court could still usurp that function (a) under Section 8, having to inquire into the existence and validity of the agreement possibly finally (though there are contrary views expressed), (b) under Section 11, whilst considering the appointment of the arbitral tribunal, having compulsorily to consider some questions bearing on the jurisdiction of the arbitrator, whilst optionally so in case of others, and (c) under Section 45, having to consider finally the issues of existence and validity whilst hearing an application for reference of the parties to arbitration. It was now left to the legislature to intervene and correct some of the anomalies. This is precisely what the Amending

Act 3 of 2016 purports to do. We shall presently see how far it succeeds in that.

Amendment Act 3 of 2016

Some of these issues have now been addressed by the Arbitration and Conciliation (Amendment) Act, 2015 (that is, Amendment Act 3 of 2016), which makes extensive amendments to the Arbitration Act, 1996. In the first place, it makes a far-reaching alteration in Section 8 of the 1996 Act insofar as the power of any judicial authority to refer the parties to arbitration, when an action is brought before it in a matter which is the subject matter of an arbitration agreement, is concerned. Though Section 8, as it originally stood prior to that amendment, did not in terms prescribe any such requirements for the judicial authority, by judicial interpretation, as we have seen above, the authorities were required to consider if the arbitration agreement is null and void or inoperative or incapable of being performed. As we have noted above, this introduced a certain dilution of the principle of *Kompetenz-Kompetenz* and separability and allowed the court to practically rule on the arbitrator's jurisdiction before the arbitrator himself could do it. Now under the amended provisions of Section 8, judicial authorities, whilst considering an application under Section 8, are merely required to consider if prima facie a valid agreement exists. The section now mandates judicial authorities to refer the parties to arbitration, if the matter before them is the subject of an arbitration agreement and a party thereto applies to them within time as provided in Section 8, 'unless it finds that prima facie no valid arbitration agreement exists'. It is now for the arbitral tribunal to consider finally, in the first place, the question of its jurisdiction, including any objections with respect to the existence or validity of the arbitration agreement, even when the parties are referred to it under a court order passed under Section 8. With that the principle of *Kompetenz-Kompetenz* is taken one step ahead to reach its fullest potential.

Insofar as the appointment provisions of the Arbitration Act, 1996 are concerned, namely, Section 11 of the Act, the Amendment Act, 2015 now restricts the inquiry of the Supreme Court or, as the case may be, the High Court, whilst considering an application for appointment of an arbitrator, to 'the examination of the existence of an arbitration agreement'. The questions of validity, it would appear are now beyond the pale of the court whilst considering the arbitrator's appointment. The matter, however, is by no means clear, since by judicial interpretation, it is still possible to expand the meaning of the word 'existence' so as to take into its fold the 'legal' existence of an arbitration agreement. It would have been far better, as we shall presently see, if the determination of the existence of the arbitration agreement and consequently, the jurisdiction of the arbitral tribunal thereunder, would have been left to be determined by the court on a prima facie consideration, as in the case of amended Section 8. The net effect of the amended Section 11, as it is presently worded, is that unlike in the case of an arbitration without reference to court, in the event of appointment of an arbitral tribunal is being sought from the court under Section 11 of the Act, it is the court which rules on the 'existence' of the arbitration agreement and thereby, on the jurisdiction of the arbitral tribunal, such determination being then binding on the arbitral tribunal.

As for Section 45 of the Act, which comes within Part II relating to the enforcement of certain foreign awards, the position remains the same as in the case of the unamended Act of 1996. As earlier, under Section 45 of the Act, a judicial authority, when seized of an action in a matter in respect of which parties have made an arbitration agreement to which the New York Convention applies, shall at the request of any of the parties refer them to arbitration unless it finds that the said agreement is 'null and void or inoperative or incapable of being performed'. Such determination would, on the principle of the *Chloro Controls*' case, be binding on the arbitral tribunal. In the case of an international commercial arbitration, thus, in a matter brought before a judicial authority in India, if it is covered by an arbitration agreement within the meaning of Section 44, the parties are required to be referred to arbitration subject to the consideration of the questions of existence, validity, and enforceability of the arbitration agreement.

The Road Ahead

Although some of the anomalies under the unamended Act of 1996, as interpreted by courts, are removed by the Amending Act 3 of

2016, the law still does not propagate the principle of *Kompetenz-Kompetenz* in its fullest expression. The fullest expression, which one possibly finds in the French approach, requires the arbitral tribunal to have the first exclusive right to rule on its own jurisdiction before any court does so, with the only exception being a case where the arbitration agreement is manifestly void or inapplicable. In this sense, the principle not only has a positive dimension, that is to say, reserving the arbitrator's power to rule on his jurisdiction, but also a negative one, namely, restricting the national courts' power to do so at the outset. The Indian law is yet to recognize this negative aspect completely. First, the dicta of the Supreme Court in the case of *Wellington Associates'* case of Section 16 being an 'enabling' provision and not an 'excluding' provision, still continue to be valid and reflected in the amended provisions of the Act. Secondly, there is now an uneven handling of the statutory provisions for judicial inquiries into the arbitrator's jurisdiction before he rules on it. Section 8 requires the court to determine the arbitrator's jurisdiction only on a prima facie consideration, whilst Section 45 mandates the court, on the principle of *Chloro Controls'* case, to finally determine the questions of existence, validity, and effect of the arbitration agreement, such determination being binding on the arbitrator. The appointment provision of Section 11, on the other hand, restricts the courts to the determination of questions of 'existence' of the arbitration agreement, possibly a throwback to the rule of *Harbour Assurance Co.* Besides, this different treatment of statutory intrusions into the arbitrator's authority does not appear to be based on any principle. For example, there is no discernible principle why a judicial authority should refer the parties to arbitration after taking a prima facie view of the existence, validity, and effect of the arbitration agreement acting under Section 8, but the court, whilst acting under Section 11, should take a final and binding view of the existence of the arbitration agreement. After all, in *Chloro Controls'* case, the Supreme Court had felt the need to place Sections 8, 11, and 45 on the same footing as a matter of principle.

How does one go from here? Whether we approach the solutions judicially or by the statutory route, it is important, as in the case of most solutions to complex issues, to go to the very basics or fundamentals of the issue. The principles of *Kompetenz-Kompetenz* and separability, in a fundamental or basic sense, simply mean that the arbitral tribunal has the exclusive jurisdiction, though not exclusive in the sense that it cannot be called into question in a court of law, to first rule on its jurisdiction before any national court is called upon to do so. The rule, as the French clearly understand it, is merely a 'rule of chronological priority'. All that it means is that in every case, it is for the arbitral tribunal to first rule on its jurisdiction, when the parties ordain it so. The national courts may come in only after the award is rendered, in a challenge to the award or its enforcement. That way the principle of party autonomy gets its fullest play and at the same time the national courts are not in any way handicapped to review the exercise of jurisdiction by the arbitral tribunal uninfluenced by the latter's own assessment of it. It achieves expeditious disposal of arbitrations with least interference by the national courts. It prevents unscrupulous parties from delaying recourse to arbitration, an expressly chosen bipartisan remedy. The French Court of Appeal, long before the international recognition of the principle of *Kompetenz-Kompetenz*, in the 1957 case of *Jules Buck et Louis Dolivet v. Eddie Constantine et Gaston Terminet dit Allain*,[30] put the matter thus:

> When the parties attributed the competence to arbitrators alone to decide on the validity of the arbitration clause [...] such attribution, which is not contrary to any principle of the ordre public, takes the place of the law for the parties [...] and cannot be derogated from [...] were the rule otherwise, a party in bad faith to the arbitration could paralyze the proceeding.

After all, thus viewed, namely, as a rule of chronological priority, the principle is open to only one criticism and that is the waste of time and money in an arbitral proceeding, which might have no legal existence or validity. But then even a seemingly existing arbitration agreement can be questioned by a party with bad faith, requiring the courts to deliver a final verdict on the arbitrability, and as a result, involving a lot of judicial time and avoidable expense to the parties. We have to simply choose here between the two options. In Indian context, considering the law's endemic delays and the propensity of Indians to litigate, one may rather err on the side of a party having to go through the arbitral machinery in an undeserving case than unsuspecting parties in practically every case having at the outset to go through a thorough and final review of arbitrator's jurisdiction at the hands of national courts. The preferred option, of course, would leave out cases where there is manifestly no arbitration agreement in place. As in the case of amended Section 8, an inquiry into the arbitrator's jurisdiction on a prima facie basis would obviate a futile resort to arbitration in such cases. Cases where the court finds that there is not even a prima facie valid arbitration agreement in existence need not go to arbitration through courts either under Section 8, 11, or 45.

Considering the amended provision of Section 8 and its parity in a fundamental sense with Section 45, it should not be difficult to go back to the *Shin-Etsu* principle laid down by the Supreme Court. It is possible to judicially so interpret Section 45 as would restrict the scope of judicial scrutiny at that stage to determination of the validity of an arbitration agreement only on a prima facie basis. Insofar as Section 11 is concerned, it would more appropriately need a statutory intervention to restrict the inquiry to a purely prima facie consideration. The original principle of the two *Konkan Railway Corporation* cases, having been already overturned by a seven judge bench, in *S.B.P. & Co.*, it may be more apposite for the legislature to intervene than to wait for an even larger bench to reconsider the whole law on the subject.

Introduction of a prima facie consideration in all three provisions, Sections 8, 11, and 45, lends not only a distinct rationality to the approach to the principle of *Kompetenz-Kompetenz* but also plain simplicity and consistency to it. While it avoids recourse to arbitration through courts in cases where the arbitration agreement manifestly does not exist, it allows the arbitration proceedings to conclude expeditiously in all cases, giving party autonomy its fullest content and yet preserves all post-award remedies to aggrieved parties, uninfluenced by the arbitrator's own assessment of his jurisdiction.

Notes and References

1. *Russell on Arbitration*, 21st ed. (Sweet & Maxwell, 2015), 2-61.
2. [1909] SC (HL) 53.
3. [1915] AC 499.
4. [1926] AC 497.
5. [1942] 1 All ER 337.

6. AIR 1953 Cal. 642.
7. (1948) ILR 2 Cal. 171.
8. AIR 1959 SC 1362 (V 46 C 193).
9. AIR 1962 SC 1810 (V 49 C 251).
10. [1993] 3 All ER 897.
11. [1993] 3 All ER 897.
12. UNCITRAL Report on Adoption of Model Law, para 151.
13. United States (Federal) Arbitration Act (FAA) § 3, 9 U.S.C. § 3 (1997).
14. 515 U.S. 938 (1995).
15. The Arbitration and Conciliation Act, 1996, 31(5).
16. The Arbitration and Conciliation Act, 1996.
17. (2000) 4 SCC 272.
18. 2002 (6) Bom CR 313.
19. AIR 2000 SC 2821.
20. (2003) 6 SCC 564.
21. (2005) 8 SCC 618.
22. (2009) 1 SCC 267.
23. *Chemical Sales Agencies v. Smt. Naraini Newar*, 2005 (1) Arb LR 193 (Delhi); *G.E. Capital Transportation Financial Services Ltd. v. Amritajit Mitra*, 2009 (3) Arb LR 51.
24. *Ranwa Construction Co. v. The Administrator*, 2006 (1) Arb LR 207 (Raj).
25. (2005) 7 SCC 234.
26. (2005) 7 SCC 111.
27. (2013) 1 SCC 641.
28. (2013) 1 SCC130.
29. Refer Fouchard Gaillard Goldman on *International Commercial Arbitration*. (2013) 1 SCC 129.
30. Cour d'appel de Paris, D. 1957. J. 566 (note J. R.), J.C.P. 1957. II. 10165 (22 January 1957).

5

Grounds for Challenging an Arbitral Award in India

Tushar Mehta

Finality of an arbitral award, scope of its scrutiny by a supervisory court, and the grounds on which such a supervisory court can interfere with an arbitral award are decisions which have consistently raised many perplexed questions among all jurisdictions in the world.

Essentially, the alternate dispute resolution (ADR) mechanism has evolved so as to ensure that the businessmen who enter into a commercial transaction with open eyes and diligence are given a redressal forum for their disputes, in which party autonomy would prevail over other technical rules, procedure, and evidence, thereby giving flexibility to adjudicating parties. Wherein, unlike a court where dispute would be adjudicated as per the procedural rules of statutes and by an adjudicator appointed as per the roaster of the said court, the parties would have the option to choose specialists or technical experts as adjudicators, who in all circumstances were considered by these businessmen as better placed persons than a judge to appreciate and understand the technical issues involved in the dispute and to provide a practical decision for its resolution. It also sought to confer finality to the resolution arrived through the process of arbitration by envisaging a very limited scope of interference by the municipal courts, who were conferred with a consolatory, supervisory jurisdiction to scrutinize an arbitral award, on limited grounds, just to ensure that no grave injustice is done to a party resorting to remedy under arbitration.

However, despite myriad advantages envisaged in the concept of arbitration, there have always been constant whisperings of dissatisfaction when it comes to implementation of this scheme of arbitration; more particularly, in the arena of implementation of the arbitral award and its finality in the eyes of the supervisory courts which have been conferred with limited jurisdiction, in every municipal law, to scrutinize the same.

As witnessed globally, the Indian arbitration law also saw, rather is still seeing, its share of ambiguity as to what would be the correct form and content of an arbitral award which would confer finality to it, without any interference by the supervisory municipal court. The problem has aggravated because in arbitration, parties chose their own procedure without taking guidance from any statute which, if followed, can insulate it from any fatal infirmities of law.

The precedents show that the law related to the 'grounds permissible under law for challenging arbitration award' did not evolve on the touchstone of statutory prescription or on literal interpretation of statutory mandate, but the same evolved through the course of successive judicial interpretation of statute—fitting and supplementing diverse fact situations in pursuit of achieving that not only is justice done but is also seen to be done. In reality, as experienced world over, in India also 'grounds permissible under law for challenging arbitration award' evolved on judge-centric approaches, adopted from time to time by various benches. These judge-centric approaches also included adoption of principles evolved by the courts of other jurisdiction which fitted into the factual situations mushrooming before Indian courts in its liberalized economy.

The literature and jurisprudence of arbitration laws shows that the parties to the proceedings have always considered the statute, that is, the Arbitration Act, to be a mandate in abstract and sought to give it a life by asserting divergent interpretations of the statute. Classic example of this approach can be found in judicial dissection between the meaning of 'venue' and 'seat' of arbitration. This branch of law evolved so as to ascertain jurisdiction of the court that would have supervisory control over an arbitration and would be competent to entertain an appeal challenging the finality of the arbitral award in such arbitral proceedings or to interfere with an arbitration proceedings at an interim stage.

Although the world over, the said distinction was not contemplated in the statutes and it is difficult to understand that businessmen, who consciously drafted and incorporated the arbitration agreement in their contract after a series of negotiations, chose to stipulate only the venue (which can be anywhere in the world as per the agreement of the parties) but remained silent on the most cardinal point, that is, seat of said arbitration.

However, the parties as per their convenience, who either wanted to invoke the jurisdiction of their preferred country or wanted to block the courts of an unpreferred country from exercising their supervisory jurisdiction—on grounds of the so-called 'statutory appellate jurisdiction' over an award—advanced their arguments through astute practitioners having a zealous allegiance to uphold their client's interest. This was in turn accepted by the superior courts and resulted in an arbitration clause being dissected into: (a) proper law of contract; (b) proper law of arbitration agreement; (c) proper law of reference; (d) the Curial law or procedural law or the Lex Fori, so as to reach and render a final statement of law that Indian courts would not have any jurisdiction over a foreign award if it is found that on the facts of a case either the juridical seat of the arbitration is outside India or the law governing the arbitration agreement is a law other than Indian law.[1] To ascertain as to whether on facts juridical seat of the arbitration is outside India, the Indian Supreme Court propounded the theory of 'Closest and Intimate connection test'.[2]

Through the aforesaid decision rendered in *Reliance Industries* case, the Supreme Court of India impliedly overruled a 15-year-old judgment rendered by it in *Bhatia International*[3] wherein the Hon'ble Supreme Court held that,

[In] cases of international commercial arbitrations held out of India provisions of Part I would apply[4] unless the parties by agreement, express or implied, exclude all or any of its provisions. In that case the laws or rules chosen by the parties would prevail. Any provision, in Part I, which is contrary to or excluded by that law or rules will not apply.

The aforesaid discussion is only to show how the law relating to arbitration is purely judge propounded and the position of law in so far as jurisdiction of Indian courts is concerned is interfering with a foreign award.

To appreciate the grounds on which such indulgence can be shown by the Indian courts, both for domestic as well as foreign awards, distinction between which would be discussed in subsequent paragraphs, it is relevant to first appreciate the process through which ADR mechanism statutorily evolved in India.

The first ADR statute was enacted in British India by way of the Indian Arbitration Act, 1899 (the 1899 Act). This pre-independent Act envisaged very restricted grounds for interfering with an arbitral award. The only grounds available under the said Act were: (a) arbitrator's misconduct and (b) improper procurement of award.

Fortunately, due to fewer litigations in those days, the phrase misconduct was constructed narrowly and with great restraint and circumspection. In interpreting these grounds, courts emphasized on judicial restraint and permitted interference only where fraud, corruption, or question of law arising on the face of the award was proved.[5]

The 1899 Act was replaced by another statutory enactment, that is, the Arbitration Act, 1940 (the 1940 Act). The 1940 Act repealed the 1899 Act and in addition to the existing grounds—that is misconduct, and improper procurement of award—the 1940 Act also mentioned that court could also set aside an arbitral award if it was 'otherwise invalid'. With the passage of time, the phrases 'arbitrator's misconduct', 'improper procurement of Award', 'and otherwise invalid' came to be construed liberally by the courts, and the Indian courts widened the scope of their judicial review power by reading into certain common law concepts while defining the said terms, which were otherwise not expressly contemplated by the statute.

Apart from the Arbitration Act, 1940, there were two other enactments of the same genre: the Arbitration (Protocol and Convention) Act, 1937 (for execution of the Geneva Convention Awards) and the Foreign Awards (Recognition and Enforcement) Act, 1961 (for enforcement of the New York Convention Awards).

In the year 1996, the Indian legislature by a consolidating and amending Act, that is the Arbitration and Conciliation Act, 1996 (the 1996 Act), consolidated all the aforesaid three acts relating to domestic arbitration, international commercial arbitration, and enforcement of foreign arbitral awards, with slight modifications, while repealing the 1940 Act and also the Acts of 1937 and 1961. The said 1996 Act was based on the United Nations Commission on International Trade Law (UNCITRAL) Model and to comply with its obligation to provide a uniform law governing the arbitration, both domestic and foreign, as well as the law relating to enforcement of foreign awards in the new borderless areas of commercial agreements. The Indian legislature mutatis mutandis adopted the grounds mentioned in the UNCITRAL Model Law, which became Section 34 of the 1996 Act. The grounds for challenging an arbitral award as mentioned under the said section inter alia provided that a court could interfere with an arbitral award if:

1. a party was under some incapacity;
2. the arbitration agreement was not valid under the law to which the parties had subjected it or, failing any indication thereon, under the law for the time being in force;
3. the party making the application was not given proper notice of the appointment of an arbitrator or of the arbitral proceedings or was otherwise unable to present his case;
4. the arbitral award dealt with a dispute not contemplated by or not falling within the terms of the submission to arbitration, or it contains decisions on matter beyond the scope of the submission to arbitration; or
5. the composition of the Arbitral Tribunal or the arbitral procedure was not in accordance with the agreement of the parties, unless such agreement was in conflict with a provision of this Part from which the parties cannot derogate, or, failing such agreement, was not in accordance with this Part.

The said Section 34 also inter alia contemplated the principles of severability as it provided that if the decisions on matters submitted to arbitration were capable of being separated from those not so submitted, the court exercising supervisory jurisdiction would be empowered to set aside only that part of the arbitral award which contains decisions on matters not submitted to arbitration.

As can be seen, the aforesaid portion of Section 34 of the 1996 Act empowered the supervisory courts to interfere with an arbitral award only on the ground of procedural irregularity; these procedural grounds did not require much judicial interpretation or literature to be developed. However, the entire jurisprudence in this regard boiled down to the portion of Section 34 which provided that an arbitral award would also be set aside if the same was in conflict with the 'public policy of India'. Though the said portion of Section 34 of 1996 Act came with an explanation that an award would be treated to be in conflict with the public policy of India only if the passing of the award was induced or affected by fraud or corruption, the expression 'public policy of India'[6] later came under strict judicial scrutiny and was given an expansive definition from time to time. It is this expression 'public policy' which gave maximum latitude to parties to challenge an arbitral award before the courts in India.

The expression 'public policy of India' first came to be interpreted by the Indian Supreme Court in the case of *Renusagar Power Co. Ltd. v. General Electric Co.*[7] In the said case, the Supreme Court of India for the first time held that an arbitral award can be set aside if it was contrary to (a) fundamental policy of Indian law, (b) the interests of India, or (c) justice or morality.

The Indian Supreme Court in *Renusagar* case gave a narrower meaning to the expression 'public policy' thereby confining judicial review of the arbitral award only to the aforementioned three grounds. It is worth noting that though *Renusagar* was decided under the Foreign Awards (Recognition and Enforcement Act), 1961, and before the enactment of the Arbitration Act of 1996, there was no material difference between the two corresponding provisions; hence, it continued to remain a relevant point of reference.

Almost ten years later, the Indian Supreme Court in *ONGC* (1) case[8] made an apparent shift from the principles laid down in its previous judgment in *Renusagar* case and held that apart from the three grounds stated in *Renusagar* case, the court would also be empowered to set aside an arbitral award on the ground of it being violative of public policy if it is patently arbitrary.

To test an arbitral award on the touchstone of 'patent illegality', the Supreme Court of India in *ONGC* case cited a caution holding that,

> [S]uch patent illegality, however, must go to the root of the matter. The public policy violation, indisputably, should be so unfair and unreasonable as to shock the conscience of the court. Where the arbitrator, however, has gone contrary to or beyond the expressed law of the contract or granted relief in the matter not in dispute would come within the purview of Section 34 of the Act.

Vide the said judgment, the Indian Supreme Court permitted the local supervisory courts to go into the merits of the case, since in the opinion of the Indian Supreme Court, what would constitute public policy was a matter dependent upon the nature of transaction and the nature of statute which can only be ascertained from the pleadings of the parties and the materials brought on record, a scrutiny of which would only enable the court to judge what is in public good or public interest and what would otherwise be injurious to the public good at the relevant point.

Resultantly, the Indian Supreme Court in *ONGC* (1) case laid down the following grounds on which an arbitral award could be challenged before a supervisory court in India:

1. The court can set aside the arbitral award under Section 34(2) of the Act if the party making the application furnishes proof that:
    i.   a party was under some incapacity;
    ii.   the arbitration agreement is not valid under the law to which the parties have subjected it or, failing any indication thereon, under the law for the time being in force;
    iii. the party making the application was not given proper notice of the appointment of an arbitrator or of the arbitral proceedings or was otherwise unable to present his case; or
    iv.   the arbitral award deals with a dispute not contemplated by or not falling within the terms of the submission to arbitration, or it contains decisions on matters beyond the scope of the submission to arbitration.

2. The court may set aside the award:
   i.   if the composition of the Arbitral Tribunal was not in accordance with the agreement of the parties, or if failing such agreement, the composition of the Arbitral Tribunal was not in accordance with Part I of the Act.
   ii. if the arbitral procedure was not in accordance with: (a) the agreement of the parties, or (b) failing such agreement, the arbitral procedure was not in accordance with Part I of the Act. However, exception for setting aside the Award on the ground of composition of Arbitral Tribunal or illegality of arbitral procedure is that the agreement should not be in conflict with the provisions of Part I of the Act from which parties cannot derogate. (c) If the award passed by the Arbitral Tribunal is in contravention of the provisions of the Act or any other substantive law governing the parties or is against the terms of the contract.
3. The Award could be set aside if it is against the public policy of India, that is to say, if it is contrary to: (a) fundamental policy of Indian law; (b) the interest of India; (c) justice or morality; or (d) if it is patently illegal.

Since the Indian Supreme Court in *ONGC* (1) case now permitted scrutiny of an arbitral award on merits in order to ascertain whether the arbitral award was contrary to public policy of India or contrary to any substantive law in force, this new window gave rise to various findings being rendered by the supervisory courts on the true meaning and purport of the expression 'public policy'—on which ground, an arbitral award could be challenged before a supervisory court. This expansive scope of judicial review of arbitral award by the supervisory court led the Hon'ble Supreme Court to once again reiterate the principles on which a supervisory court could interfere with an arbitral award in the case of *SAIL v. Gupta Brother Steel Tubes Ltd.*, (2009) 10 SCC 63, wherein the Supreme Court held:

1. In a case where an arbitrator travels beyond the contract, the award would be without jurisdiction and would amount to legal misconduct and because of which the award would become amenable for being set aside by a court.

2. An error relatable to interpretation of the contract by an arbitrator is an error within his jurisdiction and such error is not amenable to correction by courts as such error is not an error on the face of the award.

3. If a specific question of law is submitted to the arbitrator and he answers it, the fact that the answer involves an erroneous decision in point of law does not make the award bad on its face.

4. An award contrary to substantive provision of law or against the terms of contract would be patently illegal.

5. Where the parties have deliberately specified the amount of compensation in express terms, the party who has suffered by such breach can only claim the sum specified in the contract and not in excess thereof. In other words, no award of compensation in case of breach of contract, if named or specified in the contract, could be awarded in excess thereof.

6. If the conclusion of the arbitrator is based on a possible view of the matter, the court should not interfere with the award.

7. It is not permissible to a court to examine the correctness of the findings of the arbitrator, as if it were sitting in appeal over his findings.

The Supreme Court in 2011 in *Phulchand*,[9] interpreting 'public policy' under Part II of the Act, now went on to expand the test laid down in *ONGC* (1) to apply in case of foreign awards. This allowed the Indian courts to reject enforcement of a foreign award on the additional ground of 'patent illegality' devised in *ONGC* (1). The Supreme Court did not provide clear analysis of its reasons for its keen expansion of *Saw Pipes* and as to why the broad interpretation given in *Saw Pipes* is principally sounder than *Renusagar*, which though under the old Act, had the identical text to Section 48.

Phulchand came to be expressly overruled in 2013 in *Shri Lal Mahal*.[10] The wider meaning given to the expression 'public policy of India' under Section 34(2)(b) (Part I) of the Act' was held by the Supreme Court as not applicable to objections raised against the enforcement of the foreign awards under Section 48(2)(b) of the Act. The expression and concept of the phrase, though identical in Section 34(2)(b) and Section 48(2)(b), was interpreted to be narrower in cases of enforcement of foreign awards than in case of enforcement of domestic arbitral awards; contravention of law alone will not be sufficient to attract the bar of public policy, and something more than contravention of law is required for refusal of enforcement of a foreign award on the ground that it is contrary to public policy of India. *Renusagar* was thus reinstated, and the wide import of the term *ONGC* (1) ceased to apply, once again limiting the possibility of a successful challenge to enforcement of a foreign award in India. That an award must not be refused enforcement merely on the ground of erroneous application of law or on the basis of re-appreciation of evidence, and that the broad interpretations of the term 'public policy' must stay restricted to domestic awards, came to be recommended with substantial emphasis in the Law Commission of India in its 246th Report, which recommended reversion to the *Renusagar* position.

The aforesaid interpretations given by the Indian Supreme Court in *ONGC* (1) and the *SAIL* case occupied the field till recently when the Indian Supreme Court in the *ONGC* (2) case[11] added three other distinct and fundamental juristic principles which were held to be part and parcel of the 'fundamental policy of Indian law' which constituted as a sub-head of challenge under the head 'public policy of India'.

In *ONGC* (2) case, while interpreting the term 'fundamental policy of Indian law' as propounded in *ONGC* (1) case, the Indian Supreme Court held that the 'fundamental policy of Indian law', which was not succinctly interpreted in *ONGC* (1) case, would mean and include all such fundamental principles which form the basis for administration of justice and enforcement of law in India.

The Indian Supreme Court in *ONGC* (2) case referred to the following three distinct and fundamental juristic principles, which it held to be necessarily embodied as part and parcel of the fundamental policy of Indian law. The said principles enunciated by the Indian Supreme Court in *ONGC* (2) case is as under:

Judicial Approach

The Indian Supreme Court held that in every determination whether by a court or other authority that affects the rights of a citizen or leads to any civil consequences, the court or authority concerned is bound to adopt what is in legal parlance called a 'judicial approach' in the matter. The duty to adopt a judicial approach arises from the very nature of the power exercised by the court or the authority and does not have to be separately or additionally enjoined upon the for a concerned. The Indian Supreme Court held that so long as the court, tribunal, or the authority exercising powers that affect the rights or obligations of the parties before them shows fidelity to judicial approach, they cannot act in an arbitrary, capricious, or whimsical manner. Judicial approach ensures that the authority acts bona fide and deals with the subject in a fair, reasonable, and objective manner and that its decision is not actuated by any extraneous consideration. Judicial approach in that sense acts as a check against flaws and faults that can render the decision of a court, tribunal, or authority vulnerable to challenge.

Compliance of Principles of Natural Justice and Non-Application of Mind by the Arbitral Tribunal

The Indian Supreme Court in *ONGC* (2) case held that the fundamental to the policy of Indian law is the principle that a court and so also a quasi-judicial authority must, while determining the rights and obligations of parties before it, do so in accordance with the principles of natural justice. It held that non-application of mind is a defect that is fatal to any adjudication. Application of mind is best demonstrated by disclosure of the mind and disclosure of mind is best done by recording reasons in support of the decision which the court or authority is taking. The requirement that an adjudicatory authority must apply its mind is, in that view, so deeply embedded in our jurisprudence that it can be described as a fundamental policy of Indian law.

Perversity or Irrationality in the Arbitral Award Tested on the Touchstone of Wednesbury Principles

The third ground which Indian Supreme Court embodied as a part and parcel of the 'fundamental policy of Indian law' is the principle of reasonableness; commonly known as *Wednesbury* principle. The

Indian Supreme Court in *ONGC* (2) case held that a decision or an arbitral award which is perverse or so irrational that no reasonable person would have arrived at the same will not be sustained in a court of law.

In addition to the above, the Indian Supreme Court held that what is important in the context of the case at hand is that if on facts proved before them, the arbitrators fail to draw an inference which ought to have been drawn or if they have drawn an inference which is on the face of it, untenable resulting in miscarriage of justice, the adjudication even when made by an arbitral tribunal that enjoys considerable latitude and play at the joints in making awards will be open to challenge and may be cast away or modified depending upon whether the offending part is or is not severable from the rest.

Although from the reading of the dicta laid down by the Indian Supreme Court in *ONGC* (2) case, it appears that virtually all the grounds of challenge as applicable in administrative law jurisdiction are available, while challenging an arbitral award under Section 34 of the 1996 Act, however the same is not the case, as the Indian Supreme Court in subsequent case of *Associate Builders*[12] explained the meaning of perversity and irrationality in the context of scheme and purport of arbitration act to hold that an award of an arbitral tribunal would be perverse only if:

1. A finding is based on no evidence; or
2. An arbitral tribunal takes into account something irrelevant to the decision which it arrives at; or
3. Ignores vital evidence in arriving at its decision.

In *Associate Builders* case, the Indian Supreme Court while relying on its previous decisions[13] held that the test of perversity/irrationality so as to attract the application of *Wednesbury* principle would be limited to cases where findings of facts are arrived at by ignoring or excluding relevant material or by taking into consideration irrelevant material and such findings so outrageously defies logic so as to make the arbitral award suffer from the vice of irrationality incurring the blame of being perverse. In such cases, the finding rendered would be infirm in law. The Indian Supreme Court further held that if a decision is arrived at on no evidence or evidence which is thoroughly unreliable and no reasonable person would act upon it, the order would be perverse. The court in the said case however held that if in case there is some evidence on record which is acceptable and which could be relied upon, howsoever compendious it may be, the conclusions would not be treated as perverse and the findings would not be interfered with. On the strength of the aforesaid test laid down by it, the Indian Supreme Court held that:

> It must clearly be understood that when a court is applying the 'public policy' test to an arbitration Award, it does not act as a court of appeal and consequently errors of fact cannot be corrected. A possible view by the arbitrator on facts has necessarily to pass muster as the arbitrator is the ultimate master of the quantity and quality of evidence to be relied upon when he delivers his arbitral Award. Thus, an Award based on little evidence or on evidence which does not measure up in quality to a trained legal mind would not be held to be invalid on this score. Once it is found that the arbitrator's approach is not arbitrary or capricious, then he is the last word on facts.

In the judgment of *Associate Builders*, the Indian Supreme Court also gave a restricted meaning to the term *justice*, *morality*, and *patent illegality* to hold that an award would be against 'justice' only when it shocks the conscience of the court. Same would be the case in testing an arbitral award on the ground of 'morality'. It held that 'morality' would, if it is to go beyond sexual morality, necessarily cover such agreements which are not illegal but which would not be enforced in the given prevailing mores of the day. However, interference on this ground would also be only if something shocks the conscience of the court.

In so far as the phrase 'patent illegality' was concerned, the Indian Supreme Court again imparted a restricted and narrower meaning to the same to hold that only those arbitration awards which are rendered in complete and blatant contravention of the substantive law of India would result in its death knell. The Indian Supreme Court in the said case held that patent illegality in an arbitral award should and must go to the root of the matter and cannot be of a trivial nature.

On the issue of an award being 'patently illegal and opposed to public policy' on account of it being rendered against the specific terms of contract, the Indian Supreme Court in *Associate Builders* held that if an arbitrator construes a term of the contract in a reasonable manner, it will not mean that the award can be set aside on this ground. Construction of the terms of a contract is primarily for an arbitrator to decide. Unless the arbitrator construes the contract in such a way that it could be said to be something that no fair-minded or reasonable person could do, it cannot be questioned before a supervisory court.

Vide the said statement of law, the Indian Supreme Court reinstated the earlier position of law that construction of the terms of a contract is primarily for an arbitrator to decide. He is entitled to take the view which he holds to be the correct one after considering the material before him and after interpreting the provisions of the contract. The court while considering challenge to an arbitral award would not sit in appeal over the findings and decisions unless the arbitrator construes the contract in such a way that no fair-minded or reasonable person could do.

Thus, from the position of law stated by the Indian Supreme Court in a series of judgments referred hereinabove, it is clear that a domestic award rendered under the 1996 Act, can be challenged under the broad heads of 'public policy of India', including 'fundamental policy of Indian law' and 'decisions on matters not submitted or beyond matters submitted for adjudication' inter alia on the following grounds:

1. Failing to adopt 'judicial approach';
2. Deciding matters beyond the arbitrator's jurisdiction or terms of reference;
3. Deciding contrary to the terms of the contract;
4. Reflecting non-application of mind;
5. Failing to draw an inference from the facts that ought to be drawn from them or drawing an inference, which is on the face of it untenable resulting in miscarriage of justice;
6. Rendering findings that are so unreasonable, perverse, or irrational that the court would conclude that no reasonable person would have arrived at the conclusion that the arbitrator did. In other words, rendering an award that is so unfair and unreasonable that it shocks the conscience of the court;

7. Rendering an award that is vitiated by patent illegality, such illegality going to the 'root of the matter' and not being of a 'trivial nature';

8. Rendering an award that is contrary to substantive provisions of law and the provisions of the Arbitration and Conciliation Act; and

9. Acting in a capricious, arbitrary, or whimsical manner, rather than acting bona fide and dealing with the subject in a fair, reasonable, and objective manner.

The 1996 Act has now been amended vide the Arbitration and Conciliation Amendment Act, 2015 (the 'Amendment Act'). The said amendment act has though in principle retained all the grounds as judicially evolved by the Supreme Court of India in the afore-referred cases; however, in an attempt to restrict the scope of interference, it has provided that 'the test as to whether there is a contravention with the fundamental policy of Indian law shall not entail review on the merits of the dispute', and 'patent illegality' would not mean an illegality merely accruing on the ground of erroneous application of law or re-appreciation of evidence. In effect, by forbidding scrutiny on the merits of the arbitral award to ascertain violation public policy of India or patent illegality in the award, the Indian legislature has sought to take away the said portion of *ONGC* (1) case which permitted the supervisory courts to scrutinize the merits of the arbitral award so as to ascertain whether there was any violation in public policy of India or not.

However, as per scholars and academicians in India, it has always been the law that in deciding challenges to arbitration awards, courts should not enter into the merits of the dispute,[14] re-appreciate evidence, or substitute their own interpretation in place of another plausible, but contrary, interpretation of terms of contract adopted by arbitrators.[15] According to them, it has been the law for the last 116 years. Yet, this has not dissuaded courts from finding a way, by rendering an expansive interpretation of phrases such as 'otherwise invalid', 'public policy of India', and 'fundamental policy of Indian law', and so on, to embark on a detailed examination of the validity of awards. Furthermore, the proposed amendment only tells us what examination of 'fundamental policy of Indian law' does not entail. It is silent on what it does. This may lead to uncertainty as to when, and in what circumstances, if not on a review of the merits, could an award be said to be in violation of 'fundamental policy of Indian law'. In these circumstances, whether the amendment would really add something new to the law, or rein the courts in, is debatable.[16]

This takes us to the last question, whether the concepts of 'public policy of India', 'fundamental policy of Indian law', and so on as applicable in scrutinizing domestic awards by local municipal courts in India are also applicable to foreign awards. The answer to the said question lies in the statutory scheme envisaged in Part II of the 1996 Act. Under the said part, a foreign award (New York Convention Awards and Geneva Convention Awards) is binding on an Indian party only if it is enforceable. The test for enforceability provided under the said part mutatis mutandis incorporates all the grounds as are available to challenge a domestic award. This also includes grounds of 'public policy of India', 'fundamental policy of Indian law', and so on. Thus, the principles or grounds for interfering with an arbitral award, as enunciated by the Indian Supreme Court in the afore-referred cases, are also applicable to foreign awards before the same can be made binding on an Indian party and enforced in India. This position is regardless of a situation where the said foreign award may have been upheld by the supervisory courts of the country where the seat of arbitration lies and may have attained finality as per the law governing the arbitration agreement.

Notes and References

1. *Union of India v. Reliance Industries Ltd.*, (2015) 10 SCC 213; relying on *Videocon Industries Ltd. v. Union of India*, (2011) 6 SCC 161: (2011) 3 SCC (Civ) 257; *Dozco India (P) Ltd. v. Doosan Infracore Co. Ltd.*, (2011) 6 SCC 179: (2011) 3 SCC (Civ) 276; *Yograj Infrastructure Ltd. v. Sangyong Engineering and Construction Co. Ltd.*, (2011) 9 SCC 735: (2011) 4 SCC (Civ) 864; *Reliance Industries Ltd., v. Union of India*, (2014) 7 SCC 603: (2014) 3 SCC (Civ) 737; *Harmony Innovation Shipping Ltd. v. Gupta Coal India Ltd.*, (2015) 9 SCC 172: (2015) 4 SCC (Civ). 341; *Balco v. Kaiser Aluminium Technical Services Inc.*, (2012) 9 SCC 552.

2. *Enercon (India) Ltd. And Ors v. EnerconGmbh And Anr*, (2014) 5 SCC 1.

3. *Bhatia International* (2002) 4 SCC 105. This judgment is specifically overruled albeit prospectively by constitution bench of Indian Supreme Court in *Balco v. Kaiser Aluminium Technical Services Inc.*, (2012) 9 SCC 552.
4. Meaning thereby that Indian courts will have supervisory jurisdiction.
5. *Champsey Bhara & Co. v. Jivraj Balloo Spg. and Wvg. Co. Ltd.*, (1922–23) 50 IA 324: AIR 1923 PC 66.
6. '[T]here was much debate in the Working Committee of UNCITRAL on the meaning of the words "public policy", India contending that the term was much too vague, had very little to do with the law of arbitration, and should be deleted'. See Howard M. Holtzman and Joseph E. Neuhaus, *A Guide to the Uncitral Model Law on International Commercial Arbitration: Legislative History and Commentary* (Kluwer Law and Taxation Publishers, 1989), p. 977. See also the decisions in *Richardson v. Mellish*, (1824) 2 Bing 229: (1824–34) All ER Rep 258: 130 ER 294 and *Central Inland Water Transport Corpn. Ltd. v. Brojo Nath Ganguly*, (1986) 3 SCC 156: 1986 SCC (L&S) 429, where the Court held that public policy is an 'unruly horse'.

   However, the Working Committee of UNCITRAL ultimately chose to retain this ground and India incorporated it into the 1996 Act. See 'Grounds to Challenge Arbitration Awards: Will Amendments to the Arbitration Act Bring "Acche Din"?', (2015) 7 SCC J-1.
7. *Renusagar Power Co. Ltd. v. General Electric Co.*, 1994 Supp (1) SCC 644.
8. *ONGC Ltd. v. Saw Pipes Ltd.*, (2003) 5 SCC 705: AIR 2003 SC 2629.
9. *Phulchand Exports Limited v. OOO Patriot*, (2011) 10 SCC 300.
10. *Shri Lal Mahal Ltd. v. Progetto Grano Spa*, (2014) 2 SCC 433.
11. *ONGC Ltd. v. Western Geco International Ltd.*, (2014) 9 SCC 263: (2014) 5 SCC (Civ) 12, see SCC p. 278–80, paras 35 and 38–40.
12. *Associate Builders v. DDA*, (2015) 3 SCC 49: 2014 SCC on Line SC 937.
13. *Excise and Taxation Officer-cum-Assessing Authority v. Gopi Nath & Sons* 1992 Supp (2) SCC 312 p. 317, para 7. See also *Kuldeep Singh v. Commr. of Police*, (1999) 2 SCC 10: 1999 SCC (L&S) 429 p. 14, para 10.
14. *Union of India v. Bungo Steel Furniture (P) Ltd.*, AIR 1967 SC 1032; *Ispat Engg. & Foundry Works v. SAIL*, (2001) 6 SCC 347.
15. *M.P. Housing Board v. Progressive Writers and Publishers*, (2009) 5 SCC 678: (2009) 2 SCC (Civ) 652; *Associate Builders v. DDA*, (2015) 3 SCC 49.
16. See 'Grounds to Challenge Arbitration Awards'.

6

Rectification of Jurisdiction to Entertain Arbitration Applications in the Commercial Courts Act 2015

Pending Practical Re-alignment to Restore the Statutory Right to Appeal?

*Ajay Bhargava**

The Problem

The Commercial Courts, Commercial Division, and Commercial Appellate Division of the High Courts Act, 2015 (2015 Act) was passed by Parliament on 31 December 2015, and Section 1(3)[1] of the 2015 Act creates a deeming fiction by virtue of which the said Act was given retrospective effect from 23 October 2015, that is, the date on which the Commercial Courts, Commercial Division, and Commercial Appellate Division of the High Courts

* I would like to thank Jeevan Ballav Panda and Kudrat Dev for their assistance in writing this chapter.

Ordinance, 2015 (2015 Ordinance) came into force. As per Section 10(2)[2] of the 2015 Act, all applications under the Arbitration and Conciliation Act, 1996 (Arbitration Act), in the cases of domestic arbitration, shall be heard and disposed of by the Commercial Division, that is, Single Bench of the High Court. Hence, the legislature rectified the poor drafting error by providing that a Single Bench would have the jurisdiction to entertain arbitration applications, and not the Division Bench, as it is the appropriate bench to hear the appeal against an order passed on an arbitration application and cannot wear two hats of first hearing in its original jurisdiction and thereafter hearing in its appellate jurisdiction.

In this background, the retrospective effect of such rectification would mean that all applications under the Arbitration Act, in the cases of domestic arbitration, which were heard and disposed of by the Commercial Appellate Division, that is Division Bench, between the period from 23 October 2015 to 31 December 2015 were heard and disposed without jurisdiction as the correct forum was the Commercial Division, that is Single Bench of the High Court (View One). However, another view could be that the 2015 Act could not have intended upsetting the disposed litigation during the period from 23 October 2015 to 31 December 2015 and preserved the same by its savings clause under Section 23 (View Two).

The rectification of the error in the 2015 Ordinance was positively welcomed on the ground that the Single Bench has jurisdiction to hear arbitration applications as it restored the statutory right to appeal under Section 37 of the Arbitration Act, in the real sense as the Single Bench would be the First Court and the Division Bench would be the Appellate Court. However, the ambiguity and complexity on the issue of restoration of the statutory right to appeal under the Arbitration Act existed in: (a) whether the statutory right to appeal has been restored prospectively for the period beginning 31 December 2015 or even retrospectively for the period from 23 October 2015 to 31 December 2015 as the 2015 Act was to take retrospective effect from 23 October 2015, (b) whether the savings clause under the 2015 Act could be interpreted to save the acts of the Courts (Division Bench), which during the 2015 Ordinance regime, were vested with jurisdiction to entertain and dispose arbitration applications, and (c) what remedy lies or is available to the aggrieved litigants whose arbitration applications were disposed of by a Division Bench in the capacity of the First Court during the 2015 Ordinance regime, in case after the enactment of the 2015 Act, they choose to exercise the statutory right to appeal under Section 37 of the Arbitration Act which will be posted for hearing before the same or Coordinate Division Bench, now wearing the hat of the Appellate Court.

Statutory Right to Appeal under the Arbitration Act: Is It Restored for Some or All?

Section 37 of the Arbitration Act provides as hereunder:

37. Appealable orders:

1. An appeal shall lie from the following orders (and from no others) to the Court authorised by law to hear appeals from original decrees of the Court passing the order, namely:
   i.   granting or refusing to grant any measure under section 9;
   ii.   setting aside or refusing to set aside an arbitral award under section 34.
2. An appeal shall also lie to a Court from an order granting of the arbitral tribunal:
   i.   accepting the plea referred in sub-section (2) or sub-section (3) of section 16; or
   ii.   granting or refusing to grant an interim measure under section 17.
3. No second appeal shall lie from an order passed in appeal under this section, but nothing in this section shall affect or take away any right to appeal to the Supreme Court.

Therefore, Section 37 of the Arbitration Act provides to an aggrieved person the statutory right to appeal against an order passed under the various provisions of the Arbitration Act as stipulated therein. Such right of appeal, in view of the settled legal position, is not merely a matter of procedure but a substantive right. The right of appeal from the decision of an inferior court becomes vested in a party, when proceedings were first initiated before an inferior court. In this context, reliance may be placed upon the judgment of the Hon'ble Supreme Court in the case of *Hoosein Kasam Dada (India)*

Limited v. State of Madhya Pradesh.[3] Such a vested right, it was held, could not be taken away except by an express enactment or by necessary intendment.

This proposition of law was crystallised in the Constitutional Bench judgment of the Hon'ble Supreme Court in the case of *Garikapati Veeraya v. N. Subbiah Choudhary*[4] wherein the Hon'ble Court recorded its conclusions in paragraph 23, which is extracted here:

23. From the decisions cited above, the following principles clearly emerge:
    1. That the legal pursuit of a remedy, suit, appeal and second appeal are really but steps in a series of proceedings all connected by an intrinsic unity and are to be regarded as one legal proceeding.
    2. The right of appeal is not a mere matter of procedure but is a substantive right.
    3. The institution of the suit carries with it the implication that all rights of appeal then in force are preserved to the parties there to till the rest of the career of the suit.
    4. The right of appeal is a vested right and such a right to enter the superior court accrues to the litigant and exists as on and from the date the lis commences and although it may be actually exercised when the adverse judgment is pronounced such right is to be governed by the law prevailing at the date of the institution of the suit or proceeding and not by the law that prevails at the date of its decision or at the date of the filing of the appeal.
    5. This vested right of appeal can be taken away only by a subsequent enactment, if it so provides expressly or by necessary intendment and not otherwise.

In view of the aforesaid judgments as reiterated from time to time, it is well settled that the right of appeal is not a mere matter of procedure but a substantive right. Therefore, this substantive right vested in a litigant could not have been abridged or taken away. In particular context of the 2015 Ordinance, the Division Bench of the Delhi High Court in *Roger Shashoua & Ors. v. Mukesh Sharma & Ors.*,[5] observed that there is an inherent inconsistency in the reading of Section 10(2)[6] of the 2015 Ordinance, to the extent that it takes away the statutory right to file appeal under Section 37 of the Arbitration Act.

Eventually, in consonance with the aforesaid settled principles of law, the Division Bench of the Delhi High Court (even during the 2015 Ordinance regime) in *Ascot Estates Pvt. Ltd. v. Bon Vivant Life Style Ltd.*[7] (*Ascot case*) when faced with the issue whether the right of appeal conferred by Section 37 of the Arbitration Act which has been specifically preserved by Section 13 of the 2015 Ordinance[8] can be taken away by Section 10 of the 2015 Ordinance inter alia: (a) interpreted Section 10(1) and Section 10(2) of the 2015 Ordinance harmoniously with Section 13 of the 2015 Ordinance to preserve the substantive right to appeal conferred by Section 37 of the Arbitration Act and (b) read down Section 10(2) of the 2015 Ordinance holding that all applications under the Arbitration Act relating to commercial dispute of a specified value has to be adjudicated only by the Commercial Division, that is, a Single Bench of the High Court.[9] Moreover, any interpretation to the contrary would be absurd and the aforesaid reading down was finally rectified while passing the 2015 Act.

However, despite rectification of jurisdiction while passing the 2015 Act, it remains unsettled, whether the statutory right to appeal was restored prospectively, that is, only for litigants filing arbitration applications after passing of the 2015 Act on 31 December 2015 or retrospectively, that is, for all the litigants regardless of the time of filing of the arbitration applications during the 2015 Ordinance regime as it could not have been abridged in the first place by the 2015 Ordinance. The concern is that the statutory right of appeal will be of no meaning in practicality for the set of litigants whose arbitration applications were disposed of by the Division Bench during the 2015 Ordinance regime (23 October 2015 to 31 December 2015) as if they now (post 31 December 2015, that is, passing of the 2015 Act) file an appeal then the same will be listed before the same or Coordinate Division Bench (Appellate Bench as per the 2015 Act) for disposal. Thus, the need arises for a real practical realignment to actually restore the statutory right to appeal for such aggrieved litigants.

The Solution: Review Application

The Commercial Courts Act was notified on 31 December 2015 with retrospective effect from 23 October 2015 by repealing the

Commercial Courts Ordinance. As per Section 10 (2) of the Commercial Courts Act, only the Commercial Division (and not the Commercial Appellate Division) has the jurisdiction to entertain and try arbitration applications under the provisions contained in the Arbitration Act. This provision as it existed in the Commercial Courts Ordinance wrongly provided that such applications under the Arbitration Act were to be heard and disposed of by the Commercial Appellate Division. The legislature realizing such apparent error/ mistake in Section 10 (2) of the Commercial Courts Ordinance rectified the provision while enacting the Commercial Courts Act and changed the term 'Commercial Appellate Division' to 'Commercial Division'.

Interestingly, the said rectification of the error/mistake by Section 10 (2) of the Commercial Courts Act has resulted in more ambiguities and complications rather than simplifying and solving the inconsistencies and adverse implications arising therefrom. This is particularly applicable in the wrongful exercise of jurisdiction by Commercial Appellate Division (instead of the Commercial Division) during the intervening period, that is, from 23 October 2015 till 31 December 2015. Litigants who have suffered or have been aggrieved by the orders passed by the Commercial Appellate Division during such intervening period, when there was lack of clarity in the legal position, have been rendered remediless in as much as their substantive right to file an appeal against an adverse order passed by the Commercial Appellate Division has been virtually taken away. In other words, Section 37 of the Arbitration Act, which provides for a statutory right to an appeal to a party aggrieved by an order passed in an Arbitration Application, inter alia, under Section 9 of the Arbitration Act was made redundant in view of the fact that an Appeal under Section 37 of the Arbitration Act could not be heard before a Coordinate Bench (Division Bench), when the original application itself has been heard and disposed of by a Division Bench (Commercial Appellate Division).

Ground for Review: No Jurisdiction

Thus, in view of the findings in the *Ascots case* (pre-2015 Act and currency of the 2015 Ordinance) and the passing of the 2015 Act providing that the Commercial Division, that is, Single Bench shall hear all applications under Arbitration Act in domestic arbitrations, all parties who faced an unfavourable order on being heard by the Commercial Appellate Bench, that is, Division Bench between the intervening period, that is, from 23 October 2015 to 31 December 2015, should resort to filing a review application on the ground of 'patent error' stating that the Commercial Appellate Bench acted without jurisdiction as the appropriate forum was the Commercial Division, that is, Single Bench of the High Court in terms with View One. Furthermore, lack of jurisdiction is a 'patent error' recognized as a fit ground for review by courts, and the Hon'ble Supreme Court in *Raja Shatrunji v. Mohammad Azmat Azim Khan & Ors.*[10] (*Raja Shatrunji* case) held that one of the grounds for review is an error apparent on the face of record which would encompass a judgment applying the unamended law where a statute has been amended retrospectively, as follows:

> Counsel for the appellant submitted that when the High Court decided the matter, the High Court applied the law as it stood and a subsequent change of law could not be a ground for review. The appellant's contention is not acceptable in the present case for two principle reasons; first, it is not a subsequent law. It is the law which all along was there from 1952. The deeming provision is fully effective and operative as from 25 May 1953 when the 1952 Act came into force. The result is that the Court is to apply the legal provision as it always stood. It would, therefore, be error on the face of record. The error would be that the law that was applied was not the law which is applicable.

The *Raja Shatrunji* case was recently reiterated by the Bombay High Court in *VIP Industries Ltd. v. Commissioner of Central Excise, Nashik, Maharashtra.*[11] Furthermore, the Hon'ble Supreme Court in *Union of India v. Sube Ram*[12] held as follows:

> It is now settled legal position that the claimants would be entitled to the enhanced solatium and interest only if the proceedings were pending either before the Land Acquisition Officer or the court. The word 'Court' defined under Section 2(d) of the Act as on the date of Amendment Bill was introduced and Act made by Parliament, was civil court. Therefore, the question that arises is whether the High Court has jurisdiction to entertain the application for enhancement after the Amendment Act 68 of 1984 came into force. It is true that

if it were a case of a superior court having interpreted the law and the law having become final, by Order 47 Rule 1 CPC it could not constitute a ground for review of the judgment. But here is the case of entertaining the application itself; in other words, the question of jurisdiction of the court. Since the appellate court has no power to amend the decree and grant the enhanced compensation by way of solatium and interest under Section 23(2) and proviso to Section 28 of the Act, as amended by Act 68 of 1984, it is a question of jurisdiction of the court. Since courts have no jurisdiction, it is the settled legal position that it is a nullity and it can be raised at any stage.

Moreover, the Hon'ble Supreme Court in *Zuari Cement Ltd. v. Regional Director, ESIC, Hyderabad & Ors.*[13] has reiterated the well-settled principle that the issue of lack of jurisdiction even if acquiesced can be raised at any stage as it makes the order without jurisdiction non est in the eyes of law and void. Thus, all the orders passed by the Division Bench during the 2015 Ordinance regime, that is 23 October 2015 to 31 December 2015, are non est in the eyes of law for being passed without jurisdiction and may be subjected to review.

Discrimination Due to a Drafting Error

One may take the view that if courts entertain such review applications, it may lead to unsettling settled litigation as that could not have ever been the intention of the 2015 Act, and during the 2015 Ordinance regime, the Division Benches of the High Courts were well vested with the jurisdiction to hear arbitration applications at the first instance itself. However, it is pertinent to note that if the review applications are not entertained, then injustice and discrimination will be caused as: a. one category of parties (who suffered an unfavourable order between 23 October 2015 and 31 December 2015) would have lost their statutory right to appeal and are left only with discretion of the Hon'ble Supreme Court to be exercised under Article 136 of the Constitution, which also may lead to opening of floodgates and b. another category of parties (who suffered an unfavourable order post 31 December 2015) would have their statutory right to appeal as an available remedy.[14] Hence, the balance tilts in favour of filing of review applications as opposed to non-filing of review applications as it is the only way to negate 'discrimination due to drafting error', between parties approaching the court by filing arbitration applications when the error existed and when the error had been rectified. Moreover, filing of review applications is the only way how the statutory and substantive right to appeal available to an aggrieved party under Section 37 of the Arbitration Act can be protected for all (2015 Ordinance regime) and not some (post-2015 Act).

Bar to Review: Savings Clause?

The repeal and savings clause contained in Section 23 (2) of the Commercial Courts Act which provides that 'anything done or any action taken under the said ordinance, shall be deemed to have been done or taken under the corresponding provision of this Act', only adds to the confusion. Applying the aforesaid repeal and savings clause to a situation where a Commercial Appellate Division (Division bench) has heard, adjudicated, and disposed of an application under the Arbitration Act in terms of Section 10 (2) of the Commercial Courts Ordinance would be deemed to have been passed by the Commercial Division (Single Bench). Such an interpretation would also lead to an absurdity, as in that case also the substantive right to file an appeal under Section 37 of the Arbitration Act cannot still be restored back, as in fact a Division Bench has disposed of the original application and a Coordinate Bench (Division Bench) cannot sit in appeal against the same order.

Thus, even though on a standalone prima facie interpretation of the Savings and Repeal Clause under Section 23 may be that what was done during the period from 23 October 2015 to 31 December 2015 stands preserved and will not be undone, a harmonious interpretation of Section 23(2) of the 2015 Act with Section 1(3) of the 2015 Act expressly providing for retrospective effect from 23 October 2015 may unsettle what is done. Moreover, the Hon'ble Supreme Court in *M.S. Shivananda v. Karnataka State Road Transport Corporation and Ors.*[15] has held that when an Act replaces an Ordinance with express legislative intention of having retrospective effect from the date when the Ordinance was notified then the acts done under the Ordinance stand 'wholly effaced'.

***

In light of the factual context and settled principles of law, the ambiguities arising out of the positive rectification in jurisdiction (Single Bench to entertain arbitration applications and not Division Bench), while passing the 2015 Act, and the corresponding responses are summarized as follows:

1. Whether the statutory right to appeal has been restored prospectively for the period beginning 31 December 2015 or even retrospectively for the period from 23 October 2015 to 31 December 2015 as the 2015 Act was to take retrospective effect from 23 October 2015.

    First Response: the question of 'restoring' the statutory right to appeal does not arise at all because the same could not have ever been taken away in the manner done by the 2015 Ordinance.

    Second Response: The statutory right to appeal has been restored retrospectively for the period from 23 October 2015 to 31 December 2015 as the 2015 Act was to take retrospective effect from 23 October 2015.

2. Whether the savings clause under the 2015 Act could be interpreted to save the acts of the courts (Division Bench) as during the 2015 Ordinance Regime, the courts (Division Bench) were vested with jurisdiction to entertain and dispose arbitration applications.

    The savings clause under the 2015 Act cannot be interpreted to save the acts of the courts (Division Bench) as during the 2015 Ordinance regime, the courts (Division Bench) even if it is argued that then the Division Bench was vested with jurisdiction to entertain and dispose arbitration applications. Moreover, when an Act replaces an Ordinance with express legislative intention of having retrospective effect from the date when the Ordinance was notified (Section 1(3) of the 2015 Act) then the acts done under the Ordinance stand 'wholly effaced'.

3. What remedy lies/is available to the aggrieved litigants whose arbitration applications were disposed of by a Division Bench in the capacity of the First Court during the 2015 Ordinance regime, in case after the enactment of the 2015 Act they choose to exercise the statutory right to appeal under Section 37 of the Arbitration Act which will be posted for hearing before the

same or Coordinate Division Bench, now wearing the hat of the Appellate Court.

All parties who faced an unfavourable order on being heard by the Commercial Appellate Bench, that is, Division Bench, between the intervening period, that is, from 23 October 2015 to 31 December 2015, should resort to filing a review application on the ground of 'patent error' stating that the Commercial Appellate Bench acted without jurisdiction as the appropriate forum was the Commercial Division, that is, the Single Bench of the High Court.

As on date, the aforesaid ambiguities have not been settled by the courts of law, however, it may not be long before the High Courts of the country are approached to resolve the aforesaid ambiguities followed by the Hon'ble Supreme Court.

Notes and References

1. Section 1(3) of the 2015 Act 1. Short title, extent, and commencement:
   (3) It shall be deemed to have come into force on the 23rd day of October 2015.
2. Section 10(2) of the 2015 Act:
   10. Jurisdiction in respect of arbitration matter:
        Where the subject-matter of an arbitration is a commercial dispute of a specified value and:
        (2) If such arbitration is other than an international commercial arbitration, all applications or appeals arising out of such arbitration under the provisions of the Arbitration and Conciliation Act, 1996 (26 of 1996) that have been filed on the original side of the High Court, shall be heard and disposed of by the Commercial Division where such Commercial Division has been constituted in such High Court.
        (3) Court shall be heard and disposed of by the Commercial Appellate Division where such Commercial Appellate Division has been constituted in such High Court.
3. AIR 1953 SC 221.
4. AIR 1957 SC 540.
5. OMP (COMM.) No. 1 of 2015.
6. See note 2.
7. O.M.P.(I) (COMM.) No. 16 of 2015.
8. Section 13 of the 2015 Ordinance:

13. Appeals from decrees of Commercial Courts and Commercial Divisions.

(1) Any person aggrieved by the decision of the Commercial Court or Commercial Division of a High Court may appeal to the Commercial Appellate Division of that High Court within a period of sixty days from the date of judgment or order, as the case may be:

Provided that an appeal shall lie from such orders passed by a Commercial Division or a Commercial Court that are specifically enumerated under Order XLII of the Code of Civil Procedure, 1908 as amended by this Ordinance and section 37 of the Arbitration and Conciliation Act, 1996.

9. International Law Office, 'Transition from Commercial Courts Ordinance to Commercial Courts Act: Ambiguities and Implications' (26 May 2016), available http://www.internationallawoffice.com/ Newsletters/Arbitration-ADR/India/Khaitan-Co/Transition-from-Commercial-Courts-Ordinance-to-Commercial-Courts-Act-ambiguities-and-implications.

10. (1971) 2 SCC 200, para 13.

11. (2010) SCC Online Bom 1908.

12. (1997) 9 SCC 69, para 5. Also see, *Union of India v. Filip Tiago De Gama of Vedem Vasco De Gama*, (1990) 1 SCC 277 p. 14.

13. Civil Appeal Nos 5138–40/2007.

14. International Law Office, 'Transition from Commercial Courts Ordinance.

15. (1980) 1 SCC 149, paras 15, 16, 20–1.

7

Institutional Arbitration in India

The Way Forward

Deepto Roy and *Madhukeshwar Desai*

It is commonly accepted today that alternative dispute resolution (ADR) has not been successful as contemplated in resolving commercial disputes in India.[1] Considering the fact that India is on its way to become a key player in the world economy, this unacceptable state of affairs prompted the Government of India and the Parliament to initiate far-ranging amendments to the Indian Arbitration and Conciliation Act, 1996 (Arbitration Act) in 2015.[2]

Among the various causes that contributed to the present state of arbitration in India, perhaps the most significant one has been the lack of penetration of institutional arbitration in the Indian context.[3]

Ad hoc arbitration is based on the arbitration clause in the agreement without reference to a specific arbitral institution or a specific body of rules. Institutional arbitration, on the other hand, mandates arbitration administered by a specialized institution, where the arbitral process is managed by the rules under the supervision of the said institution. In its purest form, ad hoc arbitration represents a significant degree of party autonomy, and the parties can decide not just the manner of dispute settlement but also the details of procedure which will govern such dispute resolution. Institutional arbitration, to a large extent, curbs party autonomy, certainly in terms of procedure, but compensates for it with procedural certainty, guaranteeing availability of high-quality arbitrators, as well as infrastructural and administrative support.

The aim of arbitration is to resolve commercial disputes in a manner which is cost and time efficient, particularly when compared to traditional court-driven dispute resolution. This has not been the case with ad hoc arbitration in the Indian context, where it as often proved to be more expensive than litigation.[4] An examination reveals that ad hoc arbitration, in practice, suffers the same maladies as court litigations: incessant delays and adjournments, uncontrollable and unpredictable costs, and overemphasis on procedure. Added to this is the lack of accountability of the arbitrators and the absence of rules of conduct and standards of professional ethics applicable to arbitrators.[5] These fallacies negate the fundamental reasons why parties choose arbitration.[6]

The experience of most participants with arbitration in India has contributed to a widespread erosion of faith in the arbitral process.[7] Accordingly most parties, including Indian parties, prefer to opt for arbitration governed by institutions outside India.[8] In fact, today, India appears before the Singapore International Arbitration Centre (SIAC) with most number of arbitration cases.[9]

In most developed countries, institutional arbitration is the preferred form of arbitration since it is more predictable and usually more efficient than ad hoc arbitrations.[10] By contrast, more than 95 per cent of all arbitrations that happen in India are ad hoc in nature.[11]

Given the concerns with ad hoc arbitration, in particular the elements of delays and costs, the way forward for ADR in India is to increase the penetration and popularity of institutional arbitration.[12] This is a view that found support from the Ministry of Law and Justice of the Government of India, which has noted with urgency the need to develop arbitral institutions in India: 'As a result of the structured procedure and administrative support provided by institutional arbitration, it provides distinct advantages which are unavailable to parties opting for ad-hoc arbitration.'[13]

The Supreme Court of India has acknowledged that institutional arbitration can be a cost-effective solution to the increasing costs of arbitration. In *Union of India v. M/s Singh Builders Syndicate*,[14] the Court recognized that 'delays made a mockery of the process of arbitration' and held that. 'It is necessary to find an urgent solution for this problem to save arbitration from the arbitration cost. Institutional arbitration has provided a solution as the arbitrators' fees is not fixed by the arbitrators themselves on a case-to-case basis but is governed by a uniform rate prescribed by the institution under whose aegis the arbitration is held.'[15]

This chapter will outline the key shortcomings of ad hoc arbitration in an Indian context and the advantages of institutional arbitrations. It would then examine the recommendations of the Law Commission of India in relation to encouraging institutional arbitration and the need for sweeping changes in the legal framework for arbitration in India, which was carried out through the 2015 Amendment Act. The chapter concludes with a viewpoint that institutional arbitration is the way forward for India and needs to be encouraged if India wishes to establish itself as a centre for arbitration.

The Problems with Ad Hoc Arbitration

As previously stated, ad hoc arbitration is the ultimate manifestation of party autonomy.[16] Parties have the freedom to determine all aspects of the arbitration including the manner of appointment of the arbitral tribunal, manner of obtaining evidence, frequency of hearing, arbitrator fees, location, and so on. While theoretically it gives parties greater flexibility and may possibly make the arbitration more flexible, cheaper and faster than its institutional counterpart, in practice it suffers from significant shortcomings, which are briefly outlined as follows.

Lack of Certainty of Procedure

Ad hoc arbitration requires the parties to decide the applicable procedures. This remains an ideal method of dispute resolution if parties approach the arbitration in the spirit of cooperation.[17] However, once a dispute has occurred, the presumption of cooperation vanishes and the question of procedure leads to protracted conflicts and delays.

Procedural issues affecting the fundamentals of arbitration, setting the terms of reference, time for hearings, time limit for making of the award, and so on, usually consume a lot of time.[18] The chances that one of the parties will use these uncertainties to delay proceedings or cause a stalemate also increases.[19] For example, with respect to the appointment of arbitrators, if one of the parties refuses or delays doing so, while institutional rules would provide for how such a situation can be addressed, in ad hoc arbitration the parties would have no recourse but to approach a court of law.[20] This increases involvement of a court particularly in the 'pre-arbitration' phase. Further, since the arbitral tribunal has significant powers in terms of determining procedural matters, it may make the process unpredictable.[21]

Retired Judges as Arbitrators

An overwhelming majority of arbitrators in ad hoc arbitrations have been retired judges of the Supreme Court of India or the High Courts. Given that the judges are familiar with adversarial litigation, they tend to approach arbitrations in the same manner in most cases. This results in the loss of one of the fundamental features of arbitration—the spirit of settlement. Judges turned arbitrators are also much likely to permit delays and adjournments and in fact do tend to get bogged down by procedures.[22]

Costs

Ad hoc arbitration tends to be, in final count, higher than institutional arbitrations and often turn out to be higher than court proceedings. More importantly, these costs are difficult to assess when the arbitration is initiated. Expenses include administrative expenses and costs of counsel as well, which keep adding up and can end up making ad hoc arbitration prohibitively expensive.[23] Particularly, in case, one of the parties takes advantage of procedural loopholes and there is frequent recourse to court proceedings, costs can spiral out of control.[24]

Quality and Availability of Arbitrators

The quality of arbitrators has been generally poor, and in the absence of a reference point for determining their value, parties are forced to choose the best among the available ones. In fact, within the circles, a small group of effective arbitrators have been identified whom all parties wish to use. Lack of dates from such arbitrators stretches the arbitral process.[25] Added to this is the fact that there are few arbitrators with specialized or technical backgrounds, which reduces the ability of arbitral tribunals to deal with complex technical and domain-specific disputes.[26] Finally, in many cases, arbitrators are found to be not proactive enough to identify preliminary issues, are not prepared for hearings, are biased in favour of the appointing party and ultimately produce poor-quality arbitral awards.[27]

Logistics and Infrastructure

Parties spend precious organizational time and expenses having to deal with the logistics of arbitration as well as coordination and clerical work. Parties are often compelled to resort to hiring facilities at expensive hotels or similar venues, which increases the cost of arbitration.[28]

There is therefore very little doubt that in the Indian context ad hoc arbitration is an inefficient and costly method of redressal and furthermore, imposes a disproportionate onus on the disputing parties appearing before it.

Advantages of Institutional Arbitration

Availability of Pre-Established Rules and Procedures

Compared to ad hoc arbitration, institutional arbitration is more transparent and accountable, and the arbitral institution contributes significant procedural know hows.[29] Tried and tested arbitral rules,[30] which are primarily designed to maximize the efficiency of the arbitration process, are mechanically incorporated in the arbitration agreement.[31] This ensures that even if a situation arises wherein the parties have not contemplated or wherein one of the parties decide to be non-cooperative, the rules usually have fall backs, allowing resolution of issues with the intervention of the institution and permitting the arbitral process to move forward. For example, appointment and removal of arbitrators who are biased are usually matters explicitly dealt with by the rules, which fails to serve the purpose of the parties who approach the courts.[32] This repeatedly creates uniformity, certainty, and more stability.[33] Most institutions also regularly update their rules, drawing on the expertise of experienced arbitrators as well as the practical learning from precedent arbitrations.[34]

Reputation

Another inherent advantage of institutional arbitration is the reputation of the institution. This impacts any future challenges to an award of the institution. Awards issued by a well-known institution are easier to enforce.[35] Challenges from a procedural perspective are limited, if the procedures of the institution have been followed.[36]

Monitoring and Supervision

The institution performs a number of roles including determining whether there is a prima facie arbitration agreement, the number of arbitrators, appointment of arbitrators, rejection of the arbitrators, ensure that the arbitrations are conducted in compliance with the rules and replace them if necessary, determine the place of arbitration, fix and extend time limits, determine the fees and expenses of arbitrators and scrutinize awards.[37] This eliminates any procedural arbitrariness and also reduces any perception of bias.[38] Institutions ensure that the reasoning and content of the award are appropriate and comprehensively dealt with while vetting awards before they are provided to parties all relevant issues, claims, and counterclaims.[39]

Administrative and Infrastructural Assistance from the Institution

Most arbitral institutions have trained staff and case management teams to administer the arbitration.[40] Parties do not have to worry about the logistics of administering the arbitration, collection of fees, recovery of expenses, arbitration venue, and so on.[41] Most institutions also have physical facilities and support services, which allow the parties and the arbitrators to focus on resolving the dispute rather than be concerned with logistical aspects.[42] The institution is ready to assist, especially in the selection of the arbitrators.[43] Some institutions are also tech savvy to use modern technological tools, for example, e-filing of documents and petitions and video-conferencing to resolve disputes.

Quality of Arbitrators

In institutional arbitrations, arbitrators are typically appointed by the institution based on pre-specified criteria. This ensures a first level of scrutiny because only arbitrators who meet the qualification criteria of the institution would qualify for a panel. Institutions maintain extensive database of arbitrators in order to assist parties in appointment stage.[44]

Transparent Fee Structure

Institutions ensure certainty of costs through the use of expedited timelines and specified cost guidelines.[45] The remuneration of arbitrators is also set out by the institution. Since arbitrator fee is one of the largest contributors to the costs of arbitration,[46] this (along with clear timelines) is a key advantage for disputing parties.

Code of Conduct and Conflicts of Interest

The institution will have a prescribed code of conduct or rules of professional ethics, which all the arbitrators have to comply with, under the supervision of the secretariat of the institution.[47] Institutions also set behavioural norms in terms of consistency of procedure and conduct of proceedings, reducing the chances of any procedural capriciousness originating from the tribunal. Institutions ensure that the appointment of arbitrators is confirmed only if their independence and impartiality is established.[48]

Law Commission's Recommendations on Institutional Arbitration

The Arbitration Act was enacted in 1996 with a view to bring Indian arbitration law in line with international practices. The provisions of the Arbitration Act were based on the UNCITRAL Model Law on International Commercial Arbitration, and the Arbitration Act replaced a variety of out-dated laws including the Indian Arbitration Act, 1940 and the Foreign Awards (Recognition and Enforcement) Act, 1961. The stated objective of the Arbitration Act was to encourage arbitration as a cost-effective and speedy mechanism for dispute settlement. As summarized before, the law cannot be said to have succeeded for a variety of reasons.

The 20th Law Commission of India[49] was cognizant of and extremely concerned with the state of arbitration in the country, critiquing sharply the 'culture of frequent adjournment when arbitration is treated as secondary by lawyers'. Accordingly, the Law Commission advocated sweeping changes to the existing Arbitration Act, with the express aim of streamlining the process and encouraging institutional arbitration.[50] Some of the key recommendations of the Law Commission in its report were[51] encouragement of institutional arbitration as a culture; all references by a Court to arbitration, where required under the law or under the arbitration agreement to be arbitral institutions; legal sanction of an 'emergency' arbitrator; requirement that an application for appointment as arbitrator to a court to be disposed of within 60 days of filing; requirement that arbitration be commenced within 60 days of filing of any application for interim order from a court of law; and the stipulation that once the arbitral tribunal has been constituted, the court shall not entertain an application under Section 9 of the Arbitration Act (which provides for interim measures from a court of law). Instead the parties should approach the arbitral tribunal which would have wide powers of granting interim measures, which could be enforced on par with court orders.

The Law Commission further recommended that challenges to arbitral proceedings will be dealt with expeditiously, and in any event, within 12 months of notice to the respondent and the development of a model fee structure for domestic ad hoc arbitration.

The 2015 Amendments to the Arbitration Act

The Government of India made wide-ranging amendments to the Arbitration Act through the Arbitration and Conciliation (Amendment) Act, 2015 (No. 3 of 2016) (2015 Amendment) in order to facilitate timely and more cost-effective arbitration.[52] Some of the key amendments are:

Time-bound Arbitration

In terms of the newly introduced Section 29A to the Arbitration Act, the arbitral tribunal is required to make an award within 12 months from the date of initiation of arbitration, extendable to 18 months with the consent of the parties. After 18 months, it can only be extended by a court for sufficient cause. The court also has the right to order that the fees by the arbitral tribunal is reduced (by not more than 5 per cent of the fees for every week of delay) if the delay can be attributed to the actions of the tribunal. This is expected to serve as a deterrent to the arbitral tribunal and avoid unnecessary adjournments and delay. There is also provision for additional fees for the arbitral tribunal if parties agree. India is one of the first jurisdictions in the world which has specified a statutory time limit for arbitration.[53]

Fast-Track Arbitrations

The Arbitration Act now permits, in Section 29B, a fast-track arbitration process for certain disputes where the arbitration has to be concluded within 6 months.

Appointment of Arbitrator

Section 11 of the Arbitration Act originally provided that if the parties could not appoint an arbitrator then the Chief Justice of the High Court or the Supreme Court of India can do so. A new sub-section has now been added to Section 11 to the effect that an application for appointment of an arbitrator will be disposed of by the High Court or Supreme Court as the case may be, as expeditiously as possible. Endeavours should be made to close such appointment within 60 days. Furthermore, the appointment of the arbitrator shall be by the High Court or the Supreme Court (as an institution) rather than the Chief Justice of a High Court or the Chief Justice of India as the case may be. The appointment of an arbitrator has been moved from a judicial function to an administrative one.

Power of Interim Relief

Section 17 of the Arbitration Act was amended to give the arbitral tribunal the same powers as a civil court, including the power to grant interim relief as specified in Section 9 of the Arbitration Act (which means that the interim injunctions are now enforceable) for both domestic and overseas arbitrations.[54] Section 17 was also amended to state that in case an arbitral tribunal has been constituted, no court would pass interim orders related to that arbitration.[55]

Initiation of Arbitration Proceedings

Arbitration proceedings are required to be commended within 90 days of any application for interim relief by one of the parties to the arbitration. Any interim relief provided elapses at the end of this 90-day period. This would avoid a situation where parties would obtain an interim relief and then delay initiating arbitration since their interests were protected.

Guidelines on Conflict of Interest

The 2015 Amendment, in Section 12, incorporates by reference the International Bar Association (IBA) Guidelines on Conflict of Interest in International Arbitration which reflects the international best practices with respect to impartiality and independence of arbitrators. This includes the Red List (waivable and non-waivable) and Orange List (requiring disclosure) formulation of conflicts and disqualifications.[56]

Reducing the Scope of the 'Public Policy Challenge'

Under the Arbitration Act, an order of an arbitrator could be challenged on the ground that it is against the 'public policy' of India. Courts were likely to interpret this clause widely increasing the scope of challenging an arbitration award.[57] The 2015 Amendment seeks to address this by providing a fairly restrictive definition of public policy, which is restricted to the following situations: (a) the award was induced or affected by fraud or corruption, (b) the award was in contravention of a fundamental policy of Indian law or, (c) the award is in conflict with the most basic norms of morality and law.

Comprehensive Provision for Costs

Section 31A has been added to the Arbitration Act as a comprehensive provision for costs. It applies not only to the arbitration proceedings but also to the related costs of any court proceedings. The section is intended to discourage frivolous litigation.[58]

Fees Chargeable by Arbitrators

The 2015 Amendment introduces a fourth schedule which specifies the model fees chargeable by arbitrators. However, this schedule is not legally binding and needs to be incorporated into rules by individual high courts for it to be effective.

Challenge to an Award

The 2015 Amendment amends Section 36 of the Arbitration Act to the effect that the filing of an application challenging the award would not automatically stay the operation of the award. A court must grant a specific order for stay. Further, Section 34(6) has been introduced to state that any challenge to an arbitral award shall be disposed of within 12 months.

***

It is evident that the Parliament and the Government of India recognizes that if India intends to grow as a commercial superpower, it needs to develop a robust commercial dispute settlement infrastructure and inculcate confidence in its legal system. Given the lack of success of the Indian arbitral regime, the government has chosen a 'top–down' approach to initiate reform and increase the effectiveness of arbitration.[59] In this context, the changes made by the 2015 Amendment can be broadly classified under three major bundles: (a) ensuring that the arbitral process can be concluded within a strict timeline and reasonable cost; (b) reducing the scope of judicial intervention either before, during or after the arbitration to a minimum, and (c) ensuring the integrity and neutrality of arbitrators.

Along with the arbitration law, the Indian Government also came out with a law related to creation of commercial courts, the Commercial

Courts, Commercial Division, and Commercial Appellate Division of High Courts Act, 2015 (No. 4 of 2016),[60] which provides that arbitration above a particular value determined by the Central Government from time to time (but not less than Rs 10 million) shall be heard by specially qualified commercial courts.[61] This again will positively influence parties in choosing arbitration.

Prior to the amendment, the Arbitration Act, with its emphasis on party autonomy, inadvertently favoured ad hoc arbitration.[62] The 2015 Amendment reduces this party autonomy to a significant degree by introducing procedural strictures in the arbitral process.[63] This ensures an encouragement of institutional arbitration since it best suited to ensure that individual and all arbitrations take place in accordance with the provisions of the revised Arbitration Act.

The key reasons for a jurisdiction to succeed as a well-recognized venue for international arbitration include the presence of an institution of repute; volume, variety, and quality of specialist advice; a minimum intervention policy from the judiciary;[64] and a strong rule of law.[65] A jurisdiction that wishes to promote arbitration must therefore adopt a pro-arbitration policy, which needs to permeate across the lawmakers, the administrators and the Courts.[66] In addition to these key factors, a number of 'soft' factors also play a part, for example, the quality of general level of infrastructure, ease of travel, geographical location and the levels of commerce.[67] With the amendments to the Arbitration Act, the government seeks to address some of these issues, but all of it cannot of course be achieved through legislation.

There has been no strong arbitral institution which could operate within the intricacies and complications of the Indian system.[68] Parties will always be more willing to arbitrate in India if they know that there is an established institution that ensures efficiency and predictability.[69] Obviously the government has a significant role in the promotion of arbitral institutions,[70] but it cannot be the only source of impetus. (In fact, one of the key features of the internationally reputable institutions is that they enjoy a great degree of independence from state interference.) While the 2015 amendments to the Arbitration Act are far-reaching and extensive, the amendments themselves will not automatically result in the achievement of the goal for expeditious and effective arbitration. What is necessary is the development of strong, well-managed, independent institutions, which adopt international best practices and has access to internationally renowned arbitration experts.[71] The more robust the arbitral institutions are India, it is more likely for becoming a preferred arbitral destination.

Notes and References

1. 'India's journey towards becoming an international commercial arbitration hub that can rival London and Singapore has been hampered by a largely ineffective arbitration law and legal regime'. See Prakash Pillai, and Mark Shan in *Kluwer Arbitration Blog*, (10 March 2016) http://kluwerarbitrationblog.com/2016/03/10/persisting-problems-amendments-to-the-indian-arbitration-and-conciliation-act/ accessed 8 July 2016; see also, Janak Dwarkadas, 'A Call for Institutionalised Arbitration in India: A Step towards Certainty, Efficiency and Accountability', (2006) 3 Supreme Court Cases (Journal); Persisting Problems: Amendment to the Indian Arbitration and Conciliation Act', in *Kluwer Arbitration Blog*, (10 March 2016) http://kluwerarbitrationblog.com/2016/03/10/persisting-problems-amendments-to-the-indian-arbitration-and-conciliation-act/, accessed 8 July 2016.

2. 'An additional consideration that drives the reform process in India is the consideration that arbitration institutions have been very successful in other Asian countries, with Singapore and Hong Kong being considered as part of the top arbitral institutions in the world'. See Harishanker, K.S., 'Contemporary International Arbitration in Asia: A Stock Take', *Indian Journal of Arbitration Law*, 3 (1, 2014), 1 at 5. For additional analysis on these institutions and their potential, see Justin D'Agostino, 'Arbitration in Asia at Full Gallop', *Kluwer Arbitration Blog* (10 February 2014), available http://kluwerarbitrationblog.com/2014/02/10/arbitration-in-asia-at-full-gallop, accessed 8 July 2016. For an overview of the increasing popularity of institutional arbitration worldwide, see Guy Pendell, 'The Rise and Rise of Arbitration Institutions', *Kluwer Arbitration Blog* (30 November 2011), available http://kluwerarbitrationblog.com/2011/11/30/the-rise-and-rise-of-the-arbitration-institution/, accessed 8 July 2016.

3. A vital area where India is lagging behind is the lack of institutional arbitration. See Hans Raj Bharadwaj, 'Extracts from the Inaugural Address', delivered at the ICFAI Conference of 'Critical Issues in International Commercial Arbitration', 19–20 October 2007, New Delhi, in *India Council of Arbitration Journal*, 42 (3 and 4, October–December 2007,

January–March 2008). The other often-discussed factor, which has heavily contributed to India's lack of success with arbitration, is the role of the domestic Courts and their frequent interference with the arbitration process. While an examination of that issue is beyond the scope of this article, there already exists a wealth of writing that examines the issue in great detail. See generally Ajay Kr. Sharma, 'Judicial Intervention in International Commercial Arbitration: Critiquing the Indian Supreme Court's Interpretation of the Arbitration and Conciliation Act, 1996', *Indian Journal of Arbitration Law*, 3 (1, April 2014), p. 6; Ravi Shankar Sathoyamoorthy, 'When Courts Can Interfere in the Awards Passed by an Arbitral Tribunal as per the Law in India?' (21 January 2015), available http://www.mondaq.com/india/x/357928/Arbitration+Dispute+Resolution/When+Courts+Can+Interfere+In+The+Awards+Passed+By+An+Arbitral, accessed 8 July 2016); and Felipe Sperandino, 'The Jurisdiction of Indian Courts over Arbitrations Seated Outside India: An Outsider's Perspective', *Kluwer Arbitration Blog* (21 July 2014), available http://kluwerarbitrationblog.com/2014/07/21/the-jurisdiction-of-indian-courts-over-arbitrations-seated-outside-india-an-outsiders-perspective/, accessed 8 July 2016).

There is a prevalent view that Indian courts have been gradually turning 'pro-arbitration'; see generally, Gary B. Born and Suzanne A. Spears, 'International Arbitration and India: A Truly Excellent Judgement', *Indian Journal of Arbitration Law*, 1 (1, 2012) (on the decision of the Supreme Court in *Bharat Aluminum v Kaiser Aluminum*, Civ App 3678 of 2007 (judgment dated 6 September 2012); Arpan Kumar Gupta, 'A New Dawn for India: Reducing Court Intervention in Enforcement of Foreign Awards', *Indian Journal of Arbitration Law*, 2 (2, 2013), p. 10; James Rogers, 'India's Changing Outlook on International Arbitration', *Kluwer Arbitration Blog* (16 August 2011), available http://kluwerarbitrationblog.com/2011/08/16/indias-changing-outlook-on-international-arbitration/, accessed 8 July 2016; Olga Boltenko and Kartikey Mahajan, 'How the Reliance Saga Brought Clarity to Bhatia International', *Kluwer Arbitration Blog* (30 November 2015), available http://kluwerarbitrationblog.com/2015/11/30/how-the-reliance-saga-brought-clarity-to-the-applicability-of-bhatia-international/, accessed 8 July 2016; Vivekananda N. and Ankit Goyal, 'Interventionist, No More?', in *Singapore International Arbitration Centre Resources* (30 November 2011), available http://www.siac.org.sg/2013-09-18-01-57-20/2013-09-22-00-27-02/articles/201-interventionist-no-more, accessed 8 July 2016; Sujoy Chatterjee, 'Delhi Airport Metro Case: Twilight Zone of the "Pro-Arbitration Trend"', *Indian Corporate Law Blog* (19 August 2014), available http://indiacorplaw.blogspot.in/2014/

08/guest-post-delhi-airport-metro-case.html, accessed 8 July 2016; Sumit Rai, 'Indian Supreme Court Overrules Bhatia International: Or Does It?', *Blog Arbitration* (6 September 2012), available https://blogarbitration.com/2012/09/06/indian-supreme-court-overrules-bhatia-international-or-does-it/, accessed 8 July 2016; Nimoy Kher, 'The Panna Mukta Arbitration: The Indian Supreme Court Adopts a Pro-Arbitration Stance—Another Step in the Right Direction?', *Lex Arbitri Blog* (22 August 2014), available http://lexarbitri.blogspot.in/2014/08/the-panna-mukta-arbitrations-indian.html, accessed 8 July 2016; R.V. Prabhat, 'Mere Choice of Foreign Seat to Exclude Part I of the Arbitration Act, 1996: Pre Balco Arbitrations', *Indian Corporate Law Blog* (11 June 2016), available http://indiacorplaw.blogspot.in/2016/06/guest-post-mere-choice-of-foreign-seat.html, accessed 8 July 2016. In the Asian context as well, interference of courts remain a key issue; see Michael Hwang, 'Why Is There Still Resistance to Arbitration in Asia?' in *Michael Hwang SC: Selected Essays in International Arbitration* (Singapore International Arbitration Centre, 2013), pp. 20–2, available https://www.transnational-dispute-management.com/downloads/mh_selected-essays_on_ia.pdf, accessed 8 July 2016.

4. See S. Sivakumar, V.S. Jaya, and K. Konoorayar Vishnu, 'Dispute Resolution through Ad Hoc and Institutional Arbitration: An Analysis of Their Effectiveness', in *ADR: Status Effectiveness Study* (India Law Institute, 2008), pp. 80 at 84; see also Amelia C. Randeiro, 'Indian Arbitration and "Public Policy"', in *Texas Law Review*, 89 (2011), p. 726.

5. See Sivakumar et al., 'Dispute Resolution', p. 98.

6. See Namrata Shah and Niyati Gandhi, 'Arbitration: One Size Does Not Fit All: Necessity of Developing Institutional Arbitration on Developing Countries', *Journal of International Commercial Law and Technology*, 6 (4, 2011), p. 235.

7. See Justice Ashok Bhan, 'Commercial Arbitration: Need to Change the Mindset', *Indian Council of Arbitration Quarterly*, (October–December 2007), p. 2. Perhaps the most scathing criticism of the arbitral system has come from the present Attorney General of India, Mr Mukul Rohatgi, who has characterized the pre-amendment Arbitration Act as a 'complete failure' and stated that the process of arbitration in the country 'has become a joke' in a written opinion to the Government of India. He says:

I find, with my experience over the last several years, that the Arbitration and Conciliation Act, 1996 is a complete failure. Firstly, arbitration itself has become a joke in this country.

Arbitration proceedings are unduly prolonged since mostly retired judges are appointed as arbitrators and they view arbitration just like a case in court. The procedure is as elaborate as that of court. It is normal to have 50–100 sittings in arbitration, whether by a single member or a multi-member arbitration.

Quoted in Maneesh Chitter, 'Law Panel, AG Differ on Arbitration Act, Government set to Revisit Its Clauses', *Indian Express* (18 May 2015), available http://indianexpress.com/article/india/india-others/law-panel-ag-differ-on-arbitration-act-govt-set-to-revisit-its-clauses/, accessed 8 July 2016.

8. See Justice D.K. Jain, 'Arbitration: As a Concept and as a Process', *Indian Council of Arbitration Quarterly* (January–March 2007), p. 26; see also Anurag K. Agarwal, 'Making India an International Commercial Arbitration Hub', in *Livemint* (5 October 2015), available http://www.livemint.com/Opinion/TQMQvWD9Agxb0n7voHpllL/Making-India-an-international-commercial-arbitration-hub.html, accessed 8 July 2016).

9. Commentators point out to the 'happy combination of factors' which makes Singapore the most attractive seat of arbitration for Indian parties. This includes a similar common law system, awards which are enforceable in India, geographical proximity, world-class infrastructure, and the 'arbitration friendly' nature of Singapore Courts. Ben Giaretta, 'Indian Arbitration in Singapore' (April 2010), available https://www.ashurst.com/doc.aspx?id_Content=5151, accessed 8 July 2016. See also Aakansha Kumar and Krutthika Prakash, 'Giving the Award Debtor a "Choice of Remedies" in Domestic and International Arbitrations: Should India Go the Singapore Way', in *Indian Journal of Arbitration Law*, 3 (2, 2014), p. 6.

10. See Gary B. Born, 'International Commercial Arbitration', *Kluwer Law International* (2009), p. 151; see also Kinga Timar, 'The Legal Relationship between the Parties and the Arbitral Institution', in *ELTE Law Journal*, (1, 2013), p. 113.

11. See Price Waterhouse Cooper, 'Corporate Attitudes and Practices towards Arbitration in India', available https://www.pwc.in/assets/pdfs/publications/2013/corporate-attributes-and-practices-towards-arbitration-in-india.pdf, accessed 6 July 2016.

12. 'The structure and procedural predictability that is provided by institutional arbitration may have great advantages in the Indian context'. See Abhinav Bhushan and Niyati Gandhi, 'One for the Money: Renewing Institutional Arbitration in India', *Kluwer Arbitration Blog* (31 March 2014), available http://kluwer arbitrationblog.com/2014/03/31/one-

for-the-money-renewing-institutional-arbitration-in-india/, accessed 8
July 2016. See Harpreet Kaur, 'The 1996 Arbitration and Conciliation
Act: A Stop towards Improving Arbitration in India', *6 Hastings Business
Law Journal* (2010), p. 261.

13. Ministry of Law and Justice, Government of India, 'Proposed
Amendments to the Arbitration and Conciliation Act: A Consultation
Paper', available http://lawmin.nic.in/la/consultationpaper.pdf, accessed
6 July 2016. It may be noted that this comprehension is not a new
one. As far back as 2005, the Parliamentary Standing Committee on
Personnel, Public Grievances and Justice, in its 9th Report on the
Arbitration and Conciliation (Amendment) Bill, 2003 highlighted the
absence of arbitrators, huge pendency of cases, no rules as to who can
be appointed as arbitrators, arbitrator fees, time limit for making an
award, and lack of consequences for making an award within a specified
time as the key issues affecting the conduct of arbitrations in India. The
Standing Committee recommended setting up an Indian Arbitration
Commission, which will grant accreditation to professional institutions
which would conduct arbitration proceedings. The recommendations
of the Standing Commission were not implemented. See Dwarkadas,
'A Call for Institutionalised Arbitration in India', p. 2.

14. 2009(4) SCALE 491.

15. In *Union of India v. UP State Bridge Corporation*, Civil Appeal No. 8860
of 2014 (SLP Civil No. 20183 of 2012) (judgment dated 16 September
2012), the Supreme Court recognized that delay in arbitral proceedings on account of the arbitral tribunal was often encountered in India.
See also the decision of the Delhi High Court in *Ariba India Private
Limited v. Ispat Industries Ltd.*, OMP 358/2010 (judgment dated 4
July 2011), where the court favourably noted the petitioner's argument
that the parties entered into an arbitration agreement 'in the hope that
their disputes would be resolved expeditiously in a fair and reasonable
manner with reasonable and limited expenditure and costs. If these
objectives are not achieved, the whole purpose of agreeing to resolution
of disputes by arbitration gets defeated and the proceedings become
a mockery.'

16. See Aarman Patkar, 'Indian Arbitration: Legislating for Utopia', *Indian
Journal of Arbitration Law*, 4 (2, 2015), p. 28.

17. See Nigel Blackaby, Constantine Partasides, Alan Redfern, J. Martin,
and H. Hunter, *Redfern and Hunter on International Arbitration*, 5th ed.
(Oxford University Press, 2009), pp. 53–4, paras 1.155–1.157; see also
Sivakumar et al., 'Dispute Resolution', p. 89.

18. See Sanskriti Rastogi, 'Problems in the Implementation of Alternative Dispute Resolution in India', *Lex Arbitri: The Indian Arbitration Blog* (26 June 2012), available http://lexarbitri.blogspot.in/2012/06/guest-post-problems-in-implementation.html, accessed 6 July 2016.

19. See Sundra Rajoo, 'Institutional and Ad-Hoc Arbitrations: Advantages and Disadvantages', 7th International Conference on Construction Law and Dispute Resolution, Mauritius, 25–6 November, 2009, *The Law Review* (2010), pp. 547–53.

20. Delay in appointment of arbitrators is considered as the top factor in increasing the length of ad hoc arbitration proceedings. See Price Waterhouse Cooper, 'Corporate Attitudes'; See also Sivakumar et al., 'Dispute Resolution', p. 87.

21. See Michael W. Butler and Thomas W. Webster, *Handbook of ICC Arbitration: Commentary, Precedents and Materials*, 5th ed. (Sweet & Maxwell, 2005), p. 198.

22. Justice Ajit Prakash Shah, 'Need to Bring Reforms in Arbitration Law', *Indian Council of Arbitration Quarterly* (October–December 2005), p. 2. This is not an issue unique to India. Experience across jurisdictions show that selecting a retired judge as arbitrator will lead to a more formal adjudication process which is procedure driven. See Robert D. Weisman and J. David Campbell, 'To Judge or Not to Judge, Retired Judges as Arbitrators', available http://www.americanbar.org/content/dam/aba/events/labor_law/2013/02/adr_in_labor_employmentlawco mmitteemidwintermeeting/z.authcheckdam.pdf, accessed 8 July 2016.

23. See Richard J. Graving, 'The International Commercial Arbitration Institutions: How Good a Job Are They Doing?', *American University International Law Review*, 4 (2), pp. 319 at 368.

24. Price Waterhouse Cooper, 'Corporate Attitudes', p. 11.

25. Price Waterhouse Cooper, 'Corporate Attitudes', p. 11.

26. Sivakumar et al., 'Dispute Resolution', p. 90.

27. See International Bar Association, 'The Current State and Future of International Arbitration: Regional Perspectives', IBA Arb. 40 Sub-committee (September 2015), p. 11, para 1.5, available www.ibanet.org/Document/Default.aspx?DocumentUid=2102ca46-3d4a-48e5, accessed 6 June 2016.

28. Krishna Sarma, Momota Dinam, and Anshuman Kaushik, 'Development of Practice of Arbitration in India: Has It Evolved as an Effective Legal Institution?' Committee on Democracy, Development and the Rule of Law, Freeman Spogli Institute for International Studies, Stanford (123, October 2009), p. 6.

29. See International Bar Association, 'IBA Guidelines for Drafting International Arbitration Clauses', Adopted by a resolution of the IBA Council (7 October 2010).
30. Rajoo, 'Institutional and Ad-hoc Arbitrations', p. 555.
31. The major arbitration institutions have model clauses that can be directly incorporated into agreements by parties, which automatically incorporates the arbitral institution in the agreement. See IBA, 'IBA Guidelines', pp. 7–8.
32. Sarma et al., 'Development of Practice of Arbitration in India', p. 235.
33. D.N. Bhat, 'Ad-Hoc Arbitration or Institutional Arbitration? Which Is Better for India?', *Indian Council of Arbitration Quarterly* (January–March 2009), p. 5.
34. For example, the HKIAC Rules were amended in 2013 to provide for modifications in relation to emergency relief, multiparty and multi-contract arbitrations, expedited procedure, all with the aim of increased efficiency. See HKIAC Rules 2013. For an analysis, see Stephan Balthazar, 'HKIAC: What Will the New Arbitration Rules Change?', *Kluwer Arbitration Blog* (30 September 2013), available http://kluwer-arbitrationblog.com/2013/09/30/hkiac-what-will-the-new-arbitration-rules-change/, accessed 8 July 2016; Justin D'Augustino and Briana Young, 'Hong Kong Tables Amendments to Arbitration Law', *Kluwer Arbitration Blog* (3 April 2013), available http://kluwerarbitrationblog.com/2013/04/03/hong-kong-tables-amendments-to-arbitration-law/, accessed 9 July 2016. Similarly, the SIAC has amended its rules on 1 July 2016 introducing rules for multiparty and multi-jurisdictional arbitrations, joinders, and consolidation. 'Arbitration Rules of the Singapore International Arbitration Centre', 6th ed. (1 August 2016), available http://www.siac.org.sg/ images/stories/articles/rules/SIAC%20 2016%20Rules_6th%20Edition.pdf, accessed 15 July 2016. See Olga Boltenko and Priscilla Lua, 'The SIAC Rules, 2016: A Watershed in the History of Arbitration in Singapore', *Kluwer Arbitration Blog* (12 July 2016), available http://kluwerarbitrationblog.com/2016/07/12/the-siac-rules-2016-a-watershed-in-the-history-of-arbitration-in-singapore/, accessed 16 July 2016.
35. Rajoo, 'Institutional and Ad-hoc Arbitrations', p. 554. There is also evidence that ad hoc awards do not receive the same deference as institutional awards when they are presented to courts for enforcement; see Nicholas Ulmer, 'Drafting the International Arbitration Clause', *20 International Lawyer* (1986), pp. 1335, 1337; William W. Park, 'Arbitration of International Contract Disputes', *39 Business Law* (1984), pp. 1783, 1784.

36. See Kaur, 'The 1996 Arbitration and Conciliation Act', p. 278.
37. See Dwarkadas, 'A Call for Institutionalised Arbitration in India', p. 2.
38. Kaur, 'The 1996 Arbitration and Conciliation Act', p. 277.
39. Rajoo, 'Institutional and Ad-hoc Arbitrations', p. 556.
40. See Jonathon Lim, 'Are All Institutional Rules Now Basically the Same?', *Kluwer Arbitration Blog*, available http://kluwerarbitrationblog.com/2015/04/10/are-all-institutional-rules-now-basically-the-same/, accessed on 8 July 2016.
41. Rajoo, 'Institutional and Ad-Hoc Arbitrations', p. 555.
42. Sivakumar et al., 'Dispute Resolution', p. 91.
43. Shah and Gandhi, 'Arbitration', p. 235.
44. See Yves Derains, 'The Future of ICC Arbitrations', *George Washington University Journal of International Law & Economics*, 14 (1979–80), pp. 437 at 441.
45. International Bar Association, 'The Current State and Future of International Arbitration, p. 11, para 1.5.
46. Price Waterhouse Cooper, 'Corporate Attitudes', p. 11.
47. Justice R.C. Lahoti, 'International Commercial Arbitration: Challenges and Possibilities in Asian Countries (with special reference to India)', p. 3.
48. Rajoo, 'Institutional and Ad-hoc Arbitrations', p. 556.
49. *20th Law Commission of India*, Report No. 246, 'Amendments to the Arbitration Act, 1996', (August 2014).
50. For further analysis and commentary on the Law Commission's Recommendations, see Shriya Jain and Param Pandya, 'Proposed Amendments to Arbitration Law', *Indian Corporate Law Blog* (30 April 2015), available http://indiacorplaw.blogspot.in/2015/04/proposed-amendments-to-arbitration-law.html, accessed 8 July 2016; Ashutosh Ray, 'Law Commission's Report to Revamp the Indian Arbitration Experience', *Kluwer Arbitration Blog* (23 August 2014), available http://kluwerarbitrationblog.com/2014/08/23/law-commissions-report-to-revamp-the-indian-arbitration-experience/, accessed 8 July 2016. Some commentators felt that Law Commission's Report reinforces the pro-arbitration trends in India, Prakash Pillai and Umer Chaudhry, 'Law Commission's Report Reinforces the Pro-Arbitration Trends in India', *Kluwer Arbitration Blog* (9 October 2014), available http://kluwerarbitrationblog.com/2014/10/09/law-commissions-report-reinforces-the-pro-arbitration-trends-in-india/, accessed 8 July 2016; and is an 'omen of good times to come', Ashutosh Roy, 'Law Commission's Report to Revamp the Indian Arbitration Experience', *Kluwer Arbitration Blog* (23 August 2014), available http://kluwerarbitrationblog.com/2014/08/23/law-commissions-report-to-revamp-the-indian-arbitration-experience/, accessed 8 July 2016.

51. It may be noted that amendments to arbitration legislation can be a legitimate first step in revamping the arbitration regime. To be successful, such amended legislation needs to address comprehensively a host of issues, including the arbitrability of disputes, validity of arbitration agreements, powers of arbitral tribunals to order interim measures, the grounds of annulment of arbitral awards, and the scope of judicial intervention. These are what distinguish one national arbitration legislation for another. See Panagiotis Chalkias, 'Making a Favorable National Law for Arbitration: How Difficult Can It Be?', *Arbitration Blog* (21 November 2011), available https://blogarbitration.com/2011/11/21/making-a-favourable-national-law-on-arbitration-how-difficult-can-it-be/, accessed 8 July 2016.

52. For initial reaction to these amendments, which were introduced through an Ordinance (Presidential Promulgation) on 23 October 2015 and then followed up with an Act of Parliament on 31 December 2015 (effective retrospectively from 23 October 2015), see Pillai and Shan in *Kluwer Arbitration Blog*, (10 March 2016) available http://kluwer-arbitrationblog.com/2016/03/10/persisting-problems-amendments-to-the-indian-arbitration-and-conciliation-act/ accessed 8 July 2016; Paavni Anand, 'Major Changes Proposed by the Arbitration Amendment Ordinance, 2015', *Indian Corporate Law Blog* (20 October 2015), available http://indiacorplaw.blogspot.in/2015/10/major-changes-proposed-by-arbitration.html, accessed 8 July 2016; Prachi Narayan and Aditi Pal, 'Proposed Amendments to Arbitration Law: Part I', *Indian Corporate Law Blog* (22 August 2015), available http://indiacorplaw.blogspot.in/2014/08/guest-post-proposed-amendments-to.html,   accessed 8 July 2016; Prachi Narayan and Aditi Pal, 'Proposed Amendments to Arbitration Law: Part II', *Indian Corporate Law Blog* (23 August 2015), *Kluwer Arbitration Blog* (2 February 2016), available http://kluwerarbitrationblog.com/2016/02/02/s-29a-of-the-new-indian-arbitration-act-an-attempt-at-slaying-hydra/, accessed 8 July 2016, http://indiacorplaw.blogspot.in/2014/08/guest-post-proposed-amendments-to_23.html, accessed 8 July 2016; Sulabh Rewai and Poorvi Saluja, 'A Close Look at India's New Arbitration Ordinance', *Indian Corporate Law Blog* (18 November 2015), available http://indiacorplaw.blogspot.in/2015/11/a-close-look-at-indias-new-arbitration.html,   accessed   8 July 2016; Vikas Mahendra, 'Arbitration in India: A New Beginning', *Kluwer Arbitration Blog* (6 November 2015), available http://kluwerar-bitrationblog.com/2015/11/06/arbitration-in-india-a-new-beginning/, accessed 8 July 2016.

Most commentators felt that the legislation was urgently required to remedy the problems of 'costly and time-consuming commercial dispute resolution in India' and represent a significant improvement; see Vrinda Bhandari, 'Ordinances on Commercial Courts and the Arbitration Act: Analysing the Process Problems of Drafting Law', *Ajay Shah's Blog* (22 December 2015), available https://ajayshahblog. blogspot.in/2015/12/ordinances-on-commercial-courts-and.html, accessed 8 July 2016. The changes are intended to 'instil confidence in investors who had been wary of choosing India as a seat of arbitration'; Herbert Smith Freehills, 'Amendments to Indian Arbitration Law Now Effective' (5 November 2015), available http://hsfnotes.com/arbitration/2015/11/05/amendments-to-the-indian-arbitration-act-now-effective/, accessed 8 July 2016. It is a 'positive step toward more speedy and fair resolutions of disputes through international commercial arbitration in India'; Baker Botts, 'India's New Arbitration Ordinance to Instill Investor Confidence' (27 October 2015), available http://www.bakerbotts.com/ ideas/publications/2015/10/ litigation update india, accessed 8 July 2016. The reactions were not all positive. See Sumit Rai, 'India Amends Arbitration Law: Some Great, Some Absurd Changes', *Blog Arbitration* (25 October 2015), available https://blogarbitration.com/2015/10/25/india-amends-arbitration-law-some-great-some-absurd-changes/, accessed 8 July 2016; Kartikey Mahajan, 'The Arbitration Ordinance: Leaving India Vulnerable to Another White Industries', *Indian Corporate Law Blog* (27 November 2015), available http://indiacorplaw.blogspot.in/2015/11/the-arbitration-ordinance-leaving-india.html, accessed 8 July 2016.

53. It is worthwhile noting that Section 29A did not form a part of the Law Commission's recommendations and has been described as 'without parallel in any other domestic jurisdiction' and is 'a novel provision and certainly aimed at an existing weakness in the present context of extremely slow arbitrations'. See Sanjeevi Sheshadri, 'Section 29A of the New Arbitration Act: An Attempt at Slaying Hydra', *Kluwer Arbitration Blog* (2 February 2016), available http://kluwerarbitrationblog.com/2016/02/02/s-29a-of-the-new-indian-arbitration-act-an-attempt-at-slaying-hydra/, accessed 8 July 2016. Commentators however have criticized the Section as an unreasonable restriction on party autonomy which forces parties to approach courts in case the 18-month period is over, which is antithetical to legislation expressly intended to reduce the extent of Court participation in the arbitral process. Further since the reason for delays in arbitration was not as a result of the legal provisions themselves finding a solution to the problem in legislation is flawed, what is necessary is appropriate infrastructure and judicial discipline; see Rai, 'India Amends Arbitration Law'. Most notably, it appears that the Chairman of the Law Commission, Justice Shah

himself has criticized the provision, in a 'strongly worded' letter to the Prime Minister Narendra Modi, calling the provision as 'unacceptable'. See Chitter, 'Law Panel'.

54. It may be noted that recent reiterations of the institutional rules of most international arbitration rules allocate broad powers to arbitral tribunals to provide interim relief, restricting the power of the national courts to only narrow circumstances. See International Chamber of Commerce Rules of Arbitration, 2012, available http://www.iccwbo.org/Products-and-Services/Arbitration-and-ADR/Arbitration/Rules-of-arbitration/ICC-Rules-of-Arbitration/, accessed 8 July 2016; London Court of International Arbitration Rules of Arbitration Rules 2014, available http://www.lcia.org/Dispute_Resolution_Services/lcia-arbitration-rules-2014.aspx, accessed 8 July 2016; Hong Kong International Arbitration Centre, Administered Arbitration Rules, 2013, available http://www.hkiac.org/sites/default/files/ck_filebrowser/PDF/arbitration/2013_hkiac_rules.pdf, accessed 8 July 2016.

55. For a detailed analysis of these amendments, in particular to foreign seated arbitrations, see Gunjan Chhabra, 'Foreign Seated Arbitrations: Section 9 Reliefs Post Amendment, 2015', in *Indian Corporate Law Blog* (9 May 2016), available http://indiacorplaw.blogspot.in/2016/05/foreign-seated-arbitrations-section-9.html, accessed 8 July 2016. The commentator concludes that under the 2015 Amendment, parties to a foreign seated arbitration can take advantage of the provisions of Sections 9, 27(1)(a) and 37(3) of the Arbitration Act provided they have an express saving clause in their agreements.

56. For a more detailed analysis of the amended Section 12 and how it affects the independence and impartiality of arbitrators and an analysis of the decision of the Delhi High Court in *Assigna-VIL JV v. Rail Vikas Nigam Limited*, (Arbitration Petition No. 677/2015, Judgement dated 29 April 2016). On the applicability and scope of the amended Section 12, see Shubham Jain, 'Independence and Impartiality of Arbitrators: The Applicability and Scope of Section 12', *Indian Corporate Law Blog* (30 June 2016), available http://indiacorplaw.blogspot.in/2016/06/guest-post-independence-and_30.html, accessed 8 July 2016.

57. A more detailed examination of Indian Court's interpretation of 'public policy' and how it has impacted the enforcement of awards in India is beyond the scope of this article. For detailed analysis of this issue, see Amrit Mahal, 'Public Policy of India and the Arbitral Award: Fighting the Unending Battle', in *Indian Corporate Law Blog* (11 July 2016), available http://indiacorplaw.blogspot.in/2016/07/guest-post-public-policy-

of-india-and.html, accessed 8 July 2016; Ben Giaretta and Akshay Kishore, 'Public Policy in Indian Arbitration' (March 2015), available https://www.ashurst.com/doc.aspx?id_Content=11657, accessed 8 July 2016; Samir Sattar, 'Enforcement of Arbitral Awards and Public Policy: Same Concept Different Approach?', available http://www.employmentlawalliance.com/Templates/media/files/Misc%20Documents/Enforcement-of-Arbitral-Awards-Public-Policy.pdf, accessed 8 July 2016; Sidharth Sharma, 'Public Policy under the Indian Arbitration Act: In Defence of the Indian Supreme Court's Judgement in ONGC v. Saw Pipes', *Journal of International Arbitration*, 26 (1, 2009), p. 133. For an examination of the Law Commission's reasons for proposing changes to the definition of public policy, see Jain and Pandya, 'Proposed Amendments to Arbitration Law'. For an examination of the Supreme Court's move towards a narrower definition of 'public policy', see Vyapak Desai, Payal Chatterjee, and Ashish Kabra, 'Supreme Court Limits Scope of Public Policy in Foreign Arbitral Awards', Singapore International Arbitration Centre, available http://www.siac.org.sg/2013-09-18-01-57-20/2013-09-22-00-27-02/articles/337-sc-limits-scope-of-public-policy-in-foreign-arbitral-awardswards, accessed 8 July 2016).

58. Most arbitral jurisdictions are strict about responsibility for costs of frivolous litigation. In *T v. TS*, 2014 WL 7311, the Hong Kong Court of First Instance held that if a party unsuccessfully resists an arbitral award or challenges an award, or unsuccessfully seeks to reopen through court proceedings an issue already dealt with in an arbitration, it will pay all costs for such proceedings on an indemnity basis. See Aditya Kurian, 'Arbitration Reform in India: A Look at the Hong Kong Model', *International Arbitration Asia* (21 July 2015), available http://www.internationalarbitrationasia.com/articles/arbitration-reform-in-india-a-look-at-the-hong-kong-model/, accessed 8 July 2016. With respect to the proactive role that the arbitral tribunal should play in controlling the costs of arbitration, see David J. Rowe, 'The Role of the Tribunal in Controlling Arbitral Costs', *The Internal Journal of Arbitration, Mediation and Dispute Management*, 81 (2, 2015), p. 116.

59. See Rohit Singhal, Shishir Kant, and Mayank Rajput, 'Dispute Resolution in Light of the New Arbitration Act of 2015', *Long International*, available http://www.long-intl.com/articles/Long_Intl_Dispute_Resolution_in_India_in_Light_of_New_Arbitration_Act_of_2015.pdf, accessed 8 July 2016. A World Bank study in 2015 ranked India as 186th among 189 countries in terms of ease of contract enforcement; see World Bank, *Doing Business Report: Going beyond*

Efficiency, 12th ed. (2014), available https://openknowledge.world bank.org/bitstream/handle/10986/20483/DB15-Full-Report.pdf? sequence=1, accessed 8 July 2016, p. 192. See Somya Kaushik, 'Arbitration in India: The Internal Challenges, India as an International Arbitration Destination and Risk Analysis for Foreign Investors' (3 May 2013), available http://www.businessconflictmanagement.com/ blog/2013/05/arbitration-in-india/, accessed 8 July 2016.

60. Also initially issued as an ordinance on 23 October 2015. The full text is available http://www.indiacode. nic.in/acts-in-pdf/2016/201604. pdf, accessed 8 July 2016.

61. For an analysis of this legislation, see Sulabh Rewai and Pooja Salija, 'Are Commercial Courts the Answer to India's Arbitration Woes?', *Kluwer Arbitration Blog* (25 December 2016), available http://kluwer-arbitrationblog.com/2015/12/25/are-commercial-courts-the-answer-to-indias-arbitration-woes/, accessed 8 July 2016). See also Vrinda Bhandari, 'Ordinances on Commercial Courts'.

62. See Patkar, 'Indian Arbitration', p. 63.

63. It will of course need to be borne in mind that the 2015 Amendment does not go so far as to specifically recommend institutional arbitration or indeed specifically recognize arbitral institutions from a legislative perspective. It is significant that while most of the recommendations of the Law Commission were accepted in the 2015 Amendment, the recommendation that all references by a High Court or Supreme Court under Section 11 of the Arbitration Act should be to institutional arbitration was not accepted and currently the Courts are free to refer matters to ad hoc arbitration as well. This does dilute the emphasis on institutional arbitration.

64. The UK enacted the Arbitration Act, 1996 to specifically limit the circumstances in which courts could interfere in arbitral matters. See Melanie Willems, 'That's a Relief (Interim): The English Court's Approach in Arbitrations', *The Arbiter* (Spring 2014), available https://www.andrewskurth.com/insights-1084.html, accessed 8 July 2016. Singapore courts have adapted a consistently pro-arbitration approach aimed at protecting the sanctity of arbitral awards and the arbitral tribunal's jurisdiction as well as facilitating the process of arbitration. In *PT Puhanfu Indah & Others v. Newmont Indonesia Ltd. and another*, [2012] SGHC 187, the Singapore High Court held that the overarching aim of the laws of Singapore is the independence and efficiency of arbitration and that limiting challenges to awards would reduce the risk of delay and of tactical attempts to distract the arbitration process. For an analysis of the judgment, see Panagiotis Charkias, 'Singapore High Court Reaffirms

Non-Interventionist Policy: PT Puhanfu Indah & Others v. Newmont Indonesia Ltd', *Blog Arbitration* (1 December 2012), available https://blogarbitration.com/2012/12/01/singapore-high-court-reaffirms-non-interventionist-policy-pt-pukuafu-indah-vs-newmont-indonesia-ltd/, accessed 8 July 2016. See also Michael Hwang and Su Zihua, 'The Role of the Court in Arbitration Proceedings and Enforcement of Awards', Paper Presented at the 15th Malaysian Conference on Arbitration at Kuala Lumpur (21 July 2010). Similarly, in *Tjong Very Sumito v. Antig Investments Pte Ltd.*, [2009] 4 SLR (R) J 32, it was held that Singapore has an 'unequivocal judicial policy of facilitating and promoting arbitration'. Hong Kong Courts have been similarly pro-active in protecting the sanctity of arbitration. See Nick Gall, 'Hong Kong Courts: Pro-Arbitration in Principle and in Practice', *Dispute Resolution Global Guide* (Practical Law Company), available http://uk.practicallaw.com/9-620-0183?q=Hong+Kong+courts:+pro-arbitration+in+princ iple+and+in+practice, accessed 8 July 2016; Norton Rose Fulbright, 'Pro-Arbitration Decisions in Hong Kong and China', available http://www.nortonrosefulbright.com/knowledge/publications/132591/pro-arbitration-decisions-in-hong-kong-and-china, accessed 8 July 2016.

65. See Lucy Scott Morcrieff, 'Arbitration: What Makes London So Special?', *The Law Society Blog* (15 November 2012), available https://www.lawsociety.org.uk/news/speeches/arbitration-what-makes-london-so-special/, accessed 8 July 2016; Llavin C. Hirani, 'The Legal Regimes Affecting International Commercial Arbitration in Singapore and India', available www.academia.edu, accessed 8 July 2016; Ruth Stackpole Moore, 'Advantages of Hong Kong Seated Arbitrations', in *Construction Claims*, 21st ed. (November 2014), available http://www.constructionadvisoryreport.com/home/blog/2014/11/04/seated-arbitrations, accessed 8 July 2016. Singapore has also been pro-active in updating its arbitration legislation to support arbitral efficiency. See Michael Pryles, 'Singapore the Hub of Arbitration in Asia', *Singapore International Arbitration Centre*, available http://www.siac.org.sg/2013-09-18-01-57-20/2013-09-22-00-27-02/articles/198-singapore-the-hub-of-arbitration-in-asia, accessed 8 July 2016.

66. The 2010 Queen Mary College/White & Case International Arbitration Survey identified formal legal infrastructure (national arbitration law, arbitration regime, and impartiality of the legal system) as the number one driver for the choice of arbitral seat; see Mike Mcclure, 'Dubai: A Hub for International Arbitration?', *Kluwer Arbitration Blog* (23 January 2013), available http://kluwerarbitrationblog.com/2013/01/23/dubai-a-hub-for-international-arbitration/, accessed 8 July 2016. See also

Simon Greenberg, Christopher Lee, and Ramesh Weeramurthy, *International Commercial Arbitration: An Asia Pacific Perspective* (Cambridge University Press, 2011), p. 423; Michael Hwang and Su Zihua, 'Egregious Errors and Public Policy: Are the Singapore Courts too Arbitration Friendly?' in Michael Hwang SC: *Selected Essays in International Arbitration* (Singapore International Arbitration Centre, 2013), p. 38, available https://www.transnational-dispute-management. com/downloads/mh_selected-essays_on_ia.pdf, accessed 8 July 2016.

67. The excellence of the physical infrastructure at the Maxwell Chambers plays a key role in the continued popularity of Singapore as a hub for international arbitration. See 'How Singapore Became an Arbitration Hub?', *Singapore International Mediation Centre* (3 September 2014), available http://simc.com.sg/singapore-became-arbitration-hub/, accessed 8 July 2016. For the multiplicity of reasons that affect the reputation of an arbitration institution, see Michael McIllworth, 'Will the Brexit Result Hasten London's Decline as Premier Seat of International Arbitration?', *Kluwer Arbitration Blog* (24 June 2016), available http:// kluwerarbitrationblog.com/2016/06/24/will-brexit-hasten-londons- decline-as-a-premier-seat-of-international-arbitration/, accessed 8 July 2016. The author concludes that while from a legal perspective, Britain's exit from the European Union will have no impact on London as a seat for international commercial arbitration, the overall financial and economic impact, as well as possible complications in for example, visa rule will negatively impact London's position.

68. The Law Commission does identify certain Institutions which have developed in India, as follows:

> In this context, the Commission notes the establishment and working of the Delhi High Court International Arbitration Centre which started in 2009 and is now fairly established and is providing good service to its users. The Punjab & Haryana High Court has also started an Arbitration Centre in 2014 with its own set of rules. The Commission further notes the working of the Indian Council of Arbitration (ICA), which is associated with FICCI and which is one of the earliest arbitral institutions in the country. The Commission further commends the working of the Nani Palkhivala Arbitration Centre in Chennai which similarly has its own set rules, governing body and staff, and is well established in the southern India. (*20th Law Commission of India*)

69. See Kaur, 'The 1996 Arbitration and Conciliation Act', pp. 278–9. Recent experience shows that there has been some growth in the number of institutional arbitrations in India; see Ernst & Young, 'Emerging Trends in Arbitration in India', no. 4, available http://www. ey.com/IN/en/Services/Assurance/Fraud-Investigation---Dispute-Services/EY-emerging-trends-in-arbitration-in-india, accessed 8 July 2016. However, the closure of Indian offices by the London Court of International Arbitration is a negative development. Alison Ross, 'LCIA India Closes Its Doors', *Global Arbitration Review* (15 January 2016), available http://globalarbitrationreview.com/news/article/34482/lcia-india-closes-its-doors/, accessed 8 July 2016.

70. Government has played an important role in the development of arbitration in the Asia-Pacific, especially Hong-Kong and Singapore and more recently in Malaysia and South Korea, See International Bar Association, 'IBA Guidelines, p. 9, para 1.3; Harishanker, 'Contemporary International Arbitration in Asia', p. 3.

71. See Meenakshi Natesan and Gerald Manoharan, 'Making Arbitration Work', *The Financial Express* (12 May 2016), available http://www.financialexpress.com/fe-columnist/column-making-arbitration-work/253308/, accessed 6 June 2016). The more established arbitration institutions there are, the more likely India will become a preferred arbitration destination. See Kaushik, 'Arbitration in India'.

8

Emergency Arbitrator in the Indian Context

Tejas Karia

Arbitration has been hailed as a viable alternate dispute resolution by virtue of its speed, confidentiality, and the degree to which parties may exercise control over the process. Developments in the undoubtedly dynamic field of arbitration enhance these traditional benefits.

Without a doubt, the interim measures before, during, or after the arbitration play a vital role in protecting the subject matter of arbitration. For this reason, parties heavily rely upon national courts in various jurisdictions. Emergence and development of the concept of emergency arbitrator makes the arbitral process extremely responsive and addresses one of the most important aspects of a party seeking urgent interim relief with recourse to national courts.

It is common knowledge that parties to a dispute may suffer irreparable harm before they are in a position to seek interim relief from an arbitral tribunal once constituted, given the time usually consumed in the formation of such tribunal. Such lack of access to interim relief was significant, especially in cases of institutional arbitration. As an alternative, emergency arbitrator provisions and the scope of their power have put in place an efficient procedure by which a party can obtain interim relief even prior to the constitution of the arbitral tribunal. This is especially significant in jurisdictions like India, wherein the reliance and interference of the domestic courts can thus be minimized.

These provisions have particular relevance insofar as the certain interim protections typically sought before the emergency arbitrator as they are extremely time-sensitive. The existing emergency arbitration provisions of institutional rules enable a party to make an application to seek emergency interim relief even prior to the constitution of the tribunal. The institutions administering the arbitrations either accept or reject an application for seeking emergency relief. Upon acceptance, an emergency arbitrator is appointed who is empowered to hear parties and grant or reject emergency interim relief in the absence of a fully constituted tribunal.

Role of Domestic Courts

Until recently, in case a party needs an urgent interim relief prior to the constitution of a tribunal, only one option is available, that is, to seek interim relief from the relevant national courts. While this is a viable option employed by most parties to an arbitration agreement, it has certain inherent disadvantages.

Often, when arbitration is chosen as the agreed method of dispute resolution, the common intent of the parties is to reduce their exposure to the formalities, constraints, and requirements of national courts. Parties may also want to stay away from national courts due to confidentiality concerns. Often parties tend to forge facts relating to the dispute in order to seek favourable interim reliefs from a national court. This is particularly relevant in cases of non-existence of procedure for the protection of identity of the litigating parties.

Moreover, in some jurisdictions, certain types of interim relief may not be available from state courts, which are bound by their municipal law.

Earlier Attempt at Providing Urgent Interim Relief

To reduce such procedural gaps and to ensure timely delivery of awards and resolution of disputes as a whole, various arbitral institutions have time and again introduced provisions, such as 'summary arbitral proceedings for interim relief' by Netherlands Arbitration Institute (NAI)[1] or 'expedited formation of the arbitral tribunal' by London Court of International Arbitration (LCIA)[2] or 'Pre-Arbitral Referee procedure' by International Court of Dispute Resolution (ICDR).[3] While these forums achieved limited success, a platform for a newer, more uniform development was initiated in the form of emergency arbitrator.

Emergency Arbitrator

The latest attempt is the introduction of emergency arbitrator procedures which, in effect, tries to address parties' emergency needs to obtain effective relief without compromising on the benefits of arbitration.

Emergency arbitrator procedures provide a temporal solution to parties by bestowing a choice of forum in which they can seek interim relief while awaiting the constitution of a tribunal. This mode allows for parties to obtain interim relief, before the constitution of the tribunal and allows the arbitral procedure for a time-responsive mechanism.

Historical Background of the Emergency Arbitrator

The concept of emergency arbitration was first adopted by International Centre for Dispute Resolution, the international division of the American Arbitration Association (AAA) as part of its amended rules in 2006.[4] Thereafter, Stockholm Chamber of Commerce (SCC) introduced a similar provision in 2010 followed by International Chamber of Commerce (ICC) which introduced emergency arbitrator provisions in 2012. This was followed by the Hong Kong International Arbitration Centre and Singapore International Arbitration Centre (SIAC) in 2013.[5] Surprisingly, LCIA introduced the emergency arbitrator provisions only in 2014.[6] Followed by the Swiss Chambers' Arbitration Institution,[7] the Australian Centre for International Commercial Arbitration, the Mexico City National Chamber of Commerce, the Netherlands Arbitration Institute,[8] the Madrid Court of Arbitration,[9] and the Arbitration Centre of the Portuguese Chamber of Commerce and Industry.[10]

In most cases, the updated provisions for emergency arbitrators apply to a dispute automatically, by virtue of the parties selecting the relevant arbitral rules, while in cases where the parties are exempted by the provisions of the emergency arbitrators, they have to specifically opt out of the arbitration agreement. Certain adopted provisions go one step further, by applying the 'opt-out' feature in respect of the emergency arbitrator provisions retroactively. It is anticipated that this automatic inclusion/opt out formulation will encourage the approval of emergency arbitrator procedures under the arbitral regimes in which they appear.

A divergence may be seen, however, in the approach of arbitral institutions at the stage at which parties may seek to invoke emergency arbitrator provisions. For instance, under the rules of certain institutions, parties are required to submit a Notice of Arbitration before, or concurrently with a request for emergency relief [Schedule 1(1) of the SIAC Rules]. Others, in contrast, offer even greater flexibility, allowing a party to apply for interim relief before a Request for Arbitration has been filed [Appendix V, Article 1(6) of the new ICC Rules]. However, in those instances, the party seeking interim relief is typically required to submit a Request for Arbitration within a certain time period after the application for relief.

There are, however, important limitations on the emergency arbitrator's powers to grant interim relief. For example, since the same principles of jurisdiction apply to emergency arbitrators as to the arbitral tribunal, they are not able to grant interim orders over third parties to the (eventual) arbitral proceedings. This rule is expressly recognized in Article 29(5) of the revised ICC Rules, which state that the emergency arbitrator provisions apply only to signatories to the arbitration agreement or their successors.

In addition, ex parte applications—where an element of surprise is vital—are not suitable for emergency arbitrations. In such situations, parties may rely on national courts for ex-parte orders.

The emergency arbitrator provisions are evolving and feasible for commercial concerns; there appears to be an increasing convergence in approaches to the provision of pre-arbitral emergency relief. Although there may be certain practical limitations on the operation and enforcement of these provisions, the ultimate aim of emergency arbitrator procedures is to increase party autonomy and reduce the role of the national courts in arbitral proceedings, taking arbitration one step further to becoming a one-stop shop for the comprehensive and effective resolution of disputes.

Legal Framework Governing Emergency Arbitration

The legal framework governing the emergency arbitration is comprised of the institutional rules providing for emergency arbitration, the municipal laws which form part of the curial law, and the law of the state where the emergency arbitrator order or awards are enforced.

Institutional Rules Providing for Emergency Arbitration

Various institutional rules provide only basic framework for emergency arbitrator. One of the methods in which the emergency arbitrator framework obtains legitimacy is when parties choose a certain set of rules to govern the procedure of the arbitration: they implicitly choose the emergency arbitration provisions in them. Some of them are detailed as follows:

ICC

The ICC Rules in Article 29 provides for an application for *emergency measures* and clarifies that such an application by a party would lie regardless of whether the party making the application has submitted its request for arbitration. This presents a unique legal background insofar as at the time of assessment of the application, no underlying request for arbitration and, the decision on the measures will be made solely on the basis of the application.

Furthermore, the ICC Rules, at least theoretically, differ from the SIAC Rules insofar as the decision of the emergency arbitrator, because it is an order and is not referred to as an award. In terms of enforceability, Article 29(2) simply specifies that the 'parties undertake to comply with any order made by the emergency arbitrator'.

The temporality of the emergency arbitrator provisions as reflected in Article 29(6) of the Rules make it clear that the emergency arbitrator provisions would not apply to arbitration agreement concluded before the new Rules come into force. While this provision is precise, it is anticipated that problems of interpretation may arise where the arbitration agreement itself specifies that the rules applicable to the arbitration would be the ICC Rules, prevalent at the time of invocation of the Notice of Arbitration.

Article 29(6) also establishes an opt-out mechanism, that is, unless parties who are subject to the new rules specifically exclude the application of the emergency arbitrator provisions.

LCIA

In addition to the general provisions relating to emergency arbitrators which largely resemble the ICC and SIAC Rules, Article 9.6 of the LCIA Rules, 2014, provides for a two-step process for the hearing before the emergency arbitrator. In terms of the provisions, the LCIA Court shall determine the application for relief. On the application being granted, the emergency arbitrator shall be appointed within three days by the LCIA Court. Specifically, Article 9.7 of the LCIA Rules specifically states that while the emergency arbitrator is required to, if possible, consult each party in relation to the emergency arbitrator claim, the arbitrator is not required to hold any hearings (whether oral, telephonic, or otherwise).

Further Article 9.8 requires that a reasoned order be passed within 14 days of the appointment of the emergency arbitrator. The provisions contained in Article 9.14 are similar to that of the ICC Rules; however, the LCIA rules requires parties to opt-in of the emergency arbitrator provisions where the arbitration agreement has been entered into prior to 1 October 2014.

SIAC

Article 1.5 of the SIAC Rules defines an award to also include awards of an emergency arbitrator. Article 26.2 read with Schedule I of the SIAC Rules sets forth the scheme for emergency arbitrator and allows a party to obtain interim relief before the constitution of the tribunal.

Some of the examples where parties have sought recourse to emergency arbitrator provisions are as follows:

1. In an SIAC arbitration, an Indian claimant filed an application for emergency interim relief alleging non-payment on the part of the respondent to a tune $100 million. The claimant stated that it had a reasonable apprehension that the respondent would encash a bank guarantee simply as a retaliatory measure. The chairman of the SIAC determined that the application should be accepted and appointed a well-recognized international emergency arbitrator on the next day.

    Within the following day, the emergency arbitrator established a schedule for consideration of the application for emergency relief. Subsequently, a telephonic hearing was conducted and an ad-interim order was passed therein one day thereafter.

2. In another SIAC arbitration involving an Indian party and its joint venture partner from the British Virgin Islands, the Indian company initiated arbitration on the basis that the respondent had breached a shareholders' agreement and was acting in violation of its confidentiality obligation by initiating court actions. On these two grounds, the Indian claimant also filed an emergency arbitrator application.

    In less than a day, the SIAC chairman promptly appointed the emergency arbitrator who, in turn, set out a schedule for the consideration of the emergency relief application. A day later, the emergency arbitrator passed a preliminary order directing status quo and then, two days thereafter an interim award was passed. Another supplemental interim order was issued after a month thereof.

3. In an SCC arbitration involving a Dutch claimant and Cypriot respondent, the claimant filed an emergency arbitrator application to secure the claimed amount to the tune of $145 million. The SCC appointed an emergency arbitrator within 13 hours of receiving the application. An order was passed eight days after the appointment.

    The emergency arbitrator rejected two out of the four interim measures on the ground that they involved third-party entities. The remaining requests were also denied since the emergency arbitrator held that while the claimant's requests sought to prevent the respondent from alienating its real estate and shares in a company, it had failed to show the harm which would be prevented if such an order was granted. Neither did the claimant show that such harm would be irreparable nor did he show that it required urgent and imminent interim relief.

4. In another SCC arbitration involving a Swiss claimant and Swedish respondent, the claimant sought an injunction preventing the respondent from selling or creating third-party rights over a certain company which, in the claimant's view, have prejudicial effect on the claimant's interest qua a shareholders' agreement. Expressing agreement with the claimant's case, the emergency arbitrator granted the injunction.

5. In an SIAC arbitration, an Indonesian company and a Chinese company were involved in relation to a contract for the sale of coal. The applicant, being the shipper of the coal sent a formal intimation to the SIAC in the morning, filed its paper by 2 p.m. and an arbitrator was appointed by 5 p.m. on the same day. The claimant simply sought permission to sell the cargo (which was deteriorating with the passage of time) and a direction to the respondent to cooperate in allowing the cargo to leave the port. Preliminary directions were passed by the emergency arbitrator that evening and he scheduled a hearing for the next day when the injunction sought by the claimant was passed.

As detailed above, emergency arbitrator provisions differ under various institutional rules, some of the common aspects are as follows:

1. The emergency arbitrator is appointed without any input from the parties.

2. The respondent to the application has a very short time frame to respond to the application for emergency relief.

3. The emergency arbitrator has broad discretion to determine the conduct of the proceedings. In particular, the arbitrator can decide if proceedings will be on written submissions, whether any kind of hearing is required and, if so, the nature of the hearing.

4. The emergency arbitrator ceases to play any role in the arbitration once the tribunal is constituted.

Law Forming Part of Curial Law

The recognition of the emergency arbitrator concept in the municipal law which constitutes the framework of the arbitral process (curial law) is the sine qua non for the success of the emergency arbitrator procedure. Theoretically, there is strong support to the argument that the institutional rules must be in strict compliance with the law governing the arbitration.

Even aside from the strict recognition, where the emergency arbitrators are not considered by the tribunal, the effects of orders are greatly diminished. Public policy concerns may also restrict the use of the emergency arbitrator mechanism.

Law Governing Enforcement of the Decision of the Emergency Arbitrator

Regardless of the two sets of rules stated above, the law governing the enforcement of the decision of the emergency arbitrator will be pivotal in ensuring enforceability of an order of the emergency arbitrator.

Most states have adopted the New York Convention verbatim. Given that the New York Convention was drafted and agreed upon before the emergence of the concept of emergency arbitrator procedures, there remains no definitive view on whether such decisions are enforceable under the New York Convention. Further, the New York Convention abstains from clearly defining an arbitral tribunal as anything apart from a tribunal appointed by the parties. By definition, the emergency arbitrator does not meet this criterion. Further, the definition of an award under the New York Convention also does not lend any support to define the emergency arbitrator decisions as award. Hence a definitive legislative gap exists in ensuring the enforceability of the emergency arbitrator decisions. Singapore and Hong Kong are the leading jurisdictions to have addressed the legislative need.

Legal Hurdles in Relation to Emergency Arbitrator Procedures

While the emergency arbitrator mechanism is hailed as a positive development, it suffers from, in our view, four conceptual hurdles.

The first such hurdle relates to the status of the emergency arbitrator. The emergency arbitrator is by definition, not appointed by the parties. This would, therefore, mean that the arbitrator cannot be referred to as a tribunal appointed by the parties. Therefore, concerns relating to party autonomy come to the fore since the tribunal is appointed by a third-party institution, without any substantive input from the parties.

The second such hurdle relates to the status of the decisions of the emergency arbitrator. Under most municipal laws, Hong Kong and Singapore being notable exceptions, the decisions are neither considered as orders nor awards. A direct consequence of such non-recognition is the absence of strict enforceability of such decisions. However, an argument may be made that in terms of the rules agreed by the parties, the parties agree to be bound by such an order. In absence of these contractual rights, there remains little, if any, legislative support. To a large extent, evidence has appeared to the contrary, where at least in the experience of the SIAC, parties have remained in compliance with the decisions of the emergency arbitrator. It may be pointed out that such compliance is only slightly affected by Singapore's recognition of emergency arbitrator decisions. Enforcement proceedings are typically carried on in the state where the respondent's assets are located.

While the above concerns are based on lack of legislative recognition, there exists some supportive jurisprudence. There are some case laws to the effect that the decisions arising out of emergency arbitration provisions are *final* in terms of the issues they intend to address.

In *Yahoo! Inc. v. Microsoft Corporation*,[11] the US District Court held that the relief awarded by the emergency arbitrators was 'in essence final' and capable of being enforced. It held that simply because a final award may be passed in respect of the subject matter of the arbitration, the emergency arbitrator was not prevented from awarding final relief for the purpose of preserving the status quo of the subject of the dispute.

In an earlier case, the US District Court had itself ruled against the finality of a decision of the emergency arbitrator.[12]

The third hurdle, which strikes at the legitimacy of the arbitral process is the alleged *due process* concerns. There is, quite often, very limited time for the respondent to present its case. Further, failure of the respondent to appear will quite likely lead to an ex parte order. There are further concerns relating to the material on record for the emergency arbitrator to review before arriving at his decisions. Specially under the ICC Rules, where a party may seek such an order even before it files its request for arbitration implies that the arbitrator would be granting the order only on the basis of the application before it. This narrows the scope of inquiry and may not even extend to a full assessment of the validity of the arbitration agreement.

Legal Aspects in India

The concept of emergency arbitrator has been a subject of much discussion and debate in the Indian context. The Law Commission in its 246th Report had suggested an amendment be made to Section 2(1)(d) which defines 'arbitral tribunal' read as, '2(1) (d) "arbitral tribunal" means a sole or a panel of arbitrators and, in the case of an arbitration conducted under the rules of an institution providing for appointment of an emergency arbitrator, includes such emergency arbitrator'.

The Law Commission specially noted that 'this amendment is to ensure that institutional rules such as the SIAC Arbitration Rules which provide for an emergency arbitrator are given statutory recognition in India'.

However, this amendment was not made part of the Arbitration Ordinance promulgated on 23 October 2015 or a part of the subsequently passed Amendment Act. Had the amendment been passed, the proposed change along with the enforcement powers under Section 17 would have made enforcement of emergency arbitrator orders straightforward.

With no confirmation of the enforceability of the emergency arbitrator decisions or provisions relating thereto, Madras High Court Arbitration Centre (MHCAC) (Internal Management) Rules, 2014 in Rule 20 provides for interim relief by an emergency arbitrator and sets out the procedure for the same. At best, this sets out evidence of the positive attitude of the administrative side of the Madras High Court in accepting the concept of emergency arbitration. Similar provisions are evident in the Delhi International Arbitration Centre (Arbitration Proceedings) Rules, Part III-A.

The newly launched Mumbai Centre for International Arbitration in Rule 14 provides for emergency arbitrator provisions. The chairman is entitled to accept requests for seeking emergency interim relief and appoint emergency arbitrator within one business day of completion of pre-appointment formalities. These rules are largely reflective of the international practice in relation to appointment of emergency arbitrator procedures.

1. As highlighted earlier, there are significant issues relating to the enforceability of order/decisions/awards of the emergency arbitrator. The Indian experience with emergency arbitrator awards is scant and is largely confined to one case before the Bombay High Court: *HSBC PI Holdings (Mauritius) Ltd v. Avitel Post Studioz Ltd. and others*, Arbitration Petition No. 1062/2012. To better understand the context in which the decision was rendered, it may be helpful to have a brief overview of the following facts as detailed: The dispute concerned a contract between an Indian party and a foreign party, governed by Indian law, and providing for SIAC arbitration with the seat in Singapore.

2. HSBC obtained an order from the emergency arbitrator seated in Singapore freezing the accounts of Avitel, requiring Avitel to disclose information relating to their assets and deliver requested information. Avitel appeared under protest in the emergency arbitration proceedings and did not comply with the order. As the assets needing protection were based in India, HSBC needed to have the order enforced in India. Therefore, HSBC sought interim relief from Indian court in support of the arbitration along the same lines as the decision of emergency arbitrator.

3. The Bombay High Court passed interim reliefs on similar terms to those in the emergency arbitrator order. The court took the view that 'petitioner has not bypassed any mandatory conditions of enforceability', because it was not seeking to enforce the decision of emergency arbitrator. Instead, it was simply seeking interim relief under Section 9 of the Indian Arbitration Act (which, essentially, allows Indian courts to issue orders in support of the arbitration).

The order of the single judge was subsequently challenged before the Division Bench of the Bombay High Court. The appeal, on facts, was partly allowed. While this decision is encouraging, the following problems may be said to have arisen in considering this decision as a general position of the law on the issue in India.

The standards for granting emergency interim relief in the emergency arbitrator context may differ to the standard applicable under Indian law for obtaining interim relief from courts. Therefore, success before an emergency arbitrator does not necessarily mean success before the Indian courts.

1. Even where the Indian courts are inclined to order interim relief, there is no guarantee that they will order a relief that is identical to, or even substantially similar to, the order issued by the emergency arbitrator.
2. The applicability of Section 9 of the Arbitration and Conciliation Act, 1996 as amended is a pre-condition for this approach. This would mean that where the parties have excluded Part I entirely, this avenue would not be available. Where Section 9 is available, it may be better for parties to approach the court directly. That is because interim relief can be obtained from an Indian court within a few days on an ex-parte basis. On the other hand, emergency arbitrator procedures take longer (usually a few weeks) and require that the other party be given an opportunity to present its case.

***

The evolution of the emergency arbitrator provisions indicate the requirement of an arbitral procedure to fill the gap that existed between the arising of a dispute and the ability of a party to seek interim measures from the tribunal. The ability of a party to seek interim relief often sets the background in which the disputes are adjudicated or settled.

Prior to the emergence of the emergency arbitrator provisions, a party could approach only the courts for interim relief. In many circumstances, this would be a less than optimal approach for primarily three reasons: first, that the local courts are bound by the mandatory local laws which may restrict their ability to grant relief, second, most courts would require disclosure of the relevant facts in order to entertain a claim for grant of relief which may go against the parties' intent to maintain confidentiality and third, parties would be forced to litigate before a national court—the exact situation that the parties sought to avoid by subjecting their dispute to arbitration. The need for an emergency arbitral relief procedure is real and imminent.

As discussed earlier, the emergency arbitrator provisions are fairly uniform with a few differences across the institutional rules. These rules are in fact the cornerstone of the development of the concept of emergency arbitration. The real issue exists in the law governing the arbitration, which is perhaps, the most important legal source defining the nature of the decision of the emergency arbitrator and of the emergency arbitrator himself.

A purposive approach which gives effect to the primary intent of arbitration, which is to give force to the parties' agreement to arbitrate their disputes, may be advanced as a strong argument to claim the enforceability of emergency arbitrator orders. Under this paradigm, decisions of the emergency arbitrator must be enforceable. In fact, where the arbitration legislations provide mandate to a pro-arbitration attitude, this may indeed be the case. For instance, under the English Arbitration Act, 1996, the English court will grant order in support of arbitration, 'if or to the extent that the arbitral tribunal, and any arbitral or other institution or person vested by the parties with the power in that regard, has no power or is unable for the time being to act effectively'. Alternatively, parties benefit from the sort of judicial creativity displayed in *HSBC v. Avitel* and count on courts to purposively enforce the emergency arbitrator decisions within the current legal framework.

While the above are strong arguments, on a strict legal construction, it is difficult to see how an emergency arbitrator decision by itself would vest in a party the right to enforce it as it is. Unless, other jurisdictions follow Singapore and Hong Kong model and introduce the legislative amendments to support the emergency arbitrator provisions, uncertainty will surround the question of the nature and enforceability of decisions rendered by the emergency arbitrators except the hope of self-compliance for fear of antagonizing the arbitral tribunal once constituted.

It is clear that emergency arbitrator procedures do not claim to be an exclusive remedy in a situation where a tribunal has not been constituted. Institutional rules provide the emergency arbitrator decisions will not bind the subsequently constituted arbitral tribunal. Even for pure utility basis, where one party seeks to rely on the element of surprise such as in ex-parte situations, recourse to emergency arbitrator procedures is sub-optimal since all of them provide for emergency arbitrator decisions only after both parties have been given a reasonable opportunity to present its case.

Tempered by the views expressed above, while judicial interpretation in favour of various emergency arbitrator provisions is a great step forward, legislative support in India would immensely help in reinforcing the benefit of this concept.

Notes and References

1. Netherlands Arbitration Rules, 2015, Article 9 and Article 36.
2. London Court of International Arbitration Rules, 2014, Article 9A.
3. International Chamber of Commerce Rules 1990.
4. ICC Rules of Arbitration, 2012, Article 29 and Appendix V.
5. Singapore International Arbitration Centre Rules, 2013, Article 26(2) and Schedule 1.
6. London Court of Arbitration Rules, 2014, Article 9B.
7. Swiss Rules of International Arbitration, 2012, Articles 42 and 43.
8. Netherland Arbitration Institute Rules, 2010, Articles 42a and 42b.
9. Statute of the Court of Arbitration of Madrid, 2014, Article 37 and Annex. 2.
10. Arbitration Centre of the Portuguese Chamber of Commerce and Industry Rules of Arbitration, 2014, Article 5 and Appendix I.
11. *Yahoo! Inc. v. Microsoft Corporation*, United States District Court, Southern District of New York, 13 CV 7237, 21 October 2013.
12. *Chinmax Medical Systems Inc., v. Alere San Diego, Inc.*, Southern District of California, Case No. 10cv2467 WQH (NLS), 27 May 2011.

9

Rise of the Expert Witness in Alternative Dispute Resolution

Gagan Puri, Geetu Singh, and *Deepankar Sanwalka*

According to estimates, the last few years have seen a steady rise in disputes arising out of increased business activities. Besides tarnishing reputation, disputes can disrupt the business foundation, resulting in project delays, funds shortage, blocking of monies, and loss of business opportunities.

Playing Their Part: Role and Functions of an Expert Witness

According to estimates, the last few years have seen a steady rise in disputes arising out of increased business activity. Besides tarnishing reputation, disputes can disrupt the business foundation, resulting in project delays, funds shortage, blocking of monies, and loss of business opportunities. Expert witnesses are 'experts' for a reason. When court cases drag on for years of painful testimony, counterclaims, and appeals, it is the knowledge of an expert witness alone that helps you settle the case without further agonizing proceedings.

Expert witnesses are independent third parties from various relevant professional backgrounds, who objectively assess facts and matters under dispute and then act in the most reasonable and neutral interest of each party involved, rather than judging or acting as arbitrators.

Expert witnesses help conduct independent and impartial fact-finding exercises in order to arrive at a decision applying right professional diligence that serves all parties involved in their best interest. An expert can overcome shortcomings such as using an internal person, inexperience, lack of industry knowledge and independence, or lack of requisite skills.

Appointing an Expert Witness

Expert witnesses can be proactively introduced into the arbitration proceedings either by the claimants or by respondents, in order to objectively counter the damages filed by the claimants. In many cases, experts can also be appointed in unique situations where disputes are complex and arbitration tribunals choose to rely on expert evidence only to arrive at a judgment taking various aspects of the matter under dispute.

In commercial disputes involving business and financial issues, accounting, technical or economic damages, a critical success factor is the decision of the counsel regarding the selection of the testifying expert.

Command of the subject matter, professional experience, credentials, and presence as an expert are key decision criteria—all crucial to a successful outcome. The selection of a well-qualified and experienced testifying expert can provide the counsel with a significant strategic advantage, especially when that expert can draw upon the leveraged, experienced, and well-trained resources of a global and in-depth litigation consulting expertise to support their testimony.

Following are the common forms of disputes where expert witnesses can be crucial:

1. Disputes arising out of inappropriate contract terminations.
2. Disputes amongst joint venture partners or shareholders.
3. Disputes arising out of delays in project execution.

4. Disputes between private sector players and stakeholders such as the government or regulatory bodies or public sector undertaking (in case of public–private partnership projects).
5. Disputes in case of bilateral agreements.
6. Disputes arising between insurance companies and corporates for large-scale insurance claims filed by the latter.

Five best practices that expert witnesses need to follow are:

1. **Maintain independence:** Expert witnesses should maintain independence, impartiality, and transparency at all times. It is critical for expert witnesses to be completely unbiased in her or his testimony in the court.
2. **Rely on only robust and forensically obtained evidence:** It is vital for experts to scientifically collect, test, and evaluate evidence, before forming an opinion and communicating it to the judge and jury.
3. **Get their facts right:** Conduct a thorough research, collect information, and understand all important aspects of matters under dispute and assess their impact on the expert report.
4. **Adopt a fact-based yet solution-oriented approach:** It is critical for expert witnesses to clear the air and strengthen inferences that might otherwise be confusing for the jury.
5. **Consider a neutral view on position on both parties to dispute:** Staying objective, neutral, and impartial while giving their opinions before the court is one of the cornerstones of becoming an expert witness.

The Evolving Role of Expert Witnesses in Arbitrations

Mostly companies opt for arbitration proceedings either with much established international arbitration forums or local arbitrations, depending on the requirement and depth of the issue at hand.

In the last few years, there has been a globalization of arbitration forums, with London Court of International Arbitration (LCIA), Singapore International Arbitration Centre (SIAC), and International Chamber of Commerce (ICC) increasing their global footprints. In certain local jurisdictions, it has been found that as compared to their international counterparts, they still have to go a long way when it comes to the way arbitrations are conducted. They need to get the same degree of maturity and efficiency on par with their international counterparts.

Today, most of the arbitrations locally derive their tradition from age-old litigations framework and are yet to imbibe the wholesome spirit of the way international arbitrations are run. It is for this reason that in certain countries, many corporates (especially those which are dealing with overseas strategic or financial investors) still prefer international arbitrations.

While many arbitrators have increasingly started relying on independent expert evidences, the extent of use of experts in local jurisdictions is still considered low in comparison with international standards. In many cases, expert reports are relied upon, however, the experts are neither cross examined nor a conferencing process is performed between experts of both sides to reach at the maximum common ground as possible.

Where are expert services required in disputes?

1. Commenting on technical, business, and commercial aspects of the contractual terms under dispute.
2. Providing objective opinions on technical, financial, and legal matters requiring specialized knowledge or expertise.
3. Quantifying damages arising in a dispute and demonstrating an objective and scientific approach for arriving at the damages.
4. Performing relevant issue analysis, document assessment, schedule and cost analysis, cause and effect determination, resultant damage analysis, delay and impact evaluation, and cost-recovery assessment.
5. Validating delays caused in disputed projects leading to root cause for culmination into disputes.
6. Assessment of cost overruns and review of critical costs related to equipment, materials, labour, and project overheads.
7. Review of revenue sharing modules (in case of revenue sharing models with government bodies).
8. Probing into the counter party's documents and facilitating a critique of his position.
9. Issuing expert report in arbitration.
10. Providing a professional testimony before the arbitral tribunal.

Common Forms of Damages, Claims, and Quantum Computation Filed in Arbitrations

1. Quantum of damages arising from wasted expenditure or losses from past profits, especially in case of untimely contract terminations.
2. Quantum of damages arising and potential losses caused due to loss of future business opportunity, especially in case of untimely contract terminations.
3. Differences of opinions on value of businesses arising from disagreement between joint venture partners or shareholders.
4. Quantum of damages arising from non-fulfilment of obligations of one party to reimburse the other (contractor relationships), in case of cost overruns.
5. Differences in opinion of both parties (employer–contractor relationship), in case of costs overruns arising from project delays in significantly large and complex contracts.
6. Computing claims, in case of large insurance claims disputes.

The Right Time to Introduce Your Expert Witness

1. At the time of filing of claims/damages or at the time of countering or rebuttal of claims/damages during the arbitration tribunal.
2. At the time of ascertaining the heads of claims/damages much early in a hostile dispute or situation.
3. At the time of pre-dispute assessment of project delay and its commercial impact and cost overruns of projects.

Entry of the Technical Expert: Roles and Functions

Forensic engineers and architects are uniquely qualified to evaluate structural damage stemming from a variety of causes including wind events, flooding, ice and snow loading, fires and explosions, mechanical impact from vehicles and debris, ground subsidence or nearby construction. These experts investigate collapses and failures of building components, differential foundation movement, the effects of long-term deterioration on structural components, and design and construction defects.

The expertise of these professionals ranges from plan and performance review of new construction projects to surety investigations and providing a 'clerk of the works' for reconstruction efforts.

Further, construction experts can provide assistance to arbitration tribunals in formulating and developing project plan including business plan assessment and cash flow projections, as well as development of execution plans and evaluation of insurance claims and plans.

How Technical, Subject Matter, and Quantum Experts Need to Collaborate to Give a Cohesive and Conclusive View to the Arbitration Tribunals?

Most of the complex disputes require a manifold analysis to arrive at damages or claims—from a technical, specific sector business, financial and commercial perspective. Since expertise may sit with different kinds of experts it is imperative that there is consolidation of thought, views, and opinions amongst various experts so that seamless experts view (techno-commercial assessment) on the matter under dispute can be formed and presented to the arbitration tribunal. The critical point is for different experts to simplify the puzzle, translate professional views and opinions in a manner where the inputs of one expert into that of another and at the same time, the arbitration tribunal can get a holistic expert view on the matter.

Common Form of Evidence Which Experts Rely Upon

Business and Financial Experts

1. Books of account and underlying records related to the project.
2. Business plans and financial models of the target entity.
3. Relevant contracts, including back-to-back contracts signed with subcontractors.
4. Documentation supporting costs related to equipment, materials, labour, overheads, and finance costs.
5. Internal management reports on budgeted costs.
6. Management business plans and project revenue and costs models.
7. Market studies and industry trends, and performance benchmarks.

8. Critical written correspondences shared between parties prior to the dispute, during culmination of dispute circumstances, and consequentially.
9. Correspondences with bankers for project financing.

Technical Experts

1. Baseline programmes of the relevant projects under dispute.
2. Revised schedules and engineering designs.
3. Reports submitted by site engineers, contractors, and subcontractors.
4. Resource planning schedules (detailing requirement and actual utilization of material, labour, and equipment).
5. Reports submitted by geologists, civil engineers, and other third-party consultants.

Role of Experts in Construction Disputes and Claims

As the pace of business intensifies, the possibility of disputes and other complications arises proportionally. When rules are violated, unintentionally or otherwise, organizations are often exposed to risks and issues that they are not used to dealing with. Whether these challenges involve cross-border dealings with customers, joint venture partners, and foreign governments, or are localized; they may involve different business cultures and legal systems, as well as unfamiliar regulatory and accountability requirements.

This is where the role of experts comes in. They help to provide concise and proportional expert testimony on delay, disruption, loss and, expense as well as other quantum issues for organizations involved in complex capital project disputes that are prone to financial and reputational loss. This enables you to concentrate on mitigating effects of the dispute rather than dwelling on what the outcome might be.

Expert Testimony Services Help in

1. Reducing the time taken to resolve disputes and save money.
2. Enabling successful negotiations.
3. Providing a robust set of results and opinions to be used in the case.

The Increasing Demand for Expert Testimony Services

Intellectual Property Disputes

World Intellectual Property Organization defines Intellectual Property (IP) as creations of the mind—inventions: literary and artistic works and symbols: names and images—used in commerce. The IP rights are the rights that accelerate the owner of the IP asset to derive economic benefits from its use in future.

Intellectual Property Life Cycle

The IP life cycle commencing from creation, protection, enforcement, commercialization, and its awareness, has become increasingly crucial to business success. Quantitative economic analysis of the IP rights during each phase of the life cycle plays an essential role, especially at a time when these rights have been subject to greater scrutiny and higher standards of proof in a dispute or litigation.

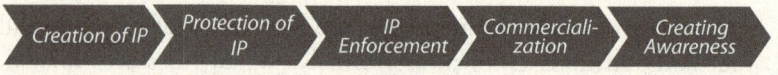

Creation of IP › Protection of IP › IP Enforcement › Commercialization › Creating Awareness

IP Now Involves 'Significant Returns'

The present global economy is driven by the power of IP, which is the gateway to growth. The value of intangible IP assets can significantly enhance the market value of the company as is evident from studies which show that the brand value of top 10 global brands individually exceeds $25 billion. As IP plays an increasingly important role in making the business unique, both business owners and courts are recognizing the true value of IP and the loss caused to right holders due to IP infringement.

Early Signs of IP Disputes

1. Are you involved in a disagreement involving valuation of an intangible asset?
2. Does your claim involve computation of reasonable royalty under FRAND terms?

3. Is there a conflict between the legal versus economic owner of the IP asset?
4. Do you notice any material loss of your revenue due to patent misuse or infringement?
5. Is your relationship with your technology partner turning hostile?
6. How do you determine lost profits and price erosion as damages?
7. Whether the licensor of the technology is attempting to abuse its monopoly power?
8. Is the existing royalty rate for the use of the brand or technology fair and reasonable?

Role of Experts in IP Disputes

1. Carry out an independent validation of the damages to strengthen the legal position of the patent holder in this matter.
2. Make the court or arbitrator understand the methodology of computing IP damages.
3. Understand the negotiations of the parties from the time the infringement began.
4. Consolidated look at the complete set of various events and facts that occurred thereafter and that could not have been known to or predicted by the hypothesized negotiators.

Role of Experts in Joint Venture and Shareholder Disputes

Any prudent strategic investor spends expecting long-term growth and financial success. However, this association also brings with it a new set of challenges and risks resulting from different realms. Lapse in corporate governance is one of the primary sources of conflict between the strategic investor and other shareholders of the investee company resulting in stress, disagreement, and eventually legal disputes. While the strategic investor expects best practices in areas of corporate governance and execution of fiduciary responsibility, some shareholders struggle with poor governance practices and are plagued with the inability to appreciate these expectations in areas of transparency, quality, timelines, and customer service.

Some of the reasons why some of these joint ventures or alliances could not sustain in the long run are:

1. Weak corporate governance standards adopted by some shareholders.
2. Disagreement, either strategic or operational in nature.
3. Technology sharing and IPR-related issues: legal versus economic ownership, fair royalty rate.
4. Dilution in shareholding and management control issues.
5. Lack of parity in size, ownership, control, and contribution.
6. Inability to appreciate best practices in areas of quality, timelines, and customer service.
7. Breach of terms of the joint venture or shareholder agreement.
8. Dominance of family members in business decision-making.
9. Lack of transparency in use of funds of the strategic investor by other partners or shareholders.
10. Difficult exit for the investors from the business.
11. Resultant litigations or arbitrations between shareholders.

Any material breach of the terms of the shareholder agreement, arising from the factors mentioned above, forces strategic investors to take a legal action against the investee company and/or other shareholders.

Role of Experts

1. Critically examine factors for failure of association with joint venture partners or shareholders.
2. Assist in firming up position on your exit strategy.
3. Assist in exercising right of inspection of books.
4. Evaluate underperformance of business plan.
5. Investigate into appropriateness of utilization of funds.
6. Providing valuation and negotiation support:
   i. Carry out pricing analysis to determine fair value of the business or the stakes held.
   ii. Carry out valuation as per the shareholder agreement and/or the local laws, as applicable.

iii. Assess the business, financial, and commercial impact of clauses in joint venture/shareholder agreements.
iv. Assist you in retaining critical written correspondence and other information in electronic form.
v. Assist in protecting your brand, technology, and other IP given without ownership transfer.

10

Med-Arb

Rajiv Shakhder

The fact that arbitration as an alternative dispute resolution (ADR) mechanism has failed to produce the desired result, though it has been in existence in India since 1899, is best exemplified by the following observations of the Supreme Court, made as far back as in 1997 in *Guru Nanak Foundation v. Rattan Singh & Sons.*[1]

> Interminable, time consuming, complex, and expensive court procedures impelled jurists to search for an alternative forum, less formal and speedy for resolution of disputes avoiding procedural claptrap and this led them to Arbitration Act, 1940 ('Act' for short). However, the way in which the proceedings under the Act are conducted and without an exception challenged in Courts, has made lawyers laugh and legal philosophers weep. Experience shows and law reports bear ample testimony that the proceedings under the Act have become highly technical accompanied by unending prolixity, at every stage providing a legal trap to the unwary. Informal forum chosen by the parties for expeditious disposal of their disputes has by the decisions of the Courts been clothed with 'legalese' of unforceable complexity.

With enactment of the Arbitration & Conciliation Act, 1996 (1996 Act), it was hoped that a course correction would occur—sadly, though, much of the expectations raised stand belied. The observations made by the Law Commission in its 246th Report are reflective of the disappointment felt by the jurists, lawyers, and litigants alike.

Resultantly, steps were taken to amend the 1996 Act. Substantive amendments were brought about in the 1996 Act with the passing of the Arbitration Conciliation (Amendment) Act of 2015 (in short, 'Amendment Act of 2015'). The Amendment Act was preceded by a series of ordinances, the last in line being the Arbitration and Conciliation (Third) Ordinance, 1996. This ordinance however stands repealed by virtue of Section 86 of the Amendment Act, 2015.

To reinforce the cause of arbitration, several amendments have been brought about in the 1996 Act. However, the amendments suggested by the Law Commission neither touched upon Part III of the 1996 Act, which deals with provisions relatable to conciliation, nor did it suggest incorporation of specific provisions pertaining to mediation. To my mind, this was a missed opportunity, with regard to the fact that mediation movement has otherwise gained momentum.

Undoubtedly, it is the perceived failure of the arbitration mechanism which has fuelled the movement for other ADR mechanisms, such as judicial settlements (including Lok Adalats), mediation, and conciliation. The legislature, on its part, took some robust steps in this behalf by amending the Code of Civil Procedure, 1908 (in short, 'the Code'), with the insertion of Section 89. The insertion of Section 89 was brought about with the enactment of the Code of Civil Procedure (Amendment) Act of 1999. This amendment was brought into force from 1 July 2002.

Section 89, in sum, takes forward the goal set forth in Article 39A of the Constitution, which, inter alia, calls upon the State to put in place legislation or schemes or even other mechanisms which ensure that opportunities for securing justice are not denied to any citizen by reason of economic or other disabilities.

Thus, Section 89 of the Code obliges a court, before whom a dispute is brought, to refer parties to any of the ADR mechanisms adverted to therein, in cases where there exist elements of settlement. The four ADR mechanisms alluded to in sub-section (1) of Section 89 are: arbitration, conciliation, judicial settlement (which includes settlement through Lok Adalat), and mediation.

That Section 89 has been poorly drafted is explicitly articulated by the Supreme Court in its judgment in *Afcons Infrastructure Ltd. & Anr. v. Cherian Varkey Construction Co. (P) Ltd. & Ors.*[2] Resultantly, the Supreme Court ended up issuing several directions in respect of the procedure to be adopted by courts, while taking recourse to the provisions of Section 89 of the Code.

Interestingly, each of the ADR mechanisms referred to above except mediation has received substantial legislative support. Save and except, for a passing reference to mediation, in Section 30 of the 1996 Act, which empowers an arbitrator to bring about a settlement between disputants, inter alia, via mediation, there are no specific provisions, in the said Act, which deal with mediation per se. However, in contrast, both Lok Adalat and conciliation are fully supported by legislative enactments.

For instance, Lok Adalats received legislative recognition after the enactment of the Legal Services Act, 1987 (in short, the 1987 Act). Similarly, as indicated above, conciliation has received legislative backing in the form of provisions contained in Part III of the 1996 Act.

Consequently, the settlements drawn up with the intercession of Lok Adalats and/or conciliators have the force of a decree. The decree, thus obtained via either of the two mechanisms referred to above, can be enforced against a recalcitrant and/or a diffident disputant with the help and assistance of courts.[3]

It is for this reason, that, in recent times, non-adjudicatory ADR mechanisms, such as mediation and conciliation have received a major fillip. Though in comparative terms, conciliation in India does not appear to have the kind of traction that mediation has. Having said so, success in mediation in India is presently confined to court-appended mediation centres. Amongst the court-appended mediation centres, which appear to have attained a high percentage of success are The Bangalore Mediation Centre and the Mediation Centres appended to various District Courts in Delhi. The Bangalore Mediation Centre,[4] between 1 January 2007 and 31 January 2016, referred 38,594 cases for mediation, out of which 30,573 were settled; which included 5,595 cases that were connected. The success rate achieved by the Bangalore Mediation Centre was thus, in the

Table 10.1 Dispute Settlement through non-adjudicatory mechanisms by Delhi District Courts

Courts	Period	Number of Cases Referred	Number of Cases Settled	Percentage of Cases Settled
Tis Hazari	22.08.2005 to 30.04.2016	67,162	36,831	62.29
Karkardooma	01.12.2005 to 30.04.2016	32,708	21,110	76.02
Rohini	02.02.2009 to 30.04.2016	26,224	13,153	62.17
Dwarka	05.07.2009 to 30.04.2016	24,370	14,834	74.53
Saket	30.04.2013 to 30.04.2016	10,849	5,613	64.01
Patiala House	01.05.2015 to 31.01.2016	976	440	45.08

Source: www.delhimediationcentre.gov.in/statistical/html

given period, in effect 78 per cent if one were to include connected cases as well. In so far as the various district courts in Delhi[5] were concerned, Table 10.1 shows the number of cases settled through non-adjudicatory mechanisms.

As against the aforesaid, the position vis-à-vis the mediation and conciliation centre appended to Punjab and Haryana High Court[6] does not appear to be as robust as one would have expected in comparison with the performance of other centres referred to above. During the period spanning between 17 March 2008 and September 2015, evidently, 8,900 cases were referred to mediation, out of which 1,772 were settled. The success rate achieved was thus approximately 19 per cent. The position of the Kerala State Mediation Centre[7] appears to be a little better. As per the data available on its website, in 2015, 21,984 cases were referred for mediation, out of which 6,119 were settled. The success rate was approximately 28 per cent. One must however indicate herein that out of 21,984 cases, 4,205 were, it appears, pending consideration at the end of 2015.

As would be evident, there are no institutions solely involved with conciliation. The only exception is, perhaps, the recognition of the status of a conciliator under the Industrial Disputes Act, 1947. Therefore, in our country, most mediation centres double-up as conciliation forums.

It must, therefore, be said that while the purist seek to draw a distinction between conciliation and mediation, there is a 'broad synonymy' between the two. The difference, if any, to my mind is essentially in the approach adopted to reach a resolution. While a conciliator who is a neutral third party attempts to bring about a settlement between the disputants, a mediator encourages the disputants to suggest their own solutions to the disputes at hand. Quite clearly, to a layman, the distinction drawn between the two processes is not one of substance but more to do with process involved in reaching the conclusion.

What is clear though is that spiralling costs, delays in pronouncement of awards, and the prolixity in court proceedings which is experienced by litigants, post the pronouncement of an award, has propelled disputants to look for an amalgam—in other words, a process which includes the attributes of both adjudicatory and a non-adjudicatory mechanism.

Consequently, lately, litigants have sought to take recourse to a Mediation-Arbitration (Med-Arb) or even Arbitration-Mediation mechanism (Arb-Med). Med-Arb[8] is a process in which a mediator changes his/her role from that of a mediator to one of an arbitrator in case mediation does not produce the desired result.

Parties often enter into such contracts and/or arrangements prior to disputes arising between them. The process has its own pros and cons. The pros being that the person who adjudicates upon disputes is the same person who attempted mediation between parties in the first place. The adjudication would therefore optimize time and, logically, costs as well.

The negatives, on the other hand, are that the person entrusted with the task of working the mediation mechanism is not able to fulfil either the role of the mediator or that of an arbitrator. The skill sets required for the two tasks are different. The mediator's role requires the person concerned to encourage disputants to arrive at a self-determined solution, whereas in an arbitration, solutions are imposed by a neutral third party.

Besides this, the biggest drawback appears to be the fear that the information supplied by the disputants during separate caucus meetings with the mediator may be used unfairly in case parties were to eventually end up in a litigation.

These drawbacks, evidently, have been successfully overcome in some countries with the help of requisite legislative intervention. A prime example[9] of one such intervention is found in the Commercial

Arbitration Act of 2010, Number 61, enacted by New South Wales. The Act, in particular, Section 27D (4)[10] provides an opportunity to the parties to step out of the Med-Arb process. In other words, once the mediation process is over, and for some reason it does not result in a resolution, any one of the parties is entitled to opt-out of the Med-Arb process. Consequently, upon failure of the Med-Arb process, any one of the parties have the option of proceeding with the agreed arbitral mechanism, albeit, with the involvement of a person other than the one who acted as the mediator.

In so far as the other drawback is concerned, which is, that the information supplied in confidence during mediation may probably be unfairly used in litigation, can, in my opinion be overcome by incorporating the necessary provision in the statute/contract which would prohibit the use of such information during trial. A provision similar to Section 81[11] of 1996 Act which pertains to conciliation proceedings should suffice to my mind.

The question which remains is would such statutory/contractual precautions do away with the risks of parties superficially engaging in mediation proceedings only to assess the strength and weakness of the opponent's case? The answer to that will perhaps be in the negative. Parties and their counsels are known to engage, ostensibly, in a mediation process only to either delay or gauge the strength and weaknesses of the opponent's case. This is distinctly a downside of the mediation process, which cannot be avoided. It is for this reason, that parties often exhibit an inclination to move away from a Med-Arb process to a converse mechanism, that is, arbitration followed by mediation, that is, Arb-Med.

Arb-Med[12] mechanism is a process where once arbitration proceedings are over and an award is drawn up, it is kept in a sealed cover till the time the parties conclude the mediation process. In case mediation is successful, the award is destroyed. Here again the same person who acted as the arbitrator engages in mediation. Critics decry the process as it not only involves costs but also results in vitiating the atmosphere and hardening of stands between litigating parties, which is undoubtedly the necessary fallout of an adjudicatory mechanism preceding a mediation process.

That Arb-Med process has resonance with a large section of disputants can be gauged from the fact that even when mediation is concerned, parties have increasingly looked for evaluative mediation.[13] One of the negatives of the mediation movement has been that it has over the years come to be dominated by litigators and it is, therefore, veering more and more towards arbitration. Since litigators are involved in the mediation process, and more often than not represent disputants before the mediator, the attempt is to stress on the rights of parties rather than what is in their interest.[14] The legal rights of parties and what is in their interest is not necessarily the same thing when looked at from the point of view of conflict resolution. It is because of this reason that mediators often evaluate for parties their chances of success in full-blown court proceedings to bring about a settlement. While an evaluative mediation process has its merits, it dilutes to a large extent the very purpose of mediation which is pivoted on the premise and belief that the disputants find their own solutions to the problem at hand. Evaluative mediation thus takes away party autonomy as the mediator and the litigators representing parties partake a domineering role which involves setting forth a predictive outcome of what would follow in the event disputants were to go to trial. Evaluative mediation, thus, in a sense has become a 'surrogate'[15] for an arbitration mechanism.

Having said so, if one were to move away from the aggressive form of mediation, which emphasizes more on rights than on what is in the interest of parties, a Med-Arb process would, to my mind, go a long way in resolution of disputes inter se parties. Much of its success would depend upon the approach of parties and their lawyers (assuming they are involved in the mediation process). If the approach is one which centres around truth, re-conciliation, and peaceful resolution of disputes, the success rate of mediation process is bound to be high. In the event mediation fails, parties could immediately thereafter proceed to arbitration, knowing fully well where they stand vis-à-vis the opposing side. To avoid unfair use of information, voluntarily supplied during the mediation process, parties could in the Med-Arb arrangement itself incorporate provisions which would prevent use of information supplied (during mediation process) in the event of a litigation erupting between them. Such provisions if incorporated would firewall to parties against unfair use of information till such time the legislature steps-in and fills this very crucial gap in the 1996 Act. In my opinion, this gap can be filled-in quite easily if the legislature were to amend Part III of the 1996

Act in a manner which would indicate that the provisions contained therein, which otherwise apply to conciliation proceedings, would apply mutatis mutandis to mediation as well.

Notes and References

1. AIR 1981 SC 2075.
2. 2010 (8) SCC 24.
3. Section 21 of the 1987 Act accords a status of a decree to a settlement recorded under the said Act. Likewise, Section 74 of the 1996 Act provides that settlements recorded by a conciliator would statutorily morph into awards, and thereupon, into a decree, which if necessary, could be executed via a court.
4. Available http://bangaloremediationcentre.kar.nic.in/statistics.html.
5. Available http://www.delhimediationcentre.gov.in/statistical/html.
6. Available http://mediationcentrephhc.gov.in/pdf/Pcrformancc%20-Chart.pdf.
7. Available http://keralamediation.gov.in/Statistics.
8. Henry J. Brown and Arthur Marriott Q.C., *ADR Principles and Practice*, 3rd ed. (Sweet & Maxwell, 2012).
9. Brown and Marriott Q.C.
10. Section 27D(4): 'An arbitrator who has acted as mediator in mediation proceedings that are terminated may not conduct subsequent arbitration proceedings in relation to the dispute without the written consent of all the parties to the arbitration given on or after the termination of the mediation proceedings.'
11. Section 81: 'Admissibility of evidence in other proceedings. The parties shall not rely on or introduce as evidence in arbitral or judicial proceedings, whether or not such proceedings relate to the dispute that is the subject of the conciliation proceedings: (a) views expressed or suggestions made by the other party in respect of a possible settlement of the dispute; (b) admissions made by the other party in the course of the conciliation proceedings; (c) proposals made by the conciliator; (d) the fact that the other party had indicated to accept a proposal for settlement made by the conciliator.'
12. Brown and Marriott Q.C.
13. Robert A. Baruch Bush, 'Substituting Mediation for Arbitration: The Growing Market for Evaluative Mediation, and What It Means for the ADR Field', *Pepperdine Dispute Resolution Law Journal*, 3 (1, 2002).
14. Bush, 'Substituting Mediation for Arbitration'.
15. Jacqueline Nolan-Haley, *Mediation: The New Arbitration* (Harvard Negotiation Law Review, 2012).

11

Limits of Arbitrability

Some Jurisdictional Issues in the Context of Public Law Remedies

Parag P. Tripathi

Arbitration per se as an alternative dispute mechanism has had a chequered history, and the tide turned decisively in its favour only in the twentieth century. This was brought about on account of a shift in jurisprudential thinking occasioned due to various reasons including docket explosions in courts, realization that for certain commercial disputes which require confidentiality and/or technical expertise, arbitration is a better remedy, and lastly by adoption and assimilation of arbitration within the broad judicial framework. The latter is important because except in technical arbitrations, as, for instance, in stock markets, sports disputes, business gilds, technical construction disputes, and so on, the human resources for conducting arbitrations are generally retired judges and practicing lawyers. In other words, a possible institutional clash of interests has been overcome by the formal legal framework of courts assimilating the arbitral alternative dispute resolution (ADR) process within its fold.

But this acceptance of arbitration as a mechanism for mainstream dispute resolution has been gradual and incremental. The classic article written by Earl S. Wolaver, 'Historic Background of Commercial Arbitration', in the 1934 issue of the *University of Pennsylvania Law Review*[1] mentions the growth and acceptance of commercial arbitration, as an acceptable alternative to court-centred litigation.

We should however not forget that it was not very far back that Lord Coke in one of his less remembered judicial utterances proceeded to lay down the principle of inherent revocability of an arbitration clause, thus, 'If I submit myself to an arbitriment ... yet I may revoke it for my act, or my words cannot alter the judgment of the law to make that irrevocable which is of its own nature revocable.'[2]

This enunciation of law in *Vynior's* case was not even founded upon the principle of ouster of jurisdiction of the court. It was a simplistic view that an arbitration clause can always be revoked. It was much later in 1746, in *Kill v. Hollister*[3] that this aspect of the ouster of jurisdiction of the court was emphasized to explain why arbitration agreements are revocable in nature. Around the same time, Lord Hardwicke in *Wellington v. Macintosh*[4] went so far as to opine that to grant discovery for the purpose of arbitration did not go well with the dignity of the court.

Interestingly, Lord Hardwicke's dictum in Wellington was simply brushed aside later in 1878 by Lord Campbell in *Scott v. Avery*[5] by simply stating that Lord Hardwicke's opinion must have been misreported. This was surely a novel, curial approach.

Fortunately, the concept of ouster of jurisdiction of court was put in a somewhat more palatable manner in that case[6] (1856), wherein Lord Campbell held that parties by contract cannot oust the jurisdiction of the court but may agree by contract that no cause of action shall arise until an arbitration reference is made and decision thereon pronounced. Lord Campbell's speech also noted a possible reason for the suspicion and hostility of the formal judicial system (with its highest seat in Westminster Hall) to arbitration:[7]

There was no disguising the fact that as formerly, the emoluments of the judges depended mainly or almost entirety of fees, and as they had no fixed salary there was great competition to get as much as possible of litigation into Westminster Hall and there was a great scramble in Westminster Hall for the division of the spoil.... And they had great jealousy of arbitration whereby Westminster Hall was robbed of those cases.

Two decades later, Lord Jessel, Master of Rolls, in *Repley v. Great Northern Rly*[8] held as follows,[9] 'Certainly these arbitrations have not been looked upon very favorably by courts of law. Many strict and some absurd rules were laid down at a period when courts of law seemed to consider a reference to arbitration to be something wrong, or as an attempt to oust the ordinary jurisdiction of the court. That period has passed away.'

Wolaver pithily reminds us of the summation of the case in favour of arbitration by one Geraud Malynes, a mercantilist of the seventeenth century, 'the trader preferred the law of merchants as a 'law not too cruell in her frowns, nor too partiall in her favours'.[10]

In other words, arbitration with its decided focus on gross commercial common sense was less likely to result as a process in a 'winner alone takes all' end result. The other potential advantage contemporaneously noted[11] which continues to hold good today is, 'Merchant affairs in controversy ought with all brevity to be decided to avoid interruption of the traffic'.

The Current Scenario

A lot of water has gone under the bridge since the rather remarkable enunciation of revocability of the arbitration clause given by the great Lord Coke in *Vynior*'s case. An important watershed was the UNCITRAL Model Law of Arbitration, 1985, which sought to give a decisive push to arbitration as an acceptable mechanism of dispute resolution and to insulate it from court interference. Further the extent of interference was also greatly reduced at the stage of challenge to the award by making very limited grounds available for bringing such a challenge. To a great extent, this insulation of arbitral awards from judicial scrutiny and of the arbitral process from judicial interference arises out of the Western economic principle of laissez faire and its concomitant principle of party autonomy in the context of protecting international trade and big-ticket foreign investments. The idea being that international trade and investment is not made hostage to the vagaries of the judicial system of a constituent state. These vagaries can range from problems on account of national jingoism, absence of an independent judiciary, absence of transparent and settled court processes and procedure (problems fortunately absent in India), and of course the vexed issue of delays in the final adjudication (an issue, with which the Indian judicial system is still coming to terms). Be that as it may, India and indeed several other countries have adopted the UNCITRAL Model Law. This brings us to the present topic, that is, interpretation of arbitrability in the context of public law remedies.

Interface with Public Law Remedies

At one end of the spectrum are the high public law remedies, like the high prerogative writs under Articles 32 and 226 of the Constitution of India. The Supreme Court has now decisively held that the existence of an arbitration clause cannot result in its automatic ouster, though the Court would only exercise such a writ jurisdiction notwithstanding the existence of an arbitration clause as an exception rather than the rule.[12] However, a second aspect of a classic public law remedy involving the adjudication of rights in rem is not free from doubt. One of the facets of this issue arises in the context of whether an allegation of fraud is arbitrable or not.

Here the Indian courts seem to have adopted a jurisprudential dichotomy: one applicable to international arbitrations and the other to domestic arbitrations. A third aspect involves the issue of arbitrability in the context of special court/tribunal remedies, like remedy of oppression and mismanagement, which is a special jurisdiction conferred on the Company Law Board/National Company Law Tribunal with the concomitant swathe of jurisdiction available to it under Section 402 of the Companies Act, including Section 402(g) conferring jurisdiction to the Company Law Board to pass such orders as it may think just and proper.[13]

The last representative aspect of interface of arbitration and public law remedies dealt with in this article relates to the concept of arbitrability in the realm of competition law (the anti-trust litigation, as it is called in the American jurisprudence). These aspects would be dealt with more fully in the later part of this chapter.

Before dealing with these aspects, it would be worth mentioning the *Kompetenz-Kompetenz* principle. Briefly put, the *Kompetenz-Kompetenz* principle is the recognition of the authority of an arbitral tribunal to determine its own jurisdiction. It is this principle that the arbitral authority can determine its own jurisdiction which firmly puts it as a true alternative to the court-based dispute resolution system. The necessary consequence of the right of an arbitral tribunal to determine its own jurisdiction is that such determination would bind a party who has not submitted itself to the jurisdiction of the tribunal or not submitted to the question of arbitrability of the dispute to the tribunal. Further reading if required can gainfully be done by referring to a thought-provoking article by Ashley Cook (a young law graduate) published in the *Pepperdine Law Review*.[14] This article deals with the positive aspect of the doctrine viz. authority of the tribunal to determine its own jurisdiction, as also the negative aspect of the doctrine, namely, the limits of the jurisdiction of the court to reopen that issue. In India, following the UNCITRAL Model Law, Section 16 as enacted provides both the positive and negative facets of this doctrine. It is for the tribunal to determine its own jurisdiction, and if the tribunal holds that it has jurisdiction, then the issue can only be challenged after the final award is passed and not before. In other words, once the tribunal holds that it has jurisdiction to entertain the dispute, the arbitration proceedings like a juggernaut must roll on.

It is interesting to note that based mainly on first principles, both the American and English courts in the cases of *First Options of Chi Inc.*[15] (US Supreme Court) and *Dallah Real Estate*[16] (UK House of Lords), respectively, have held that the arbitral tribunals have the competence to rule on their own jurisdiction.

Allegations of Fraud and its Interface with Arbitrability

Briefly stated, the point made is that a serious question of fraud requires adjudication in rem and therefore only the courts are entitled to take that final call. An allegation of fraud requires not only examination of documents but often oral evidence, both of which are best done in the public realm, that is by a court, which pronounces a judgment which is in the public domain, as are generally all the proceeding in court, which are open to all unless in exceptional cases, the court directs otherwise.

The argument runs that an adjudication of a serious question of fraud by a chosen arbitral tribunal does not subserve the greater public interest. This is similar to an argument which is often raised against mediated settlement of a dispute which is before a court. Once a mediated settlement is reached, parties can and often do claim confidentiality and the matter disappears as it were from the public domain.

In a different world, namely, the world of fine wines, a similar issue arose in the context of a greatly publicized dispute involving counterfeiting of some of the best fine wines of the world from the famed regions of Burgundy and Bordeaux of France. Some of these wines were sold in international auctions at prices as astounding as $1 million. Others were sold regularly at somewhat less astronomical but nonetheless significant prices in the range of up to $80 to 100,000 a bottle. An Indonesian wine enthusiast settled in California, one Rudy Kurniawan, proceeded to blend and bottle these top dollar counterfeit wines by mixing various vintages, in genuine but used wine bottles, repasted a counterfeit paper label and then by passed them off as genuine to the various auction houses. The whole counterfeit strategy came to light when Mr Kurniawan sought to sell a 1929 vintage of a Chateau Ponsot, a well-known Bordeaux Wine, which vintage was never produced by the Chateau.

One Mr Bill Koch, one of the biggest collectors of fine wines in the United States, with a personal collection estimated to be upwards of several million US dollars had purchased some of the most expensive wine bottles in an auction conducted by a leading American auction house. It transpires that some of these consignments had apparently been sourced from the now infamous Mr Kurniawan. On coming to know of this fraud, Mr Koch proceeded to sue inter alia the auction house, namely, Acker Merall and Condit as well as Mr Kurniawan for multimillion dollars claims. However, at the stage of discovery, the matter was settled and it was reported that both the auction house and Mr Kurniawan had agreed to pay undisclosed sums in damages. Interestingly, the infamous Rudy Kurniawan episode has since been made into a film with the rather apposite title 'Sour Grapes'.

The result was that all other individuals who were perhaps likewise duped into buying Mr Kurniawan's consignments from the various auction houses in the United States were not made privy to the details of these counterfeit wine consignments and were left without an effective remedy other than initiating individual legal proceedings afresh. This example pithily makes the case against protective confidentiality provisions without a public forum adjudication of serious issue of fraud.

The flip side however is that if an ipso facto allegation of fraud could either shut out the jurisdiction of the tribunal or compel the court to adjudicate that issue before itself, then it would make the arbitration process unworkable. In India, the judicial view seems to be that in a domestic arbitration, if a serious question of fraud arises, then the case ought not to be referred to arbitration. Thus in the case of *N. Radhakrishan*[17] (2010), the Apex Court held:

> In our view and relying on the aforesaid observations of this Court in the aforesaid decision and going by the ratio of the abovementioned case, the facts of the present case do not warrant the matter to be tried and decided by the arbitrator, rather for the furtherance of justice, it should be tried in a court of law which would be more competent and have the means to decide such a complicated matter involving various questions and issues raised in the present dispute.

Interestingly the judgment in *N. Radhakrishnan* was 'overruled' later by a Single Judge Bench in *Swiss Timing*[18] (2014) a matter which came to the court in the context of an international arbitration for the appointment of an arbitrator under Section 11(6) of the Arbitration Act. It would appear that it was not brought to the court's notice that *N. Radhakrishnan*'s case involved a domestic arbitration.

However, subsequently in the case of *RRB Energy*,[19] the Delhi High Court has held the *Swiss Timing* judgment to be inapplicable to domestic arbitrations, inasmuch as the Single Judge Bench therein had 'overruled' a prior judgment of the Division Bench in *Radhakrishnan's case*. The High Court in *RRB Energy* noted:

> In addition to this, Swiss Timing Ltd.'s case (supra) has been rendered by Hon'ble Mr Justice Surinder Singh Nijjar sitting singly as a delegate of the Chief Justice of India and his Lordship himself in a case

titled *Bihar State Govt. Secondary School Teachers Association v. Bihar Education Service Association & Ors.*; 2012 13 SCC 33 has held that a Bench of lesser number of judges cannot overrule the ratio laid down by the larger number of judges and more so in a case where collateral points are involved, yet the Hon'ble Judge has observed that the judgment in Radhakrishan's case (supra) which was rendered by a bench of two judges as being per incuriam while pronouncing judgment in Swiss Timing Ltd.'s case (supra) where his Lordship was sitting singly. For all these reasons, I feel that the view expressed in Swiss Timing Ltd.'s case (supra) would not be applicable to the facts of the case and the dispute cannot be referred to arbitral tribunal.

In an earlier judgment in *World Sport Group (Mauritius)*,[20] the Supreme Court took the view that the law laid down in the earlier cases of *Radhakrishnan* and *Abdul Kadir*[21] (1962) were decisions rendered in the context of domestic arbitrations and not under New York Convention to which Section 45 of the Arbitration Act applies. The Court held:

36. Thus, the arbitration agreement does not become 'inoperative or incapable of being performed' where allegations of fraud have to be inquired into and the said cannot refuse to refer the parties to arbitration as provided in Section 45 of the Act on the ground that allegations of fraud have been made by the party which can only be inquired into by the court and not by the arbitrator. *N. Radhakrishnan v. Maestro Engineers* and *Abdul Kadir Shamsuddin Bubere vs. Madhav Prabhakar Oak* were decisions rendered under New York Convention to which Section 45 of the Arbitration Act applies. In the case of such arbitrations covered by the New York Convention, the Court can decline to make a reference of a dispute covered by the arbitration agreement only if it comes to the conclusion that the arbitration agreement is null and void, inoperative or incapable of being performed, and not on the ground that allegations of fraud or misrepresentation have to be inquired into while deciding the disputes between the parties.

In India, therefore, it appears that as far as the domestic arbitration is concerned, a serious question of fraud or at least a serious question of prima facie fraud would not be arbitrable but in case of an international arbitration, if the arbitration clause is widely worded, it would be so. This distinction is unique to India and creates its own problems.

While on this issue as to whether a dispute which raises a serious question of prima facie fraud can be referred to arbitration,
there is another peculiarity of Indian arbitral jurisprudence which
cannot be lost sight of. The Apex Court, based on the principle of
party autonomy and the otherwise salutary doctrine that a contract
entered into with open eyes is binding on the parties, has proceeded
to hold in a catena of judgments relating back to *S. Rajan*[22] that an
arbitration agreement which leaves the process of appointment of
the sole arbitrator to the exclusive discretion of one of the parties to
the dispute is valid in law. It started with such unilateral arbitration
clauses in public sector undertakings contracts in the domestic realm.

Surely, the salutary principle that justice must not only be done
but also seen to be done would stand violated by such unilateral
appointment of clauses. However, till today, the Supreme Court has
kept its faith in the earlier line of judgments starting with *S. Rajan*
and culminating in *Raja Transport*.[23] The Delhi High Court, in its
recent judgment in *Assignia-VIL JV*,[24] has somewhat courageously
sought to put an end to such a practice in view of Section 12(5) of
the Arbitration and Conciliation Act, 1996 as amended in 2015.
Section 12(5) of the Arbitration & Conciliation Act, 1996 only
solves this issue in part.

In recent times, there has been severe criticism against distinguished arbitrators unilaterally appointed by private moneylend-
ers and hire-purchase companies, and entities lending money
to corporate borrowers in the form of Inter Corporate Deposits
(ICD) wherein such single-party-appointed arbitrators have upheld
on penal interest clauses typically providing for interest at 3 per cent
per month with monthly interests on the ground that the same was a
part of the bargain between the parties. For instance, in *Modi Rubber
Ltd.*[25] as against a principal amount of Rs 5 crores borrowed by a
corporate borrower as an ICD, the interest awarded for a period of
approximately seven months was in the region of Rs 1.72 crores,
namely, 34.4 per cent interest within a period of seven months. Such
arbitral awards do nothing to create either the acceptability of arbitration as an ADR or faith in its ability to be seen as doing justice. The
matter eventually came up in execution proceedings where the court
upheld the execution, at its extraordinary rate of interest. The Division
Bench on Appeal pointed out that since the matter had come up at

the stage of execution, the court was really helpless as it could not go behind the decree. The matter is currently pending before the Supreme Court after grant of leave and staying the recovery.

Interestingly, yet another case with the same lender is presently pending at the stage of Section 34 challenge before Delhi High Court wherein the arbitrator has upheld another similar penal interest clause of 3 per cent per month with monthly interests, which has resulted in a principle of Rs 34 lakhs ballooning into a figure of Rs 54 crores over a period of 14 years, that is, a staggering quantum of interest of 6,104 per cent or 61 times the principle. In a situation like this, it is possible that when the conscience of the court is touched, the court could be tempted to find a way out. What happens in such cases is that they sometimes end up making bad law. A jurisdictional High Court may feel that the view of the Supreme Court about validity of unilateral arbitration clauses is plainly wrong, yet the court's hands would be tied as it cannot, in view of the binding law laid down, set aside the award on the ground that the tribunal was not properly constituted. In such circumstances, the court then looks to alternative ways of setting aside such an award, as an easy way out. One of the options that present itself is that, since an issue of fraud was raised in the domestic arbitration, the tribunal had no jurisdiction to adjudicate the issue. A simple way out would be for the Supreme Court to reconsider its view and to recall its previous judgment and hold that merely by consent of parties the very appointment of a sole arbitrator cannot be left to whims of a party to the dispute.

There could be other ways out as far as this controversy is concerned. First, the issue whether a party in arbitration proceedings prima facie establishes a serious case of fraud ought to be determined by tribunal itself while dealing with the question of maintainability of the proceedings under Section 16, and if the tribunal decides to go ahead with the hearing, then its decision that prima facie, the allegation of fraud is not made out and therefore, the tribunal had jurisdiction to entertain the dispute, would be subject to challenge only at the stage of Section 34 proceedings. The second way out is for the Supreme Court in an appropriate case to partly overrule the judgment in *N. Radhakrishnan*'s case or in the alternative for the Parliament to amend the Arbitration & Conciliation Act, 1996 making it clear that the domestic tribunal can entertain questions of fraud as well. In such a case, the public interest aspect can be satisfied by providing that in the event there is a finding of fraud returned by a tribunal, the proceedings before the tribunal and the court in Section 34 proceedings will no longer be protected by confidentiality.

In any event urgent remedial steps are required to deal with a situation in domestic arbitration in India, where invariably a recalcitrant party which is not interested in going ahead with arbitration raises, the bogey of the dispute involving a question of fraud. This has now become a serious obstruction to realize the purpose of the Arbitration Act, 1996. Interestingly, as far as the law in England is concerned, as pointed out in a Newsletter published by the law firm Herbert Smith Freehills LLP,[26] there appears to be no public policy requiring the issues of fraud to be decided by the court of law alone. The only question which requires to be considered is whether the wording of the arbitration agreement itself is broad enough to include the dispute of fraud. The only exception to the rule of arbitrability of a dispute relating to fraud as mentioned in the case of *Nigel Peter Albon*[27] is where the arbitration clause is contained in the agreement itself, and as a result of fraud, the entirety of the contract along with the arbitration clause would perish.

Coincidentally in a judgment delivered during the same year in *Fiona Trust & Holding Corporation*,[28] the English Court of Appeal seems to have taken a view to the effect that even any kind of a case referred to in *Nigel Peter Albon*, the tribunal can adjudicate the issue of fraud and pass an award to declare the contract itself to be void on account of having been procured by bribery and/or forgery. The approach of the American Courts is also broadly the same.

Arbitrability and the Competition Act, 2002

The scheme of the Competition Act, 2002 is to create deterrence against anti-competitive agreements and abuse of the dominant position by an enterprise. This jurisdiction is vested in the Regulator, namely, the Competition Commission of India. The regulator not only has the jurisdiction to issue cease and desist orders but also to impose a huge financial burden in the form of a penalty which could be up to 10 per cent of the average turnover of the defaulting enterprise for the last three preceding financial years. The focus of the

Competition Act is not merely to protect any particular individual or group but the public at large, and the economy in general. It is therefore, clearly a public law concern involving high public interest.

In the United States, the Supreme Court in the classic case of *Mitsubishi Motors Corporation*[29] (1985) took a view that in international arbitration anti-trust claims were arbitrable if the dispute was captured within the four corners of arbitration clause. The reasoning which found favour with the Supreme Court was that if such a contract contained a broad enough arbitration clause, the policy favouring arbitration would override the domestic public policy against arbitrability of an anti-trust claim. It is not necessary, the Supreme Court reasoned that the arbitration clause should specifically mention or name a given statute, say Sherman Act, in order to ensure that the disputes touching upon or relating to such a statute would also be referred to arbitration.

There is a prior judgment of the United States Supreme Court, which arose in the context of Domestic Securities Suit against a brokerage firm for an alleged misrepresentation under Federal Security Act, 1933. Even though, the sale agreement in question provided for arbitration, the Supreme Court in *Wilco v. Swan*[30] held that the arbitral tribunal would not have jurisdiction. The Apex Court relied upon a provision of the Federal Security Act which expressly forbade parties from waiving complaints arising within the provisions of the Act, pursuant to a clause in their inter se private contract. The court took the view that an arbitration clause amounted to waiving a purchaser's right to bring a suit in a Federal Court under provisions of Federal Security Act. The Court also noted that the arbitration process was not structured to ensure the protection of investors' right, which was a concern vital to the public interest of the realm.

As far as Indian law is concerned, there does not appear to be any judgment of the Supreme Court on this issue. The Delhi High Court in the case of *Union of India v. Competition Commission of India*[31] (2012), which arose in the context of a complaint filed by private parties against the Ministry of Railways to the effect that the Railway Board was abusing its dominant position by increasing charges and restricting the access to its infrastructure, held that the arbitrator would not have the necessary expertise to investigate an issue involving anti-competitive practices and therefore rejected the challenge by the Ministry of Railways to the jurisdiction of the Competition Commission of India to adjudicate the complaint in this regard.

Oppression, Mismanagement, and the Arbitration Clause

The Indian Supreme Court had an occasion in the case of *Haryana Telecom Ltd.*,[32] to deal with the question whether a dispute of winding up can be referred to arbitration. The answer was an emphatic 'No', as winding up is a specific statutory remedy which can be only granted under the provisions of the Companies Act. In this backdrop, the question then arises as to whether a case of oppression and mismanagement which arises in the context of a shareholders' agreement containing an arbitration clause can necessarily be referred to arbitration.

There are earlier judgments of the Delhi High Court in the case of *In Re: Kare*[33] and *O.P. Gupta*[34] where D.K. Kapur, J. held that disputes relating to oppression and mismanagement were by their very nature not arbitrable. The court did not deal with this aspect in any great detail and proceeded to take this jurisprudential proposition as a 'given'.

In this connection, it would be worthwhile to refer to the judgment of the Supreme Court in *Booz Allen*.[35] It has been held in *Booz Allen* that disputes in rem cannot be referred to arbitration. It could arguably follow therefore that disputes in rem would include disputes in relation to oppression and mismanagement which are issues in rem. In the well-known Treatise 'Russell on Arbitration',[36] the principle is stated thus, 'Nevertheless, English law does recognize that these are matters which cannot be decided by means of arbitration and there have been decisions elsewhere that have recognized this ground'.

A single judge of the Bombay High Court in *Rakesh Malhotra*[37] held that disputes in relation to oppression and mismanagement are not per se arbitrable. However, the court proceeded to place a caveat that it is only where the Company Law Board finds that the Company Petition is either dressed up, mala fide, or vexatious that the parties can be referred to arbitration.

It may be pointed out that there appears to be a later and on apparently contrary view of the Delhi High Court in the *Vijay Sekhri* case,[38] which held that no appeal under Section 10F of the Companies Act,

1956 was maintainable against an order of the Company Law Board referring parties to arbitration. It appears from the reading of the said judgment that the attention of the court was not drawn to the previous judgments of the Delhi High Court in *Re. Kare* and the *O.P. Gupta* cases. Further, the order under challenge in the *Vijay Sekhri* case was an order simpliciter referring the dispute to arbitration without any adjudication of the issue as to whether or not the Company Petition was dressed up, mala fide, or vexatious. The judgment does not shed any light on the issue which is being dealt with in this chapter.

In a later case, the Andhra Pradesh High Court in *Triumphant Institute*[39] took the view that where the Company Law Board passes a composite order rejecting the Company Petition summarily and allowing respondent's application under Section 8 of the Arbitration Act, then an appeal under Section 10F of the Companies Act would be maintainable.

***

It is, therefore, seen that the whole focus of arbitration as an ADR mechanism has shifted from an initial suspicion, any hostility to the arbitral process, as some kind of usurper of the court system to the present, which on the whole is favourably inclined towards arbitration as a speedy and party nominated forum of dispute resolution. There are still certain 'No Go' areas as far as the jurisdiction of the tribunal is concerned, but these are severely limited and justified only by recourse to principles of high public policy.[40]

Lord Mustill in an article published in the *ICC Colloquium*[41] (1993) propounds the view that there is now a veritable partnership between arbitrators and national courts with each playing a different role at different times. The handling of arbitral disputes, according to Lord Mustill, resembles a relay race. In the initial stages, before the arbitrators are seized of the dispute, the baton is in the grasp of the court; for at that stage, there is no other organization which can take steps to prevent the arbitration agreement from becoming ineffectual. When the arbitrators take charge, they take over the baton and retain it until they have made an award. At this point, having no longer a function to fulfil, the arbitrators hand back the baton to the court so that the coercive powers of the court, if needed, can be used for enforcing the award.[42]

I would like to conclude by referring to an instructive judgment of the English Queen Bench in the case of *J. Jarvis*.[43] The plaint was for an anti-suit injunction to restrain an on going arbitration process while a parallel proceeding in a court of law was pending. An anti-arbitration injunction was sought on the ground that continuation of the arbitration would be vexatious, encourage multiplicity of proceedings, and result in potentially inconsistent verdicts. In his judgment, Jackson J noted the paramount principles of party autonomy and self-restraint by the courts as far as intervening in the arbitral proceedings was concerned. The court relied on the well-known speech of Lord Steyn in the case of *Lesotho Highlands Development Authority*.[44]

The court held under the new English Arbitration Act, 1996 though the jurisdiction of the court to restrain the continuation of arbitration proceedings has survived, but its exercise has become even more sparing than before. The 'before' which the court was referring was the law laid down in the earlier cases of *The Oranie*.[45]

The case of *The Oranie* involved a complex dispute, which was a subject of arbitration in London. At a late stage of arbitration, one of the ship owners applied for injunction to prevent arbitration from proceeding on the ground that there were concurrent proceedings between some of the parties, both in French and English Courts, and there was a grave risk of inconsistency between the court decisions and that of the tribunal.

Before the trial court, the anti-arbitration injunction was rejected principally on the ground of delay. By the time the matter reached the Court of Appeals, the arbitration proceedings had been concluded, the award had been prepared but had not yet been issued. The appeal was rejected. The single-most important factor for rejection was once again the delay, but the court also elucidated the guiding principle for grant of such stay:

> All of those observations are true, but they do not mean that the arbitration is vexatious. It is an inevitable consequence of the mandatory language of section 9 of Arbitration Act that from time to time there will be concurrent proceedings in court and before an arbitrator. Indeed, *Taunton-Collins v. Cromie* (1964) 1 WLR 633 (authority much relied upon by counsel under the old regime) would have been decided

differently if section 9 of Arbitration Act had been in force in 1994, the University of Reading proceedings would have taken a different course. In particular, Judge Bowsher would have allowed rather than dismissed Miller's application for a partial stay of the litigation. That circumstance may have caused Judge Humphrey Lloyd to refuse the application for injunction.[46]

Therefore, the English Courts in both *J. Jarvis* case as well as in the case of *Oranie* refused to injunct the arbitration proceedings even when there were continuing concurrent court proceedings. It, therefore, emerges that the courts in England are reasonably disinclined to injunct concurrent arbitration proceedings. This is particularly so, in the absence of a clear finding that the arbitration proceedings are clearly vexatious.

To conclude, one discerns a clear trend in judicial dicta where arbitration is the chosen forum of dispute resolution of increasingly limited court interference even where concurrent court and arbitration proceedings are likely to result in conflicting judgments. While making this shift, the courts have shown awareness to the ground reality that there is a much greater chance of the arbitration being concluded first and consequently arbitration verdict, being 'first past the post', as opposed to the final adjudication achieved in a court of law. Yet, there is palpably disinclination to interfere even in such concurrent arbitration proceedings.

But, on the other hand, when it comes to overwhelming public interest, in respect of areas where there are specific statutory provisions dealing with the issues of public weal as in the case of Competition Law, the statutory remedies Oppression and Mismanagement under the Companies Act, and in India at least in cases of egregious fraud, then the private forum of arbitration may have to yield to the larger public interest.

Notes and References

1. Earl S. Wolaver, 'The Historical Background of Commercial Arbitration', *University of Pennsylvania Law Review*, 132 (1932).
2. Vynior's Case, 8Co. 80a, 8Ib (1609).
3. I Wilson 129 (K.B. 1746).
4. 2 Atk. 569 (Ch. 1743).

5. 5 H.L. Cas. 811 (1856).
6. 5 H.L. Cas. 811 (1856).
7. H.L. Cas. 853 (1856).
8. 869 (Ch. 1875).
9. 31 L.T.R. (N.S.) 870.
10. Malynes, Lex Mercatoria (1622).
11. Malynes, Lex Mercatoria (1622).
12. *Union of India v. Tantia Constructions (P) Ltd.*, (2011) 5 SCC 697; Paras 33 and 34.
13. Companies Act, 1956, section 402: 'Powers of the Company Law Board on application under Section 397/398: Without prejudice to the generality of the powers of the Company Law Board under section 397 or 398, any order under either section may provide for…. (g) any other matter for which in the opinion of the Company Law Board] it is just and equitable that provision should be made.'
14. Ashley Cook, '*Kompetenz-Kompetenz*: Varying Approaches and a Proposal for a Limited Form of Negative *Kompetenz-Kompetenz*', *Pepperdine Law Review*, 17 (2014).
15. *First Options of Chi. Inc. v. Kaplan*, 514 US 938 (1995).
16. *Dallah Real Estate and Tourism Holding Company v. The Ministry of Religious Affairs, Government of Pakistan*, [2010] UKSC 46; Paras 79–85.
17. *N. Radhakrishnan v. Maestro Engineers & Ors.*, (2010) 1 SCC 72; Para 21.
18. *Swiss Timing Ltd. v. Organising Committee, Commonwealth Games*, (2014) 6 SCC 677; Para 20.
19. *RRB Energy Ltd. v. Vestas Wind Systems*, 219 (2015) DLT 516; Para 54.
20. *World Sports Group (Mauritius) Ltd. v. MSM Satellite (Singapore) Pte. Ltd.*, (2014) 11 SCC 639; Para 36.
21. AIR 1962 SC 406.
22. *S. Rajan v. State of Kerala*, (1992) 3 SCC 608; Para 12.
23. *Indian Oil Corporation Ltd v. Raja Transport*, (2009) 8 SCC 520; Para 13.
24. *Assignia-VIL JV v. Rail Vikas Nigam Ltd.*, Arb. P No. 677/2015; Para 43.
25. *Modi Rubber Ltd v. Morgan Securities & Credits Pvt. Ltd.*, (165) 2009 DLT 113.
26. 'Arbitrability of Fraud in India', available http://hsfnotes.com/arbitration/2015/12/02/arbitrability-of-fraud-in-india/.
27. SDN BHD (2007) EWHC 665FF.
28. *Fiona Trust & Holding Corporation v. Yuri Privalov & Ors.*, [2007] APP.L.R. 01/24; Para 43.
29. *Mitsubishi Motors Corp. v. Soler Chrysler-Plymouth Inc.*, 473 US 614 (1985).

30. *Wilko v. Swan*, 346 U.S. 427 (1953).
31. AIR 2012 Del 66; Para 16.
32. *Haryana Telecom Ltd v. Sterlite Industries Ltd.*, (1999) 5 SCC 688; Para 5.
33. (1974) SCC OnLine Del 101; Paras 2, 6, 7 & 8; (1977) 47 Comp Cas 276.
34. *O.P. Gupta v. Shiv General Finance*, ILR 1975 II Delhi 911; Paras 2, 4, 5 and 6.
35. (2011) 5 SCC 532; Paras 36–9.
36. Francis Russell, *Russell on Arbitration*, eds David St John Sutton, Judith Gill, and Matthew Gearing, 23rd ed. (2007), para 8.43, p. 470.
37. (2015) 192 Comp Case 516; Paras 46, 74–85, and 86–91.
38. (2010) SCC OnLine Del 3843; Paras 10–18, 24, and 28.
39. *Triumphant Institute of Management Education Pvt. Ltd. v. Inspire Educational Services Pvt. Ltd.*, (2014) 183 Comp Cas 462; Para 31.
40. See also *Redfern and Hunter on International Arbitration*, eds Nigel Blackaby, Constantine Partasides QC, Alan Redfern, and Martin Hunter, 5th ed. (Oxford University Press, 2009), p. 442.
41. Lord Mustill, 'Comments and Conclusions', in *Conservatory Provisional Measures in International Arbitration*, 9th Joint Colloquium (ICC Publication, 1993), p. 118.
42. Mustill, *Conservatory Provisional Measures in International Arbitration*, 1993.
43. *J. Jarvis & Sons Ltd v. Blue Circle Dartford Estates Ltd.*, [2007] EWHC 1262 (TCC).
44. [2005] UKHL 43.
45. The 'Oranie' and the 'Tunisie', [1966] 1 Lloyd's List LR 477.
46. The 'Oranie' and the 'Tunisie', [1996]; para 46.

12

Arbitration

An In-house Counsel's Perspective

Sanjeev Gemawat

Discourage litigation. Persuade your neighbors to compromise whenever you can. Point out to them how the nominal winner is often the
real loser—in fees, and expenses, and waste of time. As a peace-maker
the lawyer has a superior opportunity of being a good man. There will
still be business enough.

—Abraham Lincoln

Rapid globalization of the economy and the resulting significant
increase in the domestic/international trade over the last couple of
decades has posed one of the greatest challenges before the business
organizations—how to resolve disputes arising in business transactions in a timely and efficient manner with minimal financial loss.
Amidst this, popularity of arbitration as an alternate dispute resolution mechanism is evident as a large number of business organizations are considering arbitration over litigation to resolve disputes as

a part of their dispute resolution policy. During the same period, the role and relevance of an in-house counsel has transformed from one performing mainly administrative tasks to that of being a strategic decision maker for the business organizations.

This chapter is an attempt to put a perspective of an in-house counsel about the evolution of the role of in-house counsel in the present business environment and the difficulty the in-house counsel faces in framing a dispute resolution policy in the backdrop of present arbitration system in India.

In-house Counsel

An in-house counsel has seen a shift in its role from that of one performing mainly administrative tasks to that of being a strategic decision maker. An in-house counsel has to oversee the company's legal issues, be responsible for managing the internal department and the external counsel, for managing risk and safeguarding the reputation and the commercial interests of the organization, all with a global perspective and keeping a close control on the budget to maintain profitability. In this backdrop, in-house counsel is a pivotal part of the triangle: Bench—External Counsel—In-house Counsel. The increasingly commercial and strategic focus of the in-house counsel has also affected its relationship with external counsel. The financial pressure of managing an unpredictable workload with limited resources led to most of the critical and strategic decisions being taken by in-house counsel instead of external counsels. Any decision taken by the in-house counsel is always influenced by the expectations of the management; and unlike the external counsel, the in-house counsel is expected to have a business-oriented approach, to provide legal solutions with commercial and strategic focus rather than a conventional approach of saying 'Yes' or 'No' to any decision.

The challenge of an in-house counsel is to develop a dispute resolution policy which should provide a structured approach to resolve disputes efficiently and effectively. Generally, business decisions are based on varied commercial considerations and it is not easy for the in-house counsel to negotiate and conclude an agreement including dispute resolution mechanism always to its advantage.

The counsel has to consistently provide guidance for adoption of dispute resolution mechanisms proportionate to the value at stake.

Dispute Resolution Mechanisms

Not only has an in-house counsel's role changed but also the perception about dispute resolution mechanisms has seen a paradigm shift. In the past two decades, we have seen a shift from the conventional litigation to alternate dispute resolution mechanisms and arbitration being the most preferred mechanism amongst them. The reason for this shift inter alia has been that standard litigation is time consuming and costly affair, whereas arbitration is considered to be a speedy and cost-effective mechanism with the liberty to the parties to choose their own procedures for adjudication of the disputes.

Another reason for this shift in approach of choosing arbitration over standard litigation can be the change in role of an in-house counsel from that of a paper pusher. As an in-house counsel has to work as per the expectations of the management and he understands the business as well, therefore, an in-house counsel would prefer that in the event of a dispute, the same should be disposed of expeditiously. The in-house counsel would prefer an alternate dispute resolution mechanism which gives him the flexibility to carve out a procedure for expeditious disposal of issues which may arise from any contractual arrangement. The basis for this could also be the wish of the in-house counsel to keep things within his control and out of the control of outsourced lawyers. A benefit arising out of this situation could be the probability of getting the disputes settled amicably at the threshold or during the course of the proceedings as the control would not be in the hands of the outsourced counsels who are more of litigators than negotiators for pro-settlement.

Drafting of Arbitration Agreement

Today, organizations prefer arbitration to resolve disputes. Most of the organizations draft contracts with the help of an in-house team. The clause on alternate dispute resolution mechanism is included more or less by the in-house counsel until and unless the same is a policy decision which is taken by the organization at a macro level.

Thus, an in-house counsel is the end user of this clause and while drafting he has to keep in mind that the clause drafted should be one which is able to stand the test of judicial precedents laid down from time to time. The clause should be such that it is not subject to interpretation or any confusion arising out of the change in law or due to any judicial pronouncements. The clause should clearly and unambiguously include or exclude what was intended to be included or excluded. It is also very important for the in-house counsel to keep himself updated with developments taking place in law. An in-house counsel appreciates that there cannot be a straightjacket formula to include arbitration clauses in the contracts. The subject matter of the contract should be inclusive of the arbitration clause that can produce desired results.

It would not be trite to mention here that inclusion of a dispute resolution mechanism and/or any negotiations thereon can be an uphill task for an in-house counsel. Despite the fact that in case of a dispute, the way forward shall be to resort to an arbitration clause, the in-house counsel has to face the resistance of business teams as the business people are not interested in investing time or effort on such issues which are not of commercial value to them. Arbitration clauses, despite being of vital importance, are discussed at the fag end of negotiations and not much time is allotted in its discussions.

As there is no such thing as a single 'model', 'miracle', or 'all purpose' clause appropriate for all occasions, the in-house counsel is expected to carefully customize the arbitration clause considering the exigencies of a given situation, taking into account the likely types of disputes, the needs of the parties' relationship, and the applicable laws. Generally, business organizations enter into numerous types of contracts—consumer contracts (specific as well as standard-form agreements), distribution agreements, franchise agreements, supplier contracts, sales agreements, joint venture agreements, shareholders' agreements, assets sale/purchase agreement, and other commercial agreements. Each of these agreements involve different considerations for dispute resolution clauses, and different arbitration clauses are required to be developed for each of such contracts. The challenge of the in-house counsel is not only to craft the best clause to meet the particular need of the contract in the absence of effective institutional arbitrations in India but also to resist the clause dictated by the party with the greatest bargaining strength. The challenge gets further enhanced due to promulgation of conflicting doctrines by the courts whether related to public policy or otherwise. This all invariably results into pathological arbitration clauses in contracts and leads to disputes over the interpretation of the arbitration agreement resulting in the failure of arbitration clause or unenforceability of an award.

A changing trend which is appearing now is that in some situations, dispute resolution clauses are gaining importance and are becoming make or break clauses. One more reason for the acceptance of alternate dispute resolution mechanism in a contract can be attributed to the changing outlook towards such mechanisms at a global level. Most of the countries today are changing their focus to arbitration and choosing the same, especially in international contracts as the parties are not interested in going to an unknown jurisdiction and becoming subject thereto. Therefore, as a matter of choice, it is preferred to select a forum of their own choice which is possible only through arbitration.

Another reason for choosing arbitration is that the parties can go to an expert of their field with technical know-how requisite for adjudicating upon their disputes. A major reason for companies choosing arbitration over standard litigation is the time consumed in courts for disposal of the matter. Further there are numerous stages of appeal in one form or the other available to the parties to vitiate the favourable order passed in favour of a party. The pendency of litigation in courts and matters being adjudicated upon by judges who are not related to the fields of the parties may lead to orders which are not able to settle the basic controversies involved. However, the way this branch of alternate dispute resolution mechanism has evolved in today's scenario, has led to a set back to the very basic scheme of arbitration law.

Spirit of Arbitration

Arbitration as a means of settling disputes fails as generally the attitude of parties to dispute is 'try to win if you can, if you cannot, do your best to see that the other side cannot enforce the award for as long as possible'. This attitude is aided and abetted by the legal fraternity. Moreover, there should not be any hesitation in accepting the reality that business organizations (and for that matter in-house counsels) would prefer to have an arbitrator of their choice particularly in those contracts where the sole arbitrator is appointed by one of the parties to the dispute. The principles of neutrality and independence get defeated and awards would only be seen as made with the motive of favouring the party who appointed the arbitrator even though there is no apparent evidence of partiality.

Arbitration: Miniature form of Litigation

The scheme of the arbitration law is such that arbitration process which is a quasi-judicial proceeding has become more or less a miniature form of litigation. There is a scope of judicial interference at numerous levels which in turn leads the parties to approach the courts, thereby getting entangled in the web of technical complexities which was sought to be avoided.

Due to the fact that the parties have to take recourse to courts for various remedies available to them under the arbitration law, the parties prefer to engage external counsels for conducting the arbitration proceedings in the event of a dispute. The proceedings are taken forward, that is, drafting, representing, and so on is done by the external counsel. The in-house counsel becomes more or less a manager of the proceedings, that is, in the administrative capacity and the external counsel becomes the actual doer.

Besides the transfer of control to external counsels, there are other deviations which also occur to the initial thoughts of the parties which they had while going in for an alternate dispute resolution mechanism. The initial thought of having the industry expert to adjudicate upon the dispute also suffers a set back as the whole process gets entangled in procedural technicalities. The industry expert gets substituted by a retired high court judge or a leading lawyer who has prior experience of arbitration and with whom the outsourced counsels of the parties are comfortable with. It is also seen that one set of lawyers prefer appointing the same person as an arbitrator, irrespective of the nature of industry to the dispute. It is needless to mention here that these factors also contribute to the mistrust which is somehow associated with the arbitration process. The parties are not able to rule out bias by an arbitrator in favour of the party by whom he had been appointed. For this very reason, in the cases where there is a provision of a sole arbitrator or where the presiding arbitrator has to be appointed, neither party tends to agree upon the name suggested by the other party, thus leaving each other with only option to get appointment done through court.

Similarly there are numerous other stages during the arbitration proceedings which are prone to judicial interference ranging from interim relief, to appointment of an arbitrator, to getting the award enforced—thus susceptible to delays and procedural complexities.

Selection of Arbitrators

There is a growing recognition that arbitration is becoming a costly affair, which is a departure from the intent of the 1996 Act. This is particularly true in ad hoc arbitration, where the fees of the arbitrators are not regulated but decided by the arbitral tribunal with the consent of the parties. Arbitral tribunals consisting of high-profile arbitrators, such as retired judges of Supreme Court/High Courts, charge high arbitration fees coupled with holding ad hoc arbitrations at costly venues, like five-star hotels. With the selection of retired high court judges or a lawyer as an arbitrator, few other features get associated with entire set of proceedings. It is considered that arbitration gives the parties the flexibility to choose their own procedure. This flexibility many a times gets restricted when chosen arbitrators are retired judges, as knowingly or unknowingly, they get trapped in the web of procedural technicalities and as an unsaid rule they start following the procedural law. Another issue which needs to be mentioned here is that an arbitral tribunal in its sub-conscious mind is driven by the fact that as per the applicable law the award of the tribunal shall be challengeable before the courts which in effect means that an award passed by a panel of high court judges gets challenged before a district judge. Therefore, the arbitral tribunal while passing the award sometimes becomes over cautious and hyper technical which may not be beneficial.

Probability of amicable settlement of issues becomes bleak as particularly, outside lawyers tend to be more of litigators than settlement negotiators, with a different set of objectives and related skills. In-house counsel can better appreciate the underlying business interests of his organization and this becomes particularly crucial in connection with possible settlement efforts. In extreme cases, outside counsel's lack of negotiating skills may be coupled with a lack of real interest in settling, as they may have a financial interest in seeing the arbitration continue.

Arbitration: Not a Cheaper Option

Arbitration being an alternate dispute resolution mechanism is considered to be cheaper than litigation. While in fact the cost of hearing, considering the venue, has to be arranged by the parties, fee of the arbitral tribunal (still higher in case of a tribunal comprising of three arbitrators), advocate's fee and other miscellaneous expenses come out to be much higher than the cost of hearing in the normal litigation process. It is also seen that the way in which arbitration proceedings move, it becomes difficult to arrive at a common date of hearing which may be suitable to both the parties as well as the arbitral tribunal. So a good part of the hearing is spent in deciding the next date of hearing.

Earlier there were no set guidelines for determining the fees of the arbitrators. Fee was charged under different heads, namely reading fee, hearing fee, for writing award, for two hearings in case a hearing continues. In case of counterclaim, additional fee was charged. Considering these circumstances the cost of arbitration always turned out to be higher.

Arbitration Jurisprudence: Ever Evolving

Arbitration jurisprudence in India is still evolving. Besides the applicable statute this branch of law seems to be ever evolving with law getting settled through various judgments being passed at different levels of judicial system. Various judicial pronouncements have created a situation of confusion, for instance, the issue relating to applicability of Part I of the Arbitration and Conciliation Act 1996 to international commercial arbitrations. In *Bhatia International v. Bulk Trading S.A*[1] and *Venture Global Engineering Case v. Satyam Computer Services Ltd,*[2] it was held by the Hon'ble Supreme Court that all provisions of Part I of the Act shall be applicable to international commercial arbitration even if held outside India, thus making the act extraterritorial in its application.

However, this proposition was set aside by a five judge constitution bench of the Hon'ble Supreme Court in *Bharat Aluminium v. Kaiser Aluminium Technical Services*, wherein it held that Part I of Indian Arbitration Act, 1996 (Act) will have no applicability over international commercial arbitrations held outside India. This judgment was, however, made applicable to arbitration agreements executed subsequent to the date of the judgment. To the agreements executed prior, the law as laid down in *Bhatia International* stood applicable.

To overcome the drawbacks which have become linked to arbitration, various amendments have been brought to the 1996 Act such as prescribing the time period for appointment of arbitrator through court, disposal of proceedings to be made within one year extendable by six months, provision of fee schedule of arbitrators, prohibition of certain people as arbitrators, and so on.

These amendments seem to be a welcome move. What however needs to be seen is that the provisions pertaining to approaching the courts for extension of prescribed timeline should not become another pitfall. That being the situation, the pendency is more likely to increase coupled with the fact that the proceedings which have been half way may get struck in limbo as the amendments fail to deal with such situations.

Institutional Arbitration: Practically Non-Existent

There is one other mental block which probably needs to be removed. The state of arbitrations in India can be improved if recourse is taken to institutional arbitration. Ad hoc arbitration is preferred over institutional arbitration without going into the benefits which institutional arbitration has over ad hoc arbitration. Institutional arbitration provides the administrative support which is required during the arbitration proceedings such as arranging the venue, fixed fee as per the schedule of the institution, rules applicable to the institution, and so on. Therefore, the whole proceedings are streamlined and there is less space of arbitrariness which is otherwise associated with ad hoc arbitration. Further, approaching the court for certain issues can be avoided, like appointment of arbitrator as in case of institutional arbitration. In case of disagreement over appointment of arbitrator, it is the institution which has the power to appoint the arbitrator. Therefore, the time which is spent in getting the appointment through a court of law is cut short.

Despite its benefits, institutional arbitration is least opted by the parties due to high costs which are associated with it. Supporters of ad hoc arbitration also contend that it gives the parties more flexibility in terms of processes and procedures. Both these contentions do not seem to be well founded as ad hoc arbitration is more expensive due to the unregulated fee structure of arbitrators, expenses incurred on the venue of arbitration, and so on. The flexibility in terms of processes and procedures may also lead to arbitrariness.

Practical Perspective

To put forth the practical perspective of arbitration, I wish to cite an example. Two parties entering into a commercial transaction decide to provide a dispute resolution clause in their agreement. After deliberation on various points, the parties provide an arbitration clause contemplating reference of dispute to a tribunal comprising of three arbitrators out of which each party to the agreement would appoint a nominee arbitrator and the nominee arbitrators would appoint the third and the presiding arbitrator. The dispute resolution clause provides for the time frame in which the appointments have to be made by each party as well as captures the jurisdiction clause. The parties perform their respective part of the agreement. However, after some time, a dispute arises concerning the interpretation and performance of the terms of the agreement. One party to the agreement invokes the arbitration clause, nominates its arbitrator, and calls upon the other party to appoint its nominee arbitrator. The other party fails to appoint its nominee arbitrator within the stipulated time frame. However, he appoints the arbitrator before the party invoking the arbitration clause approaches the court. The two nominee arbitrators are unable to reach a consensus as to the presiding arbitrator. The parties are left with no other option but to approach the courts for appointment of the presiding arbitrator. The process of appointment of presiding arbitrator takes a period of almost four years due to one reason or the other. Meanwhile, one of the parties approaches the court with another petition seeking interim relief. This petition remains pending for considerable period of time until constitution of the arbitral tribunal.

The arbitral tribunal comprises of three retired high court judges. At the first hearing, the schedule of fee of each arbitrator is decided and the same comprises of fee under various heads like reading fee, hearing fee, fee in case of counterclaim, fee in case of hearing getting prolonged, and so on. During this whole discussion of settlement of fee, the in-house counsel who is present there, as a representative of the party, has nothing to contribute and is in a miserable position as he witnesses the cost effectiveness of arbitration process. Not to miss here the role being played by external counsel representing the parties who encourage the arbitrators to fix their fee under few more heads. The external counsels do not feel like displeasing the arbitrators even if the same is at the cost of their clients. Then comes the herculean task of fixing the dates of hearing. Since the panel has three arbitrators, arriving at a date which can be suitable to all three of them as well as the external counsels representing the parties is an uphill task. The external counsel also while deciding on the dates give preferences to matters listed before courts. However, at the time of charging the fee for an arbitration hearing, the rates of external counsels are higher as compared to appearances before any court. He is also apprehensive about the feedback he is supposed to give to the management, which he had agreed for this alternate dispute resolution mechanism on the grounds that it would be expeditious and cost effective. The plight does not end here as during each hearing it is the description of the arbitral tribunal to follow the procedural aspect as per their wish. The mechanism of pick and choose while considering the procedure to be followed is not ruled out. This situation is not uncommon and can be observed in almost all arbitration proceedings, especially ad hoc arbitrations.

After the proposed amendment in the law, it needs to be seen whether these practical issues would be catered or not.

Way Forward

Despite the dissatisfaction associated with resolving disputes through arbitration, business organizations are increasingly opting for arbitration. However, for arbitrations to be successful and sustainable in India, the need of the hour is for a robust arbitration infrastructure, which could only be provided by credible institutional framework of arbitrations to overcome the significant challenge of selection of the right arbitrator, as well as time and cost of arbitration proceedings. Arbitration proceedings in India are critically affected due to lack of availability of arbitrators with requisite industry knowledge coupled with professionalism.

References

1. (2002) 4 SCC 105.
2. (2008) 4 SCC 190.

PART II

INTERNATIONAL ARBITRATION

13

The Concept of Seat in International Arbitration

Developments in India

Vikramajit Sen and *Satyajit Gupta*

A central issue in any international arbitration is the location of the seat of arbitration. It is well-accepted that the location of the seat of arbitration can have profound legal and practical consequences and materially alter the course of dispute resolution.[1] While jurists such as Born have classified the impact of the seat on costs and convenience of parties as 'mundane', the authors believe that these issues may very well influence parties at the time of entering into the arbitration agreement. Needless to say, the choice of seat can also impact the arbitration per se.

Developments in India

The Arbitration and Conciliation Amendment Act, 2015 (the Amendment Act),[2] enacted recently by the Parliament, has once again opened the vexed question of applicability of Part I of the Arbitration and Conciliation Act, 1996 (the Act).[3] The Amendment Act makes certain sections of Part I, specifically Sections 9, 27, 37(1)(a), and 37(3) of the Act, applicable to international commercial arbitration, even if the place of arbitration is outside India unless the said sections are expressly not applied.

In the Constitution Bench judgment in the matter of *Bharat Aluminium Co. v. Kaiser Aluminium Technical Services*,[4] the Supreme Court of India had put to rest all the issues concerning applicability of Part I to foreign-seated international commercial arbitrations (ICA). The court conclusively held that Part I of the Act applies only when the seat or place of arbitration is in India. In holding so, the apex court also expressly overruled its two previous decisions in *Bhatia International*[5] and *Venture Global*.[6] The Supreme Court in *Bhatia International* had held that Part I of the Act would also apply to international commercial arbitrations held outside of India unless the parties by agreement, express or implied, excluded all or any of its provisions. The Apex Court in *Venture Global* followed the position taken by *Bhatia International* and held that foreign awards could also be challenged under Section 34, Part I of the Act.

These are in a long line of conflicting decisions given by Indian courts on the subject of seat of arbitration and its relevance in deciding the curial law. The jurisprudence on this point in other common law countries is fairly clear that in the absence of an express agreement, there is a strong prima facie presumption that the parties intend the curial law to be the law of the seat of arbitration. Since the Indian Arbitration Act does not make express mention of the word 'seat' and uses the term 'place of arbitration' instead, it has warranted examination into the real intention of the parties as to which curial law will be applicable to the arbitration proceedings. Indian courts have not been as forthright in taking a similar stand when it comes to the question of deciding the curial law. Courts in India have given differing opinions on the issue of relevance of seat of arbitration in deciding the curial law.

We will consider these judgments in order to outline the development of case laws on this point. But before that, we must gain a general understanding of the scope and ambit of relevant systems of laws applicable to or during an arbitration proceeding. The Supreme

Court discusses the area of operation of curial law in its decision in *Sumitomo Heavy Industries Ltd. v. ONGC Ltd. and Ors.*[7] The Apex Court quoted in its judgment, observations made by Lord Justice Kerr in *Naviera Amazonica Peruana S.A. v. Compania International De Seguros Del Peru*[8] thus, 'All contracts which provide for arbitration and contain a foreign element may involve three potentially relevant systems of law. (1) The law governing the substantive contract. (2) The law governing the agreement to arbitrate and the performance of that agreement. (3) The law governing the conduct of the arbitration.'[9]

The apex court further observed that, 'the proper law of the arbitration agreement governs the validity of the arbitration agreement itself, the question whether a dispute lies within the scope of the arbitration agreement; the validity of the notice of arbitration'.[10] The curial law, on the other hand, 'governs the manner in which the reference is to be conducted, the procedural powers and duties of the arbitrator and questions of evidence'.[11] The court elaborates upon the ambit of curial law further,

> [T]he conclusion that we reach is that the curial law operates during the continuance of the proceedings before the arbitrator to govern the procedure and conduct thereof. The courts administering the curial law have the authority to entertain applications by parties to arbitrations being conducted within their jurisdiction for the purpose of ensuring that the procedure that is adopted in the proceedings before the arbitrator conforms to the requirements of the curial law and for reliefs incidental thereto. Such authority of the courts administering the curial law ceases when the proceedings before the arbitrator are concluded.[12]

Case Law Analysis

Having underlined the scope and ambit of curial laws in the arbitration process, we must now go back to discussing the original matter at hand, that is, relationship between seat of arbitration and applicable curial law, especially in the light of decisions on this point by courts in India. In India, matters pertaining to arbitration are governed by the Act. It is important here to consider the scheme of the Act. The Act is divided into two parts: simplistically, Part I applies to arbitrations that take place in India, Part II applies to foreign awards. In the context of the Act, Indian curial law is mainly contained in Part I. As a natural corollary, any decision regarding the choice of curial law in an international arbitration would turn on the question of applicability of Part I.

Bhatia International (SC)

We begin our analysis with the *Bhatia International* case. This was a case where the applicability of interim measures under Section 9 of the Act to international commercial arbitration held outside India came before the courts. The Supreme Court, placing reliance upon the absence of word 'only' in section 2(2) of the Act, held that Part I would also apply to international commercial arbitrations held outside India. The Apex Court compared the Act with the UNCITRAL model law and observed,

> Article 1(2) of UNCITRAL Model Laws uses the word 'only' to emphasize that the provisions of that Law are to apply if the place of arbitration is in the territory of that State. Significantly in Section 2(2) the word 'only' has been omitted. The omission of this word changes the whole complexion of the sentence. The omission of the word 'only' in Section 2(2) indicates that this sub-section is only an inclusive and clarificatory provision. As stated above it is not providing that provisions of Part I do not apply to arbitrations which take place outside India.[13]

The Apex Court, after considering the arguments placed before it, finally held,

> To conclude we hold that the provisions of Part I would apply to all arbitrations and to all proceedings relating thereto. Where such arbitration is held in India the provisions of Part I would compulsory apply and parties are free to deviate only to the extent permitted by the derogable provisions of Part I. In cases of international commercial arbitrations held out of India provisions of Part I would apply unless the parties by agreement, express or implied, exclude all or any of its provisions. In that case the laws or rules chosen by the parties would prevail. Any provision, in Part I, which is contrary to or excluded by that law or rules will not apply.[14]

The Supreme Court, in holding so, overruled several decisions given by the High Courts of Orissa, Bombay, Madras, Delhi, and Calcutta, wherein the respective courts had held that Part I of the Act would apply only to arbitrations held in India. The Supreme Court reasoned its position in the following words,

> Such an interpretation does not lead to any conflict between any of the provisions of the said Act. On this interpretation there is no lacunae in the said Act. This interpretation also does not leave a party remediless. Thus such an interpretation has to be preferred to the one adopted by the High Courts of Orissa, Bombay, Madras, Delhi and Calcutta. It will therefore have to be held that the contrary view taken by these High Courts is not good law.[15]

Whatever the intention of the Supreme Court might have been, the *Bhatia International* decision revealed an alarmingly interventionist stand on the part of the Indian judiciary.[16] The ratio of the case railed against the very objectives of the Act, which was to provide fast, efficient, and predictable remedy to the business community in case of disputes.[17] The Supreme Court's decision to exercise jurisdiction in matters of ICAs held out of India also defeated the underlying principles of arbitration per se. Arbitration being an alternate remedy, interference by the courts should be kept at a minimal. The *Bhatia* judgment derogated from this principle and caused much angst to the business community.

Venture Global (SC)

The *Bhatia International* ratio regarding the applicability of Part I to ICAs held out of India was followed by the Supreme Court in the *Venture Global* case. In this case, applicability of Section 34 of the Act to foreign awards came under dispute before the court. The Apex Court relying on its judgment in *Bhatia* case held that all provisions of Part I including Section 34 would apply to ICAs held out of India unless the parties agree, either expressly or impliedly, to the contrary. The Apex Court underlined the reasoning behind its decision in the following words:

> In any event, to apply Section 34 to foreign international awards would not be inconsistent with Section 48 of the Act, or any other

provision of Part II as a situation may arise, where, even in respect of properties situate in India and where an award would be invalid if opposed to the public policy of India, merely because the judgment-debtor resides abroad, the award can be enforced against properties in India through personal compliance of the judgment-debtor and by holding out the threat of contempt as is being sought to be done in the present case. In such an event, the judgment-debtor cannot be deprived of his right under Section 34 to invoke the public policy of India, to set aside the award.[18]

Inventa Fischer (Bombay HC)

The issue of applicability of Section 34 to foreign awards also came up for consideration before the Bombay High Court in the matter of *Inventa Fischer GmbH and Co. v. Polygenta Technologies Ltd.*[19] The court extensively discussed the ratio laid down in *Bhatia International* and held that the challenge procedure provided under Section 34 of the Act would not be available against foreign awards. The court quoted *Bhatia International* to arrive at its ratio, 'To the extent that Part II provides a separate definition for enforcement of foreign awards, the provisions in Part I dealing with these aspects will not apply to such foreign awards'.[20]

The court, after considering the scheme of the Act and submissions put before it, held the contention that Section 34 would be attracted to a challenge against foreign award is not acceptable. The court observed that the scheme of the Act does not make remedy available under Section 34 to foreign awards. In the words of the court, 'The scheme of Arbitration Act appears to be to make the remedy for challenging an Arbitral Award provided by Section 34 available only against a domestic award made under the provisions of Part I of the Arbitration Act.'[21] However, this decision was overruled by the Supreme Court in *Venture Global* case discussed earlier.

INDTEL Technical Services (SC)

The ratio laid down in *Bhatia International* case was further entrenched by Supreme Court in its decision in *INDTEL Technical Services Pvt. Ltd. v. W.S. Atkins PLC.*[22] The appellant applied for the appointment of sole arbitrator under Section 11 of the Act. As per the facts of the case, the agreement provided that proper law of contract was to be the English law. The relevant arbitration clauses, however, were silent on proper law of arbitration agreement, seat and venue of the arbitration, and the curial law applicable to arbitral proceedings.

The respondents placed reliance upon the decision of this court in *National Thermal Power Corporation v. Singer Company & Anr*[23] wherein it was held that when an arbitration agreement is silent as to the law and procedure to be followed in implementing the arbitration agreement, the law governing the said agreement would ordinarily be the same as the law governing the contract itself. The court, however, distinguished the *NTPC* judgment and chose to apply the ratio laid down in *Bhatia International*. The court applied the *Bhatia* ratio to the facts of the case and held that applicability of Part I of the Act had not been excluded by the parties, either expressly or impliedly. Since there was no exclusion of Part I, the Supreme Court had the authority to appoint the sole arbitrator under Section 11(9) of the Act.

Sara International (Delhi HC)

There have also been decisions where the courts in India have given effect to the common law position that in the absence of an agreement to the contrary, curial law would be the law of the seat of arbitration. The Delhi High Court decision in *Sara International Ltd. v. Arab Shipping Co.(P)Ltd.*[24] is a case in point. As per the facts of this case, the parties had agreed that the arbitration will be held in Mumbai and English law would be applicable. The court considered the jurisprudence surrounding the seat of arbitration, proper law of contract, proper law of arbitration agreement, and the curial law. It also discussed English case laws and academic literature on this matter and held that,

> In view of the above discussion, the Court is of the opinion that the claimant's contention about applicability of English law as the proper or governing law for the arbitration agreement cannot be accepted. The discussion in Bhatia International and subsequent judgments and Mustill & Boyd clearly show that if the seat of the arbitration is in a different country than the laws of one, which govern the contract, the

proper law of the arbitration agreement and the curial law would be that of the former.[25]

Impact of *Bhatia* Ratio

The *Bhatia* ratio had vested an overarching power of interference in the Indian judiciary. This came to be exercised often, leading to a corpus of conflicting case laws. There was widespread ambiguity and confusion about the status of law currently applicable. Needless to say, this affected the business culture of the country. Soon enough, the courts in India began to realize the perilous impact of the *Bhatia* decision on the sacrosanct principle underlying the arbitration process, that is, providing swift and predictable resolution of disputes thereby improving the ease of doing business in India. This came to be amply reflected in subsequent decisions of our Supreme Court and high courts.

The ratio laid down in *Bhatia International* was not overruled until the SC decision in *BALCO* case which came much later in 2012. Even so, the high courts and the Supreme Court chose not to apply the *Bhatia* ratio by taking the implied exclusion route propounded by *Bhatia International.*

Judicial Trend Away from *Bhatia* Ratio

Dozco India (SC)

The Supreme Court ruling in the *Dozco India P. Ltd. v. Doosan Infracore Co. Ltd*[26] is one such case where the Apex Court chose the implied exclusion route to deviate from the ratio laid down in *Bhatia International.* The question that came before this court was regarding the appointment of arbitrators under Section 11(6) of the Act. The main issue was whether or not the Supreme Court had the jurisdiction to decide this matter. The court quoted the relevant arbitration clauses from the agreement and observed that the correct law in this regard has been discussed in *Mustill and Boyd.* The relevant paragraph from *Mustill and Boyd* that according to the court was extremely important for this particular case, is quoted as follows:

> In the absence of express agreement, there is a strong prima facie presumption that the parties intend the curial law to be the law of the

'seat' of the arbitration, i.e. the place at which the arbitration is to be conducted, on the ground that that is the country most closely connected with the proceedings. So in order to determine the curial law in the absence of an express choice by the parties it is first necessary to determine the seat of the arbitration, by construing the agreement to arbitrate.[27]

It was therefore important for the court to decide the seat of arbitration. The court interpreted the relevant arbitration clauses and arrived at a conclusion that the parties meant the seat of arbitration to be in Seoul, South Korea. The court then went into the difference between seat and venue of arbitration. It observed that the distinction between the seat and the venue of arbitration is a common feature of international arbitrations. There could only be one seat of arbitration. However, whatever may be the seat of the arbitration, the parties are free to hold meetings and arbitral hearings at a place(s) other than the designated seat. These other places are called venue(s) and decided as per the convenience of the parties. The arbitral proceedings may be held at these venues but the seat of arbitration remains the same.

The Apex Court held that from the language of the arbitration clause, it was clear that the parties intended to exclude the applicability of Part I of the Act. Hence, the ratio laid down by *Bhatia International* would not be applicable to the present case. The court therefore didn't have the requisite jurisdiction to appoint arbitrators under Section 11(6) of the Act.

Videocon Industries (SC)

The *Videocon Industries Limited v. Union of India (UOI)*[28] case was another matter where the Supreme Court chose the implied exclusion route and held that *Bhatia International* ratio would not apply. Again, the Court's jurisdiction to grant a (under Section 9 of the Act) interim relief was under dispute. In this particular case, the arbitration agreement contained a non-obstante clause which said that the arbitration agreement shall be governed by the laws of England. The Court held that this amounted to implied exclusion of Part I and hence, it did not have the jurisdiction to grant a relief under Section 9 of the Act.

Yograj Infrastructure (SC)

In *Yograj Infrastructure Ltd. v. SSANGYONG Engineering and Construction Company Ltd.*,[29] the matter concerned an appeal before the Court, under Section 37, for setting aside of a foreign award by an arbitral tribunal in Singapore. The Supreme Court, upholding the rulings by Courts below, held that since 'the parties had specifically agreed that the arbitration proceedings would be conducted in accordance with the SIAC Rules, which includes Rule 32, the decision in *Bhatia International*, and the subsequent decisions on the same lines, would no longer apply in the instant case'.[30]

BALCO (SC)

Perhaps the most widely discussed verdict on this issue was delivered by the Supreme Court in *Bharat Aluminium Company v. Kaiser Aluminium Technical Services Inc.*[31] It was also the most welcomed. The Apex Court extensively discussed the contentious issue of applicability of Part I to ICAs held out of India. It traced the development of the Act and noted that it was based on the UNCITRAL model law. It observed that, like UNCITRAL model law, the Act too has given effect to the territoriality principle. The Act, by adopting the territorial principle of UNCITRAL law, has limited the applicability of Part I to arbitrations that take place in India.

On the issue of absence of the word 'only' from Section 2(2) of the Act, the Court observed that the Indian Legislature adopted the model law with some changes. In light of those changes, the inclusion of the word 'only' in the Act would have been superfluous. Hence, the *Bhatia* argument that omission of the word 'only' would show that the territoriality principle was not adopted by the Act and was denied by the Court. In the words of the Court, 'The absence of the word 'only' which is found in Article 1(2) of the Model Law, from Section 2(2) of the Arbitration Act, 1996 does not change the content/import of Section 2(2) as limiting the application of Part I of the Arbitration Act, 1996 to arbitrations where the place/seat is in India.'[32]

The Court further elaborated upon its argument that the strict territoriality principle had been firmly embedded in the Act by placing reliance upon the scheme of the Act and ruled that 'Section 2(2) is an express parliamentary declaration/recognition that Part I of the Arbitration Act, 1996 applies to arbitration having their place/seat in India and does not apply to arbitrations seated in foreign territories'.[33]

The Court also highlights the distinction between seat and venue in the context of Section 20(3) of the Act. The said section allows parties to hold arbitral meetings, proceedings, and hearings at any place. The Apex Court observes that in an ICA seated in India, parties may, by mutual agreement, hold arbitral proceedings outside India. This, however, would not have the effect of changing the seat of arbitration, which would continue to remain in India.

The Court then envisages a scenario where the arbitration agreement designates a foreign seat and also selects the Act as the curial law governing the conduct of arbitral proceedings. In such a scenario, the Court opines,

> It would be matter of construction of the individual agreement to decide whether:
> 1. The designated foreign 'seat' would be read as in fact only providing for a 'venue'/'place' where the hearings would be held, in view of the choice of Arbitration Act, 1996 as being the curial law. OR
> 2. Whether the specific designation of a foreign seat, necessarily carrying with it the choice of that country's Arbitration/curial law, would prevail over and subsume the conflicting selection choice by the parties of the Arbitration Act, 1996.[34]

The Court, having couched the complex issue in the above words, goes on to answer it:

> Only if the agreement of the parties is construed to provide for the 'seat'/'place' of Arbitration being in India, would Part I of the Arbitration Act, 1996 be applicable. If the agreement is held to provide for a 'seat'/'place' outside India, Part I would be inapplicable to the extent inconsistent with the arbitration law of the seat, even if the agreement purports to provide that the Arbitration Act, 1996 shall govern the arbitration proceedings.[35]

Further elaborating on this point, the Court observes that even where the arbitration agreement contains a provision that the Arbitration Act, 1996 would govern the arbitral proceedings, if upon construction, the seat of arbitration is held to be outside India, Part I would remain inapplicable, and Indian Courts wouldn't have supervisory jurisdiction over arbitration or award. However, the Court also observed that, in the above situation, it would only mean that 'the parties have contractually imported from the Arbitration Act, 1996, those provisions which are concerned with the internal conduct of their arbitration and which are not inconsistent with the mandatory provisions of the English Procedural Law/Curial Law. This necessarily follows from the fact that Part I applies only to arbitrations having their seat/place in India'.[36]

The Court, while considering the matter of applicability of Part II, reiterates its position that Part I and Part II of the Act are segregated and there is no overlap whatsoever between the two parts. It is for this reason that provisions of Part I would not be applicable to foreign awards defined under Section 44 of Part II. The Court reasoned that if provisions of two parts were allowed to overlap, it would lead to distortion of the scheme of the Act.

On the question of availability of interim awards/reliefs under Section 9 of the Act, the Court ruled that since Section 9 is schematically placed in Part I of the Act, it cannot be granted a special status. Quoting the words of the Court, 'On a logical and schematic construction of the Arbitration Act, 1996, the Indian Courts do not have the power to grant interim measures when the seat of arbitration is outside India'.[37]

The Court further reasoned that by extending the applicability of Section 9 to arbitrations seated outside India, it would be dilapidating/sabotaging the territoriality principle adopted and declared by Section 2(2) of the Act. The Apex Court finally concludes saying that Part I of the Act would apply only to arbitrations which take place within the territory of India. In its concluding remarks, the Court rules that the law so declared by it 'shall apply prospectively, to all the arbitration agreements executed hereafter'.[38]

Enercon (India) (SC)

In *Enercon (India) Ltd. and Ors. v. Enercon GMBH and Anr*,[39] the Supreme Court once again considered a matter involving seat, venue, and curial law. The Court, before ruling on the issues before it, culled out the correct applicable principle from English Court decisions: 'Where the parties have failed to choose the law governing the arbitration proceedings, those proceedings must be considered, at any rate prima facie, as being governed by the law of the country in which the arbitration is held, on the ground that it is the country most closely connected with the proceedings.'[40]

The Apex Court further elaborates upon the above principle in the following words, 'It is correct that, in virtually all jurisdictions, it is an accepted proposition of law that the seat normally carries with it the choice of that country's arbitration/Curial law. But this would arise only if the Curial law is not specifically chosen by the parties.'[41]

The Court also highlights the difference between seat and venue and reiterates the observations made by it in the *BALCO* case:

> In the present case, even though the venue of arbitration proceedings has been fixed in London, it cannot be presumed that the parties have intended the seat to be also in London. In an International Commercial Arbitration, venue can often be different from the seat of arbitration. In such circumstances, the hearing of the arbitration will be conducted at the venue fixed by the parties, but this would not bring about a change in the seat of the arbitration.[42]

Once, upon construction of the arbitration agreement, it is found that the seat of arbitration is in India, the Courts in India would be vested with the exclusive supervisory jurisdiction over the arbitration. To quote the words of the Court on this point, 'The choice of seat also has the effect of conferring exclusive jurisdiction to the Courts wherein the seat is situated'.[43]

Reliance Industries (SC)

In *Reliance Industries Limited and Anr. v. Union of India (UOI)*,[44] the Supreme Court once again addressed the issue of exclusion of Part I in a matter concerning a (under Section 34) challenge to an arbitral award. The Apex Court, after construing the agreement, arrived at a conclusion that while the proper law of contract was Indian Law, proper law of arbitration agreement itself was English Law. The court also observed that relevant arbitration clauses provided specifically that English Law would govern the arbitral proceedings. Applying the *Bhatia* ratio, the Apex Court held that in this instance, the parties had excluded the applicability of Part I. The Court after construing the relevant provisions of the arbitration agreement came to a conclusion that the parties meant the seat to be in London. Therefore, as per the ratio laid down in *Videocon Industries*, the law of the seat of arbitration agreement would be the lex arbitri.

Harmony Innovation (SC)

In *Harmony Innovation Shipping Ltd. v. Gupta Coal India Ltd. and Ors*,[45] the Supreme Court once again considered a matter concerning its jurisdiction to decide matters under Sections 9, 11, and 34 of the Act. The Apex Court following the ratio laid down in *Videocon* and *Reliance* cases held that the parties had excluded the applicability of Part I of the Act.

Pricol v. Johnson Controls (SC)

In the case of *Pricol v. Johnson Controls*,[46] the Supreme Court of India declined to intervene in an international arbitration with the SIAC (Singapore International Arbitration Centre) as appointing authority, upholding the parties chosen mechanism in a decision which was marked by a degree of judicial deference towards the arbitral process.

Eitzen Bulk (SC)

In *Eitzen Bulk A/S and Ors. v. Ashapura Minechem Ltd. and Ors*,[47] the Supreme Court, after considering the facts before it, observed that two factors had excluded the applicability of Part I. The first factor being the seat of arbitration, which was in London. The second factor that contributed to the exclusion was a clause in the arbitration agreement that English law would apply. The Apex Court after applying the ratio laid down by it in the *Videocon* and *Reliance* cases, discussed above, held that there was an exclusion of Part I of the Act.

Imax Corporation (SC)

In the matter of *IMAX Corporation v. E-City Entertainment (I) Pvt Ltd*,[48] the Supreme Court considered choice of ICC Rules by the

parties, and the consequent choice of foreign seat by ICC in consultation with parties, to operate as a clear case of exclusion of Part-I of
the Act. With respect to absence of choice of seat, the Supreme Court
noted that the parties had merely chosen institutional arbitration rules,
while not choosing the seat. However, in the next stroke of furthering
party autonomy, it recognized that the parties were presumably aware
that the ICC Rules contained provisions to fix a seat of arbitration.
This power of arbitral institutions to fix a seat, employed after due
consultation and agreement of the parties, has been upheld by the
Supreme Court as a valid and binding choice of seat by and upon
the parties. The Supreme Court duly noted that the choice of ICC
Rules demonstrated willingness of the parties to choose a seat outside India. This was recognized as an exclusion of Part I of the Act,
consequently ousting the jurisdiction of Indian courts. Needless to
mention, the choice of London as a seat attracted English law as the
curial law for conduct of the arbitration proceedings.

Indus Mobile (SC)

The most recent pronouncement by the apex Court regarding the
interplay between seat and place of arbitration came in the case of
*Indus Mobile Distribution Pvt. Ltd. v. Datawind Innovations Pvt. Ltd.
and Ors.*,[49] wherein the Court discussed the BALCO, Enercon, and
Reliance judgments and read them together with the amendments to
the Act pursuant to the Law Commission Report. The primary issue
before the Court was the effect of an exclusive jurisdiction clause on
the seat of arbitration. The Court observed that

> A conspectus of all the aforesaid provisions shows that the moment the
> seat is designated, it is akin to an exclusive jurisdiction clause. Under
> the Law of Arbitration, unlike the Code of Civil Procedure which
> applies to suits filed in courts, a reference to 'seat' is a concept by which
> a neutral venue can be chosen by the parties to an arbitration clause.
> The neutral venue may not in the classical sense have jurisdiction—
> that is, no part of the cause of action may have arisen at the neutral
> venue and neither would any of the provisions of Section 16
> to 21 of the CPC be attracted. In arbitration law however, as has been
> held above, the moment 'seat' is determined, the fact that the seat is
> at Mumbai would vest Mumbai courts with exclusive jurisdiction for

purposes of regulating arbitral proceedings arising out of the agreement between the Parties. It is well settled that where more than one court has jurisdiction, it is open for parties to exclude all other courts.

Law Commission Recommendations and Amendment Act

The Law Commission of India by its 246th report[50] focused on the amendments required to the Act. One of the issues it noted was with the 'gaps' which were left with the Supreme Court's decision in *BALCO*. As many noted when the decision came out, the effect of *BALCO* is that where the assets of a party are in India and the arbitration is seated outside India, the court's refusal to exercise jurisdiction under Section 9 may leave the party with no adequate avenue for interim relief. The Law Commission recommended that the courts should have power to issue interim relief in cases where the award is likely to be enforced in India.

The court's power in India to issue interim relief has been slightly controversial in the past. The Law Commission suggested limit on the court's power to issue interim relief and recommended that once the arbitral tribunal is constituted, courts should not ordinarily entertain an application for interim relief. In such cases, the parties should approach the arbitral tribunal to seek interim relief. The Law Commission strengthened the tribunal's authority to issue interim relief by providing for effective enforcement of the tribunal's interim orders as if they were orders of the court, providing 'teeth to the interim order of the arbitral tribunal'.

The Amendment Act specifically recognizes that parties to a foreign-seated arbitration can seek the assistance of Indian courts for interim protection and for obtaining evidence, unless they specifically exclude the jurisdiction of the Indian courts to provide such assistance. The Amendment Act however limits the Indian Courts ability to provide such assistance to cases where the seat of arbitration is in a country which India recognizes in its official gazette as being a reciprocating territory for the purposes of the Act.

***

The judicial trend post *Bhatia*, as far as international arbitrations held out of India are concerned, showed a preference for interference on the part of Indian courts. This is amply evident from the judgments of Indian courts in *Venture Global, Inventa Fischer, Indtel,* and *Sara International.* This clearly had an adverse impact on the business environment prevailing in the country. It also railed against the underlying principles of arbitration as a method of speedy resolution of disputes. However, the courts soon realized their folly and made a course correction starting with their judgment in *Dozco* case. The Supreme Court instead of overruling the *Bhatia* case used its ratio to devise an implied exclusion route. The Apex Court also widened the ambit of this implied exclusion route sufficiently enough to cover all fact scenarios where an ICA was held out of India. However, the position soon changed with the Supreme Court judgment in the *BALCO* case, where the court expressly overruled its *Bhatia* decision. The *BALCO* decision, however, had only prospective applicability. The *Bhatia* ratio continued to operate for cases where the arbitration agreement had been executed before 6 September 2012. However, the judicial trend of following the implied exclusion route continued. Even in the post *BALCO* era, the Apex Court, while conceding that *Bhatia* ratio was applicable, followed the judicial trend of taking the implied exclusion route to exclude the applicability of Part I.

The recent Amendment Act changes everything, as it makes Sections 9, 27, 37(1)(a), and 37(3) applicable to international commercial arbitrations held out of India. The Amendment Act, however, allows the parties to exclude the applicability of Part I, in general, and these provisions, in particular, by mutual agreement. There is still some uncertainty over the applicability of the Amendment Act. The judicial response to agreements entered in the post-Amendment era remains to be seen.

As a suggestion, the authors would like to leave the reader with a model arbitration clause:

1. Any dispute arising out of or in connection with this [*agreement/ contract*], including any question regarding its existence, validity or termination, shall be referred to and finally resolved by arbitration seated in [•] in accordance with the Arbitration Rules of the [•] for the time being in force, which rules are deemed to be incorporated by reference in this clause.
2. The arbitral tribunal shall consist of [*an odd number, either one or three*] arbitrator(s) to be appointed by [•].

3. The language of the arbitration shall be [•].
4. For the avoidance of doubt, the arbitral tribunal may decide to convene its meetings at any other location either for convenience or for taking evidence, and so on, without affecting the agreed seat of arbitration as set out in sub-clause (1) above.
5. The provisions of Part I of the [Indian] Arbitration and Conciliation Act 1996, including Sections 9, 27, 37(1)(a), and 37(3) shall [apply/ not apply] to the arbitration/s under this clause [•].

Notes and References

1. Gary Born, *International Arbitration: Cases and Materials* (Wolters Kluwer, 2011), 535.
2. The Arbitration and Conciliation (Amendment) Act, 2015.
3. The Arbitration and Conciliation Act, 1996.
4. (2012) 9 SCC 552.
5. (2002) 4 SCC 105.
6. (2008) 4 SCC 190.
7. (1998) 1 SCC 305.
8. (1988) 1 Lloyds Law Report 116.
9. (1988) 1 Lloyds Law Report 9.
10. (1988) 1 Lloyds Law Report 9.
11. (1988) 1 Lloyds Law Report 9.
12. (1988) 1 Lloyds Law Report 9.
13. (2002) 4 SCC 105.
14. (2002) 4 SCC 105.
15. (2002) 4 SCC 105.
16. Sumeet Lall, Harsh Pratap, and Sagar Divekar, 'India: The Supreme Court of India Overrules Bhatia International and Venture Global', available http://www.mondaq.com/india/x/205912/The+Supreme+Court+Of+India+Overrules+Bhatia+International+And+Venture+Global accessed 4 July 2016.
17. Lall, Pratap, and Divekar, 'India'.
18. (2008) 4 SCC 190.
19. 2005 (2) Bom C.R. 364.
20. 2005 (2) Bom C.R. 364.
21. 2005 (2) Bom C.R. 364.
22. 2008 (10) SCC 308.
23. 1992 (3) SCC 551.

24. (2009) 3 Arb LR 81.
25. (2009) 3 Arb LR 81.
26. (2011) 6 SCC 179.
27. (2011) 6 SCC 179.
28. (2011) 6 SCC 161.
29. (2012) 12 SCC 359.
30. (2012) 12 SCC 359.
31. (2012) 9 SCC 552.
32. (2012) 9 SCC 552.
33. (2012) 9 SCC 552.
34. (2012) 9 SCC 552.
35. (2012) 9 SCC 552.
36. (2012) 9 SCC 552.
37. (2012) 9 SCC 552.
38. (2012) 9 SCC 552.
39. (2014) 5 SCC 1.
40. (2014) 5 SCC 1.
41. (2014) 5 SCC 1.
42. (2014) 5 SCC 1.
43. (2014) 5 SCC 1.
44. (2014) 7 SCC 603.
45. (2015) 9 SCC 172.
46. Arbitration Case (Civil) No. 30 of 2014.
47. 2016 SCC OnLine SC 523.
48. AIR 2017 SC 1372.
49. AIR 2017 SC 2105.
50. Available http://lawcommissionofindia.nic.in/reports/Report246.pdf.

14

Introduction to Investment Arbitration

A Perspective from India

Shreyas Jayasimha and *Radha Raghavan**

The first Bilateral Investment Treaty (BIT) was signed between Germany and Pakistan in 1959[1] and contained dispute resolution provisions only between states.[2] This epoch witnessed decolonization and the advent of the World War, represented by the coming together of two major geopolitical formations in the Western world.[3] The first BIT that incorporated Investor State Dispute Settlement (ISDS) mechanism was the Netherlands–Indonesia BIT (1968)[4] and the first BIT that included ISDS with unqualified consent to ISDS was the Chad–Italy BIT in 1969.[5]

* The authors are immensely grateful for the valuable inputs received from Chester M. Brown, Professor, International Law and International Arbitration, Sydney Law School, The University of Sydney, and to Swati Tata and Pinaz Mehta for their assistance in the research and editing of this chapter.

ISDS is an international law mechanism through which foreign investors seek redressal of investment treaty rights violation by the host state. BITs, with ISDS, are perceived to be important tools in encouraging the influx of foreign investment.[6] They have gained significant support and encouragement from global economic institutions such as the Organisation for Economic Co-operation and Development (OECD) and the United Nations Conference on Trade and Development (UNCTAD) as it is believed that BITs spur an increase in FDI by providing investor security, in particular, for developing countries. However, there have also been critics who have queried the link between BITs and increased investment.[7]

By the end of 2016, the International Investment Agreement (IIA) network consisted of 3,324 treaties,[8] including 2,957 BITs and 367 treaties with investment protection clauses like Free Trade Agreements (FTA), Comprehensive Economic Partnership Agreements (CEPA), Comprehensive Economic and Trade Agreement (CETA) and Comprehensive Economic Cooperation Agreements (CECA).

There have been innumerable endeavours to deal with investment at the multilateral level. The 1994 World Trade Organization (WTO) agreements that resulted from the 1986–94 Uruguay Round negotiations, in particular, the General Agreement on Trade in Services (GATS) and the Agreement on Trade Related Investment Measures (TRIMs), cover important aspects of investment. It was expansively discussed by the OECD at the multilateral agreement on investment (MAI) negotiations in May 1995. However, the negotiations broke down in 1997 and have not been resumed since. In 1996, at the Singapore Ministerial Conference, WTO member-countries decided to set up three new working groups, including one on investment. This was included in the Doha Development Agenda in 2001 and later dropped due to opposition from developing countries in the 2003 Ministerial Conference in Cancún, Mexico.[9] Presently, the major multilateral treaties in Asia protecting investments[10] are the Asia Pacific Economic Cooperation (APEC), Trans-Pacific Partnership (TPP), the 1987 ASEAN Agreement for the Promotion and Protection of Investments, (1987 ASEAN Agreement), and the ASEAN Comprehensive Investment Agreement, 2009 (2009 ASEAN Framework Agreement).

The global IIA regime, according to the UNCTAD Investment Report 2015,[11] has moved from an era of infancy (1950–64) to an era of dichotomy (1965–89), to an era of proliferation (1990–2007) and is now in the era of reorientation (2008–today).[12] Asian countries did not actively participate in the IIA regime till the era of dichotomy. However, India and China stayed away from BITs till much later. In fact, India signed its first BIT (also known as Bilateral Investment Protection Agreement, or BIPA) only in 1994 with the United Kingdom, and China in 1982 with Sweden.

ISDS Regimes

Investment arbitrations are conducted either on an ad hoc (non-administered) basis or through established arbitral institutions (like the International Centre for Settlement of Investment Disputes (ICSID). Appointment of the Permanent Court of Arbitration as the arbitral institution while adopting the UNCITRAL rules to govern the arbitral process has been a recurring trend.[13]

ICSID Regime

ICSID, established by the Convention on the Settlement of Investment Disputes between States and Nationals of Other States (ICSID Convention), provides facilities for arbitration and conciliation of investment disputes between contracting states and nationals of other contracting states.[14]

The executive directors of the International Bank for Reconstruction and Development (World Bank) formulated the convention and submitted it to the World Bank members for their consideration, signature, and ratification.[15] With 20 countries ratifying it, the convention came into force on 14 October 1966. Currently, 161 states have signed the convention and 153 states have ratified it.[16] Presently, India is not a signatory to the ICSID convention.

The ICSID Convention is accompanied by rules and regulations adopted by the Administrative Council of the Centre pursuant to Article 6(1)(a)–(c) of the Convention (the ICSID Regulations and Rules). The ICSID Regulations and Rules (last amended in April 2006) comprise Administrative and Financial Regulations, Rules of Procedure for the Institution of Conciliation and Arbitration Proceedings (Institution Rules), Rules of Procedure for Conciliation

Proceedings (Conciliation Rules), and Rules of Procedure for Arbitration Proceedings (Arbitration Rules).

UNCITRAL Regime

The United Nations Commission on International Trade Law (UNCITRAL) was established by the United Nations General Assembly by Resolution 2205 (XXI) on 17 December 1966 to promote areas of commercial law inter alia dispute resolution, insolvency, and sale of goods.[17] It prepares legislative and non-legislative guidance documents in these areas of law.[18]

In the area of international arbitration, the UNCITRAL has prepared a set of rules that guide arbitration procedure which is used in both ad hoc and institutional arbitrations. The UNCITRAL arbitration rules have turned out to be the second most popular choice of arbitration rules for investment arbitrations, with the ICSID rules being the most popular.[19] The rules provide guidelines with respect to appointment of arbitrators, conduct of arbitral proceedings and effect, and interpretation of awards.[20]

The UNCITRAL has three versions of the arbitration rules. They are (a) UNCITRAL Arbitration Rules, 1976; (b) the UNCITRAL Arbitration Rules, 2010; and (c) UNCITRAL Arbitration Rules 2010 (modified slightly in 2013) incorporating the UNCITRAL Rules on Transparency for Treaty Based Investor-State Arbitration.[21] The UNCITRAL Transparency Rules aim to bring about a transparent regime in international investment arbitration process and can be adopted along with either the UNCITRAL Arbitration Rules or any other arbitration rules.

Other Arbitral Institutions

The other arbitral institutions that administer investment treaty arbitrations are Arbitral Institute of the Stockholm Chamber of Commerce (SCC), International Chamber of Commerce (ICC), London Court of International Arbitration (LCIA), Moscow Chamber of Commerce and Industry (MCCI), Permanent Court of Arbitration (PCA), and the Cairo Regional Centre for International Commercial Arbitration (CRCICA). All these institutions have their own arbitration rules. LCIA adopted a revised set of arbitration rules in 2014. UNCTAD reports that LCIA, having administered a total of four investment treaty arbitrations, has concluded only one arbitration under its own rules[22] and the other under UNCITRAL rules. The PCA, having administered a total of 83 investment arbitrations till 2015, has not used its own rules in any investment arbitration.[23] The Singapore International Arbitration Centre (SIAC) has recently taken steps towards adopting arbitration rules specifically for investment arbitrations. Having released the draft SIAC Investment Arbitration Rules in early 2016 for public consultation, they came into effect on 1 January 2017.[24]

Development of ISDS

While the first publicly known arbitration under the ICSID Convention was the *Holiday Inns S.A v. Morocco*[25] in 1972, the first ICSID BIT Arbitration was *Asian Agricultural Products Ltd. v. Democratic Socialist Republic of Sri Lanka* in 1990.[26] However, it was not until the late 1990s that ISDS was invoked by many investors. With the arrival of the North American Free Trade Agreement (NAFTA) in 1994, investors began to realize the underlying power of investment treaties and the ISDS mechanism.[27] Nevertheless, it was Argentina's State 'reforms' in response to the 2001 economic and political crisis that brought BITs to the fore with the invocation of almost 40 bilateral investment treaty claims against Argentina.[28] In 1997, there were 19 known ISDS cases, by 2010 there were over 390 cases[29] and today, the number stands at 767 publicly known cases.[30] It is said that, since the beginning of 2015, almost one new ISDS case is filed per week.[31]

According to the UNCTAD Investment Report 2017,[32] the most frequently invoked IIA has been the Energy Charter Treaty (ECT), followed by the North American Free Trade Agreement (NAFTA). Among the BITs, the Argentina–United States BIT has been most frequently relied upon by foreign investors.[33] A majority of investment arbitrations in 2016 were brought under the Energy Charter Treaty, NAFTA, and the Russian Federation–UK BIT.[34] Argentina has been a respondent state in the maximum number (59) of investment arbitrations.[35] India has been a respondent state in 21 investment arbitrations of which some are ongoing, settled, or decided.[36]

Rights under a Bilateral Investment Treaty

Protection against Expropriation

An important protection granted under a BIT is protection of foreign investment against expropriation. Expropriation is a bundle of rights which balances the interest of both the host state and the investor. The sovereign right of the host government under international law to take property of a domestic and foreign investor for social, economic, political, and other reasons is recognized. Following are important considerations in determining the legality of expropriation:

1. Whether the property has been taken for a public purpose
2. Whether the acquisition was non-discriminatory
3. Whether the acquisition was in accordance with due process

The availability of compensation and duties of mitigation may also be pertinent. Expropriation is divided into multiple kinds based on the nature of the taking—direct, indirect, creeping, de facto, or a measure tantamount to expropriation.[37] Broadly, expropriation can be grouped into indirect and direct expropriation.

Direct and Indirect Expropriation

Direct expropriation is the physical seizure of property. It is also said to occur where 'the use or enjoyment of benefits related thereto is exacted or interfered with to a similar extent even where legal ownership over the assets in question is not affected, and so long as the deprivation is not temporary'.[38]

On the other hand, indirect expropriation is a result of 'the measures taken by governments which interfere with the right to the property or diminish the value of the property'.[39] The Iran–US Claims Tribunal in the *Starrett Housing* case defined indirect expropriation as follows: 'measures taken by a State can interfere with property rights to such an extent that these rights are rendered so useless that they must be deemed to have been expropriated, even though the State does not purport to have expropriated them and the legal title to the property formally remains with the original owner'.[40]

In distinguishing direct and indirect expropriation, the *Feldman* Tribunal noted that the recognition of direct expropriation, such as governmental taking over of a mine or factory or depriving the investor of all meaningful benefits of ownership and control, is easier as compared to recognition of an indirect expropriation, where governmental action interferes with broadly defined property rights and crosses the line between a valid regulation to a compensable taking.[41]

In the event of finding expropriation, the next important component of this concept that the tribunals turn to is the quantum of compensation. The quantum of compensation to be paid is calculated using various methods such as the discounted cash flow method and the net book value method. However, the legal principle behind the obligation to pay compensation is formulated differently in various BITs. While some BITs require that 'Just Compensation'[42] be the standard of compensation, other BITs refer to formulations such as 'Real Value Compensation',[43] 'Fair Market Value',[44] and Genuine Value[45] standard of compensation.[46]

Fair and Equitable Treatment

Fair and equitable treatment (FET) has emerged as one of the most important and widely invoked standard in international investment arbitration.

FET is not a new concept. One can find its genesis in the early international economic agreements such as the Havana Charter for an International Trade Organization (1948); the Economic Agreement of Bogotá (1948); and the United States Friendship, Commerce, and Navigation (FCN) treaties.[47]

What Is FET?

The obligation of fair and equitable treatment lies on the host state, imposing on it an obligation to treat the foreign investors 'fairly' and 'equitably'. A model clause, adopted in several multilateral agreements, can be found in The Draft OECD MAI, 1998, which stipulates, 'Each contracting party shall accord fair and equitable treatment and full and constant protection and security to foreign investments in their territory. In no case shall a Contracting Party accord treatment less favourable than that required by international law'.[48] With the growth of investment treaty law, the bounds of 'fair' and 'equitable' has grown to be significantly broad. The deprivation of this protection is very often raised as an issue in ISDS. It is interpreted by the tribunal based on several factors including facts of the case,[49] language of the clause in the relevant BIT, and prior broad standards set by the tribunal. FET may be incorporated into a BIT either as 'fair and equitable treatment', or 'just and equitable treatment', or 'equitable treatment'.

Scope of FET: As Defined by Different Tribunals

A summary of the scope of FET is succinctly discussed in UNCTAD's FET Series on international investment agreements quoted as follows:

1. Prohibition of manifest arbitrariness in decision-making, that is, measures taken purely on the basis of prejudice or bias, without a legitimate purpose or rational explanation;
2. Prohibition of the denial of justice and disregard of the fundamental principles of due process;
3. Prohibition of targeted discrimination on manifestly wrongful grounds, such as gender, race or religious belief;
4. Prohibition of abusive treatment of investors, including coercion, duress and harassment;
5. Protection of the legitimate expectations of investors arising from a government's specific representations or investment inducing measures although balanced with the host State's right to regulate in the public interest.[50]

It has been widely believed that the standard for determining FET is the 'international minimum standard'.[51] FET, like expropriation, is an absolute standard since it is not determined in comparison to any other standard, unlike that of National Treatment or Most Favoured Nation (MFN) protections.[52]

The *Mondev* tribunal, while setting yardsticks for the FET standard held that it may not be necessary for a state action to be in bad faith for it to be considered unfair or inequitable under the FET standard. In this regard, the tribunal stated that, 'To the modern eye, what is unfair or inequitable need not equate with the outrageous or egregious. In particular, a State may treat a foreign investment unfairly or inequitably without necessarily acting in bad faith'.[53]

On the question of 'legitimate expectations' of the investor as a component of FET, the *Saluka* tribunal, recognized that the standard of FET was closely tied to the notion of legitimate expectations. However, it also recognized the *SD Myers* tribunal's interpretation that 'the determination of a breach of the obligation of "fair and equitable treatment" by the host State must be made in the light of the high measure of deference that international law generally extends to the right of domestic authorities to regulate matters within their own borders'.[54] In doing so, the *Saluka* tribunal laid down the FET standard to be as follows: 'In order to determine whether frustration of the foreign investor's expectations was justified and reasonable, the host State's legitimate right subsequently to regulate domestic matters in the public interest must be taken into consideration as well'.

The tribunal in *Waste Management* summarized the FET standard discussed in SD Myers,[55] Mondev,[56] ADF,[57] and Loewen[58] as follows:

> Taken together, the S.D. Myers, Mondev, ADF and Loewen cases suggest that the minimum standard of treatment of fair and equitable treatment is infringed by conduct attributable to the State and harmful to the [investor] if the conduct is arbitrary, grossly unfair, unjust, or idiosyncratic, is discriminatory and exposes the [investor] to sectional or racial prejudice, or involves a lack of due process leading to an outcome which offends judicial propriety—as might be the case with a manifest failure of natural justice in judicial proceedings or a complete lack of transparency and candour in an administrative process. In applying this standard it is relevant that the treatment is in breach of representations made by the host State which were reasonably relied on by the [investor].[59]

However, despite several arbitral decisions interpreting FET, the exact standard is still unclear and evolving and it depends on the facts and circumstances of the case.[60]

Exclusion of FET

A few investment agreements have excluded FET from their text and placed reliance on national treatment for the protection of investments.

The Australia–Singapore FTA, 2003[61] and the India–Singapore CECA, 2005 are examples.[62] The reason for this exclusion is perceived to be the states' unwillingness to subject their regulatory decision making to the review of independent international arbitral tribunals.[63]

National Treatment and Most-Favoured Nation

National Treatment Clause

National treatment is a concept in international law which ensures that foreigners are given the same treatment as nationals. It is not a concept specific to investment treaties as it is used in all kinds of agreements from trade, to intellectual property, to investment.

The standard of national treatment is set on a comparative basis, which means that the standard of treatment to a foreigner is decided based on the standard of treatment meted out to nationals. This came to be known as the Calvo Doctrine and was accepted by many Latin American states. However, developed countries did not recognize this doctrine and asserted that in cases where the standard of treatment given to nationals is below customary international law, as recognized by the International Law Commission (ILC) Articles on State Responsibility, then the standard of treatment to be given to the foreigners must be the higher customary international law standard of treatment.

The wording of national treatment clauses has remained fairly consistent for many decades.[64] Some national treatment clauses include the phrase 'in like circumstances'. The objective of this insertion would be to ensure that the foreigner and national are on the same footing or 'in a like situation' before the State is obliged to accord them treatment which is equally favourable.[65]

An important question in national treatment that tribunals often face is the relevance of discriminatory intent on the part of the host state.[66] Ruling on this, the tribunal in *Siemens v. Argentina* held that intent was not a decisive or essential factor for a finding of discrimination, but what was essential was the impact of the measure on the investment.[67] However, several tribunals like those in *SD Myers*,[68] *Methanex*,[69] and *Genin* held that intent was a 'necessary prerequisite for a finding of discrimination'.[70] In any case, the burden of proving discrimination is on the claimants.[71]

Most-Favoured-Nation Clause

The most-favoured-nation clause is 'a treaty provision whereby a state undertakes an obligation towards another state to accord most-favoured-nation (MFN) treatment in an agreed sphere of relations'.[72] MFN treatment is guaranteed to the investor by the host state. It guarantees that an investor from one country would be treated the same way as it would treat an investor in another country. Thus, if a host state grants a level of protection to an investor from Country X which is higher than that granted to an investor from Country Y, then the investor from Country Y can invoke the MFN Clause in his BIT and avail the standards of treatment granted to investors from Country X. However, MFN may be invoked only if the underlying BIT grants the MFN protection.

As defined by the ILC draft articles on MFN clauses, 'Most-favoured nation treatment is a treatment accorded by the granting State to the beneficiary State, or to persons or things in a determined relationship with that State, not less favourable than treatment extended by the granting State or to a third State or to persons or things in the same relationship with that third State'. [73]

Other Rights under a BIT

A detailed analysis of all the rights under a BIT falls outside the scope of this article, but has been enlisted below for completeness. The other rights inter alia are: Full Protection and Security, recourse to State-to-State Dispute Settlement or ISDS in case of a dispute under the BIT, denial of benefits, capital transfers, and entry and sojourn of personnel in the host state.

Backlash against ISDS

There is a growing global backlash against the perceived exploitation of BITs by multinational corporations whereby national regulations are being circumvented, and developing countries are being harassed in the name of protection of foreign investors and their investments.

A significant cause for the backlash is the threat perceived by sovereign states in respect of interference by private tribunals with policy and regulatory measures adopted by governments in public interest. For instance, the Government of Australia issued the Gillard Government Trade Policy Statement in April 2011 announcing that it would no longer continue the inclusion of investor–state dispute resolution provisions in future trade agreements with developing countries.[74]

Europe's citizens also raised concerns over the proposed investment chapter in the Transatlantic Trade and Investment Partnership (TTIP) with the United States. Around 3.5 million Europeans campaigned against the TTIP, effectively stalling negotiation.[75] Massive protests and demonstrations across Europe forced authorities such as the French Government to suggest that they will not be supporting TTIP 'at this stage'.[76] One of the key arguments made by those in favour of the Brexit controversy is the prospect of avoiding the pitfalls of TTIP.

Indonesia has terminated over 60 BITs,[77] starting with the BIT it signed with the Netherlands, whilst expressing its displeasure over the 'new modus operandi of foreign investors using these treaties to threaten weak governments'.[78] From 1 January 2016 to 1 April 2017 itself, Indonesia terminated 11 treaties while India closely followed behind by terminating seven treaties.[79]

Authors like Mehmet Toral and Thomas Schultz have even questioned the assumption that BITs impose obligations only on States and not investors and have even suggested that states act as private parties in commercial contracts and therefore must be entitled to step into the shoes of a claimant.[80] Another concern arising out of this backlash against ISDS is that the current system serves only the interests of the lawyers and arbitrators, leading to a decline of faith in the fairness and efficiency of the system.[81]

However, strong and erudite responses have also been authored, defending the ISDS system in BITs, by authors such as Judge Stephen Schwebel, who have contended that 'the current approach of the EU to investor–State arbitration may be seen as questionable not only with respect to investor–State arbitration at large but in the singularities of its attempts to neuter investor–State treaties between Member States of the EU based on the dubious proposition that the levels of adjudication are the same throughout the Union'.[82]

India and BITs

India liberalized its economy in 1991, opening up most industries to foreign investment. Automatic approval of FDI up to 51 per cent in high priority industries, 100 per cent foreign equity in the energy sector and setting up of the Foreign Investment Promotion Board (FIPB) in order to act as a single window clearance for foreign investments were just some of the measures taken by the government in pursuance of its liberalization policy.[83] Further, India has signed bilateral investment protection and promotion agreements, FTAs with Singapore, Korea, Malaysia, and Japan and Trade in Services and Trade in Investment Agreement with the Association of the South East Asian Nations.[84] As an initiative to encourage foreign investment, the Government of India adopted the Make in India programme on 25 September 2014. The programme involves guiding the investors through the whole process including helping them identify areas of investment and expediting regulatory approvals, among others.[85]

The FDI inflows into India has over the years increased from $36 billion in FY 2013–14 to $45.1 billion in FY 2014–15 to $55.4 billion [86] in FY 2015–16. On the flip side, India also plays a significant role as a capital exporting country. In the year 2015–16, Indian investors made foreign investments to the tune of $ 7 billion.[87] India has signed BITs with 84 countries out of which 74 have come into force. It was only in the mid-1990s that BITs were initiated by the Government of India.[88] A look at various BITs to which India is a party will make it clear that each BIT is quite different from the other in its own way although there are many common features present.[89]

Watershed Events in India's History of Investment Treaty Arbitration

White Industries Australia Ltd. v. Republic of India[90]

In this landmark case, White Industries, an Australian investor, filed this investment treaty arbitration against the Government of India in order to enforce an ICC award passed in the investor's favour back in 2002. The investor had been trying to enforce the award for around ten years and was unable to do so. The investor claimed that long judicial delays in India were the cause of this enforcement delay.

Therefore, they used the MFN clause[91] under the India–Australia BIT to get the 'effective means' protection granted under the India–Kuwait BIT.[92] The tribunal found for the investor on the issue of long judicial delays stating that these delays amounted to a denial of effective means and thereby a denial of justice under the India–Australia BIT.[93] This case is important because it is the first case in which a BIT was effectively used against India.[94]

The Dabhol Case

Enron, through its subsidiary, entered into a power purchase agreement (PPA) with the Maharashtra State Electricity Board (MSEB) in India for the construction and operation of an electrical power plant, the Dabhol Power Project. The contract provided for dispute resolution through international arbitration. Enron was the majority shareholder in the Dabhol Power Corporation (DPC), with General Electric (GE) and Bechtel with 10 per cent stake each. In 1995, the Dabhol Power Project was cancelled by the government on grounds of lack of transparency, failure to take some clearances and high tariffs among others.

The PC and GE and Bechtel, the international sponsors of the project, commenced an international commercial arbitration proceeding against the Government of India, which was ultimately decided in favour of the investor. India successfully challenged this award in local courts. The PPA was renegotiated and once again disputes arose in the early 2000s. This time round, the cases were settled out of court with compensation of around $1 billion.[95] This project resulted in a large number of arbitration cases in many places, under multiple contracts and several bilateral investment treaties. The Indian courts collaborated in the effort by enjoining international arbitration of the disputes at the will of Indian government entities.[96]

Devas v. India[97]

Recently, Devas filed an investment treaty arbitration against the space research wing of Indian Space Research Organisation (ISRO) under the India–Mauritius BIT against the government's decision to cancel certain telecommunication contracts that it had previously granted.[98] Antrix, the commercial arm of ISRO, had entered into an agreement with Devas granting it the license to a specific frequency of satellite spectrum for the purpose of providing high-speed internet services. The agreement was terminated by Antrix, allegedly based on a decision of the Cabinet Committee on Security citing grounds of national and strategic purposes and India's essential security interests. Devas alleged that the termination was coloured with corruption at the hands of the Union government, based on a draft audit report of the Comptroller and Auditor General (CAG) which pointed out several serious financial irregularities and corruptive practices on part of the Indian government. The PCA tribunal seated in Hague has recently issued an award against India finding material breaches of the substantive provisions of the BIT. Though the award has not yet been made available in the public domain, it would be interesting to see how issues of alleged corruption have been analysed by an international investment tribunal.

IMFA v. Indonesia

Aside from being a receiver of foreign investment, India's role as a capital exporting country has also grown. Indian investors are now turning to BITs signed by India, to explore claims against the host state.[99] *IMFA v. Indonesia* is an illustration.[100] In this case, Indian investor Indian Metals and Ferro Alloys Ltd. has initiated an investment treaty arbitration against Indonesia in 2015 under the India–Indonesia BIT. The arbitration is conducted by PCA under the UNCITRAL Rules and is currently in progress.

Model BITs in India

India adopted its first model BIT in 1993. This was revised in 2003 and was called the 2003 Model BIT and further revised recently in 2015 and called the New Model BIT.

India's New Model BIT

The Government of India, with an aim to bolster the inflow of investment into the country, re-examined the existing Model BIT (2003 Model BIT) and adopted the New Model BIT in December

2015. The objective was to ensure that the country had a model BIT that instilled faith and reposed confidence in Indian and foreign investors while maintaining a balance between rights of the investors and government obligations.[101] It had to also examine it in light of the growing global criticism of the ISDS regime.[102] While some countries took measures such as denouncing ISDS, India aimed to find a middle ground which would protect both its investors and the State.[103] In light of this, the government, in April 2015, invited comments on the then-existing model BIT. The Law Commission of India in its 246th Report, dated August 2014, recognized risks to the international investment treaties due to gaps in the growing body of international investment law. Concurrently, the monetary penalty award in White Industries[104] and the receipt of numerous notices of arbitration under various BITs triggered a renewed focus on the country's BIT regime. There was also pressure from the civil society organizations, to review the regime.[105] All these events cumulatively led to the formation of a study committee to analyse and study the 2003 Model BIT.

India adopted the New Model BIT on 28 December 2015, which replaced the 2003 Model BIT and declared that all future BIT negotiations would be led by the Department of Economic Affairs so as to ensure the convergence of investment and trade issues.[106] The Government of India has, presently, notified 47 countries that it does not wish to renew its existing BITs as it intends to implement the text of the new model investment treaty and sign new BITs.[107] The background for this decision was, as the external affairs minister put it, the shocking number of cases (or disputes) that arose out of the earlier investment treaties drafted along the lines of the previous Model BITs (1993, 2003).

The New Model BIT is radically different from the 2003 Model BIT, making substantial changes to the clauses relating to scope, MFN and investment treaty protections inter alia fair and equitable treatment (FET) and expropriation. The 2003 Model BIT had envisaged only 'promotion' as an objective. The absence of 'protection' was one of the reasons for the criticism of the Draft BIT. The preamble of the Model BIT now includes 'protection' of the investment as an objective. This step will be viewed positively not only by the investors who want to invest in India but also by the Indian investors who are now actively investing outside India. Thus, 'promotion' and 'protection', considered to be the two cornerstones of a BIT, are now reflected in the Model BIT.

The Scope Clause: The 2003 Model BIT encompassed all disputes relating to any investment made by an investor of a Contracting party as long as the investment was made in accordance with the law of the Host State. The 2015 Model BIT has significantly narrowed down the ambit of the BIT to exclude, inter alia, disputes pertaining to pre-investment expenditure, law or measure of taxation, measures taken by a local government, services rendered by a governmental authority in governmental capacity, IP-related subject matters, subsidies/grants given by the government and disputes relating to governmental procurement.[108]

Fair and Equitable Treatment Clause: The 2003 Model BIT incorporated the usual fair and equitable treatment protection found in many investment treaties. The Law Commission of India noted that this ever-growing umbrella of protections along with an inconsistent interpretation of legitimate expectations under the clause, limited the legislative, regulatory, and administrative actions of the host state.[109] Thus, in the New Model BIT, the FET provision was deleted and a more general customary law protection was inserted to ensure a base level of protection for the investors.[110]

Full Protection and Security: The 2016 Model BIT also grants Full Protection and Security that extends only to the physical protection of its investor and investment and not any other obligation.[111] Moreover, any breach of any article of the treaty or of an international agreement would not amount to a violation of this clause.[112]

Exhaustion of Local Remedies: The 2016 Model BIT expressly provides for an exhaustion of local remedies clause, which ensures that arbitral tribunals are not burdened with premature claims and more importantly that the domestic courts are given the power to decide on issues of domestic law.[113]

National Treatment and MFN: The National Treatment clause which grants the investors and their investments the same protection as that provided to the investors and investments of the nationals of the host state, has been narrowed down in 2016 Model BIT to the extent that the National Treatment would be granted only if the foreign investment or the investor is in 'like circumstances' as the national investment or investor.[114]

The MFN protection that existed in the 2003 Model BIT[115] has now been removed in the 2016 Model BIT. This decision was made after a bitter experience in White Industries, where the Australian investor relied on the MFN provision in the India-Australia BIT and sought favourable protections granted under the India–Kuwait BIT. India argued that this amounted to 'treaty shopping' and that it would 'fundamentally subvert the carefully negotiated balance of the BIT' and 'be contrary to the emphasis in the BIT on domestic law'.[116] However, these arguments were not accepted by the Tribunal. On a review of the government's decision to omit the MFN clause, the Law Commission noted that a removal did not balance investment protection with regulation and suggested an inclusion of an MFN provision with its scope restricted to application of domestic measures. However, this suggestion was not taken and the government, in order to avoid borrowing of beneficial provisions by the investor, omitted the MFN provision in the New Model BIT.

Till date, all the BITs signed by India contain the MFN provision. The only ones that do not have it are India's FTAs with Singapore, Korea, and Malaysia.[117] The New Model BIT provides that there must be a minimum of five years between the date on which the investor first acquired knowledge and the date of filing of a 'Notice of Dispute', to refer the matter to investment treaty arbitration. This time period is intended to be used for exhausting available local judicial and administrative remedies. The cooling off period, that is, the time period between the notice of dispute and the notice of arbitration, is prescribed at six months.

Expropriation Clause: The New Model BIT has excluded from its purview non-discriminatory regulatory measures and measures/ awards by judicial bodies of the host state aiming to protect public interest. India had contemplated the inclusion of a clause which took away the power of the tribunal to review a host state's determination of whether the measure was made genuinely in public interest. On the recommendation of the Law Commission of India, this clause was dropped in order to ensure a fair balance of interests of the investor and State.[118]

Other Notable changes: The term 'company' has been replaced by the term 'enterprise'[119] thus moving from an 'open-ended asset-based' definition to a more limited definition that protects only those investors who have a substantial and real business presence in India.[120] The New Model BIT also reiterates that foreign investors must be in strict compliance with the host state's taxation laws.[121] Umbrella[122] and Stabilization Clauses[123] have also been excluded. The New Model BIT has incorporated Dispute Settlement within states mechanism.

***

The debate on fine-tuning the ISDS process is now enriched by the proposal for a World Investment Court.[124] India is yet to take a formal position in this debate but has to bear in mind interests of foreign investors in India and Indian investors overseas. There is a new found confidence in the resilience of the Indian Investment environment as evidenced by the proposed re-negotiation of significant DTAAs[125] and BIPAs.[126] It is critical that India remains engaged in international debates on both incremental and radical reform proposals to ensure a healthy balance of investor and host state's sovereign concerns not only in India but across the world.

Notes and References

1. Treaty between the Federal Republic of Germany and Pakistan for the promotion and protection of investments. Signed at Bonn, on 25 November 1959, available http://www.iisd.org/pdf/2006/invest-ment_pakistan_germany.pdf.
2. Germany–Pakistan BIT [1959], art 11.
3. International Institute for Sustainable Development (IISD), *Investment Treaties & Why They Matter to Sustainable Development*, available http://www.iisd.org/pdf/2011/investment_treaties_why_they_matter_sd.pdf; and Eric Neumayer and Laura Spess, 'Do Bilateral Investment Treaties Increase Foreign Direct Investment to Developing Countries?' *World Development*, 33 (10, 2005): 1567–85, esp. p. 1582.
4. Burghard Ilge, 'An Account of the EU's Engagement with Bilateral Investment Treaties', in *Rethinking Bilateral Investment Treaties: Critical*

Issues and Policy Choices, 1st ed. (Both Ends, Madhyam and Centre for Research on Multinational Corporations (SOMO), 2016).

5. Anthea Roberts, 'State to State Investment Treaty Arbitration: A Hybrid Theory of Interdependent Rights and Shared Interpretative Authority', *Harvard International Law Journal*, 55(2016).

6. IISD, available http://www.iisd.org/investment/law/treaties.aspx.

7. Peter Buckley, 'Explaining China's Outward FDI: An Institutional Perspective', *The Rise of Transnational Corporations from Emerging Markets: Threat or Opportunity?* 1st ed. (Cheltenham: Edward Elgar 2008); UNCTAD Series on International Investment Policies for Development, *The Role of International Agreements in Attracting Foreign Direct Investment to Developing Countries* (2009); and Lisa E. Sachs and Karl P. Sauvant, *BITs DDTs and FDI Flows: An Overview* (Oxford University Press, 2009).

8. *UNCTAD World Investment Report* (2017), p. 111.

9. IISD, *Investment Treaties*, p. 5.

10. *UNCTAD World Investment Report* (2016), available http://unctad. org/en/PublicationsLibrary/wir2016_en.pdf, p. 121.

11. *UNCTAD World Investment Report* (2015), available http://unctad. org/en/PublicationsLibrary/wir2015_en.pdf, p. 179.

12. *UNCTAD World Investment Report* (2015), p. 121.

13. Latham and Watkins, *Investment Treaty Arbitration: A Primer* (1563, 29 July 2013), p. 4.

14. See https://icsid.worldbank.org/ICSID/StaticFiles/basicdoc_en-archive/ ICSID_English.pdf.

15. *ICSID Convention, Regulations and Rules*, available https://icsid.world-bank.org/ICSID/StaticFiles/basicdoc/CRR_English-final.pdf.

16. ICSID, Database of Member States, available https://icsid.worldbank. org/en/Pages/about/Database-of-Member-States.aspx.

17. UNCITRAL, *Guide to UNCITRAL: Basic Facts about the United Nations Commission on International Trade Law*, available http://www. uncitral.org/pdf/english/texts/general/12-57491-Guide-to-UNCIT-RAL-e.pdf, accessed 30 June 2017.

18. UNCITRAL, *Guide to UNCITRAL*.

19. UNCTAD, *Investment Policy Hub*, available http://investmentpo-licyhub.unctad.org/ISDS/FilterByRulesAndInstitution, accessed 30 June 2017.

20. UNCITRAL Arbitration Rules available http://www.uncitral.org/ uncitral/en/uncitral_texts/arbitration/2010Arbitration_rules.html.

21. UNCITRAL Arbitration Rules.

22. LCIA concluded the case of *TS Investment Corp. v. Republic of Armenia* in 2011, using its own rules – UNCTAD, *Investment Policy Hub.*
23. UNCTAD, *Investment Policy Hub.*
24. SIAC December 2016 Press Release, 'SIAC Announces Official Release of the SIAC Investment Arbitration Rules, 2017' (30 December 2016), available http://www.siac.org.sg/images/stories/press_release/SIAC%20 Announces%20Official%20Release%20of%20the%20SIAC%20 Investment%20Arbitration%20Rules.pdf.
25. *Holiday Inns S.A. and others v. Morocco*, ICSID Case No. ARB/72/1.
26. ICSID Case No, ARB/87/3, 4 ICSID Rep. 245 (1997).
27. IISD, *Investment Treaties*, p. 6.
28. UNCTAD, 'Latest Developments in Investor-State Dispute Settlement, IIA Monitor No. 4' (2005), p. 3, available http://unctad. org/en/docs/webiteiit20052_en.pdf, accessed 30 June 2017.
29. IISD, *Investment Treaties*, p. 6.
30. UNCTAD, *Investment Report 2017*, p. 114.
31. Burghard Ilge and Kavaljit Singh, 'An Account of the EU's Engagement with Bilateral Investment Treaties', in *Rethinking Bilateral Investment Treaties: Critical Issues and Policy Choices.*
32. UNCTAD, *World Investment Report 2017*, p. 116.
33. UNCTAD, *World Investment Report 2017*, p. 115.
34. UNCTAD, *World Investment Report 2017*, p. 116.
35. UNCTAD, *World Investment Report 2017*, p. 115.
36. UNCTAD, *World Investment Report 2017*, p. 115.
37. '"Indirect Expropriation" and the "Right to Regulate" in International Investment Law', *OECD Working Papers on International Investment*, 2004/04, OECD Publishing, p. 4.
38. *Técnicas Medioambientales Tecmed, S.A. v. The United Mexican States* (2003) ICSID Case No. ARB (AF)/00/2.
39. Guzman Carrasco, Gonzalo, *Indirect Expropriation in Free Trade Agreements: The U.S. Trade Act of 2002 and Beyond*, Revista Colombiana de Derecho Internacional, 2004, (004), p. 281.
40. *Starrett Housing v. Iran*, [1983] ITL 32-34-1, (Interlocutory Award, 19 December 1983).
41. *Marvin Feldman v. United Mexican States* [2002] Case No. ARB. (AF)/99/1), para 100.
42. See China–Tunisia BIT 1998, Art. 6: '(1) Neither Contracting Party shall nationalize, expropriate or subject the investments of an investor of the other Contracting Party to any measures having an equivalent effect (hereinafter referred to as 'expropriation') unless the following

conditions are complied with: [...] (2) The measures are taken against just compensation.'

43. See Slovenia Turkey BIT 2004, Art 4: '[...] 2. Such compensation shall amount to the real value of the expropriated investment at the expropriated investment at the time immediately before the expropriatory action was taken or became known. (Emphasis added.)'.

44. See ASEAN, *Comprehensive Investment Agreement* (2009), Art. 14: '[...] 2. The compensation referred to in sub-paragraph 1(c) shall: (a) be paid without delay; (b) be equivalent to the fair market value of the expropriated investment immediately before or at the time when the expropriation was publicly announced, or when the expropriation occurred, whichever is applicable;[...]'.

45. See Netherlands–Oman BIT 2009, Art 4: '[...] c) ...Such compensation shall represent the genuine value of the investments affected immediately before the date the measures or impending measures became public knowledge and shall, in order to be effective for the claimants, be paid and made transferable, without undue delay, to the country designated by the claimants concerned and in the currency of the country of which the claimants are nationals or persons or in any freely convertible currency accepted by the claimants.'

46. Expropriation, UNCTAD Series on Issues in International Investment Agreements II. 2012 available http://unctad.org/en/Docs/unctaddiaeia2011d7_en.pdf, p. 43.

47. Fair and Equitable Treatment, UNCTAD Series on International Investment Agreements II, 2012 available http://unctad.org/en/Docs/unctaddiaeia2011d5_en.pdf, p. 5.

48. Draft OECD Multilateral Agreement on investments, (1998), clause IV(1) (which also includes the Full Protection and Security Standard).

49. *Mondev International Ltd. v. United States of America*, ICSID Case No. ARB(AF)/99/2, 11 October 2002, para. 118, 'A judgment of what is fair and equitable cannot be reached in the abstract; it must depend on the facts of the particular case'.

50. Fair and Equitable Treatment, UNCTAD Series on International Investment Agreements II, 2012 available http://unctad.org/en/Docs/unctaddiaeia2011d5_en.pdf, p. xvi.

51. Marcela Klein Bronfman, *Fair and Equitable Treatment: An Evolving Standard*, (Max Planck UNYB 10, 2006), p. 623.

52. Marcela Klein Bronfman, *Fair and Equitable Treatment: An Evolving Standard* (Max Planck UNYB 10, 2006), p. 622.

53. *Técnicas Medioambientales Tecmed, S.A. v. The United Mexican States*, (2003) ICSID Case No. ARB (AF)/00 Para 153.

54. *S.D. Myers, Inc.*, 40 ILM 1408, para. 263.
55. *S.D. Myers, Inc. v. Government of Canada*, 40 ILM 1408.
56. *Mondev International Ltd. v. United States of America*, ICSID Case No. ARB(AF)/99/2, 11 October 2002.
57. *ADF Group Inc. v. United States of America*, ICSID Case No. ARB (AF)/00/1.
58. *Loewen Group, Inc. and Raymond L. Loewen v. United States of America*, ICSID Case No. ARB(AF)/98/3.
59. *Waste Management, Inc. v. United Mexican States* (Number 2), ICSID Case No. ARB(AF)/00/3, Award, 30 April 2004, para 93.
60. Kavaljit Singh, *An analysis of India's New Model Bilateral Investment Treaty, Rethinking Bilateral Investment Treaties: Critical Issues and Policy Choices* Kavaljit Singh and Burghard Ilge (eds), p. 88.
61. Australia-Singapore FTA, 2003, Article 3 available <http://www.austlii.edu.au/au/other/dfat/treaties/2003/16.html>.
62. UNCTAD Series on Issues in International Investment Agreements II, Fair and Equitable Treatment, 2012.
63. UNCTAD Series on Issues in International Investment Agreements II, Fair and Equitable Treatment, 2012.
64. Rudolph Dolzer and Christopher Schreuer, *Principles of International Investment Law* (2nd Edition, Oxford University Press, 2012), p. 178.
65. *UPS v. Canada*, Award, 24 May 2007.
66. Rudolph Dolzer and Christopher Schreuer, *Principles of International Investment Law* (2nd Edition, Oxford University Press, 2012), p. 184.
67. *Siemens v. Argentina* [2007].
68. *SD Myers v. Canada*, [2009] , 40 ILM (2001) 1408 (First Partial Award, 13 November 2009).
69. *Methanex v. USA*, [2005], 44 ILM (2005) 395 (Final Award, 3 August 2005).
70. Alex Genin, *Eastern Credit Limited, Inc. and A.S. Baltoil v. The Republic of Estonia*, ICSID Case No. ARB/99/2.
71. Rudolph Dolzer and Christopher Schreuer, *Principles of International Investment Law* (2nd Edition, Oxford University Press, 2012), p. 184.
72. International Law Commission, Draft Articles on Most-Favoured-Nation Clauses (hereinafter ILC Draft Arts.), (1978), available http://legal.un.org/docs/?path=../ilc/documentation/english/reports/a_33_10.pdf&lang=EFS.
73. Draft articles on most-favoured-nation clauses (Yearbook of the international Law Commission, 1978, Vol. II, Part Two) 21.
74. Gillard Government Trade Policy Statement, April 2011, p. 14.

75. Nick Dearden, *You thought TTIP was dead? With Brexit we'll get the same thing, on steroids*, available https://www.theguardian.com/commentisfree/2016/jul/08/ttip-dead-brexit-brussels-free-market.

76. Owen Jones, *Protest never changes anything? Look at how TTIP has been derailed*, available <https://www.theguardian.com/commentisfree/2016/may/05/protest-never-changes-anything-derailing-ttip-trade-agreement>.

77. Available http://globalarbitrationnews.com/indonesia-the-end-of-bilateral-investment-treaties-the-end-of-bilateral-investment-treaties-20150202/.

78. Ben Bland and Shawn Donnan, *Indonesia to terminate more than 60 bilateral investment treaties Multinationals accused of bullying developing countries*, Financial Times, available https://www.google.co.in/url?sa=t&rct=j&q=&esrc=s&source=web&cd=1&cad=rja&uact=8&ved=0ahUKEwimvuaWuIbOAhUJQY8KHWhqBXYQFggdMAA&url=http%3A%2F%2Fwww.ft.com%2Fcms%2Fs%2F0%2F3755c1b2-b4e2-11e3-af92-00144feabdc0.html&usg=AFQjCNFUIsR03KN8GvIGTCDMZgfUzdgXnA&sig2=wA7lVa4ZVoAOkRtb6gmYZw.

79. World Investment Report, 2017, p. 112.

80. Mehmet Toral and Thomas Schulz, *The State, a Perpetual Respondent in Investment Arbitration? Some Unorthodox Considerations* in *The Backlash Against Investment Arbitration: Perceptions and Reality*, pp. 577–602, (Michael Waibel, Asha Kaushal, Kyo-Hwa Liz Chung, and Claire Balchin, eds).

81. Mehmet Toral and Thomas Schulz, *The State, a Perpetual Respondent in Investment Arbitration? Some Unorthodox Considerations* in *The Backlash Against Investment Arbitration: Perceptions and Reality*, pp. 577–602, (Michael Waibel, Asha Kaushal, Kyo-Hwa Liz Chung, and Claire Balchin, eds).

82. Judge Stephen Schwebel, *The outlook for the continued vitality of investor state arbitration*, Arbitration International LCIA, 2016, 32, 1–15.

83. Prabhash Ranjan, *India's Bilateral Investment Treaty Programme—Past, Present, and Future, Rethinking Bilateral Investment Treaties: Critical Issues and Policy Choices*, Kavaljit Singh and Burghard Ilge (eds), p. 104.

84. Prabhash Ranjan, 'Most Favoured Nation Provision in Indian Bilateral Investment Treaties: A Case for Reform'[2015], *Indian Journal of International Law*.

85. Available http://www.investindia.gov.in/ accessed 30 June 2017.

86. Quarterly Fact Sheet (Fact Sheet on Foreign Direct Investment), Department of Industrial Policy and Promotion available

http://dipp.nic.in/sites/default/files/FDI_FactSheet_OctoberNovember December2016.pdf accessed 30 June 2017.

87. Investment Report 2016 Annex Table 2.

88. UNCTAD available <http://investmentpolicyhub.unctad.org/IIA/ CountryBits/96> accessed 30 June 2017.

89. Bilateral Investment Treaties And India, available http://www. nishithdesai.com/fileadmin/user_upload/pdfs/Bilateral_Investment_ Treaties_and_India.pdf.

90. UNCITRAL, Award of 30 Nov. 2011, Final Award available http:// italaw.com/documents/WhiteIndustriesv.IndiaAward.pdf.

91. India–Australia BIT, art 4(2).

92. India–Kuwait BIT, art 4(5).

93. Shalaka Patil and Pratibha Jain, 'Bilateral Investment Treaties and their impact on the Global Economy', Chapter 14, available http://www. nishithdesai.com/fileadmin/user_upload/pdfs/Research%20Articles/ Bilateral%20Investment%20Treaties.pdf.

94. Prabhash Ranjan, 'Most Favoured Nation Provision in Indian Bilateral Investment Treaties: A Case for Reform', *Indian Journal of International Law,* 2015.

95. Jayati Ghosh, *India's Bilateral Investment Treaties: Worst Fears Realised,* available http://triplecrisis.com/indias-bilateral-investment-treaties- worst-fears-realised/.

96. Bettauer, Ronald J., *India and International Arbitration: The Dabhol Experience* available https://www.questia.com/library/journal/ 1P3-2200933641/india-and-international-arbitration-the-dabhol- experience.

97. *CC/Devas (Mauritius) Ltd., Devas Employees Mauritius Private Limited and Telecom Devas Mauritius Limited v. India,* UNCITRAL.

98. Available http://investmentpolicyhub.unctad.org/ISDS/Details/484.

99. Prabhash Ranjan, Antrix- Dewas A BIT of protectionism, *The Wire,* 09 August 2016, available http://thewire.in/57586/antrix-devas-a-bit- of-protectionism/.

100. It may be noted here that *IMFA v Indonesia* is not the first claim brought by an Indian investor. Mr. Ashok Sancheti (an Indian inves- tor) had previously brought claims against Germany (in 2005) and UK (in 2007–2008) under the Germany–India BIT and the UK–India BIT, respectively. However, these proceedings were discontinued.

101. Available https://www.mygov.in/sites/default/files/master_image/ Model% 20Text%20for%20the%20Indian%20Bilateral%20 Investment%20Treaty.pdf.

102. Saurabh Garg, Ishita G. Tripathy, and Sudhanshu Roy, *The Indian Model Bilateral Investment Treaty: Continuity and Change, Rethinking Bilateral Investment Treaties: Critical Issues and Policy Choices*, p. 73.

103. Saurabh Garg, Ishita G. Tripathy, and Sudhanshu Roy, *The Indian Model Bilateral Investment Treaty: Continuity and Change, Rethinking Bilateral Investment Treaties: Critical Issues and Policy Choices*, p. 75.

104. *White Industries Australia Ltd. v. The Republic of India*, UNCITRAL, Final Award (November 30, 2011).

105. Prabhash Ranjan, 'Most Favoured Nation Provision in Indian Bilateral Investment Treaties: A Case for Reform' [2015] *Indian Journal of International Law*.

106. Available http://finmin.nic.in/sites/default/files/ModelTextIndia_BIT%20%281%29.pdf?download=1.

107. 'India Seeks Fresh Treaties with 47 Nations', *Economic Times* (27 May 2016).

108. Model BIT 2016, art. 2.4.

109. Law Commission of India Report No. 260, (Para 3.1.1); J.R. Picherack, 'Expanding Scope of the Fair and Equitable Treatment Standard: Have Recent Tribunals Gone Too Far?'[2008], *Journal of World Investment and Trade* (Volume 9, Issue 4, p. 255) G. Mayeda, 'Playing Fair: The Meaning of Fair and Equitable Treatment in Bilateral Investment Treaties', [2007] *Journal of World Trade* (Volume 41, pp. 273, 291).

110. 'India Releases a New Model BIT' available http://www.norton-rosefulbright.com/knowledge/publications/136918/india-releases-a-new-model-bit.

111. Model BIT 2015, art. 3.2.

112. Model BIT 2015, art. 3.3.

113. *Encana v. Ecuador*, Article 2(2)(c) – UN Charter on economic rights.

114. Model BIT 2015, art. 4.1.

115. Model BIT 2003, art 4(2).

116. *White Industries v. India*, available http://www.italaw.com/sites/default/files/casedocuments/ita0906.pdf.

117. Prabhash Ranjan, 'Most Favoured Nation Provision in Indian Bilateral Investment Treaties: A Case for Reform' [2015] *Indian Journal of International Law*.

118. Ashutosh Ray, *Unveiled: Indian Model BIT* [2016].

119. Model BIT 2015, art. 1.3.

120. Law Commission of India Report, pp. 8–9.

121. Model BIT 2015, art 11(iii).

122. Umbrella Clause—A clause that 'guarantees compliance with contractual obligations. Under an Umbrella Clause, a violation of an investment contract between the host state and an investor can be

considered as a violation of the BIT. In other words, it can convert a contract claim into a treaty claim'—Kavaljit Singh, *An Analysis of India's New Model Bilateral Investment Treaty, Rethinking Bilateral Investment Treaties: Critical Issues and Policy Choices* Kavaljit Singh and Burghard Ilge (eds), pp. 91–2.

123. Stabilization Clause—A clause that 'prohibits the host state to unilaterally change the laws and regulations related to an investment project'– Kavaljit Singh, *An Analysis of India's New Model Bilateral Investment Treaty, Rethinking Bilateral Investment Treaties: Critical Issues and Policy Choices* Kavaljit Singh and Burghard Ilge (eds), p 92.

124. Gabrielle Kaufmann-Kohler and Michele Potestà, *Can the Mauritius Convention serve as a model for the reform of investor-State arbitration in connection with the introduction of a permanent investment tribunal or an appeal mechanism? Analysis and roadmap,* [2016] CIDS Research Paper, 6; See also M. Sornarajah, *An International Investment Court: panacea or purgatory?* [2016], CCSI Columbia FDI Perspectives, Perspectives on topical foreign direct investment issues (No. 180, 15 August 2016).

125. 'DTAA India to Renegotiate Tax Treaty with Singapore: Jaitley', the *Hindu* (16 May 2016). Available http://www.thehindu.com/business/dtaa-india-to-renegotiate-tax-treaty-with-singapore-jaitley/article8607096.ece 'India and Cyprus renegotiate double taxation avoidance agreement' (1 July 2016) https://www.pwc.in/assets/pdfs/news-alert-tax/2016/pwc_news_alert_01_july_2016_india_cyprus_dtaa_renegotiation_press_release.pdf.

126. 'India Seeks Fresh Treaties with 47 Nations' (27 May 2016) available http://economictimes.indiatimes.com/news/economy/foreign-trade/india-seeks-fresh-treaties-with-47-nations/articleshow/52458524.cms.

15

Allocation of Costs in International Arbitration

Sonal Kr. Singh and *Manish Lamba*

Resolving of disputes through international commercial arbitration can be an expensive affair. It can involve expenses for several technical and legal services. Moreover, since the parties have opted for a private means of dispute resolution, they will have to pay fees and incur expenses of the arbitrators.[1] Cost has been defined, by Halsbury's Laws of England, as the sum of money which the court orders one party to pay to another party in respect of the expenses of litigation incurred.[2] Since most arbitration proceedings are convoluted, the legal fees incurred by the parties can be substantial.

Allocation of costs in international arbitration is an area that requires greater analysis and research given the lack of a universal or singular approach adopted by the arbitral tribunals world over in the allocation of the said costs. The said issue gains even more prominence in view of the colossal amounts being allocated towards costs by arbitral tribunals which are borne by the parties to the arbitration agreement ultimately adding to the costs of the arbitral process.[3]

Arbitration costs can be procedural costs, that is, arbitrator's fees, expenses, and administrative fees and party's costs, that is, attorneys and experts fees and expenses. Arbitration fees are on a rise in the International Commercial Arbitration and are a growing source of user disaffection.[4]

Given that arbitration is essentially the result of an agreement between the parties, it could be said that it is the parties' written agreement that should prevail over any decision of the arbitral tribunal on the allocation of costs but there could arise a situation where there are mandatory provisions contained in the arbitration statute of the seat of the arbitration,[5] and whether in such a situation, it is the parties written agreement or the mandatory provisions that will take precedence on any decision of the allocation of costs by the arbitral tribunal.[6]

The endeavour of the present chapter is therefore to shed light over such issues by examining awards rendered by arbitral tribunals in different jurisdictions with special emphasis on the practices adopted in the Indian jurisdiction.

Considerations for Allocation of Costs

While allocating costs there are various considerations the tribunal has to take into account before arriving at a decision as to which party would bear the costs. The first and foremost factor which affects the tribunal's decision is the agreement between the parties. If the parties to the dispute have an agreement or a clause in the agreement which specifically relates to costs, then such an agreement would be considered as a primary factor while deciding the dispute as to costs. There are generally following five aspects to consider in the agreement between the parties:

The Parties Written Arbitration Agreement

The tribunals would consider and give due weightage to the agreement, if any, as to allocation of costs among the parties. The tribunals would usually uphold the arrangement of costs as detailed in the agreement between the parties unless the same is contrary to the provisions of law.

The Applicable Institutional Arbitration Rules

The tribunals would also give due regard to the rules of the institutions incorporated by parties into their agreement. The rules of most arbitration institutions give broad discretion of allocation of reasonable costs; however, there are minute differences between them.[7]

Procedure Agreed by Parties/Terms of Reference

Where the arbitration rules or law require the parties to agree upon or requires the tribunal to direct the terms of reference in relation to allocation of costs. Then the arbitrator/tribunal at the conclusion of the proceedings, while deciding the issue of costs, is bound by the terms of reference agreed upon.

Applicable Laws

The tribunals also have to be very careful while deciding the question of costs. They have to bear in mind the applicable laws which would govern the arbitration. The decision on costs by the tribunals has to be in accordance with the applicable laws on costs in arbitration and not be contrary to the same.

Additional Rules Adopted

The parties may agree on the application of other rules or guidelines such as the IBA Rules on the Taking of Evidence in International Arbitration or the IBA Rules on Party Representation in International Arbitration.[8] Therefore, the tribunals would be bound by such rules especially if these contain a proviso to costs.

Cultural Expectations

Parties may have unspoken expectations in respect of costs. These may well be coloured by the parties origins.[9] Since international arbitration involves parties from varied cultures and nationalities, each party may have different expectations especially when it comes to allocation of costs. Such expectations should be addressed early on in the arbitration by the tribunals.

Allocation of Costs: International Aspect

There exists no universal rule for the allocation of costs in arbitration (including both the arbitration costs and the parties legal fees and expenses); however, under most modern arbitration rules, the tribunal has been given the power to impose costs sanctions for non-compliance with the applicable procedure. The rules of most arbitral institutions permit arbitrators to assess costs against the losing party in a manner that they consider appropriate.[10]

The tribunals will refer to the rules under which the arbitration is being conducted. Different approaches have been adopted by various arbitration institutions around the world while deciding the issue of costs. The International Chamber of Commerce (ICC) Arbitration rules gives power to the tribunal to fix the costs of arbitration in its final award and decide which party would bear it and in what proportion.[11] Thus, it is clear that the parties under these rules have to wait until the final award to know who and in what proportion they have to bear the burden. On the other hand, the International Centre for dispute Resolution (ICDR) International Arbitration Rules give the power to the arbitral tribunal to award reasonable costs for legal representation of a successful party and apportion such costs among the parties.[12] Thus, the institution follows 'the loser pays' principle which is also followed by other arbitral institutions, such as UNCITRAL[13] and ICDR,[14] which is very distinct from the approach followed by the ICC. Thus, it can be seen that arbitral tribunals generally have wide discretion unless the parties have entered into an agreement on costs.

One could say that the starting point for any decision on the allocation of costs would be the agreement between the parties or applicable institutional arbitration rules. However, the arbitration rules and other factors determining costs are not same, thus adding to the different approaches followed by arbitral tribunals in allocation of costs. For instance, the 2015 China International Economic and Trade Arbitration Commission (CETAC Rules), German Institution of Arbitration (1998 DIS Rules), London Court of International Arbitration (2014 LCIA Rules), Permanent Court of Arbitration (2012 PCA Rules), 2010 UNCITRAL Rules all include an express, rebuttable presumption that the successful party will be entitled to recover its reasonable costs, whereas the International Chambers of Commerce (ICC Rules), Hong Kong International Arbitration Centre (HKIAC Rules), International Centre for dispute Resolution (ICDR), Stockholm Chamber of Commerce (SCC), Singapore International Arbitration Centre (SIAC Rules) simply authorize the arbitral tribunal to make an award apportioning costs but do not contain any presumption on their allocation.

The rules of most arbitral institutions permit arbitrators to assess costs against the losing party in a manner that they consider appropriate. Since an assessment of costs can only be made after a determination that one party or the other will prevail on the merits, it is not surprising that, in the ordinary arbitration, little attention is paid to the issue of legal fees and other costs until the very end.[15]

The standard for costs allocation under most arbitration rules is usually one of reasonableness and tends to be applied by considering whether the costs incurred are reasonable and proportionate in the context of the value of the claim and the overall importance and complexity of the matters in dispute. In assessing whether the amount of work done is reasonable, tribunals may take into account various factors such as the length and conduct of oral hearings, the parties approach to determining the preliminary issues, relevance of evidence, and document production.[16]

The decision of awarding costs by tribunals in international commercial arbitration is usually driven by the parties express agreement, their agreement in reference to arbitration rules if any, and the *lex arbitri* of the seat of arbitration. The arbitrators' approaches to the allocation of costs are also often influenced by practice in the courts and/or under the laws of the countries of origin of the parties and the arbitrators or of the place of arbitration.

Analyses of awards rendered in different jurisdictions reveal the following general practices followed by arbitral tribunals:

1. Costs follow the event (also known as the *English Approach*): A general principle of the law of costs that a party who is substantially successful in litigation is entitled to costs. It is a principle only, as in costs, barring a statute to the contrary, the determination is a matter of judicial discretion.[17] The ICC Report[18] points

out that the 'Costs follow the event' approach has been adopted despite the fact that the ICC and majority of other major institutional rules do not contain a presumption in favour of the recovery of costs by the successful party; or

2. The American Rule: The other main approach to cost allocation is the American Rule. Under this rule, each party bears its own arbitration costs and fees, irrespective of the outcome of the case. The exception is in case of fraud or abusive process. A number of investment treaty tribunals have endorsed this approach, for example, *Romak v. Uzbekistan, MCI Power v. Ecuador and Anderson v. Costa Rica*;[19] or

3. Tribunals acknowledge an agreement of the parties towards the allocation of costs; or

4. Tribunals also assess the reasonableness of the costs claimed by the successful party, the procedural behaviour of the parties and whether they conducted the arbitration in an expeditious and cost-effective manner and whether they rejected a settlement offer.

Arbitral tribunals in different jurisdictions have been taking into account different factors before deciding the issue of allocation of costs. Few of the factors which usually affect the decision of costs are:

Parties Conduct

Parties conduct is one of the prime factors influencing the decision of costs by tribunals. The tribunals would usually consider the conduct and behaviour of the parties prior to the initiation of the arbitration. The tribunals would usually favour the party which had tried to settle the dispute and taken maximum steps to prevent the conflict making it subject to arbitration. For example, in recent award rendered by a tribunal under the UNCITRAL arbitration rules, the tribunal directed the respondent to cover the costs of the arbitration which were approximately over $11 million. Regarding the allocation of costs for legal representation and assistance of the parties, the tribunal considered that the egregious nature of the measures taken by the respondent in breach of the Energy Charter Treaty entitled the claimants with a part of their costs and ordered reimbursement of $60 million, that is, approximately 75 per cent of the claimant's costs.[20]

Guidance from Principles of Cost Allocation

The tribunals also take into account the principles of cost allocation prevalent at seat of the arbitration. These principles are taken into account by the tribunals not as the law that they are bound to follow but as principles guiding them to arrive at a fair decision.

Agreement Between the Parties

The agreement between the parties is an important factor that the tribunals consider before deciding the issue of costs. This agreement plays a paramount role in helping the tribunal decide as to which party would bear the costs and in what proportion. To understand such agreement better, this is the clause that was found in one of the awards: '"The contracting parties shall each bear their respective expenses and fees. In the event the arbitrator renders an award for only one party, the costs of the arbitration shall be borne by the other party". The tribunal considered that this agreement prevailed over Article 31 of the 1998 ICC Rules.'[21]

Behaviour of Parties During Arbitral Proceedings

More than often the tribunal takes into account the behaviour of the parties while awarding the costs. The uncooperative and unacceptable behaviour would also have the winning party paying the costs irrespective of having claims decided in their favour.

> Examples of conduct that gave rise to cost shifting include: (i) uncooperative behaviour, resulting in unnecessary delays; (ii) failure to pay advance on costs; (iii) refusal to participate in drafting terms of reference and procedural arrangements; (iv) failure to reply to document production requests; (v) failure to appear at the hearing in person; (vi) abandoning of claims very late in the proceedings; (vii) failure to abide by major time limits; (viii) disregard of standard procedural rules; (iv) lack of professional courtesy; (v) failure to provide timesheets to substantiate claims for legal fee; (vi) withholding of evidence needed by another party; (vii) obscuring of the factual and legal situation; (viii) persistence in arguing on issues already determined by procedural orders; (ix) bad or ill-timed submissions; and (x) unreasonable conduct that fell short of bad faith.[22]

Complexity of the Case

The tribunals under various awards are also seen to consider the complexity of the case at hand. While deciding whether the matter is complex, the tribunals consider the length of the hearings, amount in dispute, number of issues that require to be settled, applicable laws, and so on.

Reasonableness of Costs

The tribunals consider whether the costs claimed/incurred are reasonable or not. The majority of tribunals attached considerable importance to whether the fees were substantiated, differentiated, well documented, and supported by evidence.[23]

A review of the aforesaid factors would reveal that there is no straightjacket formula which is applied by the tribunals. The factors taken into consideration by arbitral tribunals are diverse. Some tribunals accord primacy to the written agreement between the parties while some have kept the conduct of the parties as the principal factor in the allocation of costs thus ignoring the applicable institutional rules.

Allocation of Costs in Arbitrations in India

Commercial arbitrations have become fairly popular in India, particularly in relation to large number of commercial contracts. Majority of arbitrations in India relate to infrastructure and construction contracts, particularly those with government entities, including public sector undertakings.

Arbitration in India is governed by the Arbitration and Conciliation Act, 1996. The Arbitration and Conciliation (Amendment Act), 2015[24] has brought about changes in the provisions relating to the allocation of costs. The Indian Judiciary had also been time and again suggesting the legislature to move towards a new cost regime. 'The suggestion to the legislature is to formulate a mechanism, that anyone who initiates and continues a litigation senselessly, pays for the same. It is suggested that the legislature should consider the introduction of a "Code of Compulsory Costs".'[25] The legislature by way of the Amendment Act, 2015 has introduced explicit provisions dealing with allocation of costs.

In order to understand the concept of allocation of costs in India, it becomes important to analyse the provisions both prior and post the amendment. Section 31(8) of the 1996 Act reveals that the Indian Arbitration statute prior to the 2015 amendment contained no clear-cut provisions relating to allocation of costs of the arbitration proceedings. Section 31 merely stated that in the absence of an agreement of the parties to the contrary, arbitration costs are to be fixed by the arbitral tribunal. This provision leaves a lot of discretion with the arbitral tribunal as to the costs of arbitration. The tribunal may decide what costs may be paid, by whom and to whom, and in what manner the same may be paid. These costs would constitute the fees and expenses of arbitrators and witnesses, legal fees and expenses, institution's administration fees (if any), and any other expenditure in connection with arbitral proceedings and awards. The principal factor to be taken into consideration seemed to be the written agreement between the parties, as the Act made it clear that the said provisions come into play only in the absence of any agreement of the parties to the contrary. The Act also directed the arbitrators to simply fix the costs of the arbitration without specifying any methods or factors to determine costs thus according primacy to the written agreement between the parties and giving unfettered discretion to the arbitrators to award costs. The Act also lacked any system to regulate the fees of the arbitrators thus adding more uncertainty in the costs of the arbitration proceedings. In fact, the Supreme Court of India while disapproving the practice of unregulated fees structures of arbitrators, in *Union of India v. M/S Singh Builders Syndicate*,[26] expressed the dire need to have in place a system to regulate the unregulated fees of the arbitrators resulting in the high costs of the arbitral process thus hampering the growth of arbitration as an effective alternate form of dispute resolution. The Hon'ble Supreme Court observed:

The large number of sittings and charging of very high fees per sitting, with several add-ons, without any ceiling, have many a time resulted in the cost of arbitration approaching or even exceeding the amount involved in the dispute or the amount of the award. When an arbitrator is appointed by a court without indicating fees, either both parties or at least one party is at a disadvantage. Firstly, the parties feel constrained to agree to whatever fees is suggested by the Arbitrator, even if it is high or beyond their capacity. Second, if a high fee is

242 Sonal Kr. Singh and Manish Lamba

claimed by the Arbitrator and one party agrees to pay such fee, the other party, who is unable to afford such fee or reluctant to pay such high fee, is put to an embarrassing position. He will not be in a position to express his reservation or objection to the high fee, owing to an apprehension that refusal by him to agree for the fee suggested by the arbitrator, may prejudice his case or create a bias in favour of the other party who readily agreed to pay the high fee. It is necessary to find an urgent solution for this problem to save arbitration from the arbitration cost.

It is unfortunate that delays, high cost, frequent and sometimes unwarranted judicial interruptions at different stages are seriously hampering the growth of arbitration as an effective dispute resolution process. Delay and high cost are two areas where the Arbitrators by self regulation can bring about marked improvement.

The Supreme Court has also been in favour of regulating and minimizing the costs of arbitration. The Court suggested methods to regulate the fees of arbitrators in order to bring about certainty of costs in arbitration. In *Sanjeev Kumar Jain v. Raghubir Singh Charitable Trust*,[27] the Hon'ble Supreme Court, allowing an appeal against an order of a high court awarding unreasonable costs of litigation in favour of a party, denounced the practice of awarding high costs in arbitration and went on to observe,

Costs in Arbitration matters

23. We have referred to the effect of absence of provisions for award of actual costs, on civil litigation. At the other end of the spectrum is an area where award of actual but unrealistic costs and delay in disposal is affecting the credibility of an alternative dispute resolution process. We are referring to arbitration proceedings where usually huge costs are awarded (with reference to actual unregulated fees of Arbitrators and Advocates).

28. Though what is stated above about arbitrations in India may appear rather harsh, or as an universalisation of stray aberrations, we have ventured to refer to these aspects in the interest of ensuring that arbitration survives in India as an effective alternative forum for disputes resolution.

Examples are not wanting where arbitrations are being shifted to neighbouring Singapore, Kuala Lumpur, etc., on the ground that more professionalized or institutionalized arbitrations, which get concluded expeditiously at a lesser cost, are available there. The remedy for healthy development of arbitration in India is to disclose the fees structure before the appointment of Arbitrators so that any party who is unwilling to bear such expenses can express his unwillingness. Another remedy is Institutional Arbitration where the Arbitrator's fee is pre-fixed. The third is for each High Court to have a scale of Arbitrator's fee suitably calibrated with reference to the amount involved in the dispute. This will also avoid different designates prescribing different fee structures. By these methods, there may be a reasonable check on the fees and the cost of arbitration, thereby making arbitration, both national and international, attractive to the litigant public. Reasonableness and certainty about total costs are the key to the development of arbitration.

The Arbitration and Conciliation Act, 1996 contained no provision which laid down the ceiling on costs, usually the tribunal would take guidance from Civil Procedure Code (CPC) in this regard. Section 35 and 35-A of the Civil Procedure Code, 1908 provides the monetary cap for costs that can be awarded in favour of a successful party while the Arbitration and Conciliation Act, 1996 contained no provision which laid down the ceiling on costs; usually the tribunal takes guidance from CPC in this regard.

The amended Indian Arbitration statute contains detailed provisions regarding the allocation of costs bringing about the much needed reforms in this area. The 246th Law Commission Report suggested insertion of provisions detailing the costs to be awarded in proceedings under the Arbitration & Conciliation Act, 1996. The amendments replaced the Section 31(8), where the tribunal's power to award costs was found. Based on the recommendations contained in the 246th Report, the Arbitration and Conciliation (Amendment) Act, 2015 has amended Section 31(8) and inserted Section 31A in the Arbitration Act, which gives the tribunal the power to determine whether costs are payable by one party to another and the quantum of such costs. The explanation to Section 31A (1) reiterates the preamendment position that costs would include the fees and expenses of the arbitrators, courts and witnesses, legal fees and expenses, administration fees and any other expenses incurred in connection with the arbitration, court proceedings or the award. Section 31A (2), which is an addition, thereafter stresses on the 'loser pays' principle. Section 31A (3) sets out the circumstances that the tribunal/court is required to keep in mind while awarding costs, including factors such as conduct of the parties, the frivolity of the respective cases put forward by the litigants and whether a reasonable settlement offer has been refused. Insertion of the latter two provisions is an attempt to toughen the existing costs regime and bring it in compliance with international practices.[28]

Perusal of the newly added Section 31A of the Indian Arbitration Statute reveals that explicit provisions relating to the allocation of costs have now been provided for. The Act adopts as a general rule, the approach popularly known as the 'English Approach' or costs follow the event however gives the arbitrators the discretion to order differently, provided they deliver reasons in writing for the same. The amended provisions also provide for factors that can be taken into consideration by the arbitral tribunals such as the delaying tactics of the parties to the arbitration proceedings in order to promote time and efficiency of the arbitral process. The Amended Act further contain a mandatory provision to the effect that parties cannot agree on paying the costs in any event unless that agreement is made after the dispute arises. The amended provisions are in addition to the provisions for costs in the Civil Procedure Code, 1908.[29] The amended act also contains a schedule containing the fee structures of the arbitrators thus bringing more certainty about costs in the arbitration proceedings.

After analysing the provisions of the Amendment Act, 2015 it is clear that there has not been a great divergence from the position earlier under the 1996 Act. However, the Amendment Act, 2015 have invigorated and elevated the cost regime from what was earlier incorporated under the Civil Procedure Code.

Since awards rendered by arbitral tribunals in India are not either published or accessible, one can examine the issue of allocation of costs in international arbitration by analysing the decisions rendered by the courts in India while deciding the objections to arbitral awards. Review of the decisions rendered by the courts in the Indian Jurisdiction reveal that in some of the cases, the courts have accorded primacy to the terms of reference between the parties to submit their dispute to arbitration. In *Burn Standard Company Ltd. v. Mc Dermott*

International Inc. and Ors.,[30] the issue at hand was whether the court had the power to relieve the petitioners of the fees payable under the ICC rules, that is, whether the court is empowered not to insist upon the enforcement of the ICC rules and compel a party to pay inequitable fees. The Calcutta High Court upheld the arbitration agreement between the parties that provided that the arbitration would be governed by the ICC rules and dismissed the challenge of the petitioners.

In a recent judgment of the Delhi High Court, the court upheld the arbitrator's decision to award legal costs and arbitration costs in favour of the respondent in an arbitration conducted under the ICC rules. The court held,

> Last contention urged by VALE/AMCI was on the costs awarded by the learned arbitrator premised on the plea that since SAIL gave up certain claims, at best proportionate costs should have been awarded. It is urged that the dispute being bonafide, parties should have been left to bear their own costs. The argument is repelled for the reason that it fell within the domain of the Arbitrator to decide which party would bear the cost.[31]

In another judgment of the Calcutta High Court, the court upheld the decision of the arbitrator to award costs as they were in concurrence with the written agreement between the parties.[32] The courts in India have also taken the conduct of the parties into consideration while considering the decision of costs. In *Thyssen Krupp Werkstoffe GMBH v. Steel Authority of India*,[33] the Delhi High Court taking into consideration the conduct of the petitioner during the arbitration proceedings granted costs of the proceedings before the court on actual basis and directed the parties to file an affidavit as to the costs incurred by them for the proceedings before the court.

Review of the above stated decisions indicates that the courts in the India have upheld the arbitrator's decision to award costs in favour of one party keeping in mind factors such as the conduct of a party or the written agreement between the parties. However no singular approach seems to have been followed. Statistically, a study conducted by Ernst and Young in India revealed that in 90 per cent of the arbitration matters, parties have to bear their own costs. In 6 per cent of the proceedings, the arbitration tribunals apportion only costs of the proceedings between the parties and in 4 per cent of the cases, only costs followed the event (that is, the unsuccessful party pays all the costs incurred during the arbitration process).[34]

***

The approach of the arbitral tribunals/courts in India as well as in other jurisdictions towards allocation of costs in arbitrations remains inconclusive. There are various factors, which the court and the tribunals take into consideration while allocating costs. The arbitral tribunals/courts generally strive to strike a balance while awarding costs so that there is a deterrent for a party who has dragged the other party into litigation and also a satisfaction to the successful party by awarding a reasonable cost that it has incurred in the arbitration. However, allocation of costs in international arbitration still remains an area for which there could not be a defined approach. Due to huge amounts involved in commercial disputes, it may be generally appropriate for the parties to take into consideration laws applicable to the arbitration proceedings, the applicable arbitral rules, agreement between the parties, if any, while making submissions as to the cost.

Notes and References

1. Micha Bühler, 'Awarding Costs in International Commercial Arbitration: An Overview', *ASA Bulletin*, 22 (2, 2004), pp. 251–79, esp. p. 251.
2. Ananya Kumar and Divyam Agarwal, 'Towards a New Costs Regime', available http://www.thestatesman.com/mobi/news/122732-story.htm.
3. Historic arbitral award rendered on 18 July 2014, an arbitral tribunal sitting in Hague under the auspices of the Permanent Court of Arbitration (PCA) held unanimously that the Russian Federation breached its international obligations under the Energy Charter Treaty (ECT) by destroying Yukos Oil Company and appropriating its asset. The tribunal ordered the Russian Federation to reimburse Yukos Oil Company $60 million in legal fees which represents 75 per cent of the fees incurred in the said proceedings and over 4.2 million in arbitration costs.
4. Robert H. Smit and Tyler B. Robinson, 'Cost Awards in International Commercial Arbitration: Proposed Guidelines for Promoting Time and

Cost Efficiency', *The American Review of International Arbitration*, 20, pp. 267–84, esp. p. 267.

5. Also referred to as *lex arbitri*.

6. For example, Section 60 of the English Arbitration Act provides that a clause, requiring a party to pay all or part of the costs of the arbitration, is valid only if made after the dispute has arisen. Section 74(8) of the Hong Kong Arbitration Ordinance provides that an agreement, requiring a party to pay all or part of costs of arbitration in any event, is valid only if made after the dispute has arisen. The Indian Arbitration Amendment Act 2015 Section 31(A) (5) also provides a mandatory provision that an agreement as to costs to be paid by the parties can only be made after the dispute has arisen.

7. ICC, 'Commission Report Decisions on Costs in International Arbitration', *ICC Dispute Resolution Bulletin* (2, 2015).

8. ICC, 'Commission Report Decisions on Costs in International Arbitration', n. 7.

9. ICC, 'Commission Report Decisions on Costs in International Arbitration', n. 7.

10. Lawrence W. Newman and David Zaslowsky, 'Assessing Costs in International Arbitration', *New York Law Journal*, 243 (2014), available http://www.americanbar.org/content/dam/aba/events/international_law/2014/04/aba-nysba-international-boot-camp/CrossBorder3.auth-checkdam.pdf.

11. Refer to Article 37(4).

12. Refer to Article 28.3.

13. Refer to Article 38.

14. Refer to Article 31.

15. Refer to Article 31, n. 10.

16. Victoria Clark, 'Reducing the Cost of Arbitration: Could Cost Allocation Be the Answer?' available http://www.blplaw.com/expert-legal-insights/articles/reducing-cost-arbitration-cost-allocation-answer.

17. See http://www.duhaime.org/LegalDictionary/C/CostsFollowTheEvent.aspx.

18. ICC, 'Commission Report Decisions on Costs in International Arbitration'.

19. Matthew Hodgson, 'Counting the Cost of Investment Treaty Arbitration', Global Arbitration Review Online News, available http://www.allenovery.com/SiteCollectionDocuments/Counting_the_costs_of_investment_treaty.pdf.

20. *Hulley Enterprises Ltd. (Cypress) v. The Russian Federation* (18 July 2014).

21. ICC, 'Commission Report Decisions on Costs in International Arbitration'.
22. ICC, 'Commission Report Decisions on Costs in International Arbitration'.
23. ICC, 'Commission Report Decisions on Costs in International Arbitration'.
24. Arbitration & Conciliation (Amendment) Act, 2015 was notified in the Gazette of India on 1 January 2016 and is deemed to have come into force from 23 October 2015.
25. (2014) 8 SCC 470.
26. 2009(4) SCC 523.
27. 2012(1) SCC 455.
28. Kumar and Agarwal, 'Towards a New Costs Regime'.
29. Sections 35 and 35(A) of the Civil Procedure Code, 1908 contain provisions that give discretion to the Courts to levy costs on parties to the suit.
30. AIR 1997 Cal 145.
31. MANU/DE/1790/2013: *Vale Australia Pty. Ltd. v. Steel Authority of India*. The arbitration was conducted under the rules of the ICC.
32. AIR 1956 CAL 11.
33. 168(2010) DLT 250.
34. Ernst & Young LLP, 'Emerging Trends in Arbitration in India', available http://www.ey.com/Publication/vwLUAssets/EY-FIDS-Emerging-trends-in-arbitration-in-India/$FILE/EY-Emerging-trends-in-arbitration-in-India.pdf.

16

International Arbitration with an Indian Connection

*Sheila Ahuja**

By way of introduction and as a note of caution, it is important to clarify the scope of this chapter, which is not intended to be an all-encompassing guide to the relevant sub-topics set out herein. Instead, its purpose is to provide guidance on the current framework of international arbitration with an Indian connection, and to identify issues that are topical and the subject of recent discussion, debate, controversy, and of course, jurisprudence.

The appropriate start to this chapter on international arbitration with an Indian connection is to explain exactly what we mean when we use the phrase 'international arbitration'.

Following is a definition of the relevant terminology that tends to be adopted to distinguish between the different types of arbitration proceedings with an Indian connection:

* This chapter has benefitted from, and could not have been possible without, the helpful assistance of Shreya Aren, Chantal du Toit, and Arun Mal of Allen & Overy.

Domestic Arbitration

Pure domestic arbitration: where the parties are all Indian and the seat of arbitration is in India. International commercial arbitration seated in India: where at least one of the parties is 'non-Indian' and the seat is in India.

International Arbitration (or Foreign Arbitration)

1. International commercial arbitration seated outside India: where at least one of the parties is international, that is 'non-Indian', and the seat is not in India.

There has been a question about whether an 'international commercial arbitration' can be one that is seated outside India, or whether the term as adopted in the Indian Arbitration and Conciliation Act, 1996 (IACA) should presuppose an Indian seat, on the basis that the term appears only in Part I of the IACA 1996. This question has been addressed by the recent amendments to the IACA 1996 and the answer lies in the proviso to Section 2(2) of the IACA 1996, a provision we will refer to at various points in this chapter, which provides that certain sections in Part I 'shall also apply to international commercial arbitration, even if the place of arbitration is outside India'. This statement clearly illustrates that an international commercial arbitration can be seated outside India.

2. International arbitration (seated outside India): this term encapsulates any arbitration which is not seated in India (whether the seat of that arbitration is in a New York Convention[1] Member-State or not) and is irrespective of the nationality of the parties.

It is pertinent to note in this regard that there is a current issue as to whether an arbitration where all the parties are Indian nationals can be seated outside India. The question has been asked of the Supreme Court of India (Supreme Court) in the pending decision of *Sasan Power*. Until the issue is finally decided by the Supreme Court, we can only set out our analysis and current understanding of the issue by reference to the jurisprudence that is available at the time of publishing this chapter, which is discussed later in the chapter.

This chapter intends to address some of the issues that arise in the context of international arbitration proceedings where there is some connection to India. That connection to India can manifest itself in several ways:

1. where one or more of the parties are of Indian nationality;
2. where the transaction which contains a submission to international arbitration is in some way connected to India (for example, location of business operations, location of performance of obligations, location of assets, and so on);
3. where the dispute which is the subject of international arbitration proceedings bears some connection to India or certain relief sought at some stage of the arbitration bears some connection to India;
4. where one of the chosen laws to govern some aspect of the transaction is Indian law; and/or
5. where one or more components of the agreement to arbitrate are Indian (for example choice of Indian institutional rules).

There may of course be other ways in which a connection to India is established. The aim of this chapter is to address the specific issues which arise for the parties' consideration when contemplating or actually getting involved in an international arbitration that has one or more connections to India.

The IACA 1996: Introduction and Reforms

The reforms to the IACA 1996 in the form of the Arbitration and Conciliation (Amendment) Act 2015 were published on 31 December 2015 following the assent of the President of India (referred to as the IACA Reforms for convenience), although they took effect retrospectively from 23 October 2015. The IACA Reforms have been a prevailing topic of much discussion since October 2015 when the Arbitration and Conciliation (Amendment) Ordinance 2015 was promulgated. Much has been said and written about the amendments, their intended scope, and predictions as to the direction that Indian jurisprudence might take.

In this section, we summarize briefly for ease of reference only those amendments to the IACA 1996 which relate to international arbitration.

Proviso to Section 2(2): Scope of Part I of the IACA 1996

Section 2(2) of the IACA 1996 provides that Part I of the IACA 1996 will apply when the place of arbitration is in India. Against the background of a contentious history as explained ahead, a proviso has been added to this sub-section by the IACA Reforms to make clear that Part I does not mandatorily apply to international commercial arbitration matters seated outside India. The proviso states that, unless there is an agreement to the contrary, the provisions of the IACA 1996 which relate to interim relief (Section 9), court assistance in taking evidence (Section 27) and appealable orders (Section 37(1)(b)[2] and Section 37(3)) will also apply to international commercial arbitration matters even if the place of arbitration is outside India. This means that the remainder of Part I does not apply to international commercial arbitration matters seated outside India.

Section 9: Interim Relief in International Arbitration

Section 9, which allows parties to apply to the Indian courts for interim relief, now extends to international commercial arbitration matters seated outside India (and, as stated at paragraph 0 below, possibly also to international arbitration matters where all the parties are Indian), unless the parties otherwise agree.

This section has been revised in two important ways. First, it has been amended to state that once a court has passed an order for any interim measure, the arbitral proceedings have to be commenced within 90 days of such order or within such further time as the court may determine. Second, it has been amended to state that the court will not entertain an application for interim relief once the arbitral tribunal has been constituted unless it finds that the interim relief which would be ordered by the arbitral tribunal would not be efficacious.

What we do not see in the IACA Reforms, in the context of interim relief, is a provision recognizing emergency arbitration proceedings. Against the backdrop of a number of emergency arbitrator proceedings with an Indian connection, as well as institutional rules recognizing this avenue for interim relief (see the Arbitration Rules of the Indian Council of Arbitration

2016 as well as the rules of the Mumbai Centre for International Arbitration 2016), there was much speculation about whether the IACA Reforms would provide for the recognition of emergency arbitrators and decisions rendered by them. It was in fact proposed by the Law Commission of India (the Law Commission) that the definition of 'arbitral tribunal' be amended to include the following language: 'in the cases of an arbitration conducted under the rules of an institution providing for appointment of an emergency arbitrator, includes such emergency arbitrator'. However, this proposal was not accepted. Thus, the IACA 1996 as amended does not prima facie acknowledge the concept of an emergency arbitrator, although it remains to be seen whether the definition of 'arbitral award' in Section 2(1)(c) which includes that an interim award will be construed broadly by the courts to also encompass an emergency arbitrator's award.

Part II: Foreign Awards

In the context of Part II of the IACA 1996, which deals with foreign awards, the most significant amendment is that of Section 48 relating to the grounds by which enforcement of a foreign award may be resisted. Section 48 has been amended to include a definition of public policy, and the legislature has now confirmed through this amendment that in this context the 'public policy' ground should be construed narrowly. An explanation has also been added to Section 48, which provides that 'patent illegality' is no longer a ground for setting aside a foreign award, although it is retained in the context of a pure domestic award, as per the new Section 34(2A). A further explanation states that the test as to whether there is a contravention of the fundamental policy of Indian law shall not entail a review of the merits of the dispute.

The Law Commission's proposed reform to Section 48 included a time limit for determining enforcement applications within a one-year period from the date a notice for an application for enforcement was served (akin to its counterpart Section 34 relating to challenges to domestic-seated arbitral awards). However, for reasons that are not explained, this provision did not make it through to the IACA Reforms as passed.

Seat and Governing Law

Introduction and Terminology: Seat or Venue?

This topic relates to the effectiveness and sanctity of the choice of 'seat', or 'place' as is the term used in Section 2(2) of the IACA 1996, of an international arbitration.

The choice of words as between 'seat' and 'place', on the one hand, and 'venue', on the other hand, has itself led to some controversy. The classic distinction of seat (which denotes the legal place of arbitration) and venue (which refers to the physical location of hearings) has been the subject of jurisdictional hurdles and challenges in arbitration proceedings. Subject to exceptions in limited circumstances, the general principle is that a choice of 'seat' brings an arbitration proceeding into the legal framework of the chosen state, whereas a choice of 'venue' merely suggests a particular location for the hearing of an arbitration proceeding. The former is one of the most important concepts in arbitration and remains constant throughout the duration of an arbitration, whereas the latter is merely a logistical issue which may vary throughout the life of an arbitration.

The English Law Position

The distinction between the two concepts as a matter of English law is clear. *Redfern & Hunter on International Arbitration* (6th ed.) states categorically at paragraph 3.56 that 'the seat of the arbitration is … intended to be its centre of gravity'.

Russell on Arbitration explains,

> In England it is essential for an arbitration to have a 'seat', which is the geographical location to which the arbitration is ultimately tied…. As the seat is the legal, rather than the physical place of arbitration proceedings, hearings can be held in other jurisdictions. The seat of arbitration is often specified in the arbitration agreement by the selection of a particular place or country in which the arbitration is to be held. In the absence of clear words or significant indications to the contrary, there is a strong presumption that the place where the arbitration is to take place will constitute its seat.[3]

This distinction between seat and venue was also observed by the Court of Appeal in England as early as 1988 in *Naviera Amazonica*

Peruana S.A. v. Compania International de Seguros del Peru,[4] where it approved the following paragraph from *Redfern and Hunter on International Arbitration*:

> The preceding discussion has been on the basis that there is only one 'place' of arbitration. This will be the place chosen by or on behalf of the parties; and it will be designated in the arbitration agreement or the terms of reference or the minutes of proceedings or in some other way as the place or 'seat' of the arbitration. This does not mean, however, that the Arbitral Tribunal must hold all its meetings or hearings at the place of arbitration. International commercial arbitration often involves people of many different nationalities, from many different countries. In these circumstances, it is by no means unusual for an Arbitral Tribunal to hold meetings—or even hearings—in a place other than the designated place of arbitration, either for its own convenience or for the convenience of the parties or their witnesses.... It may be more convenient for an Arbitral Tribunal sitting in one country to conduct a hearing in another country—for instance, for the purpose of taking evidence.... In such circumstances each move of the Arbitral Tribunal does not of itself mean that the seat of arbitration changes. The seat of arbitration remains the place initially agreed by or on behalf of the parties.

The Indian Law Position

As a matter of Indian law, in the pre-eminent decision of *Bharat Aluminium Company v. Kaiser Aluminium Technical Service, Inc.*[5] (*BALCO*),[6] a five-judge constitutional bench, citing the above paragraph of *Naviera Amazonica*, held at paragraph 72 that a choice of seat does not mean that all arbitration proceedings must take place at the seat, and that the arbitrators are at liberty to hold meetings at a place which is convenient to all concerned.

Ambiguity in the Choice

However, various courts have struggled to give meaning to ambiguous clauses which do not clearly demarcate what the seat of an arbitration proceeding should be versus its venue.

A well-known English authority in this area is the case of *Roger Shashoua and others v. Mukesh Sharma*,[7] where it was held that despite it being contended that "'venue" is not synonymous with "seat" ...

in an arbitration clause which provided for arbitration to be conducted in accordance with the Rules of the International Chamber of
Commerse (ICC) in Paris (a supranational body of rules), a provision
that the venue of arbitration shall be London, United Kingdom did
amount to the designation of a juridical seat'.

An example of the interplay between the choice of 'seat' and 'venue'
in the Indian context is the heavily cited judgment of *Enercon (India)
Ltd & Ors v. Enercon GmbH & Anr*[8] (*Enercon*). By way of brief background, Enercon (India) Ltd (Enercon India) and Enercon GmbH
were involved in disputes which led to a series of parallel proceedings
initiated in India as well as England in which they sought anti-suit
injunctions as well as declaratory relief concerning the validity of the
arbitration clause (in circumstances where there was a dispute as to
whether the agreement containing the arbitration clause had been
properly concluded between the parties).

Enercon India commenced proceedings before the Bombay High
Court and the Daman Trial Court, in which it sought a declaration
that the relevant underlying contract had not been properly concluded and thus no valid agreement to arbitrate existed between the
parties. Enercon GmbH in response commenced proceedings under
Section 45 of the IACA 1996 requesting the Indian courts to refer
the matter to arbitration on the basis that there was a valid agreement
to arbitrate. At the same time, it also commenced proceedings before
the English Commercial Court requesting that it grant an anti-suit
injunction in respect of the proceedings in India and also constitute
a tribunal pursuant to the arbitration clause. Initially, the English
Commercial Court granted an ex parte anti-suit injunction, but this
was subsequently discharged. The English Commercial Court stayed
its proceedings pending the conclusion of the Indian proceedings,
relying on an undertaking by Enercon India, that it would take steps
to ensure that the Indian proceedings were concluded expeditiously.[9]
Meanwhile, the Indian proceedings progressed up the system to the
Supreme Court.

A question arose before a two-judge bench in the Supreme Court
as to what the seat of arbitration was, against the backdrop of a
clause which provided in its operative part: 'The venue of the arbitration proceedings shall be in London ... the provisions of Indian
Arbitration and Conciliation Act, 1996 shall apply'. The Bombay

High Court had delivered a judgment saying that London was the venue of arbitration (but not the seat) and that for the same reason the English courts would have concurrent jurisdiction.

In a judgment that considered a variety of Indian and English authorities, the finding of the Supreme Court (handed down by Former Justice Surinder Singh Nijjar) was that a choice of 'venue' in London was not sufficient to displace the application of Part I of the IACA 1996 in circumstances where the arbitration agreement expressly provided that the IACA 1996 shall apply (in particular, Chapters III, IV, V, and VI). It was held at paragraph 105 as follows:

> Learned senior counsel has rightly pointed out that unlike the situation in Naviera Amazonica (supra), in the present case all the three laws: (i) the law governing the substantive contract; (ii) the law governing the agreement to arbitrate and the performance of that agreement (iii) the law governing the conduct of the arbitration are Indian. Learned senior counsel has rightly submitted that the curial law of England would become applicable only if there was clear designation of the seat in London. Since the parties have deliberately chosen London as a venue, as a neutral place to hold the meetings of arbitration only, it cannot be accepted that London is the seat of arbitration. We find merit in the submission of Mr. Nariman that businessmen do not intend absurd results. If seat is in London, then challenge to the award would also be in London. But the parties having chosen Indian Arbitration Act, 1996—Chapter III, IV, V, and VI; Section 11 would be applicable for appointment of arbitrator in case the machinery for appointment of arbitrators agreed between the parties breaks down. This would be so since the ratio laid down in Bhatia will apply, i.e., Part I of the Indian Arbitration Act, 1996 would apply even though seat of arbitration is not in India. This position has been reversed in BALCO, but only prospectively. BALCO would apply to the agreements on or after 6 September 2012. Therefore, to interpret that London has been designated as the seat would lead to absurd results.

Although this judgment subsequently formed the basis of extensive debate as to whether this set a precedent in India that the use of the word 'venue' was insufficient to conclusively effect a choice of seat of arbitration, the better view is that the judgment was correct in deciding that 'venue' in this particular case could not mean seat because the parties had expressly agreed that the IACA 1996 should apply. In fact, what can be observed from the finding above is that the Supreme Court did not merely conclude that the word 'venue' was a reference to the physical location and could not mean seat; rather, it looked at the entirety of the arbitration clause, which also provided for the application of the IACA 1996, and construed the choice of seat accordingly.

Seat v. Governing Law

Having established the significance of the choice of seat where does that leave us in terms of India's recognition of the consequences of a choice of seat?

In short, the Indian courts have been slow to fully acknowledge the parties' choice of a foreign seat, or more accurately, to recognize that such choice of a foreign seat constitutes a choice of exclusive submission to the arbitration laws of that chosen country, and consequently an exclusive submission to the supervisory jurisdiction of the courts of that country (to the exclusion of the jurisdiction of all other courts including the Indian courts other than where submission to such other courts is compatible with the supervisory jurisdiction of the courts of the seat). We refer here to this as the 'seat approach'.

As set out ahead, there is an alternative approach (the governing law approach) which provides that, in choosing for the laws of a particular State to govern the parties' agreement to arbitrate, the arbitral legislation of that State is imported into the arbitration proceedings arising from that agreement to arbitrate. In those circumstances, the choice of seat is seen to be relevant only insofar as mere procedural matters are concerned, which would be governed by the law of the seat. This is explained further below in the context of India, who has followed this approach until recent times.

The Pre-1996 Regime: The Statutory Embodiment of the Governing Law Approach (the 1937, 1940, and 1961 Acts)

It is helpful to begin with the regime which existed prior to the enactment of the IACA 1996 and was comprised of the following three statutes: the Arbitration (Protocol and Convention) Act

1937 (the 1937 Act), the Arbitration Act 1940 (the 1940 Act), and the Foreign Awards (Recognition and Enforcement) Act 1961 (the 1961 Act).

Under this regime, domestic awards were governed by the 1940 Act, while foreign awards were governed by (a) the 1937 Act, in respect of those awards falling under the Geneva Convention on the Execution of Foreign Arbitral Awards (the Geneva Convention)[10] and (b) the 1961 Act, in respect of those awards subject to the New York Convention on the Recognition and Enforcement of Foreign Arbitral Awards (the New York Convention).[11]

The crucial point to note here is the way in which a distinction was drawn between domestic and foreign awards. Section 9(b) of the 1961 Act expressly provided that the 1961 Act would not apply to 'any award made on an arbitration agreement governed by the law of India'. Thus, prior to the enactment of the IACA 1996, India had adopted the governing law approach, in that it determined whether an award was a domestic award or a foreign award by reference to the law that governed the arbitration agreement from which the award arose.

As will be seen from the developments that followed, while the IACA 1996 technically moved away from statutory recognition of the governing law approach with an aim to transition to the seat approach, the Indian courts' jurisprudence has led to the emergence of what can at best be called a hybrid approach.

An important starting point in following the history of Indian jurisprudence on this topic is the judgment of *National Thermal Power Corporation v. Singer Company and Ors*[12] (*NTPC v. Singer*). This judgment serves to confirm India's adoption of the governing law approach pre-IACA 1996.

The Supreme Court held in this judgment that the courts of the country whose substantive law governed the arbitration agreement had 'exclusive competence' in respect of all matters arising under the arbitration agreement, subject only to the concurrent jurisdiction exercised by the courts of the seat of arbitration in respect of matters of procedure.[13] In this case, the Supreme Court found that:[14]

All substantive rights arising under the agreement including that which is contained in the arbitration clause are, in our view, governed by the laws of India. In respect of the actual conduct of arbitration, the procedural law of England may be applicable to the extent that the ICC Rules are insufficient or repugnant to the public policy or other mandatory provisions of the laws in force in England. Nevertheless, the jurisdiction exercisable by the English courts and the applicability of the laws of that country in procedural matters must be viewed as concurrent and consistent with the jurisdiction of the competent Indian courts and the operation of Indian laws in all matters concerning arbitration in so far as the main contract as well as that which is contained in the arbitration clause are governed by the laws of India.

When read as a whole, it can be seen that the judgment places some emphasis on the fact that the agreement to arbitrate[15] did not designate a seat of arbitration and instead provided (in the operative part) that: '[t]he arbitration shall be conducted at such places as the arbitrators may determine'. Nonetheless, the principle that emerges is that the choice of governing law of the agreement to arbitrate would dictate the question of whether the resulting award constituted a domestic or foreign award, depending on whether that choice was made in favour of India or elsewhere.

Notwithstanding that *NTPC v. Singer* is a decision from the pre-1996 regime, it has been cited in various Indian judgments, including in recent years (albeit largely in respect of agreements to arbitrate that were concluded prior to the IACA 1996 coming into force).

Introduction of the IACA 1996

India implemented the IACA 1996 to replace the previous regime of the 1937, 1940, and 1961 Acts with a view to provide for a unified statute in respect of domestic arbitration and international arbitration (and thus domestic and foreign arbitral awards), as well as to update the content of its arbitration legislation to reflect to some degree the provisions of the UNCITRAL Model Law on International Commercial Arbitration (then the 1985 version, which was amended in 2006, after the IACA 1996 had come into force).

Section 2(2) of the IACA 1996 states that '[t]his Part [that is Part I] shall apply where the place of arbitration is in India'. The Model Law provision is differently worded, at Article 1(2): 'The provisions of this Law, except articles 8, 9, 17H, 17I, 17J, 35, and 36, apply only if the place of arbitration is in the territory of this State'.

By Section 2(2), the IACA 1996 intended to shift the arbitration regime in India from the governing law approach to the seat approach. However, owing to the omission of the qualifying language contained in the Model Law (to limit the application of the domestic portion of the Model Law only to domestic arbitration proceedings), Section 2(2) of the IACA 1996 became subject to a significant amount of litigation, the effect of which has been to revert to a governing law approach, or alternatively to adopt somewhat of a hybrid approach between the seat and governing law approaches, leaving numerous parties in a plethora of uncertainty. Unsurprisingly, this provision ultimately became one of the main drivers for the IACA Reforms.

The judicial treatment of Section 2(2), as well as its ultimate amendment by the IACA Reforms, is dealt with in the remainder of this section.

The *Bhatia* Principle

In the well-known case of *Bhatia International v. Bulk Trading S.A.*[16] (*Bhatia*), the Supreme Court was faced with an appeal against a judgment from the Madhya Pradesh High Court, which arose from 'an arbitration clause which provided that arbitration was to be as per the rules of the International Chamber of Commerce.... Parties agreed that the arbitration be held in Paris, France'. Notwithstanding the choice of a seat in Paris, the first respondent filed an application in India under Section 9 of the IACA 1996 against the appellant and the second respondent seeking, inter alia, an order of injunction restraining those parties from 'alienating, transferring and/or creating third-party rights, disposing of, dealing with and/or selling their business assets and properties'.

It was against this background that the Supreme Court was asked to decide the imperative question of whether the provisions of Part I could apply to an arbitration seated outside India. In a judgment handed down by Variava J, it was held by a three-judge bench as follows:[17]

> To conclude, we hold that the provisions of Part I would apply to all arbitrations and to all proceedings relating thereto. Where such arbitration is held in India the provisions of Part I would compulsorily apply and parties are free to deviate only to the extent permitted by

the derogable provisions of Part I. In cases of international commercial arbitrations held out of India provisions of Part I would apply unless the parties by agreement, express or implied, exclude all or any of its provisions. In that case the laws or rules chosen by the parties would prevail. Any provision, in Part I, which is contrary to or excluded by that law or rules will not apply.

Application of the *Bhatia* Principle

The decision in *Bhatia* led to a floodgate of cases through the doors of the Indian courts, which had the difficult task of deciding, on a case-by-case basis, whether they could assert jurisdiction in respect of the underlying arbitration proceedings in circumstances where there was no express exclusion of Part I of the IACA 1996. The key question, therefore, was: What constituted an 'implied exclusion' of Part I of the IACA 1996?

Of the many cases decided on this point, a number of the prominent ones are discussed below.

Hardy Oil and Gas Limited v. Hindustan Oil Exploration Company Limited and 3 Ors[18]

This was a judgment of the Gujarat High Court, in which the single judge grappled with the task of applying the *Bhatia* test to an agreement to arbitrate. The arbitration agreement provided that: (a) save for the arbitration clause, the proper law of the substantive agreement was Indian law; (b) the 'place' of arbitration was London; and (c) the law governing the arbitration agreement was English law. The single judge held as follows:[19]

However, their Lordships observed in Para 32 that in cases of international commercial arbitrations held out of India provisions of Part I would apply unless the parties by agreement, express or implied, exclude all or any of its provisions. In that case laws or rules chosen by the parties would prevail. Any provision, in Part-I, which is contrary to or excluded by that law or rules would not apply. Thus, even as per the decision relied upon by learned advocate for the appellant, if the parties have agreed to be governed by any law other than Indian law in cases of international commercial arbitration, the same would prevail. In the case on hand, it is very clear even on plain reading of Clause 9.5.4 that the parties' intention was to be governed by English law in respect of arbitration. It is not possible to give a narrow meaning to this clause as suggested by learned Senior Advocate Mr. Thakore that it would apply only in case of dispute on Arbitration Agreement. It can be interpreted only to mean that in case of any dispute regarding arbitration, English law would apply. When the clause deals with the place and language of arbitration with a specific provision that the law governing arbitration will be the English law, such a narrow meaning cannot be given. No other view is possible in light of exception carved out of Clause 9.5.1 relating to arbitration. Term Arbitration, in Clause 9.5.4 cannot be taken to mean arbitration agreement. Entire arbitral proceedings have to be taken to be agreed to be governed by English law.

Therefore, the Gujarat High Court followed a governing law approach to justify the exclusion of Part I of the IACA 1996.

Venture Global Engineering v. Satyam Computer Services Limited[20]

The principal issue in the judgment of *Venture Global Engineering v. Satyam Computer Services Limited* (*Venture Global*) was whether a foreign award rendered outside India could be the subject of proceedings in India brought under either Section 9 or Section 34 of the IACA 1996, both of which are contained in Part I. Although the shareholders' agreement was governed by the laws of the State of Michigan, United States, and the agreement to arbitrate provided for binding arbitration before the London Court of International Arbitration (LCIA), the Supreme Court placed significant emphasis on the following 'non-obstante' (that is, overriding) clause, which provided that 'notwithstanding anything to the contrary in this agreement, the shareholders shall at all times act in accordance with the Companies Act and all other applicable Acts/rules being in force in India at any time'.

Giving effect to the *Bhatia* principle, the Supreme Court held that Part I applied to the proceedings (see paragraph 37). In particular, the Supreme Court found that the non-obstante clause regarding the applicability of Indian law would 'override' the entirety of the Shareholders Agreement (including the agreement to arbitrate) and thus, Indian law was held to apply to the enforcement of the award:[21] 'Necessarily, enforcement has to be in India, as declared by this very section [referring to the non-obstante clause] which over-rides every other section in the shareholders agreement.... In terms of the decision in *Bhatia International* we hold that Part I of the Act is applicable to the award in question even though it is a foreign award.'

Given the unique circumstances in which the *Bhatia* principle was applied here (that is, insofar as the decision turned on the Supreme Court's interpretation of the non-obstante clause), it should have been the case that *Venture Global* did not develop a general binding precedent but one that was instead confined to its facts. However, the reality has been quite the opposite; *Venture Global* has been the source of much controversy in several subsequent cases involving the question of the applicability of Part I of the IACA 1996 to arbitration proceedings seated outside India. This was until *BALCO* declared the *Venture Global* judgment bad law.[22]

Videocon Industries Limited v. Union of India and Anr[23]

In the judgment of *Videocon Industries Limited v. Union of India and Anr* (*Videocon*), the Supreme Court held that where the parties to an arbitration agreement had chosen a foreign seat of arbitration and provided for a foreign law to govern that arbitration agreement, even where the law governing the remainder of the contract was Indian law, this '*necessarily implie*[d]' that the parties had agreed to exclude the application of Part I of the IACA 1996:

> The learned Single Judge of the Gujarat High Court in Hardy case referred to para 32 of the judgment in *Bhatia International v. Bulk Trading S.A.* and observed that once the parties had agreed to be governed by any law other than Indian law in cases of international commercial arbitration, then that law would prevail and the provisions of the Act cannot be invoked questioning the arbitration proceedings or the award.
>
> In our opinion, the learned Single Judge of the Gujarat High Court had rightly followed the conclusion recorded by the three-Judge Bench in *Bhatia International v. Bulk Trading S.A.* and held that the District Court, Vadodara did not have the jurisdiction to entertain the petition filed under Section 9 of the Act because the parties had agreed that the law governing the arbitration will be English law.

In the present case also, the parties had agreed that notwithstanding Article 33.1, the arbitration agreement contained in Article 34 shall be governed by the laws of England. This necessarily implies that the parties had agreed to exclude the provisions of Part I of the Act. As a corollary to the above conclusion, we hold that the Delhi High Court did not have the jurisdiction to entertain the petition filed by the respondents under Section 9 of the Act and the mere fact that the appellant had earlier filed similar petitions was not sufficient to clothe that High Court with the jurisdiction to entertain the petition filed by the respondents.

Subsequent judgments have placed strong reliance on the *Videocon* decision for a variety of reasons, including the language of the agreement to arbitrate, the helpful application of the *Bhatia* principle which led to an implied exclusion of Part I of the IACA 1996, and the clarity of the reasoning of the Supreme Court.

It is fair to conclude that this was one of the key judgments which brought about a turning point in the attitude of the Supreme Court, in construing agreements to arbitrate outside India and interpreting the *Bhatia* principle to refuse jurisdiction absent a clear indication that Part I was not intended to be excluded.

Yograj Infrastructure Limited v. Ssang Yong Engineering and Construction Co Ltd[24]

In *Yograj Infrastructure Limited v. Ssang Yong Engineering and Construction Co Ltd* (*Yograj*), the Supreme Court was invited to interpret the meaning of an arbitration clause which provided that[25] the 'arbitration shall take place in Singapore' and 'shall be conducted in English in Singapore in accordance with the Singapore International Arbitration Centre (SIAC) Rules as in force at the time of signing of this agreement'. One of the questions before it was whether this provision constituted an express or implied exclusion on the operation of Part I of the IACA 1996, that is, whether the *Bhatia* principle could be invoked to exclude Part I.

The Supreme Court held, in an agreement where the parties agreed that the arbitration proceedings would be governed by a foreign curial law (being the Singapore International Arbitration Act), that:[26]

Having agreed to the above, it was no longer available to the appellant to contend that the 'proper law' of the agreement would apply to the arbitration proceedings. The decision in *Bhatia v. Bulk Trading*, which was applied subsequently in *Venture Global Engg. v. Satyam Computer Services Ltd.* and *Citation Infowares Ltd. v. Equinox Corpn.* would have no application once the parties agreed by virtue of Clause 27.1 of the agreement that the arbitration proceedings would be conducted in Singapore, that is, the seat of arbitration would be in Singapore, in accordance with the Singapore International Arbitration Centre Rules as in force at the time of signing the agreement.

In conclusion, the Supreme Court held that Part I of the IACA 1996, including Section 42, was not applicable in this case.

Dozco India Private Limited v. Doosan Infracore Company Limited[27]

In *Dozco India Private Limited v. Doosan Infracore Company Limited* (*Dozco*), the Supreme Court once again considered the question of whether Part I would be applicable in circumstances where the agreement to arbitrate provided that disputes would be settled by arbitration in Seoul, Korea, pursuant to the ICC rules and where the agreement was governed by Korean law.

The Supreme Court held that where the seat of arbitration was foreign, this was[28] 'clearly indicative of the express exclusion of Part I of the Act'. It concluded that the clear language of the agreement to arbitrate[29] 'spells out a clear agreement between the parties excluding Part I of the Act' and that there would be 'no question of applicability of Section 11(6) of the Act'.

Reliance Industries Limited & Anr v. Union of India[30] and *Union of India v. Reliance Industries Limited & Anr*[31]

The decisions that brought greatest clarity to the *Bhatia* test and have somewhat put this matter to rest are the two related decisions of the Supreme Court in *Reliance Industries Limited & Anr v. Union of India*, which was rendered in 2014 (*Reliance I*), and *Union of India v. Reliance Industries Limited & Anr* (2015) 10 SCC 213 which was decided the following year (*Reliance II*).

The cumulative effect of both decisions is that where the parties have agreed either that the seat is outside India or that the law governing the arbitration agreement is not Indian law, the parties are deemed to have excluded the application of Part I of the IACA 1996 in their agreement to arbitrate. These decisions significantly narrow the scope of the *Bhatia* principle and are addressed in the relevant order of chronology below.

Reliance I

In *Reliance I*, the Supreme Court confirmed that Indian courts do not have jurisdiction to set aside an arbitral award in circumstances where the parties have (a) agreed to refer their disputes to arbitration with a seat in London and (b) provided for English law to govern their arbitration agreement.

The brief factual background to this is that the parties entered into two production-sharing contracts (PSCs) in respect of off-shore oil and gas fields in 1994. Each of the PSCs contain the following provisions:

32.1   Subject to the provisions of Article 33.12, this Contract shall be governed and interpreted in accordance with the laws of India.

32.2   Nothing in this Contract shall entitle the Government or the Contractor to exercise the rights, privileges and powers conferred upon it by this Contract in a manner which will contravene the laws of India.

33.12   The venue of conciliation or arbitration proceedings … shall be London, England. The arbitration agreement … shall be governed by the laws of England.

The PSCs were subsequently amended in 2004/2005 to change the 'venue/seat' of arbitration from London to Paris. Three of the four parties to the PSCs were in dispute and an arbitration was commenced in 2010. At a hearing in 2011, the parties to the arbitration agreed that the 'juridical seat (or legal place)' of arbitration for the purposes of the arbitration proceedings would be London, England, and entered into a consent award to that effect, which was also signed by the arbitral tribunal. Subsequently, the arbitral tribunal rendered its first substantive award on the arbitrability of several disputes. The Union of India commenced proceedings in the Delhi High Court challenging this award under Section 34 of the IACA 1996, despite the juridical seat (and thus, the mandatory place for challenging the award) being London, England. A single judge found in favour of the application of Part I to the award in question. The matter thereafter proceeded to the Supreme Court by way of a Special Leave Petition.

The Supreme Court found that in light of the prospective nature of the decision in *BALCO*[32]—which held that Part I of the IACA 1996 does not apply to foreign-seated arbitration proceedings arising from arbitration agreements entered into after 6 September 2012— the bench was bound by the law laid out in the *Bhatia* judgment. As explained earlier, the operative finding in *Bhatia* was that '[i]n cases of international commercial arbitrations held out of India provisions of Part I would apply unless the parties by agreement, express or implied, exclude all or any of its provisions'.

Applying the *Bhatia* test, the Supreme Court held[33] that once the parties had 'consciously agreed' that the juridical seat of the arbitration would be London and that the arbitration agreement would be governed by the laws of England, this 'would clearly show that the parties have by express agreement excluded the applicability of Part I of the [IACA 1996]' and it was thus no longer open to them to contend that the provisions of Part I of the IACA 1996 would also be applicable to their arbitration agreement.

A consistent theme in this judgment is the reliance placed on the dual elements of foreign seat and foreign law governing the arbitration agreement, which constitutes the clearest jurisprudential formulation of the hybrid approach between seat and governing law. This approach was reinforced, and arguably taken further, by the *Reliance II* decision, as is explained later in the chapter.

The Supreme Court criticized the Delhi High Court for not applying the ratio of the law laid down in *Videocon*. In holding that it was bound by the ratio in *Videocon*, the bench also observed that the *Videocon* judgment was subsequent to and made upon consideration of *Venture Global*, a judgment relied upon heavily by the Delhi High Court and the Union of India in asserting the application of the IACA 1996 (paragraph 48).

Following a close examination of the other provisions within Article 33 of the PSCs, the Supreme Court bolstered its finding that the parties intended to exclude the IACA 1996 by selecting the Permanent Court of Arbitration to act as the appointing authority (rather than the Chief Justice of India) as well as through their choice of the UNCITRAL Arbitration Rules to govern the arbitration proceedings.[34]

Harmony Innovation Shipping Ltd v. Gupta Coal India Ltd[35]

The Supreme Court in *Harmony Innovation Shipping Ltd v. Gupta Coal India Ltd* (*Harmony*) considered a clause which provided that '[i]f any dispute or difference should arise under this charter, general average/arbitration in London to apply.... This contract is to be governed and construed according to English law. For disputes where total amount claim by either party does not exceed $50,000 the arbitration should be conducted in accordance with small claims procedure of the London Maritime Arbitration Association.'

The Supreme Court analyzed most of the judgments in this section, and held, *inter alia*, that[36] '[t]he issue has to be tested, as we perceive, on the parameters of the law laid down in the cases of Videocon Industries Ltd (supra), Dozco (supra) and Reliance Industries Ltd (supra) [that is, *Reliance I*]'.

In its finding, the Supreme Court held that[37] 'interpreting the clause in question on the bedrock of the aforesaid principles it is vivid that the intended effect is to have the seat of arbitration at London. The commercial background, the context of the contract and the circumstances of the parties and in the background in which the contract was entered into, irresistibly lead in that direction.'

It went on to conclude that[38] 'applying the principles laid down in *Bhatia International* and scanning the anatomy of the arbitration clause, we have arrived at the conclusion that the courts in India will not have jurisdiction as there is implied exclusion'.

Reliance II

The second judgement concerning *Reliance*, as mentioned above, there is a second judgment concerning Reliance and the Union of India—*Reliance II*—which the Supreme Court has deemed a 'sequel' to *Reliance I*. This judgment confirms that the parties had excluded the application of Part I such that the Indian courts had no jurisdiction in respect of the arbitration proceedings. In comparison to its predecessor, *Reliance II* arguably goes further, and evolves the hybrid approach in *Reliance I* of seat and governing law construed together, by declaring a principle that Part I of the IACA 1996 will not apply to an arbitration agreement where the seat is outside India or if the law governing the arbitration agreement is not Indian law.

The additional facts (to those in *Reliance I*) upon which *Reliance II* arises are that following the decision in *Reliance I*, the Delhi High Court dismissed three underlying petitions under Part I as not maintainable—two of these petitions were under Section 34 (one of which was the subject of *Reliance I*) and one was under Section 14.

The Union of India sought to revive the Section 14 petition by contending that the *Bhatia* principle would govern the arbitration agreement and, accordingly, Part I (or at least Section 14) would be applicable. The Union of India also argued that London could not be said to be the seat of arbitration as: (a) the consent award designating London as the 'juridical seat' was contrary to Article 34.2 of the PSCs (which required amendments to be in writing and signed by all parties), as the Oil and Natural Gas Corporation (ONGC), whilst a party to the PSCs, was not a signatory to the consent award (not being a party to the arbitration proceedings); and (b) in any event, Article 33.12 of the PSCs simply referred to the 'venue' being London, which could not be construed to mean the 'seat' of arbitration.

The Supreme Court rejected the Union of India's appeal in light of the Court's finding in *Reliance I*, that Part I of the IACA 1996 had been excluded by the parties, it was not open to the Union of India to argue that Part I of that Act was now applicable. On this basis, the Supreme Court found that the Union of India's Section 14 application was not maintainable.

The finding as to the exclusion of Part I was consistent with a series of well-settled Indian authorities, including *Videocon*, *Dozco*, *Yograj*, and *Harmony*.

Importantly, in *Reliance II*, the Supreme Court went further than in *Reliance I* by holding that the last paragraph of *BALCO* (which makes the application of the judgment prospective) is now to be read with two caveats, both emanating from paragraph 32 of *Bhatia*, namely, that:[39]

[W]here the Court comes to a determination that the juridical seat is outside India or where law other than Indian law governs the arbitration agreement, Part-I of the Arbitration Act, 1996 would be excluded by necessary implication. Therefore, even in the cases governed by the Bhatia principle, it is only those cases in which agreements stipulate that the seat of the arbitration is in India or on whose facts a judgment cannot be reached on the seat of the arbitration as being outside India that would continue to be governed by the Bhatia principle. Also, it is only those agreements which stipulate or can be read to stipulate that the law governing the arbitration agreement is Indian law which would continue to be governed by the Bhatia rule.

In this regard, the Supreme Court repeated a finding made in *Reliance I* that 'it is too late in the day to contend that the seat of arbitration is not analogous to an exclusive jurisdiction clause', as laid down in the well-known English case of *C v. D*.[40]

Finally, the Supreme Court endorsed Reliance Industries Limited's submission that the Union of India was prohibited from bringing the Special Leave Petition in respect of the Part I question by virtue of the doctrine of res judicata. In particular, the Court found that the Union of India's reliance on the Supreme Court judgment of *Mathura Prasad Bajoo Jaiswal v. Dossibai N.B. Jeejeebhoy* (1970),[41] to argue that res judicata would not attach to questions relating to jurisdiction, was misplaced as the effect of Article 34.2 of the PSCs (dealing with amendment to the PSCs) raised 'at best a mixed question of fact and law and not a pure question of jurisdiction unrelated to facts'.[42]

The Supreme Court in *Reliance II* has thus made further strides in narrowing the scope of interference from the Indian courts in international arbitration proceedings. On one view, the judgment has a broader scope than *BALCO*, both in terms of the lack of limitation on its temporal effect (although it appears to refer to the application of the *Bhatia* principle only, which suggests it applies to agreements to arbitrate pre-6 September 2012, this is not beyond doubt as the operative paragraph—paragraph 20—also refers to *BALCO*) as well as the substantive test adopted (in that whereas the *BALCO* test relies on the choice of seat by the parties to determine whether or not Part I of the IACA 1996 applies, the *Reliance II* test results in an exclusion of Part I where the seat of arbitration and/or governing law of agreement to arbitrate is foreign).

Videocon Industries Limited and Ors v. Union of India, Ministry of Petroleum & Natural Gas and Ors[43]

The May 2016 decision of the Delhi High Court (Division Bench) in *Videocon Industries Limited and Ors v. Union of India, Ministry of Petroleum & Natural Gas and Ors* (*Videocon II*) is the latest in a series of decisions that have been rendered by various courts across different jurisdictions in disputes arising from a PSC between the Union of India, on the one hand, and *ONGC, Videocon Industries Ltd, Cairn India Ltd, and Ravva Oil* (Singapore), on the other hand.

The preceding decisions related to the question of which courts had supervisory jurisdiction over arbitration proceedings. Although the seat of arbitration in the PSC was Kuala Lumpur, one party alleged that an order of the arbitral tribunal had the effect of shifting the seat to London. The governing law of the PSC was Indian law and that of the agreement to arbitrate was English law. The Kuala Lumpur High Court found that the seat had indeed shifted to London, which decision is, as at the time of authoring this chapter, pending appeal in the Malaysian Court of Appeal. Meanwhile, the same question was asked in the Indian courts, and the Supreme Court held that Kuala Lumpur remained the seat, while London was a mere venue for hearings.

In the current proceedings, two matters were at issue:

1. The arbitral tribunal suggested that a hearing be held in Colombo for which the consent of the parties was sought, but the Union of India objected and insisted that hearings be held in Kuala Lumpur and approached the Delhi High Court seeking a direction preventing the tribunal from meeting in Colombo; and
2. Cairn filed an application before the arbitral tribunal to quantify costs following the rendering of an arbitral award but the Union of India argued that the tribunal was functus officio after the arbitral award had been passed and lacked jurisdiction to entertain further applications. The arbitral tribunal held by majority that it had jurisdiction over the application, and the

Union of India approached a single judge of the Delhi High Court for an anti-arbitration injunction.

The single judge granted the direction against any hearing being held in Colombo and issued an anti-arbitration injunction.

A division bench held on appeal that the decisions of the single judge were incorrect. It held that the Indian courts had jurisdiction because the PSC governed by Indian law was incorrect, and that the curial remedies available to the parties were in Kuala Lumpur—the seat of arbitration—and under the Malaysian Arbitration Act. It held that 'a gridlock exists as of today because the Supreme Court of India has held that the seat of arbitration is Kuala Lumpur and not London. The Court of Competent Jurisdiction in Kuala Lumpur has held that the seat of arbitration is London and not Kuala Lumpur. The Courts in India cannot resolve this dispute'.

Eitzen Bulk A/S v. Ashapura Minechem Ltd & Anr[44]

The final judgment worth noting in this section is that of *Eitzen Bulk A/S v. Ashapura Minechem Ltd & Anr* wherein Ashapura Minechem Ltd (Ashapura) filed a suit in the Indian courts claiming that the contract and arbitration clause were illegal, null, and void ab initio. An interim injunction was initially granted but the suit was ultimately dismissed for want of jurisdiction. Subsequently, an arbitral award was rendered against Ashapura. Ashapura commenced proceedings before the District Judge in Jamnagar, Gujarat, under Section 34 and filed a writ petition before the Gujarat High Court seeking an injunction to restrain Eitzen from enforcing the arbitral award overseas. At the same time, Eitzen approached the Bombay High Court seeking enforcement of the arbitral award in India (having successfully sought enforcement in other foreign courts) which Ashapura contested. Separately, Ashapura had a similar dispute with another entity in respect of which it also contested enforcement proceedings. The decisions in the lower courts arising from these three parallel proceedings became the subject of consolidated appellate proceedings before the Supreme Court. The issue in question was whether Part I of the IACA 1996 had been excluded by the parties.

In this case, the parties had opted for arbitration in London and for English law to govern the arbitration. The Supreme Court observed that such a situation had been held to have excluded Part I of the IACA 1996 in *Reliance I*. The Supreme Court also relied on and cited *Reliance II*. It held as follows:[45]

> In this case the losing side has relentlessly resorted to apparent remedies for stalling the execution of the Award and in fact even attempted to prevent Arbitration. This case has become typical of cases where even the fruits of Arbitration are interminably delayed. Even though it has been settled law for quite some time that Part I is excluded where parties choose that the seat of Arbitration is outside India and Arbitration should be governed by the law of a foreign country ... the law is too well settled and with good reasons, for us to take another view. We do not wish to endorse 'a recipe for litigation and (what is worse) confusion'.

The Supreme Court went on to observe that the mere choosing of the seat attracts the law applicable to such location and it would not be necessary to specify which law would apply to the arbitration proceedings. It held that its conclusion was further supported by the reference in the arbitration clause to an 'Umpire', whose decision would be final and binding in the event that the arbitrators appointed by the parties did not agree. The Court observed that the IACA 1996 does not make any provision for an umpire and the parties' intention was clearly to refer to an umpire under Section 21 of the English Arbitration Act 1996.

The *BALCO* Regime: Prospective Application of the Seat Principle

As is evident from the above, following *Bhatia* and subsequent extensions of the ruling in a number of cases, the Indian courts had exercised wide jurisdiction in relation to international arbitration proceedings seated outside India, for example, in respect of the granting of interim injunctions, appointment of tribunal members, and the review of foreign arbitral awards. It also led to a long line of Supreme Court and High Court decisions on what factors (such as choice of foreign seat or foreign law to govern the contract or the arbitration agreement) would give rise to an 'implied exclusion' of the applicability of Part I of the IACA 1996.

The Supreme Court in December 2011 referred this question of principle for consideration by a five-judge Constitution Bench in the *BALCO* judgment, which is arguably the most significant arbitration-related decision of the Supreme Court to date. In a 177-page judgment which addresses numerous issues—and serves as the leading authority on many different principles as a result—one of the key findings of the Constitution Bench was that Part I of the IACA 1996 was applicable only to arbitrations which take place within the territory of India. This was a ground-breaking decision which brought much-awaited clarity in the country and internationally. The Court decided as follows:[46]

> [W]e are of the considered opinion that the Arbitration Act, 1996 has accepted the territoriality principle which has been adopted in the UNCITRAL Model Law. Section 2(2) makes a declaration that Part I of the Arbitration Act, 1996 shall apply to all arbitrations which take place within India. We are of the considered opinion that Part I of the Arbitration Act, 1996 would have no application to International Commercial Arbitration held outside India. Therefore, such awards would only be subject to the jurisdiction of the Indian courts when the same are sought to be enforced in India in accordance with the provisions contained in Part II of the Arbitration Act, 1996. In our opinion, the provisions contained in Arbitration Act, 1996 make it crystal clear that there can be no overlapping or intermingling of the provisions contained in Part I with the provisions contained in Part II of the Arbitration Act, 1996.

> With utmost respect, we are unable to agree with the conclusions recorded in the judgments of this Court in Bhatia International (supra) and Venture Global Engineering (supra). In our opinion, the provision contained in Section 2(2) of the Arbitration Act, 1996 is not in conflict with any of the provisions either in Part I or in Part II of the Arbitration Act, 1996. In a foreign seated international commercial arbitration, no application for interim relief would be maintainable under Section 9 or any other provision, as applicability of Part I of the Arbitration Act, 1996 is limited to all arbitrations which take place in India. Similarly, no suit for interim injunction simpliciter would be maintainable in India, on the basis of an international commercial arbitration with a seat outside India.

We conclude that Part I of the Arbitration Act, 1996 is applicable only to all the arbitrations which take place within the territory of India.

> As mentioned in the above excerpt, the Supreme Court also held that it would not be possible for parties to seek interim measures from the Indian courts in relation to foreign-seated arbitrations.

However, the sting in the tail of this landmark decision was that it was only to apply prospectively to all the arbitration agreements executed thereafter, that is after 6 September 2012. Although this prospective application was suggested to provide comfort and certainty to those parties who entered into agreements to arbitrate on the understanding of the law as it stood pre-*BALCO*, this meant that the much-needed reform to the Indian position would only really take effect a number of years from the time of the *BALCO* decision, when prospective agreements to arbitrate started coming before the Indian courts.

Given the recent nature of the decision coupled with the significant backlog of cases at the Supreme Court, it would not be surprising if some time lapses before we find an authoritative decision on a post-*BALCO* arbitration agreement. Thus, for the time being, the Indian courts continued to grapple with the jurisdictional questions that arose from agreements to arbitrate, and those circumstances called for some other means of reform.

The IACA Reforms: Further Confirmation of the Seat Principle

The proviso to Section 2(2) inserted into the IACA 1996 by way of the IACA Reforms was intended to resolve this protracted debate about the meaning of Section 2(2). The proviso states:

> Provided that subject to an agreement to the contrary, the provisions of sections 9, 27, and clause (a) of section (1) and sub-section (3) of section 37 shall also apply to international commercial arbitration, even if the place of arbitration is outside India, and an arbitral award made or to be made in such place is enforceable and recognised under the provisions of Part II of this Act.

The proviso is intended to put beyond doubt the principle that the domestic provisions of the IACA 1996 (save for three sections: sections 9, 27, and 37(1)(a)[47] and (3)) do not apply to a foreign-seated arbitration.

However, the text of the proviso appears to qualify the reference to a foreign-seated arbitration by another criterion which is that the arbitration should be an international commercial arbitration. Thus, while it is now clear that a choice of foreign seat in an international commercial arbitration would not import the provisions of Part I of the IACA 1996 (save for the few provisions identified above), the position as regards the ability to make and effect a choice of a foreign seat in an arbitration between or amongst only Indian parties remains to be clarified at the Supreme Court level. To this extent, there are two high court judgments that are important to highlight.

Addhar Mercantile Private Limited v. Shree Jagdamba Agrico Exports Pvt Ltd[48]

The first is the Bombay High Court's decision in *Addhar Mercantile Private Limited v. Shree Jagdamba Agrico Exports Pvt Ltd* (*Addhar*). In this case, the Bombay High Court considered an agreement between two Indian parties which provided for disputes to be submitted to 'arbitration in India or Singapore and English law to be [*sic*] apply'.[49]

The Bombay High Court decided that the arbitration had to be conducted in India. The basis for this decision was the finding in *TDM Infrastructure Private Limited v. UE Development India Private Limited*[50] (*TDM Infrastructure*) where the Supreme Court held, in the context of Section 28(1)(a) of the IACA 1996,[51] that 'the intention of the legislature [of the IACA 1996] appears to be clear that Indian nationals should not be permitted to derogate from Indian law. This is part of the public policy of the country.'

The Bombay High Court examined the arbitration clause and found that if they decided the seat was Singapore, then English law would have applied pursuant to the clause, which would be contrary to the finding in *TDM Infrastructure*. Thus, finding that parties had to conduct their arbitration in India, the Bombay High Court held as follows:[52] 'I am of the view that the arbitration has to be conducted in India, under Section 28(1)(a), the arbitral tribunal will have to decide the disputes in accordance with the substantive law for the time being in force in India. In my view the said agreement which provides for arbitration in India thus does not violate Section 28(1)(a).'

Given the lack of certainty of choice of seat in the arbitration clause, it would be a stretch to conclude that this judgment sets any precedent in respect of two Indian parties and their ability to agree a seat outside India and the consequence of such an agreement.

In any event, the Bombay High Court's decision arguably misconstrued the purpose and effect of Section 28(1)(a) of the IACA 1996 on two fronts. The sub-section in question (a) is intended to address the law applicable to the substance of the dispute, rather than the law applicable to the arbitration itself, and (b) falls within Part I of the IACA 1996, which would only apply where the seat of arbitration was in India (as has now been confirmed by various judicial authorities including *BALCO* and *Reliance II*, which are dealt with later in this chapter). This meant that if the Bombay High Court decided that the seat of arbitration could be Singapore, then the parties would not fall within the purview of Section 28(1)(a) to begin with. In fact, the decision in *TDM Infrastructure* has received criticism from the arbitral community for its interpretation of the effect of Section 28(1)(a), and that interpretation has now (incorrectly) been followed by the Bombay High Court in *Addhar*.

Although an appeal to the Bombay High Court's decision in *Addhar* was attempted, the Supreme Court did not give leave to hear an appeal to this judgment.

Sasan Power Limited v. North American Coal Corporation India Pvt. Ltd [53]

The second judgment is the case *of Sasan Power Limited v. North American Coal Corporation India Pvt. Ltd* (*Sasan Power*) decided by the Madhya Pradesh High Court. In this judgment, the Madhya Pradesh High Court held that two Indian parties were permitted to choose a seat of arbitration in London (under the ICC arbitration rules). This was on the basis that the law laid down in *TDM Infrastructure* was not 'applicable' and also on the basis that [54] 'the Supreme Court in the case of *Atlas Exports Industries v. Kotak & Company*[55] has laid down the principle to the effect that two Indian companies can enter into an agreement by having the seat of arbitration in a foreign country'. The material aspect of the *TDM Infrastructure* decision has already been addressed above.

By way of background, the *Atlas Exports Industries v. Kotak & Company* [56] (*Atlas v. Kotak*) judgment involved two Indian parties arbitrating a dispute in London in accordance with the arbitration rules of the Grain and Food Trade Association Limited. The arbitration clause was contained in a set of standard terms and incorporated into their contract, to which a third and foreign party was also privy, by reference.

Upon enforcement proceedings being pursued in India, a two-judge bench of the Supreme Court was asked to decide whether such an agreement to arbitrate in London as between the two Indian parties in dispute was contrary to the provisions of the Indian Contract Act 1872 (the Contract Act), and in particular Section 28, which provides that a contract which has the effect of excluding a remedy available to a party at ordinary law is void,[57] in that the Indian parties were compelled to arbitrate in a foreign country and therefore impliedly denied an available remedy in India. (It was also said that such an agreement would be opposed to Indian public policy and therefore unlawful pursuant to Section 23 of the Contract Act.)

The Supreme Court in the *Atlas v. Kotak* case found that the agreement to arbitrate was not contrary to the Contract Act, as it fell within the purview of Exception 1 to its Section 28, such that the right of the parties to pursue a legal remedy was not excluded by an agreement which provided for arbitration. The bench held as follows:[58]

> The case at hand is clearly covered by Exception 1 to Section 28.
> Right of the parties to have recourse to legal action is not excluded
> by the agreement. The parties are only required to have their dis-
> putes adjudicated by having the same referred to arbitration. Merely
> because the arbitrators are situated in a foreign country cannot by
> itself be enough to nullify the arbitration agreement when the parties
> have with their eyes open willingly entered into the agreement.

In *Sasan Power*, the question before the Madhya Pradesh High Court was whether, in circumstances where there existed an agreement to arbitrate in London, the lower court erred in holding that the parties' agreement to arbitrate was covered by Part II of the IACA 1996 and thus attracted its Section 45,[59] such that a suit filed by the appellant in respect of their dispute was rightly dismissed, or whether the agreement to arbitrate was null, void, and inoperative as contemplated under Section 45, such that the suit filed by the appellant was maintainable. The basis for the proposition that the agreement to arbitrate was null, void, and inoperative was that two Indian companies could not agree to arbitrate in a foreign country and reference was made here to *TDM Infrastructure* and the Indian Contract Act. The proposition to the contrary, that the agreement to arbitrate was valid and did invoke Section 45, was made in reliance on the *Atlas v. Kotak* decision.

The single judge relied on the *Enercon* decision (discussed above) and observed that 'if it is found that the intention of the parties was to resolve their dispute through arbitration, then it is the bounden duty of the Court to give effect to the intention of the parties' (paragraph 62). This of course is a paramount principle of party autonomy which forms the cornerstone of any agreement to arbitrate.

The Madhya Pradesh High Court[60] analysed the clause and referred to a vast number of other authorities (note to the contrary that the single judge in *Addhar* only referred to the one authority of *TDM Infrastructure*) and ultimately held, in favour of upholding the agreement to arbitrate by two Indian parties abroad, as follows:

1. The *TDM Infrastructure* decision was not applicable, as it was a judgment only for determining jurisdiction under Section 11 of the IACA 1996 and nothing more.
2. It was bound by the decision of the Supreme Court in *Atlas v. Kotak*, and the fact that that judgment related to an agreement to arbitrate under the auspices of the 1940 Act was irrelevant as it nevertheless constituted a binding precedent.
3. It is clear that based on the seat of arbitration, the question of permitting two Indian companies/parties to arbitrate out of India is permissible.[61]
4. It is found by us that parties by mutual agreement have decided to resolve their dispute by arbitration and when they, on their own, chose to have the seat of arbitration in a foreign country,

then in view of the provisions of Section 2(2) of the Act of 1996, Part I of the Act, will not apply in a case where the place of arbitration is not India and if Part I does not apply and if the agreement in question fulfils the requirement of Section 44 then Part II will apply and when Part II applies and it is found that the agreement is not null or void or inoperative, the bar created under Section 45 would come into play and if bar created under Section 45 comes into play then it is a case where the Court below had no option but to refer the parties for arbitration as the bar under Section 45 would also apply and the suit itself was not maintainable.[62]

Following the *Sasan Power* decision, on one view it remains crystal clear that two Indian parties can choose to arbitrate with a foreign seat, on the basis that *Atlas v. Kotak* continues to be a binding Supreme Court judgment that is good law. However, apart from the issue of the judgment being handed down pursuant to the 1940 Act regime, in *Atlas v. Kotak*, while the arbitration indeed involved two Indian parties (and therefore was not an international commercial arbitration), the agreement to arbitrate in the contract involved a third and foreign entity incorporated in Hong Kong. Thus, it may be argued that this judgment has its limitations, although it is difficult to see how the ratio decidendi of the judgment, at the heart of which was the fact that the parties in question were purely domestic, could be successfully questioned on this ground.

Nonetheless, it would be helpful if the Supreme Court would put the matter beyond doubt by confirming that the principle in *Atlas v. Kotak* applies equally in respect of the IACA 1996 regime, as well as in a situation where there is no foreign party involved even in the agreement to arbitrate. In that regard, the Madhya Pradesh High Court judgment in *Sasan Power* was appealed to the Supreme Court by way of a Special Leave Petition. Arguments before the Supreme Court were concluded in March 2016 and a judgment has been reserved but not yet handed down. All that can be said at this stage is that this is a space to watch. As a final point on this matter, it also remains to be seen whether this topic may be the subject of further legislative amendment.

Interim Measures

Section 9 of the IACA 1996

Introduction and the applicable test: This provision is derived from the UNCITRAL Model Law, although it has been amended by the IACA Reforms with the addition of two sub-paragraphs. It is intended to be invoked in the event an interim measure is needed prior to the commencement of arbitral proceedings or during the course of such proceedings, or even after the rendering of an award (but prior to enforcement proceedings being commenced in respect of the award).

This provision is intended to protect the subject matter of the arbitral proceedings; however, it is not intended to capture the award of substantive relief that should properly be the subject of final relief in the arbitral proceedings.

One of the key considerations by parties choosing a seat of arbitration in a dispute with an Indian connection is whether or not recourse to interim relief before the Indian courts would be available to them. The key advantage to being able to seek interim relief before an Indian court is that where a party's assets are situated in India and a foreign court is unable to assert jurisdiction over them for some reason, then a party need not be left remediless as it can approach an Indian court for relief in respect of those assets (such that they are not dissipated over the life of the proceedings, for example).

The disadvantages of allowing a situation where an Indian court may be entitled to grant interim relief in respect of a foreign arbitration proceeding are: (a) that proceedings are sometimes commenced in India under the disguise of interim relief but with the motive of bringing the underlying dispute (which should have been subject to the jurisdiction of an arbitral tribunal or another supervisory court) to the Indian courts instead and (b) the Indian courts may of their own assert broader jurisdiction over a matter where they were only entitled to grant interim relief. One can, for example, see how in *Bhatia* the Supreme Court intended to assert jurisdiction in Section 9, interim relief application, in respect of a foreign-seated arbitration agreement, but in its ratio decendi held that all of Part I would apply to a foreign-seated arbitration, which then became the default starting position taken in subsequent decisions applying the *Bhatia* principle.

In granting an injunction under this section, and consistent with many other jurisdictions, three principles must be satisfied:

1. The person seeking interim measures has made out a prima facie case.
2. A balance of convenience lies in his favour.
3. The person, in the absence of such interim measures sought, would suffer irreparable loss and injury.

Relief before Commencement of Arbitral Proceedings

Prior to the IACA Reforms, the position was that a party could seek interim relief before the commencement of arbitral proceedings, although that party had to show a manifest intention to take recourse to arbitral proceedings within a reasonable time. What was considered a reasonable time depended on the circumstances of each case, including the nature of the dispute, the relief sought, and the background of the case.

This requirement of reasonable time has now been superseded by the 90-day period (or such other longer time period as the Indian court may determine) provided by the newly inserted Section 9(2) pursuant to the IACA Reforms. This sub-section was meant to be a provision which had the effect of elapsing the interim relief obtained if arbitration proceedings were not commenced within the 90-day period following the grant of such relief. However, the Law Commission's draft language to this effect was not imported into Section 9(2) and instead Section 9(2) only provides, 'Where, before the commencement of the arbitral proceedings, a Court passes an order for any interim measure of protection under sub-section (1), the arbitral proceedings shall be commenced within a period of ninety days from the date of such order or within such further time as the Court may determine'.

Absent any language which addresses the consequence of non-compliance with the 90-day time period for the commencement of proceedings, the effect of this provision is that a party, upon the expiry of the 90-day period, will need to seek a further appearance in the relevant Indian court to 'vacate' the interim relief order, on the basis that no arbitration proceedings have been commenced within the said 90-day or such other period, so as to give effect to the intention behind Section 9(2).

Relief after the Constitution of an Arbitral Tribunal

The new Sub-section 9(3) provides that once the arbitral tribunal has been constituted, the court 'shall not entertain' an application for interim relief, unless it finds that 'circumstances exist which may not render the remedy provided under Section 17 efficacious'. Again, like its counterparts in other jurisdictions,[63] India has incorporated this provision to ensure that recourse to the courts is sought only in limited circumstances once an arbitral tribunal has been constituted.

Given this sub-paragraph would now apply also to an international commercial arbitration seated outside India, there is a question as to what to make of the reference to Section 17 (which, as a Part I provision, should only apply to a domestic-seated arbitration). The correct construction must be to substitute the reference to Section 17 with the equivalent provision of the arbitral legislation of the seat which empowers the tribunal to grant interim relief. The appropriate reading of this sub-paragraph in the context of a foreign seat would therefore be that if the remedy sought by a party from an arbitral tribunal under the provisions of the law of the seat of its arbitration would not be efficacious, then that party may seek recourse from the Indian courts.

Relief after the Making of the Arbitral Award

Section 9(1) also indicates that a party may seek recourse to interim relief 'after the making of an arbitral award but before it is enforced in accordance with Section 36.

As with the reference to Section 17 above, the reference to Section 36 (also contained in Part I) here assumes the context of a domestic award. Thus, in the same manner, the appropriate reading of the provision in the context of a foreign-seated award must be that Section 9 may be availed after the arbitral award is rendered but before it is enforced in accordance with the applicable enforcement procedure (which in the Indian context, would be a reference to Sections 47 and 48 in Part II of the IACA 1996).

Availability of Section 9 in a Foreign Seat

Many jurisdictions expressly provide that their courts are competent to grant interim relief in arbitration proceedings that are seated outside their jurisdiction.[64] Prior to the IACA Reforms, the language of the IACA 1996 had not been clear and reliance had to be placed on the courts' jurisprudence in ascertaining whether or not parties to a foreign-seated arbitration could approach an Indian court for interim relief.

In the pre-*BALCO* regime, the *Bhatia* principle imported the availability of Section 9 (as well as the rest of the Part I provisions) into the Indian courts' jurisdiction in the case of a foreign-seated arbitration. Following the decision in *BALCO*, however, the entirety of Part I—including Section 9—was precluded upon the choice of a foreign seat of arbitration.[65]

As a result of the IACA Reforms, a party to an international commercial arbitration with a seat outside India can now avail itself of Section 9, unless it has entered into an agreement to the contrary. Thus, in respect of a party to an international commercial arbitration seated outside India, but with an Indian connection, one of the first questions to consider is whether or not to contract out of the application of Section 9. Note that this consideration is to be made at the time of drafting the agreement to arbitrate (and although in principle an agreement can be reached at the time of commencement of a dispute, in practice, this is rare).

Identification of the 'Competent Court'

Another aspect of relevance in the context of Section 9 is the identification of the appropriate 'competent court' in India before which interim relief proceedings should be brought. The point has been above that one of the key purposes of availing of Section 9 relief is to prevent assets being dissipated over the life of the arbitration, in circumstances where only an Indian court can prevent such dissipation.

However, when we refer to an 'Indian court', what exactly do we mean? A court of competent jurisdiction within India that would appear to be most appropriate to take jurisdiction in that regard must be identified. Amongst the choices of courts of competent jurisdiction, we have:

1. the courts of the place where the respondent resides or has its principal place of business;
2. the courts of the place where the respondent's assets are located;
3. the courts of the place where the cause of action arose; and
4. in the context of an arbitration seated in India, the courts of the place that has supervisory jurisdiction over the arbitration.

The *BALCO* judgment,[66] which serves as authority for more than just one proposition, states at paragraph 96 by reference to Section 2(1)(e) (that is, the definition of 'Court' in the context of Part I) that the legislature intended to give jurisdiction to two courts: the courts of the place where the cause of action arose and the courts where the arbitration takes place. On the other hand, with respect to the enforcement of foreign awards under Section 47, the competent court would be the court having jurisdiction over the subject matter of the award, that is, the court within whose jurisdiction the asset/person is located, against which/whom the enforcement of the foreign award is sought (paragraph 97). This would, for instance, be the court within whose jurisdiction any immovable property is situated (Section 16 of the Code of Civil Procedure) or, in the case of movable property such as shares in an Indian company, the court within whose jurisdiction the defendant resides (Section 20 of the Code of Civil Procedure). Thus, a party seeking relief under Section 9 must consider which of the competent courts would be the most appropriate to bring proceedings.

However, the effect of Section 42 must also be addressed here. By Section 42, irrespective of what the remainder of the IACA 1996 or any other law states, where an application in respect of an arbitration agreement is made under Part I to a court, that court alone shall have jurisdiction over the arbitral proceedings and all subsequent applications arising out of that agreement and the arbitral proceedings shall be made in that court and in no other court. What happens in a situation where a party seeks interim relief prior to commencement of the arbitration pursuant to Section 9 from one court having supervisory jurisdiction but subsequent to the arbitral award from the same arbitration it seeks enforcement from a different court which is the court of the place of assets of the losing party? Would the party be precluded by Section 42 from approaching the enforcement court? The answer in respect of a foreign award is that any application for enforcement from a court of the place of assets of the losing party would not be a 'Part I' application, and would therefore fall outside the purview of Section 42 (note that Section 47 has its own definition of a 'Court'). Thus, the two situations can co-exist in harmony.

Scope of Relief under Section 9

Most of the matters covered by Section 9(ii) in respect of which a party can seek relief are fairly self-explanatory and maybe invoked without significant controversy, save for one aspect which is dealt with below. Given that these provisions find their roots in the UNCITRAL Model Law, other jurisdictions have also approached these provisions with a somewhat consistent attitude.

There is one exception to the non-controversial nature of Section 9(ii) and that is in the context of an injunction or stay of arbitral proceedings. One question that often arises is whether Section 9 is the right avenue for an anti-suit injunction, an anti-arbitration injunction, or a stay of arbitration proceedings. On its face, the section is broad enough to cover this type of relief, as Section 9(ii)(d) specifically provides for an 'interim injunction', and Section 9(ii)(e) envisages 'such other interim measure of protection as may appear to the Court to be just and convenient'.

Even if Section 9 were broad enough to cover injunctions or stays of arbitral proceedings, there is an overriding matter in the context of this chapter which is whether such a power could be invoked by an Indian court in circumstances where the seat of arbitration was outside India. There is authority to the effect that Section 9 is not applicable where the place of arbitration is outside India.[67] However, now that the IACA Reforms expressly provide for the application of Section 9 to a foreign-seated arbitration, we must address the question of what the scope of this provision is vis-à-vis an injunction or stay (that is, even where the seat is foreign).

In *Bhatia* (Para 29), the Supreme Court observed that, 'section 9 does not permit any or all applications ... there cannot be applications under section 9 for stay of arbitral proceedings or to challenge the existence or validity of arbitration agreements or the jurisdiction of the Arbitral Tribunal. All such challenges would have to be made before the Arbitral Tribunal under the said Act'. This observation was cited with approval in *Videocon*.

In a judgment of the Karnataka High Court in *Deccan Asian Infrastructure (Mauritius) Inc v. BPL Communications Ltd (Deccan)*,[68] it was also held that Section 9 should not be read to allow applications for a stay of arbitration proceedings:

> A clear reading of the provision shows that stay of the arbitration proceedings cannot be said to be an interim measure that could be granted under section 9. The section does not contemplate such an order to be granted in favour of a party. It has to be kept in mind that the provisions of the Act are designed to reduce to an acceptable minimum the interference of the Courts with the conduct of arbitration and the finality of awards. It is recognised that in the interest of justice and the healthy arbitral system there should be only a limited scope for recourse to Courts. But it is also recognised particularly in response to international commercial opinion that the parties having chosen their Tribunal should not be allowed to evade the decision of the Tribunal or obstruct or delay the decision.

Thus, it appears that the starting point is that an Indian court should not accept jurisdiction under Section 9 to entertain an application for a stay or injunction. However, as is the case with every rule, there are exceptions. The *Deccan* judgment itself went on to recognize that if a power does exist to grant a stay of arbitral proceedings, such power should only be exercised in rare or exceptional cases. Indeed, if an attempt is made to trawl through the jurisprudence, one can find examples of situations where at some stage an anti-arbitration injunction has been granted under the purview of Section 9.

One example is in the case of *Maharashtra State Electricity Board v. Datar Switchgear Ltd*,[69] where the Bombay High Court recognized that a residuary power existed in Section 9(ii)(e) to grant a stay of arbitral proceedings and stated in reliance on an English authority,[70] that:

> This decision does support the proposition that in an appropriate case, where the circumstances warrant the passing of an order as stringent as a stay of the arbitral proceedings, the Court in the exercise of its power under section 9 of the Arbitration and Conciliation Act, 1996 can impose such sanctions to secure due compliance with an order of the Arbitral Tribunal. This power must, however, in my view, be wielded with extreme caution and circumspection. Therefore, though I am of the opinion that the Court under section 9 of the Act does have the power in an exceptional case to impose sanctions against a recalcitrant party, such as by the grant of a stay of the arbitration proceedings to secure compliance with an interim order for the furnishing of security, that power has to be exercised with caution and circumspection. A default in effecting payment cannot be a ground in itself to justify the exercise of a power as stringent or serious in its ramifications. There has to be an element of bad faith, or contumacious conduct. That may be for instance where despite being possessed of means, a party refuses to comply with an order to furnish security.

Three further points should be made in this context:

1. Rather than Section 9, there is authority to state that the correct avenue for injunctive relief would be the Code of Civil Procedure, and in particular Order 39 (or Order XXXIX), Rules 1 (Cases in which temporary injunction may be granted) and 2 (Injunction to restrain repetition or continuance of breach), where relief for restraint of arbitral proceedings may be granted if the conditions set out therein are satisfied.[71] It is noted, however, that there is no specific reference in these provisions to the restraint of proceedings, let alone arbitral proceedings.
2. In an application for a stay or an injunction, Section 9 or Order 39 may be invoked in conjunction with Section 151 of the Code of Civil Procedure, which gives an Indian court the inherent power to make such orders as may be necessary for the 'ends of justice or to prevent the abuse of process of the Court'.
3. There are judgments that discuss the scope of authority to order a stay or injunction in respect of arbitral proceedings by invoking Section 45 of the IACA 1996.

These points are discussed further in the next section.

Interim Relief Relating to Restraint of Proceedings

As set out above, different routes have been pursued by parties seeking relief in the form of restraining proceedings relating to an agreement to arbitrate, whether that be a restraint of the arbitration proceedings themselves or a restraint of court proceedings in breach of an agreement to arbitrate.

Anti-Suit Injunctions

In terms of restraining court proceedings generally, whilst a lot can be said in terms of the considerations that arise in its respect, that is not the purpose of this chapter. Rather, it suffices here to briefly set out the principles established by the Indian courts in respect of anti-suit injunctions, as summarized neatly in the judgment of *Modi Entertainment Network and Another v. W.S.G. Cricket Pte. Ltd*[72] (Modi Entertainment Network):

1. In exercising jurisdiction to grant an anti-suit injunction the court must be satisfied of the following aspects:
    i.   the defendant, against whom the injunction is sought, is amenable to the personal jurisdiction of the court;
    ii. if the injunction is declined the ends of justice will be defeated and injustice will be perpetuated; and
    iii. the principle of comity—respect for the court in which the commencement or continuance of action/proceeding is sought to be restrained—must be borne in mind.
2. In a case where more forums than one are available, the Court in exercise of its discretion to grant anti-suit injunction will examine as to which is the appropriate forum (forum conveniens) having regard to the convenience of the parties and may grant anti-suit injunction in regard to proceedings which are oppressive or vexatious or in a forum non-conveniens.
3. Where a jurisdiction of a Court is invoked on the basis of jurisdiction clause in a contract, the recitals therein with regard to exclusive or nonexclusive jurisdiction of the court of choice of the parties

are not determinative but are relevant factors and when a question arises as to the nature of jurisdiction agreed to between the parties the court has to decide the same on a true interpretation of the contract on the facts and in the circumstances of each case.

4. A court of natural jurisdiction will not normally grant anti-suit injunction against a defendant before it where parties have agreed to submit to the exclusive jurisdiction of a court including a foreign court, a forum of their choice in regard to the commence-ment or continuance of proceedings in the court of choice, save in an exceptional case for good and sufficient reasons, with a view to prevent injustice in circumstances such as which permit a contracting party to be relieved of the burden of the contract; or since the date of the contract the circumstances or subsequent events have made it impossible for the party seeking injunction to prosecute the case in the court of choice because the essence of the jurisdiction of the court does not exist or because of a vis major or force majeure and the like.

5. Where parties have agreed, under a non-exclusive jurisdiction clause, to approach a neutral foreign forum and be governed by the law applicable to it for the resolution of their disputes aris-ing under the contract, ordinarily no anti-suit injunction will be granted in regard to proceedings in such a forum conveniens and favoured forum as it shall be presumed that the parties have thought over their convenience and all other relevant factors before submitting to non-exclusive jurisdiction of the court of their choice which cannot be treated just as an alternative forum.

6. A party to the contract containing jurisdiction clause cannot normally be prevented from approaching the court of choice of the parties as it would amount to aiding breach of the contract. Yet when one of the parties to the jurisdiction clause approaches the court of choice in which exclusive or non-exclusive juris-diction is created, the proceedings in that court cannot per se be treated as vexatious or oppressive nor can the court be said to be forum non-conveniens.

7. The burden of establishing that the forum of choice is a forum non-conveniens or the proceedings therein are oppressive or vexatious would be on the party so contending to aver and prove the same.

Anti-Arbitration Injunctions

There have been judicial attempts to define the circumstances in which the Indian courts can grant an anti-arbitration injunction: the first is in the context of the court's powers under the Civil Procedure Code, and second is in the context of Section 45. This sub-section addresses the former, whilst the latter (that is Section 45) is addressed ahead.

The recent and widely reported decision of *McDonald's India Private Limited v. Vikram Bakshi and Ors*[73] (*McDonald's*) merits discussion as a starting point in this sub-section. This judgment concerned an application for an anti-arbitration injunction made pursuant to Order 39 Rules 1 and 2 of the Code of Civil Procedure.

By way of appeal to a first instance decision that had been widely regarded as a move away from a pro-arbitration stance, a Division Bench of the Delhi High Court in the case of *McDonald's* set aside the interim anti-arbitration injunction granted by a single judge against arbitration proceedings initiated by McDonald's in London pending the disposal of a suit already before the Company Law Board in India or until a status quo order passed by the Company Law Board was vacated.

The division bench considered that in determining whether or not to uphold the injunction granted by the single judge, it needed to take note of points 6 and 7 in the principles pertaining to anti-suit injunctions set out in the judgment of *Modi Entertainment Network*. It stated that:[74]

[W]hen one of the parties to a contract containing a jurisdiction clause approaches the court of choice in which exclusive or non-exclusive jurisdiction is created, the proceedings in that court cannot per se be treated as vexatious or oppressive. Furthermore, the burden of establishing that the proceedings in the forum of choice are oppressive or vexatious would be on the party so contending to aver and prove the same.

It also referred to the English judgment of *Albon (T/A NA Carriage Co.) v. Naza Motor Training SDN BHD* 2008 (1) Lloyds Law Reports 1, in which the English courts observed as follows:

It is said that the caution exercised by the court relating to anti-suit injunctions should be increased or even re-doubled in the case of anti-arbitration injunction. It is further said that the judge is effectively case managing the arbitration and that it should be for the arbitrators, not the English Court, to decide whether the arbitration should proceed pending resolution of the genuineness of the JVA.

In granting the relief at first instance, the single judge found, inter alia, that the agreement to arbitrate was prima facie incapable of being performed or inoperative until questions put before the Company Law Board were decided. Amongst its considerations was the fact that McDonald's had invoked Sections 9 and 45 proceedings but subsequently withdrawn them. The Delhi High Court held[75] when setting aside the injunction:

Courts need to remind themselves that the trend is to minimize interference with arbitration process as that is the forum of choice. That is also the policy discernible from the 1996 Act. Courts must be extremely circumspect and, indeed, reluctant to thwart arbitration proceedings. Thus, while courts in India may have the power to injunct arbitration proceedings, they must exercise that power rarely and only on principles analogous to those found in sections 8 and 45, as the case may be, of the 1996 Act. We have already indicated that the circumstances of invalidity of the arbitration agreement or it being inoperative or incapable of being performed do not exist in this case.

This non-interventionist approach can be contrasted with a decision that is widely citedin *Union of India v. Dahbol Power Company*.[76] In this matter, the Delhi High Court appears to have granted an anti-arbitration injunction, sought under Order 39 Rules 1 and 2 read with Section 151 of the Code of Civil Procedure, restraining the advancement of a London-seated arbitration, pending the decision of the Supreme Court on a question of jurisdiction concurrently being raised in the arbitration. The Delhi High Court held[77] that it being a 'Court of equity has inherent powers to injunct a party from proceeding further with oppressive proceedings in a foreign country especially when temporary deferment thereof is not going to make much difference'. It is noteworthy that this decision was criticized in the *McDonald's* decision for the observation that the courts have inherent jurisdiction that can be exercised whenever the circumstances are vexatious or oppressive.

Section 45 of the IACA 1996

As to a restraint of court proceedings in breach of an agreement to arbitrate, the provision that is most relevant in the context of international arbitration proceedings is Section 45 of the IACA 1996, which sets out the power of a judicial authority to refer the parties to arbitration and provides as follows:

> Notwithstanding anything contained in Part I or in the Code of Civil Procedure, 1908 (5 of 1908), a judicial authority, when seized of an action in a matter in respect of which the parties have made an agreement referred to in section 44, shall, at the request of one of the parties or any person claiming through or under him, refer the parties to arbitration, unless it finds that the said agreement is null and void, inoperative or incapable of being performed.

This provision is in Part II of the IACA 1996 and thus applies only to an international commercial arbitration. Its counterpart provision in respect of domestic arbitration is contained in Section 8 of the IACA 1996.

This provision has been the subject of some judicial history; it has not, however, been the subject of any amendment by way of the IACA Reforms.

The Nature of a Section 45 Finding: Prima Facie or *Ex Facie?*

The first question that arises in this context is whether the finding as to the validity of the agreement to arbitrate takes the nature of a prima facie finding or an ex-facie finding. This question was considered in the matter of *Shin-Etsu Chemical Co. Ltd v. Aksh Optifibre Ltd and Anr.*[78]

The Supreme Court[79] found that if it were to be held that a finding under this section should determine the question conclusively, then 'it is obvious that, until such a pronouncement is made, the arbitral proceedings would have to be in limbo. This evidently defeats the credo and ethos of the Act, which is to enable expeditious arbitration without avoidable intervention by judicial authorities'.

It stated that if a finding under this section were to be treated as final, then a competent court at the enforcement stage 'might decline to go into the same question'. It also observed[80] that principles analogous to res judicata might preclude a party from raising the defence under Section 48(1)(a) that the agreement to arbitrate was not valid under the law to which the parties have subjected it.

Interestingly, the Supreme Court analysed the position in a number of other jurisdictions which contained a comparable provision also derived from the UNCITRAL Model Law. In light of the above reasons, and because a Section 45 hearing was determined only on the basis of affidavits and to the exclusion of oral evidence, the Supreme Court found that[81] 'it would be preferable to hold that Section 45 requires only a prima facie view of the matter as to the absence of the vitiating factors contemplated therein'.

The Meaning of 'Any Person Claiming through or under Him'

Another key decision on the scope of Section 45 is *Chloro Controls India Private Limited v. Severn Trent Water Purification Inc. & Arv.*[82] Although this judgment served several important purposes, one of the key findings was in relation to the language in Section 45, namely, 'any person claiming through or under him'.

The Supreme Court found in this judgment that non-parties could be bound by an agreement to arbitrate, so that it referred all the parties involved to arbitration, including those that were not party to the agreement to arbitrate.

The Supreme Court[83] cautioned that non-signatories would only be bound in exceptional circumstances. As set out below, it held that the general concept that only parties to the arbitration agreement can be party to an arbitration reference was subject to exceptions:

> A non-signatory or third party could be subjected to arbitration without their prior consent, but this would only be in exceptional cases. The Court will examine these exceptions from the touchstone of direct relationship to the party signatory to the arbitration agreement, direct commonality of the subject matter and the agreement between the parties being a composite transaction. The transaction should be of a

composite nature where performance of mother agreement may not be feasible without aid, execution and performance of the supplementary or ancillary agreements, for achieving the common object and collectively having bearing on the dispute. Besides all this, the Court would have to examine whether a composite reference of such parties would serve the ends of justice. Once this exercise is completed and the Court answers the same in the affirmative, the reference of even non-signatory parties would fall within the exception afore-discussed.

In a case like the present one, where origin and end of all is with the Mother or the Principal Agreement, the fact that a party was non-signatory to one or other agreement may not be of much significance. The performance of any one of such agreements may be quite irrelevant without the performance and fulfilment of the Principal or the Mother Agreement. Besides designing the corporate management to successfully complete the joint ventures, where the parties execute different agreements but all with one primary object in mind, the Court would normally hold the parties to the bargain of arbitration and not encourage its avoidance. In cases involving execution of such multiple agreements, two essential features exist; firstly, all ancillary agreements are relatable to the Mother Agreement and second, performance of one is so intrinsically inter-linked with the other agreements that they are incapable of being beneficially performed without performance of the others or severed from the rest. The intention of the parties to refer all the disputes between all the parties to the arbitral tribunal is one of the determinative factor.

Where the agreements are consequential and in the nature of a follow-up to the principal or mother agreement, the latter containing the arbitration agreement and such agreements being so intrinsically intermingled or inter-dependent that it is their composite performance which shall discharge the parties of their respective mutual obligations and performances, this would be a sufficient indicator of intent of the parties to refer signatory as well as non-signatory parties to arbitration.

Null and Void, Inoperative or Incapable of Being Performed

The Supreme Court in *World Sport Group (Mauritius) Limited v. MSM Satellite (Singapore) Pte Ltd* 2014 (11) SCC 639, observing that the expressions 'null and void', 'inoperative' and 'incapable of being performed' mirror the wording in the New York Convention (Article II.3 in particular), referred to various authorities in order to ascertain the meaning of the expressions. The following paragraphs from the judgment are self-explanatory:

33.   *Redfern and Hunter on International Arbitration* (Fifth Edition) published by the Oxford University Press has explained the meaning of these words 'inoperative or incapable of being performed' used in the New York Convention at page 148, thus:

'At first sight it is difficult to see a distinction between the terms "inoperative" and "incapable of being performed". However, an arbitration clause is inoperative where it has ceased to have effect as a result, for example, of a failure by the parties to comply with a time limit, or where the parties have by their conduct impliedly revoked the arbitration agreement. By contrast, the expression "incapable of being performed" appears to refer to more practical aspects of the prospective arbitration proceedings. It applies, for example, if for some reason it is impossible to establish the arbitral tribunal.'

34.   Albert Jan Van Den Berg in an article titled 'The New York Convention, 1958: An Overview' published in the website of ICCA,[84] referring to Article II(3) of the New York Convention, states:

'The words "null and void" may be interpreted as referring to those cases where the arbitration agreement is affected by some invalidity right from the beginning, such as lack of consent due to misrepresentation, duress, fraud, or undue influence.

The word "inoperative" can be said to cover those cases where the arbitration agreement has ceased to have effect, such as revocation by the parties.

The words "incapable of being performed" would seem to apply to those cases where the arbitration cannot be effectively set into motion. This may happen where the arbitration clause is too vaguely worded, or other terms of the contract contradict the parties' intention to arbitrate, as in the case of the so-called co-equal forum selection clauses. Even in these cases, the courts interpret the contract provisions in favour of arbitration.'

35.   The book *Recognition and Conferment of Foreign Arbitral Awards: A Global Commentary on the New York Convention* by Kronke, Nacimiento, et al.(ed.) (2010) at page 82 says:

'Most authorities hold that the same schools of thought and approaches regarding the term null and void also apply to the terms inoperative and incapable of being performed. Consequently, the majority of authorities do not interpret these terms uniformly, resulting in an unfortunate lack of uniformity. With that caveat, we shall give an overview of typical examples where arbitration agreements were held to be (or not to be) inoperative or incapable of being performed.

The terms inoperative refers to cases where the arbitration agreement has ceased to have effect by the time the court is asked to refer the parties to arbitration. For example, the arbitration agreement ceases to have effect if there has already been an arbitral award or a court decision with res judicata effect concerning the same subject matter and parties. However, the mere existence of multiple proceedings is not sufficient to render the arbitration agreement inoperative. Additionally, the arbitration agreement can cease to have effect if the time limit for initiating the arbitration or rendering the award has expired, provided that it was the parties' intent no longer to be bound by the arbitration agreement due to the expiration of this time limit.'

Finally, several authorities have held that the arbitration agreement ceases to have effect if the parties waive arbitration. There are many possible ways of waiving a right to arbitrate. Most commonly, a party will waive the right to arbitrate if, in a court proceeding, it fails to properly invoke the arbitration agreement or if it actively pursues claims covered by the arbitration agreement.

Circumstances in Which a Section 45 Application Could Be Granted

The Indian courts have found that even if a court has jurisdiction under the Civil Procedure Code to entertain a suit, once a request is made by the parties to refer the matter to arbitration, the court would be obliged under Section 45 to refer the matter to arbitration unless it found that the agreement to arbitrate was null and void, inoperative or incapable of being performed.[85] It has also noted that even if no formal application was made and an objection was filed in the suit stating that the arbitration has already commenced, that would itself amount to a request made by a party to refer the matter that had already commenced to arbitration. In other words, no formal application under Section 45 was necessary for invoking its effect.[86]

In a rather unique setting, the judgment of *The Board of Trustees of the Part of Kolkata v. Louis Dreyfus Amateurs SAS & Arv.*[87] relates to an anti-arbitration injunction sought in respect of a bilateral investment treaty (BIT) claim. The application was to restrain a respondent from taking further steps in the BIT arbitration.

The Calcutta High Court considered the jurisdiction of the civil court to decide on the existence of the foreign agreement to arbitrate (under the BIT) pursuant to Section 45. It observed that the circumstances under which an anti-arbitration injunction could be granted were as follows:

1. If an issue is raised whether there is any valid arbitration agreement between the parties and the Court is of the view that no agreement exists between the parties.
2. If the arbitration agreement is null and void, inoperative or incapable of being performed.
3. Continuation of foreign arbitration proceeding might be oppressive or vexatious of unconscionable.

While the facts of the decision are not in themselves relevant in this context, this authority stands for the proposition that the IACA 1996 can be invoked in respect of investment treaty disputes. Notably, no objection was raised to the jurisdiction of the Indian courts to determine the application pursuant to Section 45 on the ground that it was a BIT arbitration.

Finally, the Supreme Court has confirmed that Section 5 of the IACA 1996 (which bars intervention by judicial authority in an agreement to arbitrate) would be applicable equally to international arbitration which falls within the scope of Part II of the IACA 1996.[88]

Enforcement of Foreign Awards and Public Policy

Enforcement of Foreign Awards

Section 48 of the IACA 1996

Section 48 addresses the conditions for enforcement of foreign awards and sets out the grounds by which an Indian court can refuse enforcement of a foreign award. This is another provision that originates from the UNCITRAL Model Law, save for the

amendments which are discussed in Section 48, as amended by the
IACA Reforms, as follows:

1. Enforcement of a foreign award may be refused at the request
    of the party against which it is invoked, but only if that party
    furnishes to the court proof that:
    i.   the parties to the agreement referred to in section 44 were,
          under the law applicable to them, under some incapacity, or
          the said agreement is not valid under the law to which the
          parties have subjected it or, failing any indication thereon,
          under the law of the country where the award was made;
    ii.   the party against which the award is invoked was not
          given proper notice of the appointment of the arbitrator
          or of the arbitral proceedings or was otherwise unable to
          present his case;
    iii. the award deals with a difference not contemplated by or
          not falling within the terms of the submission to arbitra-
          tion, or it contains decisions on matters beyond the scope
          of the submission to arbitration. Provided that, the deci-
          sions on matters submitted to arbitration can be separated
          from those not so submitted, the part of the award which
          contains decisions on matters submitted to arbitration may
          be enforced;
    iv.   the composition of the arbitral authority or the arbitral
          procedure was not in accordance with the agreement of
          the parties, or, failing such agreement, was not in accor-
          dance with the law of the country where the arbitration
          took place or;
    v.   the award has not yet become binding on the parties, or has
          been set aside or suspended by a competent authority of the
          country in which, or under the law of which, that award
          was made.
2. Enforcement of an arbitral award may also be refused if the court
    finds that:
    i.   the subject matter of the difference is not capable of settle-
          ment by arbitration under the law of India;
    ii.   the enforcement of the award would be contrary to the
          public policy of India.

Explanation 1. For the avoidance of doubt, it is clarified that an award is in conflict with the public policy of India, only if:

i.   the making of the award was induced or affected by fraud or corruption or was in violation of section 75 or section 81; or
ii.   it is in contravention with the fundamental policy of Indian law; or
iii. it is in conflict with the most basic notions of morality or justice.

Explanation 2. For the avoidance of doubt, the test as to whether there is a contravention with the fundamental policy of Indian law shall not entail a review on the merits of the dispute.

3.   If an application for the setting aside or suspension of the award has been made to a competent authority referred to in clause (e) of sub-section (1) the Court may, if it considers it proper, adjourn the decision on the enforcement of the award and may also, on the application of the party claiming enforcement of the award, order the other party to give suitable security.

The IACA Reforms

The amendments to the provisions relating to the enforcement of foreign awards constituted one of the most significant aspects of the IACA Reforms. The reason for this is two-fold:

The amendments relate to the conduct by the Indian courts in respect of foreign awards, and have thus gained the most attention from the international community; and the amendments, in particular the definition of 'Court' and 'public policy', when compared against their domestic counterparts, offer different treatment to foreign versus domestic awards (in favour, it is thought, of foreign awards).

The most notable omission in the IACA Reforms is the lack of a provision imposing a time limit on the consideration of an application for enforcement of a foreign award (as contained in its counterpart provision in respect of domestic awards in Section 34(6), which imposes a one-year time limit for the disposal of a setting aside application).

The remainder of this sub-section deals with the scope of the 'public policy' ground, as this is by far the most controversial and highly debated aspect of Part II. In some ways, the controversy has now been put to rest with the implementation of the IACA Reforms, which are also addressed below in the specific context of the 'public policy' phrase. As such, although the judicial history pre-dating the IACA Reforms is addressed here, both in the context of domestic awards and foreign awards, it is only addressed briefly and in order to provide context to the IACA Reforms.

What remains to be seen is whether the Indian courts will give effect to the intention behind the IACA Reforms and how this will manifest itself by means of future judgments.

Public Policy

India vs. the International View

It appears that India is one of the few jurisdictions to have codified its definition of the phrase 'public policy', and such codified definition that India has adopted constitutes a hybrid definition as between the civil and common law approaches.

The IBA Subcommittee on Recognition and Enforcement of Arbitral Awards produced a 'Report on the Public Policy Exception in the New York Convention' in October 2015 (the Report), which surveyed a number of countries (over 40, although the report suggests it is an on-going exercise) to examine their interpretation of the 'public policy' exception in the New York Convention, given that the instrument itself (intentionally) contains no definition.

Interestingly, besides India, only two other jurisdictions have codified a definition of the phrase: the UAE and Australia. As to the extent to which there is uniformity across jurisdictions in their treatment of the meaning of public policy, what the report suggests is that in the vast majority of countries surveyed, a violation of public policy implied a violation of what were considered to be 'fundamental' or 'basic' principles, although the precise scope of these definitions varied as between jurisdictions depending on whether they were civil or common law countries. In civil law countries, 'public policy' generally referred to basic principles or values upon which the foundation of society rests, without precisely naming them. On the other hand, common law countries referred to more precisely identified, although still very broad, values, such as justice, fairness, or morality. India seems to have adopted a combination of the approach of both the civil law and common law countries by referring more generally to the 'fundamental policy of Indian law' as well as setting out certain more precise grounds such as morality, justice, fraud, and corruption.

As regards foreign arbitral awards, the report states that many jurisdictions drew a distinction between domestic public policy and international (or transnational) public policy, the purpose being to narrow the scope of the public policy exception in the case of recognition and enforcement of foreign awards.

The IACA Reforms in respect of the definition of 'public policy' were the subject of a supplemental report to the Law Commission as a result of two of the then recent judgments which gave cause to reconsider the meaning of public policy, albeit as used in Section 34 (rather than section 48) of the IACA 1996. These judgments—*ONGC Limited v. Western Geco International Limited*[89] (*ONGC v. West Geco*) and *Associated Builders v. Delhi Development Authority*[90] (*Associated Builders v. DDA*)—are dealt with briefly below.

As the supplemental report highlights, the term 'public policy' was not defined either in the IACA 1996 before the reforms were implemented or in any other statute. Thus, the codification of the definition of the term is a novel concept. The judgments set out below go some way in demonstrating why the Law Commission thought it necessary to adopt this approach, notwithstanding that this was an untested territory.

Ultimately, it is hoped that this provides the judiciary with the much-needed defined scope of the term as well as an appropriate demarcation between domestic arbitration and international arbitration.

Renusagar Power Plant Ltd v. General Electric Co.[91]

Until 2011, the meaning of public policy in relation to the enforcement of foreign awards was as declared in *Renusagar Power Plant Ltd v. General Electric Co.* (*Renusagar*), a case decided under Section 7(1)(b)(ii) of the 1961 Act (that is, the predecessor to what is now Part II of the IACA 1996). In *Renusagar*, the Supreme Court held that enforcement of a foreign award would be refused if it was contrary to (a) fundamental policy of Indian law, (b) the interests of India, or (c) justice or morality. Thus in order to attract the bar of public policy, the enforcement of the award had to invoke something more than a violation of Indian law.

ONGC Ltd v. Saw Pipes [92]

Renusagar was distinguished in the subsequent Supreme Court case of *ONGC v. Saw Pipes* (*Saw Pipes*) in 2003, which held that, for the purposes of setting aside domestic awards under Part I of the IACA 1996, a broader meaning must be given to the term 'public policy'.

The Supreme Court held that the term as used in Part I should be interpreted in the context of the jurisdiction of the court where the validity of the award challenged before it becomes final and executable, in contrast to the enforcement of an award after it becomes final. It considered that in the context of setting aside a domestic award, adopting a narrow interpretation of public policy would render some provisions of the IACA 1996 nugatory, and thus added a new category of 'patent illegality' to the *Renusagar* meaning of public policy. Even though the Supreme Court stated that illegality of a trivial nature would not be sufficient, the decision effectively opened the door to enable a review of arbitral awards on the merits.

However, its scope was confined to domestic arbitral awards until *Phulchand Exports Limited v. OOO Patriot* was decided in 2011.

Phulchand Exports Limited v. OOO Patriot [93]

In *Phulchand Exports Limited v. OOO Patriot* (*Phulchand*), the Supreme Court decided that the broader *Saw Pipes* meaning of public policy under Part I of the IACA 1996 should also apply to the grounds for refusing the enforcement of foreign awards under Part II: in other words, that enforcement of a foreign award could be refused if it was patently illegal.

The decision was widely criticized as being contrary to international practice and generated widespread debate as to the vulnerability of foreign awards to review on the merits by Indian courts at the enforcement stage.

Shri Lal Mahal Ltd v. Progetto Grano Spa [94]

In *Shri Lal Mahal Ltd v. Progetto Grano Spa* (*Shri Lal Mahal*), the Supreme Court clarified that the 'public policy of India' grounds for resisting the enforcement of foreign awards, under Section 48 should be given a narrow meaning.

Shri Lal Mahal requested that the Supreme Court refuse enforcement of two foreign awards made by the Grain and Feed Trade Association, claiming that the awards were contrary to the express provisions of the contract entered into between the parties and thereby contrary to the public policy of India under Section 48(2) (b) of Part II of the IACA 1996. The question for the Supreme Court was whether the scope of the expression 'public policy of India' was wide enough to encompass this situation, such that it should refuse enforcement of the awards.

The Supreme Court confirmed that Section 48 did not permit a review of foreign awards on the merits. This is in contrast with the scope of public policy under Section 34 of Part I of the IACA 1996, pursuant to which the Indian courts could set aside domestic arbitral awards if they contain a 'patent illegality'.

The Supreme Court in *Shri Lal Mahal* overruled *Phulchand* and endorsed the narrow meaning of public policy with respect to the enforcement of foreign arbitral awards under Part II of the IACA 1996, as adopted by *Renusagar*. In summary, enforcement of a foreign award could only be refused by the Indian courts if such enforcement would be contrary to (a) the fundamental policy of Indian law, (b) the interests of India, or (c) justice or morality. The Supreme Court confirmed that '[t]he scope of inquiry under Section 48 does not permit review of the foreign award on the merits.... While considering the enforceability of foreign awards, the court does not exercise appellate jurisdiction over the foreign award'.

Some observers questioned the basis on which the Supreme Court in this case overruled a prior judgment of its own court. The distinction lies in the number of judges sitting in each case:

Phulchand involved a two-judge bench, whereas *Shi Lal Mahal* and *Renusagar* both involved three-judge benches.

ONGC v. Western Geco[95]

In *ONGC v. Western Geco*, the Supreme Court considered the meaning of public policy in the context of Section 34 (that is, in respect of domestic awards). The Supreme Court restated the *Saw Pipes* approach to the meaning of the term 'public policy' and adopted a wide construction in respect of one of the grounds of public policy—the 'fundamental policy of Indian law'. A three-judge bench said that the phrase should include all fundamental principles which provide a basis for the administration of justice and enforcement of law in India.

Without giving the term an exhaustive meaning, the Supreme Court set out three 'distinct and fundamental juristic principles that must necessarily be understood as a part and parcel of' the 'fundamental policy of Indian law': (a) a 'judicial approach', that is a judicial authority must act bona fide and deal with the subject in a fair, reasonable, and objective manner, and cannot act in an arbitrary, capricious, or whimsical manner, and further that its decision is not actuated by any extraneous consideration; (b) the principle that any determination by a judicial or quasi-judicial authority must be in accordance with the principles of natural justice, to which besides the *audi alteram partem* rule, one of its facets is that the authority must apply its mind to the facts and circumstances at hand while taking a view one way or another; and (c) the principle that a decision which is so perverse or irrational that 'no reasonable person would have arrived at the same' will not be sustained in a court of law (adapted from the Wednesbury principle in administrative law).

On this basis, the Supreme Court held that if the arbitrators failed to make an inference which should have been made or have made a prima facie wrong inference, then the arbitral award would be open to challenge. Therefore, this decision allowed for increased interference with a domestic arbitral award.

Associate Builders v. DDA[96]

In this judgment, also under Section 34 of the IACA 1996, a two-judge bench of the Supreme Court followed the decision in *ONGC v. Western Geco*. In *Associate Builders*, the Supreme Court reversed a decision of the Delhi High Court on the ground that Section 34 of the IACA 1996 does not normally permit the courts to review findings of fact made by arbitrators. It clarified that 'when a court is applying the "public policy" test to an arbitral award, it does not act as a court of appeal and consequently errors of fact cannot be corrected'.

It further held that an award based on little or no evidence that does not 'measure up in quality to a trained legal mind' would not be held to be invalid on that basis.

In the process, the Supreme Court clarified the law on the definition of 'public policy'. In particular, it said that an award can be set aside if it is: (a) contrary to the fundamental policy of India (reiterating the principles articulated in *ONGC v. Western Geco*, and in particular that the arbitrator must adopt a judicial approach and that he must not act perversely); (b) contrary to the interests of India, which concerns India as a member of the world community in its relations with foreign powers; (c) contrary to justice and/or morality (that is when it shocks the conscience of the court or it relates to an immoral contract); or (d) patently illegal (being a non-trivial contravention of the substantive law of India, a contravention of the IACA 1996, or a situation where the tribunal does not decide the dispute in accordance with the terms of the contract).

Despite the welcome clarification to the scope of the term 'public policy', the decision nonetheless received some degree of criticism as the Supreme Court appeared in the process of the Section 34 application to entertain contentions based on the merits of the dispute, even though these contentions were eventually dismissed.

The IACA Reforms

In its 246th Report dated August 2014 (the 246th Report), the Law Commission suggested substantial amendments to Section 34 of the IACA 1996. The Law Commission suggested that the 'patent illegality' test be retained only in relation to domestic arbitral awards and be construed in a narrower fashion than the principles established in the *ONGC v. Saw Pipes* regime.

In February 2015, the Law Commission responded to the *ONGC v. Western Geco* and *Associate Builders* judgments by issuing a supplement to its 246th Report (as introduced earlier in the chapter). In this supplement, the Law Commission stated that its suggested amendments in the 246th Report were based on the assumption that the other terms such as 'fundamental policy of Indian law' or conflict with 'most basic notions of morality or justice' would not be widely construed. It stated that a clarification needed to be included to ensure that the term 'fundamental policy of Indian law' was not widely construed. Therefore, the Law Commission further suggested that Section 34 be amended to also state that '[f]or the avoidance of doubt, the test as to whether there is a contravention with the fundamental policy of Indian law shall not entail a review on the merits of the dispute'.

In this regard, the IACA Reforms accepted the suggestions put forth by the Law Commission in the 246th Report and the supplement relating to the interpretation of public policy, and this acceptance has manifested in the current revised language of Section 48.

The Role of Arbitral Institutions

Introduction and Historic Preference for Ad Hoc

It is considered stating the obvious when said that India has seen a preference for ad hoc over institutional arbitration. This is for historic reasons—when there were few or no arbitral institutions present in India which had the means or reputation to effectively facilitate arbitration proceedings, particularly in the international arbitration context, such that all faith and hope was left to the Indian courts.

Recent times have suggested that there may be a change in this trend and a turn towards giving more prominence and hope of a meaningful role to arbitral institutions. This is addressed further ahead.

Ad Hoc versus Institutional Arbitration: A Brief Comparison

There are arbitral institutions which exist to provide arbitration services (essentially as 'administrators'), either as their sole or principal purpose (for example, the London Court of International Arbitration, that is the LCIA) or as ancillary to other functions of a trade or professional association (for example, the International Chamber of Commerce, or ICC). An arbitration which is conducted under the ambit of an arbitral institution is referred to as an 'institutional arbitration'. In an institutional arbitration, the institution will supervise the arbitration and its arbitration rules will govern the proceedings. These rules provide the procedural framework for how the arbitration is to proceed.

In contrast, an ad hoc arbitration is one in which there is no institution involved. In this case, the party may choose a particular set of rules (for example, the UNCITRAL Arbitration Rules) or opt not to choose any rules. If no rules are chosen, the procedure is governed by the law of the seat of arbitration. In the Indian context, previous decades saw many an arbitration clause drafted to provide for a seat within India and for the arbitration to run under the auspices of the IACA 1996 (or indeed its predecessor legislation, the 1940 Act).

While institutional arbitration proceedings are considered to be more efficient as they provide a degree of institutional oversight over the proceedings, one of the disadvantages of institutional proceedings is the additional expense incurred due to the fees charged by the institution, and in some cases, additional delay at the tail end of the arbitration proceedings when the institution 'scrutinises' the arbitral award before it is rendered to the parties. Ad hoc arbitration proceedings often have the attraction of lower cost (although this is not always the case taking into account arbitrators' fees and in circumstances where various institutional rules set limits on the rate of such arbitrators' fees). However, this should be contrasted with the problem of speed and efficiency, which even without the institutional scrutiny process is suffered to a significant degree by parties particularly where the intervention of courts is resorted to at many a stage if not every stage of the arbitration proceeding (which in an institutional world may involve the arbitral institution instead).

International Institutions Currently in India or Soon to Be

Notwithstanding the historic preference in India, there are now significant efforts to steer the country in the direction of institutional arbitration. The following concrete steps are evidence of this:

ICC's presence in India: the Indian national committee of the ICC is one of its most active chapters in India. The ICC has formed an Indian Arbitration Group aimed at reinvigorating the presence of the ICC International Court of Arbitration and its dispute resolution services in India.

ICA steps up efforts: the Indian Council of Arbitration (ICA), which is regarded as one of the leading institutions founded in India, has taken active steps to position itself as the predominant choice for domestic institutional arbitration in India. Its rules have been revised as recently as April 2016, which serves to align the ICA very well with its international counterparts.

The setting up of LCIA India: while the first move by an international institution in India was the setting up of the LCIA India office in 2009, unfortunately this establishment closed its doors as of June 2016. Nonetheless, it has set the scene for further developments by institutions in India.

SIAC in India: the Singapore International Arbitration Centre (SIAC) took steps to establish a liaison office in Mumbai, India. This office does not administer arbitration proceedings but rather acts as a marketing and administrative arm of its Singapore head office, so as to provide some level of an on-the-ground service to its Indian clientele.

MCIA established: while the LCIA India was closing its doors, on the one hand, the Mumbai Centre for International Arbitration (MCIA) was being established, on the other. This is a joint venture between the Government of Maharashtra and the legal and business communities. Its focus is on administering India-related arbitrations to international standards at a competitive cost. Its new institutional rules came into force as of June 2016, while the formal opening of the centre took place in late 2016.

Notes and References

1. Convention on the Recognition and Enforcement of Foreign Arbitral Awards, New York, 1958.
2. See paragraph ahead for why this should be a reference to Section 37(1)(b) rather than 37(1)(a).
3. *Russell on Arbitration*, 24th ed. (Sweet & Maxwell), pp. 94–5.
4. [1988] 1 Lloyd's Rep 116 (CA), p. 121.
5. (2012) 9 SCC 552.

6. *BALCO* was a decision of a five-judge constitutional bench of the Supreme Court given on 6 September 2012. The decision came about in the context of related cases that were referred to a larger bench of the Supreme Court by a two-judge bench which expressed reservations regarding the *Bhatia* principles.

7. [2009] EWHC 957 (Comm) paras 25 and 26.

8. (2014) 5 SCC 1.

9. *Enercon GmbH v. Enercon (India) Limited*, [2012] EWHC 689 (Comm); and *Enercon GmbH v. Enercon (India) Limited*, [2012] EWHC 3711 (Comm).

10. The Geneva Convention on the Execution of Foreign Arbitral Awards was signed in 1927 and came into force in 1929. The notifications of territories in the Official Gazette made under the 1937 Act remain valid for the purposes of Chapter II of Part II of the IACA 1996.

11. The New York Convention was adopted in 1958 and came into force in 1959. Pursuant to Section 44(b), the applicability of the convention is restricted to territories which have been notified in the Official Gazette and declared to be territories to which the convention applies. Todate there are 50 'notified' countries as per Article VII(2) of the New York Convention, the Geneva Convention does not apply between contracting States to the New York Convention.

12. (1992) 3 SCC 551.

13. (1992) 3 SCC 551 para 25.

14. (1992) 3 SCC 551 para 51.

15. (1992) 3 SCC 551 para 4.

16. (2002) 4 SCC 105.

17. (2002) 4 SCC 105 para 32.

18. (2006) 1 GLR 658.

19. (2006) 1 GLR 658, para 11.3.

20. (2008) 4 SCC 190.

21. (2008) 4 SCC 190, paras 44 and 47.

22. See paragraphs 158 and 198 of *BALCO*.

23. (2011) 6 SCC 161.

24. (2011) 9 SCC 735.

25. (2011) 9 SCC 735 para 47.

26. (2011) 9 SCC 735 para 55.

27. (2011) 6 SCC 179.

28. (2011) 6 SCC 179, para 15.

29. (2011) 6 SCC 179, para 20.

30. (2014) 7 SCC 603.

31. (2015) 10 SCC 213.

32. This judgment is addressed below.
33. *Reliance Industries Limited & Anr v. Union of India*, paras 43 and 58.
34. *Reliance Industries Limited & Anr v. Union of India*, paras 43 and 58, para 38.
35. Civil Appeal Nos. S131-S133 as 2016 (Arising out of SLP (Civil) Nos. 2210-2212/2011)) (2015) (9) SCC 172.
36. Civil Appeal Nos. S131-S133 as 2016 (Arising out of SLP (Civil) Nos. 2210-2212/2011)) (2015) (9) SCC 172, para 35.
37. Civil Appeal Nos. S131-S133 as 2016 (Arising out of SLP (Civil) Nos. 2210-2212/2011)) (2015) (9) SCC 172, para 46.
38. Civil Appeal Nos. S131-S133 as 2016 (Arising out of SLP (Civil) Nos. 2210-2212/2011)) (2015) (9) SCC 172, para 52.
39. *Union of India v. Reliance Industries Limited & Anr* (2015) 10 SCC 213, para 20.
40. [2007] EWCA Civ 1282.
41. 1 SCC 613.
42. *Union of India v. Reliance Industries Limited & Anr* (2015) 10 SCC 213, para 21.
43. Delhi High Court decision dated 3 May 2016 in FAO (OS), 450/2015 and FAO(OS) 519/2015).
44. Civil appeal nos. 5131–3 as 2016 (Arriving out of SLP (Civil) Nos. 2210-2212/2011)), MANU/SC/0583/2016.
45. Civil appeal nos. 5131–3 as 2016 (Arriving out of SLP (Civil) Nos. 2210-2212/2011)), MANU/SC/0583/2016, paras 29 and 30.
46. *Bharat Aluminium Company v Kaiser Aluminium Technical Service, Inc.* (2012) 9 SCC 552, paras 194–6.
47. Note that the reference to Section 37(1) (a) appears to be erroneous and must have been intended to be a reference instead to Section 37(1)(b).
48. Bombay High Court decision dated 12 June 2015 in Arbitration Application No. 197 of 2014 along with Arbitration Petition No. 910 of 2013) MANU/MH/1978/2015.
49. Bombay High Court decision dated 12 June 2015 in Arbitration Application No. 197 of 2014 along with Arbitration Petition No. 910 of 2013) MANU/MH/1978/2015, para 3.
50. (2008) 14 SCC 271, para 20.
51. Section 28(1)(a) of the IACA 1996 states that where the place of arbitration is situated in India, in an arbitration other than an international commercial arbitration, the arbitral tribunal shall decide the dispute submitted to arbitration in accordance with the substantive law for the time being in force in India.
52. (1996) 28(1)(a) of the IACA, para 9.
53. (2016) (2) Arb LR 179 (MP).

54. (2016) (2) Arb LR 179 (MP), para 2.
55. (1999) 7 SCC 61.
56. (1999) 7 SCC 61.
57. Section 28 of the Indian Contract Act states: 'Every agreement, by which any party thereto is restricted absolutely from enforcing his rights under or in respect of any contract, by the usual legal proceedings in the ordinary tribunals, or which limits the time within which he may thus enforce his rights, is void to that extent.

Exception 1. This section shall not render illegal a contract, by which two or more persons agree that any dispute which may arise between them in respect of any subject or class of subjects shall be referred to arbitration, and that only the amount awarded in such arbitration shall be recoverable in respect of the dispute so referred'.
58. *Atlas Exports Industries v. Kotak & Company.*
59. Section 45 of the IACA 1996 states:

Notwithstanding anything contained in Part I or in the Code of Civil Procedure, 1908 (5 of 1908), a judicial authority, when seized of an action in a matter in respect of which the parties have made an agreement referred to in Section 44, shall, at the request of one of the parties or any person claiming through or under him, refer the parties to arbitration, unless it finds that the said agreement is null and void, inoperative or incapable of being performed.
60. *Sasan Power Limited v. North American Coal Corporation India Pvt. Ltd* 2016 (2) Arb LR 179 (MP).
61. *Sasan Power Limited v. North American Coal Corporation India Pvt. Ltd* 2016 (2) Arb LR 179 (MP), para 55.
62. *Sasan Power Limited v. North American Coal Corporation India Pvt. Ltd* 2016 (2) Arb LR 179 (MP), para 70
63. See Arbitration Act 1996 (England), Sections 44(5)–(6) *(Court powers exercisable in support of arbitral proceedings)*; International Arbitration Act (Singapore), Sections 12A(6)–(7) *(Court-ordered interim measures)*; and Arbitration Ordinance (Cap. 609) (Hong Kong), Section 45(4) *(Article 17J of the UNCITRAL Model Law (Court-Ordered Interim Measures))*.
64. See, for example, Arbitration Act 1996 (England), Section 2(3) *(Scope of application of provisions)*; International Arbitration Act (Singapore), Sections 12A(1)(b) and 12A(3) *(Court-Ordered Interim Measures)*; and Arbitration Ordinance (Cap. 609) (Hong Kong), Sections 45(2) and 45(5)–(8), Article 17J of the UNCITRAL Model Law (Court-Ordered Interim Measures).
65. *Bharat Aluminium Company v. Kaiser Aluminium Technical Service, Inc.* (2012) 9 SCC 552, paras. 195–6.

66. This judgment is addressed above.

67. *Kitec Industries (India) Ltd v. Unicor Gmbh Rahn Plastmaschinen & Anr1999* (48) DRJ 316. See also *Bharat Aluminium Company v. Kaiser Aluminium Technical Service*, Inc. (2012) 9 SCC 552, para 195.

68. (2005) 2 Arb LR 450, para 14.

69. (2003) 2 Bom CR 81, para 52.

70. *International Ltd v. International Industrial Food Co. Sal* (1989) 1 All. E.R. 613, in the context of an English provision analogous to section 9 of the IACA 1996.

71. See *Ardy International Pvt. Ltd v. Inspiration Clothes & U* (2006) 1 SCC 417. This judgment also clarified that section 8 of the IACA 1996 is not the appropriate avenue, though this is not a provision considered any further in this chapter.

72. 2003 (1) Arb. LR 533 (SC) 11–12.

73. Delhi High Court decision dated 21 July 2016 in FAO (OS) 9/2015 and CM No. 326/2015; MANU/DE/1684/2016.

74. Delhi High Court decision dated 21 July 2016 in FAO (OS) 9/2015 and CM No. 326/2015; MANU/DE/1684/2016, para 37.

75. Delhi High Court decision dated 21 July 2016 in FAO (OS) 9/2015 and CM No. 326/2015; MANU/DE/1684/2016, para 59.

76. Delhi High Court decision dated 5 May 2004 in I.A. No. 6663/2003 in Suit No. 1268/2003.

77. Delhi High Court decision dated 5 May 2004 in I.A. No. 6663/2003 in Suit No. 1268/2003, para 23.

78. (2005) 7 SCC 234.

79. (2005) 7 SCC 234, para 72.

80. (2005) 7 SCC 234, para 15.

81. (2005) 7 SCC 234, para 78.

82. (2013) 1 SCC 64.

83. (2013) 1 SCC 64, paras 73–4, 76.

84. Available www.arbitration-icca.org/media/0/12125884227980/new_york_convention_of-1958_overview.pdf.

85. *World Sport Group (Mauritius) Limited v. MSM Satellite (Singapore)* Pte Ltd 2014 (11) SCC 639.

86. *World Sport Group (Mauritius) Limited v. MSM Satellite (Singapore)* Pte Ltd 2014 (11) SCC 639.

87. Calcutta High Court decision dated 29 September 2014 in GA 1997 as 2014 and CS NO. 220 of 2014.

88. *Chatterjee Petrochem Co. and another v. Haldia Petrochemicals Ltd and others* (2014) 14 SCC 574, para 31.

89. (2014) 9 SCC 263.
90. (2015) 3 SCC 49.
91. (1994) Supp (1) SCC 644.
92. (2003) 5 SCC 705.
93. (2011) 10 SCC 300.
94. Civil Appeal No. 5085 of 2013 (2014) 2 SCC 433.
95. (2014) 9 SCC 263.
96. 2014 (4) ARBLR 307(SC).

PART III

MEDIATION

17

Commercial Mediation

An Evolving Frontier of Alternative Dispute
Resolution in India

Allison M. Malkin and *D. Gracious Timothy*

The principles and practice of mediation are not new or even contemporary concepts, with consensual forms of dispute resolution
observed in traditional societies dating back centuries. Even before
litigation or trial advocacy, informal means of resolving disputes
through the use of third-party interventions were familiar to nearly
every society. Exploring the concepts inherent within commercial
mediation and its scope in India exposes itself to several key concerns
raised by commercial and business entities. How are alternative dispute resolution (ADR) mechanisms being utilized to address disputes
currently and how are these various mechanisms understood within
the legal and business community? More specifically, how can mediation be utilized as an instrument for boosting commercial growth
and business in India to achieve its fullest potential?

India is a powerful emerging economy with fertile and appealing
markets. Increasingly, rapid globalization is demanding commercial

integration on multiple levels. The rapid expansion of technology, including e-commerce, and more frequent international business partnerships, has brought the need for collaborative dispute resolution processes to the fore. It is, therefore, both relevant and necessary to locate and cultivate commercial mediation in India within a broader global context, identifying domestic Indian statutes and frameworks impacting mediation in the commercial sphere.

Mediation is progressing to the top as the first choice for dispute settlement because it has to. Corporate entities are expected to secure positive settlement outcomes at lower costs, minimizing risks with shareholder assets. It is becoming increasingly necessary that businesses draw a line under conflict budgets and opt for progressive, more effective outcomes. In addition, legal practitioners are becoming convinced that extemporaneous early conflict resolution is more efficient, especially in terms of client satisfaction. Therefore, mediation merits further exploration and potential utilization in India, given the sea of existing commercial[1] disputes and those impending.

Fundamental to this investigation of commercial mediation in India is the development of an understanding of the roles of various stakeholders; in-house counsel, mediation advocates, the commercial parties themselves and significantly, the key qualities and designations of the mediator. These stakeholders operate in a variety of environments and as such, the scope of the application of commercial mediation is both broad and inclusive. For many years, mediation has suffered misperceptions. Bringing clarity, therefore, to the concept and its application in the legal and commercial context is indispensable. This chapter deals with these concerns providing a firm base for users and practitioners to make threshold decisions about choosing mediation.

This chapter does not conclude that mediation is appropriate in all matters of commercial dispute nor does it suggest that mediation supplants other forms of dispute resolution.[2] This chapter does, however, make a case for deepening the understanding of mediation and its application in commercial disputes as a means of offering additional tools from which to draw upon in an increasingly complex world. Mediation has proven to be an extraordinary process of reaching a settlement when conducted by a skilled mediator, assisted by a trained advocate, and participated by informed users. The authors share a strong belief in the promise of commercial mediation and the increasingly valuable inputs that can be made in employing this approach in India.

Mediation: Perceptions and Myths versus Reality

Mediation and Other Forms of Alternative Dispute Resolution

Mediation is just one of many alternative forms of dispute resolution in practice in India, and around the world. Mediation's associates include negotiation, expert determination, dispute review boards (DRBs), lok adalats, and arbitration. It is seen that amongst the Alternative Dispute Resolution (ADR) family, arbitration is the most widely adopted method for business and commercial disputes, domestic and international. However, users have time and again expressed that arbitration in India appears to be the equivalent of going to court, with many of the same advantages and disadvantages. They are lengthy, expensive, formal, and adversarial. So, what could then be considered ADR in the true sense? It is not arbitration. It is surely the use of mediation, which is relaxed, faster, less expensive, and gives parties full control over the outcome of the dispute. However, despite the fact that mediation works and the very institution is in place, it is either rarely used or has been perceived wrongly for reasons known and unknown. Repeatedly, research and practice uncover popular myths surrounding mediation and consensual dispute resolution (CDR), more generally. Many of these false impressions have been succinctly assumed in the following series of statements:

True or False?

1. Mediation is a softer approach to justice.
2. Mediation yields a lesser form of justice.
3. Suggesting mediation makes disputants appear weak and unsure of their potential for success at trial.
4. What I say in mediation can be used against me at a later date.
5. It's too late for us to go to mediation.
6. That mediators need to be lawyers or judges.

7. I'm nervous that a mediator will make the wrong decision.
8. It doesn't work and it's a waste of time.

The misperceptions above are a handful of the common myths surrounding mediation. They are fuelled by a lack of conceptual and procedural understanding of mediation on the part of advocates and users more generally; the opposing nature of mediation and adversarial processes causing reluctance; fears associated with financial implications in commercial disputes preventing the inclination to try mediation and concerns surrounding the process being unfamiliar and, therefore, being an invaluable use of time.

What is mediation then? Although it does not have one agreed upon definition,[3] simply phrased, it is a voluntary process of facilitated negotiation between disputing parties where the selected or appointed mediator (the third party) has no vested interest in the outcome of the dispute. The goal of mediation is a consensual settlement. Though the decision to settle in mediation is always voluntary, the decision to enter into mediation may even be suggested or mandated by a court. Alternatively, parties may elect to enter into mediation in a private capacity by either entering into a mediation agreement for future disputes or once a dispute has arisen.[4]

Mediation is utilized in a range of areas from divorce and family disputes to intellectual property and environmental conflict. Unlikely as it may seem, the principles of mediation in commercial disputes are the same as in the aforementioned. Likewise, in all of these cases, whatever may be the type of dispute, the advantages of mediation remain the same: risk avoidance, conservation of expenses, prevention of delay, and escaping the stress of a lawsuit. As a backdrop to the discussion, a range of qualitative and quantitative properties characterize the mediation process as shown in Table 17.1.

The process of mediation is applicable in various contexts, and equally, the mediator may exercise a variety of styles and approaches in the process.[5] Facilitative and evaluative mediation styles exist on a sliding scale.[6] Facilitative mediators guide parties through the negotiation, encouraging parties to move beyond their own positions to consider the positions, interests, and needs of the other side. A degree of reality testing[7] of the parties' assertions takes place where hypothetical outcomes have the opportunity to be examined. Evaluative

Table 17.1 Universal Properties Associated with the Process of Mediation

Qualitative Characteristics	Quantitative Characteristics
• Active participation by parties who own the process (self-determination) • Preserves future relationships • Flexible in nature • Creative and giving scope for option generation • Informal process • Bespoke or tailor-made • Highlights areas of commonality	• Confidential process • Efficient and structured • Identifies underlying positions, interests, and needs of parties from a neutral perspective • Cost-effective: costs of mediation are most often shared equally between parties; huge cost-saving potential in avoiding litigation

Source: Authors.

mediators may be more directive in negotiations by drawing attention to the substantive issues and arguments in a dispute and driving parties towards practical settlement options. Both have their place and offer benefits depending on the dispute, whether the mediation is court-connected or private, the subject matter of the dispute, and the stage of the mediation process. In spite of required neutrality, the preparation, personality, and powers of persuasion held by the mediator absolutely impact each process. The varied and flexible approach of mediation processes make it the only tailored alternative in which the diverse needs of parties are truly and holistically met.

Reflecting on the list of false impressions above, a more accurate series of statements might look something like this.

1. Mediation offers disputing parties a unique opportunity to find a negotiated settlement which addresses the specific needs of their dispute.
2. A mediator is not a judge or an arbitrator nor does the mediator hold any power to make binding decisions. A mediator's job is to assist the parties in reaching a solution that works best for them because the parties hold the power to control the outcome and not the mediator.
3. Suggesting mediation is progressive and allows for the preservation of relationships, costs, resources, and time.

4. Mediation can prevent future conflict between parties.
5. Mediators, notably commercial mediators, often come from legal backgrounds; however, the field is occupied by an array of professionals with diverse backgrounds such as lawyers, journalists, engineers, social workers/activists, judges, and so on.
6. It is never too late to go to mediation. The decision to mediate may be considered at any stage, wherever evaluated to be appropriate or considered to be helpful.

It is the flexible and bespoke nature of the mediation approach that offers the scope for powerful results commercially, emotionally, and interpersonally. The qualities listed above capture some of what makes mediation uniquely beneficial when compared with other popular ADR methods. Quoting Sriram Panchu, senior advocate at High Court of Madras, who shares his perspective about the aptness of mediation through an illustrative analogy: '[T]he point is that the roots and symptoms of conflict differ from case to case. The treatment must be appropriate for each case instead of herding all of them through a civil procedure code system. Somewhat like the treatment of a medical problem, proper evaluation and diagnosis and appropriate prescriptions from a range of conflict resolution methods is needed.'[8]

Mediation among Other Forms of ADR

ADR in its myriad forms shares the commonality of sitting outside formal adversarial channels of court-led trial processes. Disputants may choose from a range of alternatives as is relevant to the field of a particular dispute, the stage of advancement and the particular details of a dispute. It would be remiss to exclude a mention of other popular ADR methods, briefly explained hereunder.

Arbitration is a private process involving the selection of a third-party—neutral(s)—with no vested interest in the outcome of a dispute.[9] After listening to and reviewing the submissions of all parties, the arbitrator is tasked with producing an award which is binding in nature. Arbitration agreements are negotiated in advance of the process and are recognized by the Indian courts as per the Arbitration and Conciliation Act, 1996, (1996 Act), in addition to the Indian Contact Act, 1872. Arbitration can also be found in combination with other forms of ADR. For example, Med-Arb (mediation-arbitration) is a process whereby disputants are offered mediation as a primary settlement option and in the event that no agreement is reached, parties accept an arbitral award. The mediation and subsequent arbitration, should it be required, are conducted by the same person. The neutral and impartial mediator changes hats to then proffer a binding decision.[10]

An Expert Determination involves selecting a neutral third party with specialist knowledge in a particular field. Akin to arbitration, these experts evaluate the merits of disputing parties and recommend a report on the dispute. Commercial entities often agree on provisions for expert determination during contract negotiation. In some ways, it offers parties in dispute an early assessment and evaluation of the merits of their case before they pursue legal action.

A DRB is a work-site dispute adjudication process, comprising of members selected by the contracting parties at the commencement of a project. Generally, the members undertake a regular visit to the site and are, therefore, actively involved throughout the project. It is also a creature of contract; however, its decision does not have the status of an arbitral award or a court decree. While DRBs are commonly related to the construction industry, DRBs are now found in the maritime industry, build-operate-transfer (BOT) or build-own-operate-transfer (BOOT) concession projects, financial services industry, operational and maintenance contracts.

With the explosion of e-commerce in recent years, provisions to address issues between consumers and businesses and between commercial entities are developing at an increasing pace. ODR[11] mechanisms bring parties together online and offer arbitrative, mediative, or consumer complaint settlement options depending upon the area of dispute. Potential also exists for the resolution of disputes between commercial businesses working together internationally. ODR in India is gradually developing in real time with world standards so as to remain competitive in the global market. A burgeoning area to engage as technology continues to advance and the stage is set in the Indian arena.[12]

To appreciate the differences between litigation, arbitration, and mediation, the table below is helpful to understand them in contrast to each other as shown in Table 17.2.

Table 17.2 Comparison between Judicial Process and the Flagships of ADR

Judicial Process	Arbitration	Mediation
Judicial process is an adjudicatory process where a third party (judge/other authority) decides the outcome, for example, a court or a tribunal.	Arbitration is a quasi-judicial adjudicatory process where the arbitrator(s) is appointed by the court or by the parties to decide the dispute.	Mediation is a negotiation process and not an adjudicatory process. The mediator facilitates the process. Parties participate directly in the resolution of their dispute and decide the terms of settlement.
Procedure and decision are governed, restricted, and controlled by the provisions of the relevant statutes. For example, the Code of Civil Procedure, 1908, the Indian Evidence Act, 1872.	Procedure and decision are governed, restricted, and controlled by the provisions of the Arbitration & Conciliation Act, 1996. Parties may agree on the applicability of other procedural statutes.	Procedure and the process of a settlement are not controlled, governed, or restricted by statutory provisions thereby allowing freedom and flexibility.
The decision of the third party is binding on the parties.	The award in arbitration is binding on the parties.	A binding settlement is reached only if parties arrive at a mutually acceptable agreement. Parties may agree on morphing the said settlement into an arbitral award on agreed terms.[13]
Adversarial in nature, as the focus is on past events and determination of rights and liabilities of parties.	Adversarial in nature as the focus is on the determination of rights and liabilities of parties.	Collaborative in nature as the focus is on the present and the future and resolution of disputes is by mutual agreement of parties irrespective of rights and liabilities.

Personal appearance or active participation of parties is not always required. For example, during a trial for witness statement and cross-examination.	Personal appearance or active participation of parties is not always required. For example, during trial stage.	Personal appearance and active participation of the parties is the cornerstone of the process.
A formal proceeding held in public and follows strict procedural stages.	A formal proceeding held in private following strict procedural stages. The process may be subject to confidentiality.	A non-judicial and informal proceeding held in private with flexible procedural stages. The entire process is confidential in nature.
The decision is appealable.	Award is subject to challenge on specified grounds.	Decree/Order in terms of the settlement is final and is not appealable.
No opportunity for parties to communicate directly with each other.	No opportunity for parties to communicate directly with each other.	Optimal opportunity for parties to communicate directly with each other in the presence of the mediator.
Involves payment of court fees.	Does not involve payment of court fees.	In the case of settlement in a court-annexed mediation, the court fee already paid is refundable as per the rules.

Source: Mediation and Conciliation Project Committee, Supreme Court of India, 'Mediation Training Manual of India', New Delhi, paras 20–2.

The Driving Force of Commercial Parties to Adopt Mediation

The outlook towards mediation has much improved in the recent years. Once upon a time, the process was considered to have 'failed' if parties did not reach a settlement; however, now, commercial parties approach mediation with an open mind, irrespective of the dispute getting settled there. Even though a settlement may not materialize, mediation benefits the parties by helping understand each other's perspectives; narrowing down the issues; paving the way to consider partial resolutions on negotiable issues; and even making it worth invoking the next dispute resolution step, without wounding the relationship. Numerous factors such as these may drive parties to consider mediation and work towards a settlement are noted here:[14]

1. It is often said that if a party wants an on-going relationship in cooperation with the other, winning a case (or a battle) against them is the last thing one should do. This serves only to prolong hostility between the parties. Mediation doesn't merely conclude matters. Whilst securing the parties' future relations, mediation *resolves* matters.

2. The costs and flaws of the legal system in the main suit and connected matters (such as interim applications, parallel legal actions, and so on).

3. Delays having pernicious effects on the business and exchequer. Commercial parties may, therefore, tend to strongly prefer avoiding losses rather than acquiring gains.

4. The ability of a party to wear down the other with heavy litigation affecting business and financial status. The 'winner takes it all' aspect of judicial decisions can be quite counterproductive, creating a peculiar incentive to adopt mediation.

5. Exposure from a court decision in the public record as to who was 'right' and who was 'wrong' can have repercussions on future business, reputation, and otherwise.

6. Court findings against a party may trigger further litigation in collateral matters, inviting additional court actions from several other parties who see an advantage in the findings of the court.

7. Given the number of institutional inflexibilities and rigorous procedures, courts are rendered incapable of addressing a variety of issues. Everything submitted to the court in the form of a plaint is eventually converted into a claim of right or an accusation of fault.[15]

8. The implications that the Arbitration and Conciliation (Amendment) Act, 2015 (Arbitration Amendment Act) has on mediations/conciliations will be more psychological and strategic

in the authors' point of view, as the Arbitration Amendment Act made no amendment to the conciliation part of the 1996 Act. Before the amendment, stakeholders lamented over several issues and called for greater efficiency, transparency, and accountability in arbitration. Now that it is actually here, many will also wish otherwise: strict timelines, checks and balances over the appointment of arbitrators, no automatic stay on the award on filing of an application to set aside an award under Section 34 of the Act, narrower grounds of challenge, enforceability of interim orders of an arbitral tribunal, and so on. With the amendments in place, mediations will be taken much more seriously. It would no longer be seen as a mere step to just get over with before one can institute a lawsuit or a notice of arbitration.

The Aversions of Commercial Parties to Adopt Mediation

India faces an unprecedented explosion of litigation, and electing litigation, which places greater emphasis on winning battles than considering future relationships, as the preferred method of dispute resolution in India, suggests social, legal, and cultural impediments to the endorsement of mediation. What is more, mediation is either underutilized or utilized too late in the process. It isn't often channeled through the right person(s) and applied in a non-conducive environment. Necessary preparations are normally ignored and proper pre-mediation meetings are snubbed, all of which points to the fact that there is a lack of willingness to give mediation an honest try. Lawyers, clients, and the courts, all have an equal role to play in embracing the advantages of mediation, and most importantly, have the responsibility to do it the right way. Having explored some of the myths and misconceptions surrounding the practice of mediation, there is an overarching need for greater awareness around the process and benefits of mediation.

India's history, culture, business practices, economy, the ease of doing business,[16] and the current state of the judicial system, each has an impact upon the endorsement of mediation in the commercial sphere. In commercial disputes, the reasoning behind the hesitation to adopt mediation to resolve disputes may point to the following facts:

1. General lack of awareness of the process and the potential benefits of mediation.
2. Lack of confidence and belief in the process. A misplaced conviction that mediation cannot work, and is therefore, not worth trying.
3. The absence of uniform standards of professionalism and codes of conduct, leading to a lack of credibility and reliability in the process. Therefore, having a sense that mediation is unregulated and can rather do more harm than good due to perceived lack of legitimacy in the process.
4. A misconception that mediation is contrary to the culture/foundations of the legal field.
5. Fear of wasting finances, time, and resources on a process like mediation to which parties are complete strangers, thus, preferring a court decree.
6. Worry amongst commercial disputants that mediation signifies a sign of weakness.
7. A previous negative experience in mediation (or a version of mediation), which for instance, led to the claimant making heavy comprises to secure a settlement.
8. Lack of encouragement and support from the advocate representing the party, who has no background or knowledge of the nuances of mediation and its practice.
9. Commercial disputants live and breathe their conflict over weeks, months, years, and in some cases, decades. Over time, the sense of righteousness may increase, leading parties to assert a disproportionately favourable view of the likelihood of a positive outcome in court, causing a hesitation to engage in mediation. Equally, a need for retribution may become enhanced, thus, mediation, which encourages collaboration and compromise, may hold less appeal. Similarly, parties whose positions become further entrenched over time, may be increasingly hesitant to engage in mediation.
10. Where commercial parties are already under the advice of lawyers, mediation may be seen as yet another cost to bear. Understandably, additional cost implications may give rise to increased aversion towards mediation.

The uptake of commercial mediation as a valued and viable alternative to litigious processes has been met with initial resistance within the business community in countries around the world. With increased education around the potential benefits of mediation, and conscious effort made to adjust the attitudes and behaviour promulgating litigation as 'best' practice, commercial mediation stands to win over the hearts and minds of ADR users, lawyers, and the justice system more broadly. According to Dr Justice Dhananjaya Y. Chandrachud, 'Above all, there has to be a realisation that the service that is rendered by the legal profession is in the cause of justice to the common man. The needs of litigants must occupy a position of pre-eminence. Any method of ADR which ensures expeditious and inexpensive justice to the ordinary litigants must, therefore, be supported.'[17]

Commercial Disputes and Mediation

Current State of Affairs

The explosion and pendency of litigation in civil courts has, for many reasons, made it unfeasible to deal with cases within a reasonable timeframe. It is a household saying that the judicial system is overburdened and unable to cope with the demands of litigants. According to the National Judicial Data Grid, nearly 7.5 million civil cases are pending in the courts in India (see Figure 17.1).[18] Of those, nearly 0.68 million cases have been pending for more than 10 years, and around 1.2 million cases have been pending before the courts between 5 and 10 years (see Table 17.3). These numbers are indeed staggering and discouraging to any litigant, investor, or businessman. In fact, it is no longer just a 'number' but a reason to fear the judicial system and the greatest hindrance from access to justice. In the midst of this, a weak system of ADR has failed the dispute resolution system in India.

Adopting mediation has become much more pressing in a country like India in its present state of affairs, as also lamented by the Supreme Court of India in *Salem Advocates Bar Association v. Union of India*:[19] '[K]eeping in mind the laws' delays and the limited number of judges who are available, it has now become imperative that

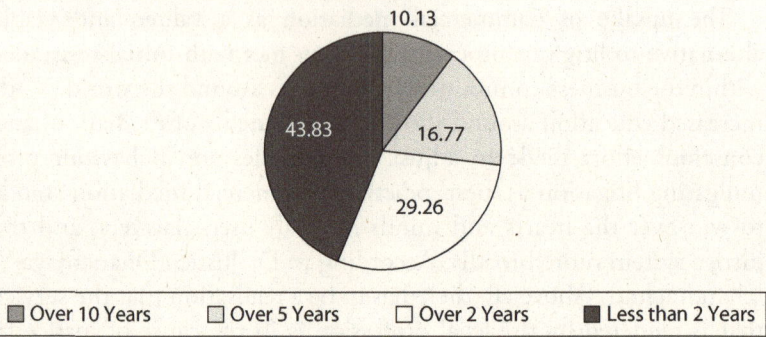

Figure 17.1   Pending Cases in India Based on the Number of Years in Pendency
Source: National Judicial Grid.

Table 17.3   Pending Cases in India Based on Their Nature and Number of Years in Pendency

Particulars (cases pending)	Civil Cases	Criminal Cases	Total Cases	Percentage
Over 10 years	67,1187	159,2024	226,3211	10.13
Between 5 to 10 years	117,8882	256,8077	374,6959	16.77
Between 2 to 5 years	222,6825	430,9653	653,6478	29.26
Less than 2 years	339,9215	639,2369	979,1584	43.83
Total pending cases	**747,6105**	**1486,2123**	**2233,8228**	**100**

Source: National Judicial Grid.

resort should be made to Alternative Dispute Resolution mechanism with a view to bring to an end litigation between the parties at an early date'. Clearly, arrears have grown to serious numbers and with significant consequences, therefore, compelling the exploration of appropriate methods of resolving disputes, such as mediation, which serves as an alternative and sometimes a complement to litigation.[20]

The dialogue on the need for mediation, however, tends to be motivated by the inconceivable docket of litigation before the courts, therefore, deriving its rationale as a tool for reducing the arrears of cases in courts. Rescuing the courts from its incapacity to handle the gigantic load of cases before it is not what mediation campaigns. Alleviating the burden of arrears is only one of its inspirations. Mediation as a complement to the judicial system achieves other fundamental purposes which are of an equal, if not greater, importance.

Mediation presents itself as an answer to some of the most daunting challenges encountered by commercial entities. It has delivered satisfaction and its efficacy has proved to be remarkable, though its prevalence has emerged only in the past few decades. India has many miles to cover before businesses widely accept mediation as an appropriate mechanism to resolve disputes, and in the long run, take the 'pledge to mediate' as an expression of their resolve to amicably settle disputes. Borrowing from Francis Burnett, 'At first people refuse to believe that a strange new thing can be done, then they begin to hope it can be done, then they see it can be done—then it is done and all the world wonders why it was not done centuries ago'.

Salient Features of a Commercial Dispute

A commercial dispute is, generally, a conflict or controversy giving rise to litigation, which involves a commercial entity (like a corporation, a company, or a partnership). Their exclusive nature may be attributable to the entities involved, the high stakes counted in, the magnitude and scale, the wide jurisdictional implications of being domestic or international in nature, the multiplicity of parties, and elements like the very subject matter of the dispute. Construction, engineering and design, defence procurement, concession projects, consultancy services, distribution, and licensing are some of the most prevalent examples of commercial relationships which, unfortunately, yield commercial disputes and illustrate certain salient features.

In mediations relating to commercial disputes, the mediators and advocates bring a distinct set of skills to the table and are often familiar with the basic concepts of commercial laws, business operations, and broad functioning of commercial entities. Commercial disputes demand mediation professionals with an exposure to the manners in which businesses perceive and operate and why they take a decision they take in a given scenario.

The principle features of any commercial dispute are often shared and must be given heed to. Recognizing these topographies, largely appearing in commercial disputes, is essential to address them (or avoid them) since they can be the reason for unproductive mediations. In-house counsels typically play a title role in mitigating these conditions, tackling obstacles and making necessary preparations.[21] Here are some of the most apparent features of commercial disputes:

1. Rarely are commercial disputes only about the money or the contract. There is always something more to the story which is often the cause and the reason why a dispute arose or aggravated. These influencers can be reputation and face-saving, fear, dominance, egos, and charged emotions.

2. Commercial parties tend to present entrenched positions, especially if they are large commercial entities or business groups. These anchored positions may be extreme and stated with absolute terms, appearing unreasonable. For example, parties produce inflated claims on the premise that they can quote excessive damages and would only consider a more reasonable figure if the opposing party can give them enough reason to do so. Massive entities, like a construction giant, generally have a 'take it or leave it' approach and are hasty about lawsuits.[22]

3. Hierarchies matter. A personnel's seniority in rank and age can influence a junior official's views, suggestions, and his responses, who has been in direct contact with the dispute. It may lead to a distortion in the overall understanding of ground realities, suppressing a junior's insightful contribution. The dynamics with hierarchical structures must, therefore, be carefully handled during pre-mediation and mediation meetings.

4. Commercial reputation has major implications and may take different forms. An entity may avoid amicable settlements so as to not appear weak to its competitors or potential disputants. However, reputation may also be the driving force to resolve disputes as soon as possible to avoid negative implications on a company's standing and goodwill. Priorities must, therefore, be evaluated keeping in mind the benefits of confidentiality in consensual processes which may even benefit reputations in keeping matters discreet.

5. The fact that an entity is in a competitive business, losing the opposing party to a competitor may be damaging at many levels.

In such cases, a continuing relationship or rather ensuring that the opposing party does not tag with a competitor may be crucial.

6. Membership in industry associations (like the International Trademark Association) or a chamber of commerce may be important. Generally, industry associations have policies governing the actions of their members. If the disputing parties are associated with a common association or chamber, the commitments made to be a part of such an association or chamber may channel a faster resolution.

7. A dispute arising from a fault of an official lower in the hierarchy may be easier to approach as compared to a dispute arising out of an action sanctioned by an official of higher ranks. Nonetheless, it is not about the people who are the cause of the dispute but rather the people who have the authority to decide to end the dispute.

8. Top management can be hesitant about taking part in mediations—either because they do not want to sit across the table from their counterparts or because they feel they are too senior to partake in mediation sessions.

The Diversity of Mediation

Even as mediation has come to be a dominant force in settling cases such as family matters, community conflicts, and industrial disputes, it is gradually becoming a major competitor and force in settling commercial disputes. In all of these various types of cases, commercial or otherwise, the principles are identical irrespective of the labels and so are the advantages: avoiding risks, costs, delays, and the trauma of litigation. Differences are generally seen in the technique, approach, the preferences of parties, the mediator, and so on.

The need for industry sensitization about mediation has been a constant effort which has gained quite a bit of popularity in India, though more so internationally. It is mediation emerging as a significant dispute resolution narrative. In the recent times, cases related to domestic goods, real estate, education, telecom, and banking sectors are being mediated and settled through mediations as a substitute to traditional litigation.[23]

The proverbial light of mediation has many beams and prismatic colours—be its cost-effectiveness, efficacy, interest-based approach, or self-determination, all are exquisitely good for commercial parties' needs be it a small-scale industry or a multimillion dollar empire, a distribution enterprise or a construction giant.

Mediation in the Consumer Business

Whatever be the type of business, consumer relationships are of a paramount priority for good and successful businesses. Many corporates (such as eBay[24] and PayPal[25]) have focused much energy on programmes dedicated to addressing customer complaints and dissatisfaction. Such programmes encourage their customers and officials to communicate with each other when there is a problem with a transaction. Ordinarily, a company official, who is not associated with the dispute, handles the problem at the first level based on the company's policy and directs it to a mediator if the problem has escalated or when the dispute is larger than the usual. These are generally handled through an ODR platform, which is helping many companies resolve disputes arising from eCommerce and those which are cross-border in nature.[26]

Mediation as a dispute redressal method answers some very relevant concerns any business has when it meets a dispute with its customer or client—addressing misunderstandings; preserving good relationship; providing a neutral go-between for buyers and sellers; mitigating damage to the company's goodwill and trust in the community; reduction of premature negative feedback; reputation in the market; and saving time, resources and costs associated with the dispute.

Mediation in Construction Disputes

Virtually every construction project commences with a spirit of cooperation and a commitment. The contractor, owner, and the consultant enthusiastically commit to the future. Nonetheless, that disputes crop up during design and construction phase is almost always the case. It is believed that significant sums amounting to millions of rupees are incarcerated only in disputes relating to the construction sector in India.[27] Infrastructure projects in India are hamstrung with schedule delays and, therefore, cost overruns.[28] Problems including site acquisition, approvals, and resource shortages are the primary logjams faced by project stakeholders.

At what stage can parties use mediation? Although any dispute resolution method is most commonly understood as a post-project practice, mediation can be tried even while the project is on-going which can almost have a therapeutic effect and help shift the project back on track. It could become effortless for a business, owner, contractor, or consultant, to simply consider mediation as a preferred dispute resolution step before engaging adversarial processes in the form of arbitration or litigation. Parties may adopt an expert advisory mediation, where mediators provide participants with technical or legal information and benchmarks, advice on the merits of the case, suitable settlement terms, and likely outcomes if the matter proceeds to determinative proceedings such as arbitration or litigation.[29] The real incentive for parties to consider mediation in a construction dispute lies in the time and cost savings attributed to successful mediations.

Mediation for the Public Sector Undertaking

A state-owned enterprise in India is called a public sector undertaking (PSU) or a public sector enterprise. These companies are owned (or majority-owned) by the Union of India, or one of the many state governments, or both. It is often said that the government is the biggest litigant and the huge expenditure involved makes a huge draft on the public exchequer. Repeatedly, it is pointed out that the indifference of the government compels people approach courts in search of relief.

In its 126th Report on 'Government and Public Sector Undertaking Litigation Policy and Strategies', the Law Commission of India expressed the need to have a litigation policy to avoid litigation or reduce it at any cost which will bring down the load on the court system resulting in the reduction of expenses on judicial set up.[30] The most recent formulation of the National Litigation Policy, 2015 is under consideration of the government with a view to bringing down pendency and reducing government litigations.[31]

The present propensity in PSUs, however, is always 'not to settle and compromise', even if it is the most commercially viable solution in the overall benefit of the company. The sheer size, locations, and sometimes nodal privileges of PSUs can create a massive business clog, locking up assets, slowing projects, and ultimately affecting the economy. PSUs need a comprehensive dispute management and resolution plan.[32] Interestingly, the litigation policy under construction suggests that disputes be first placed before the highest authority in the public sector, such as the managing director (MD), making it the MD's responsibility to settle the issue without the litigation. In cases where litigation cannot be avoided, the policy suggests that ADR methods like mediation must be considered. It is expected that litigation policy would dispel the fears of audit, scrutiny, and corruption charges, which have immobilized officials from making sensible commercial decisions, afflicting the resources and finances of PSUs. Another way is to constitute a committee of high-level officials, functioning with immunity, who can deliberate and recommend the use of mediation in appropriate cases and who have the authority to settle by giving reasons. This, of course, is an area that merits further exploration.

Mediation in Contractual Disputes

Almost all commercial disputes are contract based, and be it any sector or industry such as manufacturing and production, consultancy, or sale of goods and services, business contracts come with opportunities for disputes. In all these cases, mediation can be an essential add-on to the dispute resolution mechanism under the terms of the contract. Arbitration is surely a valuable tool, but it is not a panacea. Often arbitrations are costlier than litigation and afflicted by other drawbacks, namely, costly procedures, high fees, heavy documentation, and so on. The award-debtor cannot get over a 'bad decision' so easily. Hence, a less hostile and less confrontational method like mediation could prove to be an advantage considering its benefits, especially because it gives the parties the opportunity to have control over the outcome.

Having a voluntary process in which parties to a dispute work with a mediator who assists them in finding ways to resolve their conflict is a solution-oriented mechanism and commercially sensible, because mediation is not a win/lose determination, unlike litigation or arbitration. Moreover, mediation presents a brilliant avenue for resolution of contractual disputes and even claims based on equitable principles (in which case arbitrations are generally out of the question[33]). In complex issues where an arbitration or litigation is inevitable, engagement in mediation at the right stage can narrow down the problem, and often, parts of a larger issue can be segregated and more effectively settled through facilitated negotiations. Besides, a vast majority of disagreements that arise in contractual disputes are not over legal issues but are rather technical in nature and could benefit from facilitated negotiations. Sometimes, the issues at hand may be concerning fairness or equity. Take for example a delay claim made by a contractor which often includes 'requests for equitable adjustment'. In the given situation, the actual disagreement is not what is lawful but what would be an 'equitable' remedy given the circumstances.

Commercial mediation is fast growing and has adapted itself to many kinds of settings with the same foundational principles. This is also why many industries and sectors have turned to adopt mediation. Mediation could, after all, appear innocuous and strange to someone who is unfamiliar; however, the correct awareness can encourage the use of mediation.

The Role of an In-House Legal Counsel in Mediation

The general counsels or in-house legal counsels can play a much greater role in resolving disputes than in litigation. A company's counsel (sometimes personnel from the contracts department) who is well acquainted with the business operations and the fact of the matter is commercially sensitive and can also be assumed to be business oriented. Thus, their involvement is necessitated in all cases of dispute between the company and others.

Being familiar with the company's dispute from its very start, and how it eventually escalates into being referred to an adversarial process, is an advantage of in-house counsels. They perceive these disputes in a much broader picture: an unresolved difference leads to a disagreement, disagreement causes problems, unresolved problems become disputes, unresolved disputes become a conflict, and unresolved conflicts can ultimately lead to situations involving violence.[34] The beauty of mediation lies in the fact that mediation can be adopted even at the very beginning when 'differences' arise between the parties. In-house counsels can adopt or propagate such a 'nip it in the bud' policy, and to do so, would have to be prepared to advise their company about the advantages and disadvantages of mediation and its potential for quick resolution. For that purpose, they must realize the different obstacles that usually feature in commercial disputes and work around them as a necessary step to take things forward. In places where such policies are grounded, in-house counsels are required to confirm the failure of amicable methods before advancing into litigation.

Business and commercial entities may adopt the use of mediation as a firm practice by negotiating mediation clauses in all their agreements (by revisiting dispute resolution clauses in executed agreements or by proposing mediation clauses in future agreements). In-house counsels are commonly involved in the drafting of agreements, and their inputs may include the inclusion of a well-structured mediation clause. Many companies, through the benefit of their in-house lawyers, take the pledge to mediate as a part of promoting best governance, speedy settlement, and uncompromised justice. The pledge is a non-binding commitment to channel resources to manage and resolve disputes through mediation with a view to establishing and propagating a sustainable dispute management and resolution process. The International Institute for Conflict Prevention and Resolution (CPR) propagated the mediation pledge internationally encouraging companies to first adopt amicable channels of resolving disputes.[35] In India, the Indian Institute of Arbitration and Mediation (IIAM), Cochin, and the India International ADR Association have formulated the 'Pledge to Mediate' which is to principally use mediation as their first try to resolve disputes.[36] The concept is a driving force for corporates to re-evaluate their priorities of good corporate governance, goodwill generation, and costs reduction.

What is more? When a dispute is in fact taken to a mediator, one of the company's representatives is most likely to be the in-house lawyer. Therefore, mediation offers in-house lawyers greater participation and more responsibility to play a role in the resolution of the company's disputes. Their role becomes indispensable with them being fully conversant with the workings of the company, both commercially and legally.

The Decision to Mediate

Why to Choose Mediation?

Mediation presents unique characteristics as a dispute resolution mechanism but does not pose itself as a panacea. The justifications for the use of mediation in commercial conflicts are many, and its exceptionality is demonstrated through the preservation of on-going relationships—where much is at stake, therefore, making it commercially sensible to settle; where the case is complex due to the technicality involved; where the case demands a creative solution to the problem at hand that would not be possible through adjudication; and resource (time and costs) management is a crucial concern. The basic tenets of mediation have thus far been identified as including overarching benefits of giving control of the process over to the parties with the added comfort of flexible choices of settlement options, under the umbrella of confidentiality, and with the promise of saving time and costs, in one efficient process.

Delving more deeply into the benefits for commercial parties yields further concrete incentives for consideration. Parties in commercial disputes face possibilities of loss of income due to the expensive and time-consuming nature of the conflict. More concerning to some is the risk of public exposure, which can lead to loss of reputation, income, and future investment. The confidential nature of commercial mediation minimizes that risk as the substance of discussions and negotiations are kept within the room. Commercial mediation is especially useful in disputes where litigation has been pending over long periods of time and parties are already facing high legal bills.

The acronym BATNA, Best Alternative to a Negotiated Agreement,[37] characterizes this concept as having thought through 'the standard against which any proposed agreement should be measured'.[38] How far parties are able or willing to shift their positions and what are their real underlying interests? These more fluid and creative processes are entirely absent in court-based litigation or arbitration, where lawyers and advocates speak on behalf of disputants, and a judge imposes a decision. The legal process inherently takes control of the process away from the parties, 'dehumanizing the participants, terminating relationships and undermining sources of community'.[39]

In addition, skilled mediators assist disputants to consider the true impacts of conflict on their individual and collective commercial interests and help focus a clearer picture of the key issues which stem from underlying positions, interests, and needs of the parties. A mediator brings new energy, ideas, and constructive ways of communicating to the table. A neutral third person occupying the space in between disputants cannot be underestimated in a commercial dispute. The mediator plays a powerful role in humanizing 'the other' and helping each side to feel acknowledged in the process, as the acknowledgement of feelings and emotions are of paramount importance in situations of conflict.

Considering the laws of probability, there is never a 100 per cent guarantee of success at trial, however optimistic parties may be in this regard. Outcomes are dependent upon factors such as the sitting judge, whose particular view on the issues at hand cannot possibly be accurately predicted. When parties are able to shift their perceptions of the probability of winning at trial by even a limited percentage, the parameters of negotiation change dramatically. All of a sudden, a simple cost analysis can paint a more sobering picture of the future, should a mediated settlement fail to be achieved. This is an important form of reality testing which mediators often employ and which is highly effective for disputants evaluating the merits of proceeding to trial. This opportunity does not exist in court proceedings where it is a case of pleading your case and waiting for a decision, without discussion.

Business parties and commercial mediation professionals will point out much more benefits of mediating commercial disputes, all of which give reasons for the trend (or the need) to adopt mediation. To give a concise summary, these potential benefits of commercial mediation include:

1. Eliminating unwanted publicity and damage to reputation.
2. Customizing the process to manage the resolution of the dispute.
3. Confidentiality securing the proceedings.
4. Improving the communication, especially in cross-border and cross-cultural disputes.
5. Avoidance of timely and expensive litigation or arbitration.
6. Separating the people from the problem, and bringing the focus on key issues/positions and underlying interests and needs.

7. Providing a conducive atmosphere for generating creative and durable solutions.
8. Preservation of relationships and possibility for future business dealings.
9. Increasing value of the future business with or without the partner in dispute.

The Decision to Mediate: Appropriate or Inappropriate?

Users and advocates are frequently faced with the question of the appropriateness of mediation—whether it is suitable to mediate, and if yes, what is the right stage to initiate it? With so many pros and cons to evaluate against the hovering uncertainty, the decision to mediate can be a tough one to make. Having said that, a dispute resolution mechanism (whichever it may be) will be appropriate where its procedures, aims, and values suit the necessities of a party's given situation. To proceed with making such a decision would require some pilot effort on which the decision may be founded:[40]

1. To ensure that the users understand the process of mediation: what it is about, what it involves, its pluses and minuses.
2. An acknowledgement of the possibility of meeting agreeable solutions with the other party.
3. An adequate understanding of the legal strengths and weaknesses of the case and the ramifications.
4. Sufficient evaluation of stakes involved requiring the efficiency of time and costs and assessing the alternatives available to meet the expectations.
5. Recognizing on-going cooperative relationships, being aware of the willingness to continue and the importance of continuing them. This is also pertinent when a party has already received an invitation to mediate.
6. An understanding of the business and its practices and the commercial impact of the party's actions.

Without gathering the initial data, an assessment of whether to mediate or not may hold repercussions at the end of the line. This early information provides parties and their advocates a base reasoning on which to make that calculated decision and not simply by relying on clichéd arguments of saving time and costs, which, although necessary, are not sufficient motivators.

If mediation is given the green signal, the next deliberation must consider when to mediate. This may be either, before, in between, or after the formal arbitration or litigation proceedings have concluded and must be carried out with the correct rationale as to why. There are several considerations to make at this stage:[41]

1. That there is sufficient information available about the claim, defence, or counterclaim. If not, would a disclosure be necessary to fill in the gaps to be able to understand the viewpoint and counter-viewpoints? Adequate data is helpful in providing a broad picture of the real needs and interests.
2. That parties understand the issues raised by each other and acknowledge the counterperspectives (however, they may disagree with those perspectives) on the canvas of facts.
3. Would the involvement of non-parties be necessary at any stage?

One must also consider cases when and where mediation would work best and advance to opt for the same as a practical solution. Sometimes parties may have no conflicting interest with respect to the way in which their dispute is to be dealt with and might choose the same mechanism. But, it may not be so in other situations. Such subjective realities are difficult to manage.

When and where mediation may be most suitable is illustrated through the situations given hereunder.

1. Where relationships matter: adversarial methods are harsh and can create a rift in the relationship because, almost always, it involves a chain reaction of mudslinging activity.
2. Where resources are limited and important: protracted expenditure of time, costs, and resources can even defeat parties who have strong cases (or think that they do). Mediation may, therefore, be a sensible option as a first-try. There is a dogmatic ideology which suggests that an opening offer to mediate is an indicator of weakness. The 'don't blink first' approach is, however, inconsiderate of the benefits and opportunities that mediation presents to both parties. Of course, dishonest motives of a party entering into a

mediation can make the process futile, and in such situations, mediation could be strategically inappropriate at that point.

3. When prior negotiations have taken place and possible settlements were discussed, however, parties lost momentum due to reasons like loss of trust or a sudden imbalance between parties. Mediation can be an appropriate process to employ when negotiations have failed, and in such cases, mediation may achieve the results negotiations could not. When negotiations fail, the dispute may scatter, leaving gaps and unexplored areas, further escalating the situation if given time to do so. A timely mediation, with the help of the mediator, ties it all together.

4. When certain methods like interim injunctions and other applications are successfully sought by a party, this pressure-building tactic may have a persuading effect on the other party to consider negotiating a settlement as a viable option.

5. A favourable decision rendered by a contractually appointed DRB[42] or an expert determination, prior to a legal suit or arbitration, can have a strong persuasive impact towards settling the case.

6. At the pre-trial stage (when parties have pleaded their case fully and are about to enter the stage of evidence), parties are much more aware of the realities of their cases. Examination-in-chief and cross-examinations are, generally, eye-openers for a party, and the preparations at this stage, gives the parties a fair idea about how the final arguments will pan out, hinting upon the likelihood of a favourable decision. Usually, reality sets in at this point and the case is revisited with a fresh perspective. Having said that, the circumstances of a particular case may make it more sensible to have mediation earlier rather than later in the adversarial process. Parties may be better able to evaluate their case after the evidence stage or if the preparation of the pleading itself is going to be a costly affair (requiring an expert report and massive documentation) it may make more sense to mediate first.

7. Before a final order is passed or a decree is made, when a party is facing the risk of an adverse decision, at which stage a party feels the need to save face in public and is looking at one more opportunity to salvage the confidentiality of the dispute. The peril of litigation and an adverse judgment is a factor that may drive all forms of litigation to an amicable settlement, since it often proves to be expensive both for the claimant and the respondent.

Although it is not possible to specify conditions and circumstances which would guarantee its effectiveness, many scenarios can bring one to understand when mediation works best and the kind of scenario where it can be persuasively tried with the other party.

In many cases, mediation would not be suitable, either due to a legal bar, because of the type of remedy being sought or simply because it would be an impediment to the process of mediation:[43]

1. Where the issue is with respect to the interpretation of a statute.
2. A party is seeking a declaratory relief to declare a legal right to be binding on another party and in rem.
3. Where the need is a binding precedent or judicial law.
4. Where there is a need for an urgent interim measure. A party can, however, consider mediating once the urgent interim relief is granted in its favour.
5. Where one party has absolutely no merit in the case and does not have a bona fide dispute.
6. Where there are dishonest and mala fide motives to mediate. Take, for instance, a party not making proper and sufficient disclosures or to simply take the advantage of delay.
7. The case is criminal in nature, therefore, necessitating the court's jurisdiction.
8. Where the remedy being sought is constitutional in nature, like a writ.

Mediation is an attractive first-protocol method to employ where there is an existing relationship or willingness to continue one. The above points are not straightjacket rules of when and in what situations might mediation be efficacious. They are general constructs and key indicators of the appropriateness of mediation. Many experts in mediation would readily agree that mediation may not be the right answer in every dispute. Rather, mediation is thought of as a prized instrument in a dispute resolution armoury, with the prospect of being deployed with efficiency in appropriate scenarios.

Olé! Online Dispute Analysis[44]

The International Mediation Institute (IMI), Netherlands,[45] has designed several mediation tools to provide assistance and guidance to users, mediators, mediation advocates, mediation providers, and mediation trainers. The tools provide an online platform for those who are considering mediation, those who are practising or advising, and for those providing institutional services. One of these tools is 'Olé! Online Dispute Analysis' which is instrumental in examining and evaluating specific disputes in order to determine the best possible way forward.

Securing a Mediation Agreement

The most auspicious time for discussing mediation and dispute resolution is when parties are negotiating a commercial deal. Although parties are optimistic and forward thinking, they are sometimes not in the mood to postulate worst case scenarios. Yet, deals do go sour, there are changes in circumstances (sometimes fundamental), political and economic environments vary from time to time, and conflicts emerge over personalities. In business, therefore, it becomes necessary to negotiate a dispute resolution clause, including mediation and other forms of ADR, without which business relations can come to a standstill.[46]

It is common for a mediation to commence through the invocation of a mediation clause under the terms of a contract-executed pre-dispute. Such mediation clauses or mediation agreements oblige a responding party to mediate on the invitation of the other.[47] However, a disputant may either refuse to mediate on an invitation from one party or he can withdraw from the process even if a mediation clause or an agreement exits.[48] Parties can choose to have their own tailored provisions in the agreement to mediate, agree on a mediation institution that offers mediation services, select specific mediation rules of any institution by which they would prefer to mediate, or plainly agree to mediate ad hoc over any dispute or differences that arise between them. A basic agreement between parties will express their willingness to enter into mediation that the parties would follow the agreed procedure and be bound by the confidentiality covenants, with the options to include provisions about the appointment of the mediator, payment of the mediator's fees, and so on.

A mediation agreement may either appear in the form of a clause in the main contract, or as one of the subclauses in a dispute resolution clause appearing in the main contract, or even as an independent agreement appended to the main contract. These are pre-dispute arrangements or agreements to mediate future disputes. Parties in trade, business, and commerce are aware of the possibilities of disputes arising because of the relationships they enter into. Therefore, having a CDR clause is an investment commercial parties make to ensure speedy resolution of differences. In fact, entering into an agreement to mediate reflects the confidence that parties have for each other that they can themselves take control of problems and come to a mutually agreeable solution amicably.

Mediation is not always the sole vehicle used to resolve a certain dispute, and another phase of resolution usually follows mediation as a back-up system if mediation does not settle all the issues. Parties agree on multistep dispute resolution clauses wherein the dispute resolution forum escalates from consensual methods to more adversarial modes of resolving disputes from negotiation to mediation to expert or panel determination to arbitration or litigation, where each subsequent process is triggered by a failure of the previous. Commercial entities may prefer following this practice of giving consensual methods full effort before embarking upon more combative methods. Businesses entering into cross-border transactions, for instance, are likely to come upon unforeseen circumstances and may benefit from mediation which resolves such problems quickly and amicably, and which is also part of a larger dispute resolution agreement, should matters escalate.

In mediation, not all disputes see the light at the end of the tunnel and remain unresolved either partially or fully. Hence, differences left unresolved agree to be referred to the next adopted mechanism. However, where no mediation agreement exists, parties may mutually agree upon submitting their case to mediation after the dispute has arisen (agreement to mediate an existing dispute). Parties can arrive at an agreement to mediate at any stage: pre, mid-, or post-proceedings of a lawsuit or an arbitration.

When parties have already agreed to mediate an existing or a future dispute, they may also benefit from entering into further agreements consideration of the following aspects of a mediation:[49]

1. That the mediator appointed by the parties must be impartial and independent and the mediator shall follow whatever may be the procedure designated by the parties.

2. Who will pay the costs of the mediation and how will the parties execute this?
3. What procedural rules will apply to the mediation? Which institutional rules will govern the mediation procedure? Which institution will the matter be referred to?[50]
4. That the entire proceedings shall be protected by confidentiality and be without prejudice.
5. Parties may even be more specific about the role of the mediator and certain procedural aspects relating to the conduct of the proceedings, for instance, the mediator may generate options and give evaluations, parties can invite witnesses and have documentary evidence and persons appearing on behalf of the disputing parties must have the authority to settle at the mediation proceedings.
6. The terms of any settlement agreement shall be in writing.
7. Provisions dealing with the remuneration of the mediator.

The concept of party autonomy, therefore, governs the constitution of each mediation. By their agreement, parties determine the very personality of the process: the number of mediators and their identities, the ambit of their roles and duties, and all the other features of the procedure. With some early planning, parties can agree to mediation so that when dispute do arise, relationships can be secured, differences can be clarified, and interactions can be resumed.

Frequently Asked Questions about Mediation

What Role Does a Mediator Play?

The role of a mediator is as multifaceted as it is demanding. Mediators are simply third-party neutrals that facilitate negotiated settlements between disputing parties. She or he has no vested interest in the outcome of a particular dispute and may be selected or appointed from a list of approved and qualified mediators acceptable to all sides in the dispute. Mediators do not impose decisions and cannot force participants in a process to settle; however, through the employment of a range of facilitative and evaluative techniques, assist the group in moving towards a consensual resolution. From the moment of appointment, the ability of a mediator to establish trust between him/herself and the parties and foster trust and belief in the

Table 17.4   Holistic Characteristics of an Effective, Competent Mediator

Personal Traits of a Mediator	Professional Skill Set of a Mediator
• Trustworthy, open, and non-judgmental	• Ethical and neutral third party
• Clear and effective communicator	• Analyse and distill underlying interests and needs of disputants
• Empathetic	• Perceptive facilitator who tests realities
• Respectful and calm	
• Adaptable, creative, and dynamic	• Evaluates interests and may direct negotiations towards creative settlement options
• Intuitive and sensitive to the needs of others	
• Persuasive	• Problem solver

Source: Authors.

promise of commercial mediation are of utmost importance. Right from the point of the mediator's selection, the attitudes, behaviours, and actions of a mediator greatly impact the process that follows (see Table 17.4).[51]

Another point for consideration connects to the relevant question of how, if business people and advocates are already skilled negotiators, these professionals benefit from the presence of a mediator. Direct negotiations are rewarding only if parties entering negotiations have mutual trust and have a relatively similar understanding of the nature of the conflict and an objective assessment of the situation. Commercial parties and advocates may find it difficult to move beyond these difficulties, especially when both parties are on different pages. This convergence of trust and understanding does not always exist. In most cases, here is when negotiators will need assistance from a neutral third-party mediator in advancing their interests and building a bridge across the gaps.

It is, therefore, useful to examine the roles of a mediator in sequence: before the mediation begins, during the mediation, and upon conclusion of the mediation process.

Pre-mediation Roles and Responsibilities of a Mediator

A mediator ensures that there are no ethical reasons or conflicts of interests present to prevent them from carrying out the mediation in a neutral and impartial manner. At this point, mediators educate themselves about the dispute by reading any statements submitted by the parties,[52] seeking clarity wherever necessary. As part of the preparation, a mediator may create a timeline of events in the dispute, note key stakeholders, assess possible power dynamics perpetuating imbalance, and evaluate relevant financials in an effort to gain a better understanding of the various factors at play. Are there obvious relational issues to be aware of? What has been gained from conversations with mediation advocates? What cultural challenges may be present? Are there any triggers of bias that may need addressing? Do the contents of the dispute raise any other alarms?

Roles and Responsibilities of a Mediator during the Mediation

At this point, the mediator has already prepared the parties for the day of the mediation, and now must set the scene by creating a safe and secure environment, an open and positive atmosphere, and present a clear agenda. The mediator initiates a round of introduction inviting all attendees to introduce themselves by the names they would prefer to be called with during the mediation proceedings. The mediation agreement is signed, if it has not been already, and a review of the confidentiality protocol is conducted, with any questions related to the structure of the day addressed. The personal qualities noted earlier are critical at this early stage as the mediator seeks to bring everyone to the table literally and figuratively by creating a trusting, non-judgmental atmosphere pregnant with the possibility of settlement. The mediator describes the nature of caucuses or private sessions, the choice that parties retain to terminate the mediation, and equally, the choice they have to keep the mediation agreement open to continue their discussions, should a settlement not reach in the first session. Above all, the mediator reminds parties that this process is theirs to own, and settlement will be generated through their willingness, openness, and the determination to do so.

During the mediation, the mediator uses a range of skills and tools. 'Research on mediator behaviours suggests three distinct but overlapping substantive domains for mediator activity: issue identification and agenda setting, proposal shaping, and proposal making. Mediator interventions in all of these domains have been associated with favourable mediation outcomes.'[53] What key issues have been identified and agreed upon in discussions and how are these captured visually for the benefit of the parties? What numerical figures have been deliberated? What underlying issues need further attention? How are parties communicating with each other, are their imbalances in power inhibiting progress in negotiations? For each of these questions, the mediator possesses a skill set to capture, reframe, reflect, and propose possible ways forward in the negotiation.

As the mediation progresses and parties move towards agreement, the mediator is aware of the mood and state of interaction between the parties.[54] There may come a point where the negotiations appear ripe for settlement and the mediator's strategy, perhaps one of evaluative or facilitative direction, assists in guiding parties towards consensual resolution. Once reached, the mediator asks important questions including how the agreement will be implemented and over what timeframe, have all of the points for agreement been noted in language acceptable to each party, can the agreement be drawn and signed on the spot, and if not, when and how will this happen?

Roles and Responsibilities of a Mediator Upon Conclusion of the Mediation

There are many roles a mediator may play upon conclusion of a mediation, each dependent upon the settlement option generated. If an agreement is reached and signed by all parties, the mediator's role is ultimately finished. If the mediation agreement is left open, the mediator follows up with parties in the agreed timeframe for further discussions and to possibly establish another day for mediation. The mediator may shuttle between the parties to a point where agreement can be reached and there is no need for a further joint session.

Therefore, a mediator brings structure to the negotiation process through his process management skills, including his ability to dissect the impasse, guiding the parties and the advocates through every stage. Table 17.5 explores 12 stages of 'mediator moves':

Role of an Advocate in Mediation

Connecting parties in mediation with an advocate is extremely useful and empowering. Mediation is user-centric with the user in

Table 17.5[55]   The Multistage Process a Mediator Undergoes from Initial
Contact with Parties to the Closing of the Mediation Agreement

Stage 1: Establishing relationship with the disputing parties	Make initial contacts with the parties Build credibility Promote rapport Educate the parties about the process Increase commitment to the procedure
Stage 2: Selecting a strategy to guide mediation	Assist the parties to assess various approaches Assist the parties in selecting an approach Coordinate the approaches of the parties
Stage 3: Collecting and analysing background information	Collect and analyse relevant data about the people, dynamics, and substance of a conflict Verify the accuracy of data Minimize the impact of inaccurate or unavailable data
Stage 4: Designing a detailed plan for mediation	Identify strategies and consequent contingent moves that enable the parties to move towards agreement Identify contingent moves to respond to situations peculiar to the specific conflict
Stage 5: Building trust and cooperation	Prepare disputants psychologically to participate in negotiations Handle strong emotions Check perceptions and minimize effects of stereotypes Build recognition of the legitimacy of the parties and issues Build trust Clarify communication
Stage 6: Beginning the mediation session	Open negotiation between parties Establish an open and positive tone Establish ground rules and behavioural guidelines Assist the parties to vent their emotions Delimit the topic areas and issues for discussion Assist the parties in exploring commitments, salience, and influence
Stage 7: Defining issues and setting an agenda	Identify broad topic areas of concern for the parties Obtain agreement on the issues to be discussed Determine the sequence for handling the issues

(Cont'd)

Table 17.5 *(Cont'd)*

Stage 8: Uncovering hidden interests of the disputing parties	Identify the substantive, procedural, and psychological interests of the parties Educate the parties about each other's interests
Stage 9: Generating options for settlement	Develop an awareness among the parties of the need for multiple options Lower commitment to positions or sole alternatives Generate options using either positional or interest-based bargaining
Stage 10: Assessing the options for settlement	Review the interests of the parties Assess how interests can be met by available options Assess the costs and benefits of selecting options
Stage 11: Final bargaining	Reach agreement through incremental convergence of positions, final leaps to package settlements, development of a consensual approach, or establishment of procedural means to reach substantive agreement
Stage 12: Achieving formal settlement	Identify procedural steps to operationalize the agreement Establish an evaluation-and-monitoring procedure Formalize the settlement and create an enforcement-and-commitment mechanism

Source: Authors.

control of the process and the outcome. It is, therefore, possible to participate in mediation with or without the presence and assistance of an advocate. In fact, parties may choose to consult an advocate in a pre or post-mediation setting and then participate in the mediation by themselves, seeking legal advice from an advocate again before the signing of any settlement agreements negotiated by the parties themselves. However, the presence and participation of an advocate, from the time of making the decision to mediate until the conclusion of the mediation proceedings, brings a new dimension of efficiency and adeptness to the process as well as to the user's experience in mediation. Advocates, who are well versed with the nuances of negotiation and mediation and are trained in CDR, adopt a more cooperative and problem-solving approach instead of one that is competitive or adversarial, focusing on a party's interests. These professionals are often referred to as 'Mediation Advocates'.[56] Above all, advocates are mindful of the boundaries circumscribing the party's negotiation limits, beyond which things could possibly become regrettable. The following points broadly capture the role of an advocate in mediation:

1. An advocate is able to examine the legal as well the non-legal consequences of a particular action or conduct.[57] Advocates have knowledge about the party's legal rights and the strengths and weaknesses of the case. Depending on the nature of the dispute, an advocate may suggest various feasible legal alternatives for a party's consideration, particularly with reference to their best and worst case scenarios, evaluate the suitability of the case for mediation, and assist the party in making the decision to mediate.

2. A preliminary meeting between the mediator, the party, and the advocate can help set the stage, deduce the key issues, highlight the legal corollaries, and identify the relevant areas which would need more information. The advocate may then prepare a brief presenting the party's statement of interest and positions.

3. An advocate's mediation assistance may also be in the form of managing client's expectations and reality testing from time to time when they know that their clients are being unrealistic in the given circumstances.

4. An advocate is a trained professional who can analyse the facts and circumstances, process the information exchange, notice the pattern of the discussion, identify negotiable and non-negotiable stands, and grasp the actual points of conflict. His skill set is, therefore, a necessary addition in a mediation through which an advocate may evaluate not just his client's case but that of the other party's case too, deciphering their strategic stands.[58]

5. An advocate may assist a party address fundamental questions which may be as important as the mediation itself: Which mediator? What kind of mediator? Which team? What to expect from the other side?

6. Although mediation is a simple process, it is surrounded by many procedural issues and a corpus of legalities that operate in parallel: the validity and enforcement of the agreement to mediate or

dispute resolution clause, confidentiality of the process, validity and enforceability of a mediated, settlement agreement. These complexities are ever so high in international commercial mediations in which the involvement of two or more jurisdictions creates many more puzzles to solve. The overarching regulations that frame a mediation process are, therefore, many to consider in international commercial scenarios.

7. It is not the mediator's role to give legal advice or support the unrepresented. Therefore, it is always best to have an advocate in the team, especially when the other party has a legal representation. The absence of an advocate can be disadvantageous in many cases affecting the undercurrents of the negotiation since almost all cases involve issues of legal rights, and an advocate may very well protect the party's rights while advancing the party's interest. It is not an easy job to manage the expectations, protect rights that are not easy to compromise, generate solutions, persuade the other side, rationalize the proposals and counterproposals, and sidestep any dissuasions. Advocates play a key role in keeping it all together.

What about the Confidentiality in Mediation?

The role of confidentiality in mediation is among the most critical aspects setting the process apart from other ADR methodologies and adversarial processes. Mediation agreements include a confidentiality clause, which may be tailored to meet the needs of individual parties. With the signing of an agreement to mediate, parties may provide for and protect the content of the discussions and disclosures in pre-mediation meetings and during the mediation itself from being raised in subsequent hearings or trials. In addition, the Indian Arbitration and Conciliation Act, 1996, acts as a guardian in this regard with several of its provisions providing protective layers of confidentiality to the whole process.[59] As for court-referred matters, confidentiality is sourced from the rules of the court drawn under the Code of Civil Procedure, 1908 (CPC), for the purpose of regulating court-referred mediations.[60]

Just as commercial parties are unable to disclose information outside of the mediation, mediators, who are privileged to all confidential information shared by the parties during the mediation, are also bound by confidentiality. The benefits of this aspect of confidentiality in the process are three-fold. Firstly, parties enter into discussions knowing they are free to share information without prejudice which may heighten the likelihood of reaching settlement; second, information shared in caucuses or private sessions with the mediator is not circulated to other parties without the party's consent; and third, all of the information exchanged cannot be used against parties at a later date as mediators may not be called upon to testify in court, should the dispute go to trial. Should confidentiality be breached at any point, parties have the option to pursue legal action against the defaulter.

Mediation reinforced by confidentiality delivers other benefits to commercial parties in mediation, which not only distinguish it from other dispute resolution processes but are the foundations of mediation:

- Protection from public exposure.
- Protection of commercial reputation.
- Promotion of an open environment where parties can share information frankly without fear of reprisal, should a trial result at a later date.
- Encourage parties to actively participate in the mediation.
- Multifaceted discussions between the collective, and in caucuses or private sessions, are confidential, therefore, adding strategic value to the process.

What Does a Mediation Process Look Like?

Mediation is a custom-built approach to CDR, inherently flexible and informal in nature. There does exist, however, a sense of structure and form which helps the mediator and the participants to guide themselves through the process: there are four functional stages of mediation inherent within this diagram, which are: Introduction and Opening statement, Joint Session, Separate Session, and Closing.[61] A useful representation of the mediation process and the different stages is shown in Figure 17.2.

Settlement Agreement and its Enforceability

Mediation offers parties in dispute the opportunity to negotiate their way to mutually arrive at a solution by giving parties complete control

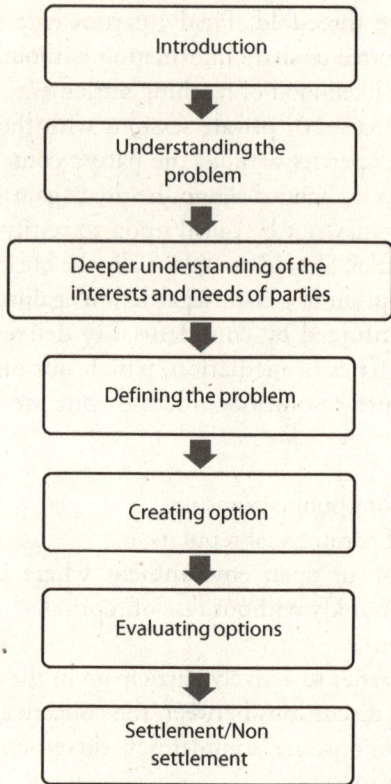

Figure 17.2   A Condensed View of the Various Stages of Mediation Process
Source: Authors.

over the process. When successful, a mediation results in a mediated settlement agreement. There are two fundamental attributes that commercial parties or ADR users look for in a dispute resolution mechanism—neutrality of the forum and/or the third party and the likelihood of obtaining enforcement. Mediation as an institution addresses these worries with prudence and pragmatism, maximizing the value it brings to dispute resolution and constantly configuring itself to the necessities of users.

Although uncommon, parties may in unforeseeable and rare circumstances not honour the terms of settlement and deviate from acting in accordance with it. Therefore, it is possible that a certain party breaches the agreement by not performing its obligations.

Developments like these concern users about the enforceability of mediated settlement agreements as a matter of protecting their interests. These are junctures where mediation is most often tested by users against the wide range of dispute resolution mechanisms available.

Figure 17.3 graphically represents the categories of enforcement of mediated settlement agreements in court-annexed and private mediations.

Enforceability in Court-Annexed or Court-Referred Mediations

Settlement agreements in court-referred[62] matters are enforced as a court decree on recording the terms of settlement between the disputing parties.[63] Basically, once a settlement is reached in the course of mediation, the same is reduced to writing, signed by both the parties and directed back to the court. The court then records the settlement and passes a decree on the premise of the terms of settlement. The decree is then final and binding, and no revision or appeal whatsoever lies against such decree.[64]

In an international commercial dispute scenario, if one party is required to initiate judicial enforcement in a foreign territory because of the recalcitrance of the other party, a consent decree delivered by the courts in India is likely to be enforced by foreign courts, either in accordance with a bilateral or multilateral understanding between India and other nations for the recognition and enforcement of foreign judgments[65] or simply out of respect for a state (Comity of Nations)[66] or in order to do justice to the parties.[67] On the other side, where a foreign party is seeking to enforce a foreign judgment in Indian courts, including a judgment on agreed terms, the Code of Civil Procedure, 1908, provides a statutory framework for the enforcement of judgments and the execution of decrees passed by competent courts in foreign states.[68]

Enforceability in Private Mediation

A settlement reached at a pre-litigation stage in a private mediation is a contract which is binding and enforceable between the parties. Because the parties in mediation are empowered to frame their own

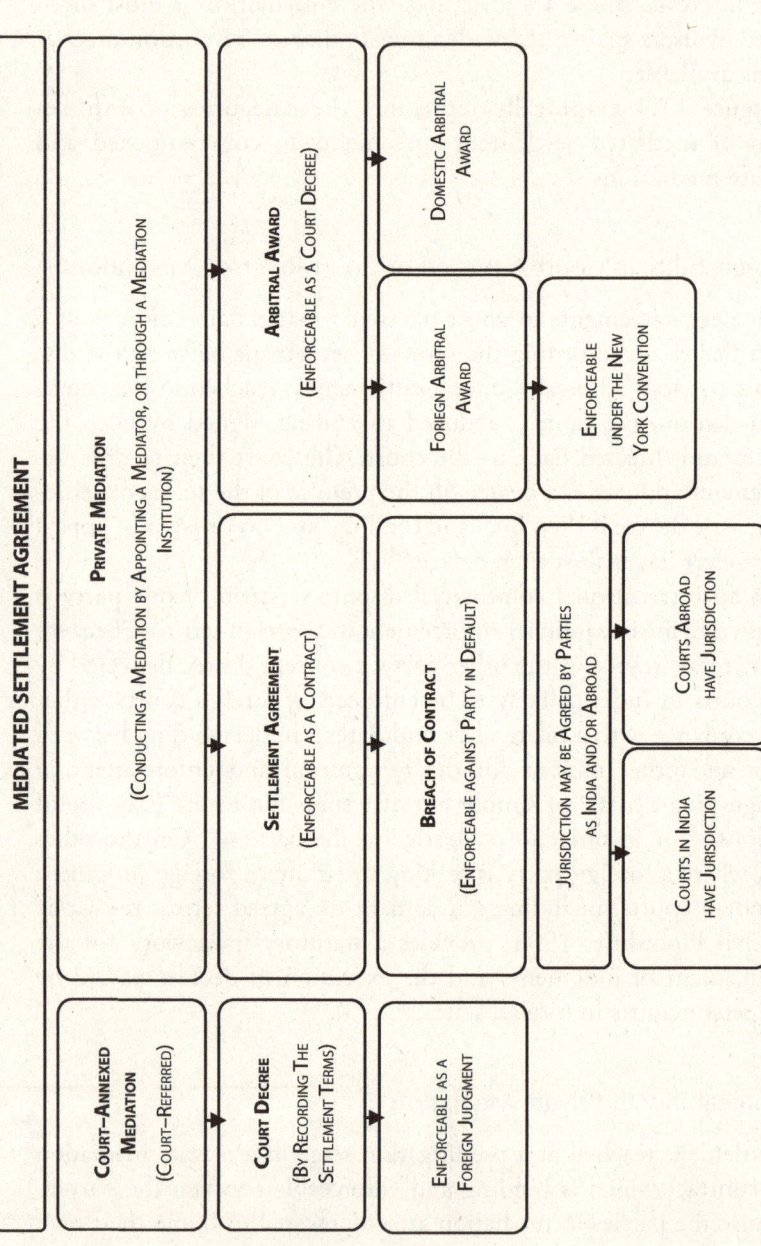

Figure 17.3 Different Enforcement Pathways for Mediated Settlement Agreements in Both Cout-annexed and Private Mediations

Source: Authors.

terms of settlement, it often is the case that the settlement agreement itself incorporates a mechanism to address non-compliance of the terms therein. Optimistically, since the resolution is a consequence of voluntariness and a complete understanding of the terms, mediated settlement agreements are willingly complied by the parties without the need to trigger any statutory mechanism of enforcement. In mediation, parties do not get a result to which they have not agreed to.

However, if a party refuses compliance of the settlement agreement, the party asserting its rights through the agreement would have to file a suit for specific performance or seek damages for breach of the agreement, like in a case of breach of contract. In such cases, the party alleging breach will have to initiate appropriate legal proceedings in accordance with the law for seeking enforcement of the settlement agreement. Generally, a settlement agreement achieved in and through mediation does not experience the problems faced in an arbitration or litigation where the award or judgment is invariably challenged.

Parties may also ask for embodiment of the settlement agreement in the form of an arbitral award.[69] It means that a settlement agreement shall have the same effect and status as if it were an arbitral award on agreed terms on the substance of the dispute rendered by an arbitral tribunal.[70] The arbitral award is final and binding on the parties and the same is endorsed under the Code of Civil Procedure, 1908, in the same manner as it were a decree of the court.[71]

International Commercial Mediation

With the phenomenal increase in cross-border contracts, investments, trade, and collaborations, India has witnessed a humungous growth in international commercial transactions. With such rapid upsurge in India's commerce and trade, commercial disputes involving high stakes, perhaps foreseeably, are increasing. As a result, ADR mechanisms have become more crucial for businesses operating in India as well as those doing businesses with Indian firms. Amongst the various ADR options, international commercial mediation[72] is a vital enhancement for international dispute resolution and may be considered the most suitable for commercial conditions.

In practice, to elucidate on the procedure involved in an international mediation, parties make a reference to a recognized mediation centre or institution to administer the mediation. Some of the acclaimed institutions in India and abroad are the Indian Institution of Arbitration and Mediation (Cochin), the Centre for Advanced Mediation Practice (Bangalore), Singapore International Mediation Centre (SIMC), London Court of International Arbitration (LCIA), and the International Chamber of Commerce (ICC). These organizations administer mediation as per their own institutional rules and guidelines. For non-administered international dispute resolution processes, even United Nations Commission on International Trade Law (UNCITRAL) has issued the UNCITRAL Conciliation Rules, 1980.[73] These rules contain a procedure for the appointment of mediators from a panel of accredited mediators (unless specifically appointed by the parties). The mediation would either have a venue within the institution or anywhere else the parties can mutually agree upon. This process with the institution can also commence even without having any prior agreements about mediation if the parties agree to mediate with an institution after the dispute has arisen. It goes without saying that the said forum provided by a mediation institution is also available for administering domestic mediations.

Advantages over Other Forms of Dispute Resolution Methods

Arbitration, another form of ADR, is a quasi-judicial procedure, where the parties in a dispute present their case in law and facts to an arbitrator, who makes an award which is final and binding on both parties.[74] Despite the probability of enforcing international arbitral awards, several traits of arbitration are a cause of difficulty, generally, because it involves more than one legal system due to which the choice of forum and the applicable laws are left unpredictable (without the cooperation between the parties). In addition to the problems of choice of forum and applicable laws, international businesses may perceive arbitration as too lengthy, costly, and antagonistic. In international dispute resolution clauses, by and large, mediation clauses precede arbitration as a first protocol in commercial disputes. The default advantages of mediation, such as saving time and costs, preserving reputation, and protecting a relationship, are much more appealing and sensible for parties locked in an international commercial dispute. In international arbitration and litigation, the financial consequences are massive and it is the biggest worry of a company, even when the merits of the case maybe tilting over to its end. Then there are some companies who come to realize about the seat of arbitration being in a third country only in the advent of dispute and in fear of cost implications they resort to temporary strategies such as anti-arbitration injunctions and termination of contracts. Realistically, the benefits of mediation have a greater realization in international commercial conflicts. Unlike international commercial arbitration and litigation, parties are not caught in a maze of jurisdictional, choice of law, and other procedural concerns which can sometimes cause so much exertion that the real issue is either blindsided or deferred. The advantage that mediation brings is the focus on the facts that matter, seeking an agreeable solution, over and above the densities of international arbitration and litigation. It curtails procedural and auxiliary concerns, promoting the development of consensual resolutions through open dialogue, while sustaining a friendly business relationship.

Mediation is perhaps the most effective way of resolving international commercial disputes since it is easily transposable to an international setting, where parties can resolve not only issues relating to law and facts but also issues that an adjudicative process is unequipped or incapable of settling. These may include issues such as emotional concerns, personal interest, and intangible feelings. Moreover, business and commerce across borders entail not only multi-jurisdictional factors but also language differences, cultural diversities, varied business practices, and regional perspectives. All of these elements impact upon the nature of the international commercial dispute. Such inherent dynamics and various complexities are often orphaned by adversarial methods. On the other hand, a mediator may explore these areas and bring about an expeditious and resourceful resolution. Mediation carefully addresses these issues, focusing on the underlying content and intangible factors of culture that may have caused the dispute in the first place. Take, for instance, a cross-cultural miscommunication where an individual from one culture misinterprets a message from a person belonging to another culture.[75] Disputes arising from an email that was misconceived due to cultural differences is not uncommon and it is, in fact, often the case.[76] Arbitration or litigation which are rights-based and strictly on the basis of law and facts become hamstrung when met with such challenges. On the contrary, cultural sensitivities are addressed and processed in international mediations which ultimately translate into negotiated settlements. It is through a mediator that misunderstandings can be clarified and counterviews can be acknowledged and understood.

Enforceability of Settlement Agreements Arising Out of International Commercial Mediation

The conversation about international commercial mediation also revolves around another important aspect, pertaining to a successfully mediated settlement agreement and whether it can be enforced? A settlement agreement which is an outcome of a mediation is indeed enforceable in India in terms of a contract, or an executable court decree, or even an arbitral award. However, in a case where a mediated settlement agreement needs recognition and enforcement outside the Indian jurisdiction, there appears to be a lacuna which is why the United Nations Commission on International Trade Law (UNCITRAL) is deliberating on the development of an international convention or a standardized international instrument which would provide for cross-border recognition and enforcement of mediation agreements.[77] The working group at the UNCITRAL has been discussing several proposals, and, while the idea is definitely pro-mediation, concerns persist about the scope and intricacies of having an international instrument governing the enforceability of settlement agreements resulting from international commercial mediations.[78]

Nevertheless, there is another way of looking at this situation: the Arb-Med-Arb mechanism, which combines the advantages of arbitration and mediation. Under the Arb-Med-Arb mechanism, parties who have commenced arbitration are to refer their dispute to mediation from the arbitration. If the outcome is successful, parties refer the process back to arbitration where their settlement agreement is recorded before the arbitral tribunal as an enforceable 'consent award' or an 'award on agreed terms' under the 1958 Convention on the Recognition and Enforcement of Foreign Arbitral Awards (New York Convention).[79] The New York Convention gives binding recognition and effect to arbitral awards and provides for its enforcement in the member countries. The concept of Arb-Med-Arb is delivered by various institutions in different jurisdictions.[80]

The Mediation Infrastructure in India

Mediation and CDR, in general, are surging around the world, however, it is doing so at different rates. The 'buzz' around mediation in India is louder than ever. Mediations, whether private, institutional, or court-annexed, are thriving in the growing awareness from regularly organized seminars, symposiums, competitions, training, and a number of other events that are putting together a community of mediation professionals and infrastructure.

Despite the fairly widespread awareness of mediation and its potential advantages, fostering a mediation culture takes time. Equally, building trust in ADR users, practitioners, and organizations. The litigation culture in India is dominant, and therefore, resistance to change might not only come from people unwilling to try their disputes through an unacquainted process or by corporations or ADR users where business practice or dispute resolution policies might just be simply adversarial or combative but even by legal practitioners who may not have experienced or been made aware of the advantages of mediation.

The first step in the development of a mediation culture is in the making of legal foundations through legislations and rules requiring disputing parties to, at least, consider mediation. Law acts like a pillar in supporting mediation by giving it recognition, credibility, and legitimacy. Although a specific law on mediation is yet to be enacted, the Arbitration and Conciliation Act, 1996, is the cornerstone of mediation. In addition, the Mediation and Conciliation Project Committee (MCPC) consisting of Supreme Court and High Court Judges and senior advocates are making headway in advancing policy matters relating to mediation.[81] In time, as mediation culture takes root, a supportive infrastructure surfaces from court initiatives and business groups; ventures emerge either independently or linked to the government. Judges and legal practitioners become increasingly acquainted and comfortable with mediation as a credible form of dispute resolution and mediation is gradually considered in a wider range of subject matters, including high-stake disputes. To address the demand, mediation institutions and service providers emerge offering panels of qualified mediators and practitioners, developing independent standards, and improving the quality of mediation as an institution. Mediation in India is in the process of taking root, and, it is believed that mediation is entrenched enough to gradually morph into an advanced mediation culture, deepening market penetration in a diversity of areas, and developing a specific species of legislation on mediation to further implant CDR practice. At that stage, legal practitioners, ADR users, ADR professionals and proponents will find themselves comfortable with the use of mediation given the infrastructure which will be supporting mediation.

Institutional and Court-annexed Mediation in India

Institutional mediation is a recent occurrence in the Indian context and is taking its course in the growing market for CDR. Two institutions in India have taken big leaps in bringing international standards of institutional mediation to India. Their international affiliations are with some of the top mediation institutions around the world, cooperating and encouraging a mutual development of mediation. The IIAM is one of the pioneering institutions in India, providing ADR services since 2001. With IIAM based out of Cochin, Bangalore has the Centre for Advanced Mediation Practice (CAMP) providing high-quality mediation services. When parties wish to refer a dispute to be settled through mediation, they can mutually agree to adopt the mediation rules of any institution or adopt an institution to administer the mediation case under its mediation rules. Once the matter is referred, an institution conducts professional case management under a competitive and transparent fee structure. It arranges all the logistics, facilities, and services required to conduct mediation proceedings smoothly. In the event parties are unable to jointly agree on a mediator, the institution helps the parties choose a mediator from a panel of domestic and international mediators. An institution, therefore, facilitates an effective mediation with its services tailored to the needs of the user.

On a different platform, the courts in India provide for mediation services integrated within the judicial system. Reference to mediation by a court may be made at a given stage of a litigation,[82] and when the court does make such reference, the mediation process is called 'court-annexed mediation' or court-referred mediation'. Such recourse requires the court to consider and record the nature of the dispute. In fact, it is also possible for the court to refer cases long pending from a list of long causes (which would take several years to come up for trial). Court-annexed mediation, therefore, provides an additional forum in the same judicial system for a faster and more effective delivery of justice. Court-annexed mediations have given great relief to courts from the burden of its case load and at the same time have been overwhelmingly successful in achieving positive results.[83] Courts were generally viewed as the place where one should go if he or she is seeking justice. Now, however, with the court's supportive role, users are more likely to accept and try mediation (even pre-litigation) after seeing that courts are at the forefront of encouraging mediation. The judiciary has taken the lead role in legally affirming and propagating mediation. These court-annexed mediation schemes are normally governed by rules made under the CPC.[84]

Choosing a Mediator and Your Mediation Advocate

Which mediator and what kind; which mediation advocate and why?[85] Asking the right questions prior to mediation is as important, if not more, as the mediation itself. Choosing a mediator and a mediation advocate is a key consideration for a commercial party without which the mediation experience may not yield satisfactory outcomes.[86]

In commercial cases, especially those dealing with complexities and technicalities, it is possible to appoint a mediator who has a specialized subject expertise that may be useful in procuring an expedient and balanced resolution. In sophisticated and complex cases, such as multi-party and multi-issue commercial disputes, parties may prefer a mediator with process skills to handle a convoluted case and having the subject-matter competence to understand the legal and technical aspects of the dispute. In addition, the mediator's experience in the area of conflict; training appropriate to the conflict; the style of mediation, whether facilitative, evaluative, or transformative;[87] the fee schedule; and conflict of interest are considerations that may be employed in choosing a mediator. Whatever these considerations may be, it is crucial that parties are able to trust the mediator. Mediation requires sharing a great deal of confidential information—the case, its strengths and weaknesses, the limitations—with the mediator, making trust an issue of overriding importance.

Primary considerations of the parties must be credibility and competence, both of which generate trust. Whoever or whatever kind of mediator, parties must clear any conflict of interest on the part of the mediator. Parties may either appoint a mediator on their own or agree upon a mediation institution to provide a mediator from its panel of accredited and experienced mediators. Besides, there are independent mediators in private practice. They set their own fee schedule and develop their own rules for guiding mediations. In fact, it is often best to consider using an independent mediator when parties are on a low budget and may be unable to afford full-fledged services of an institution and when they are readily agreeable to a date, time, and place.

The IMI (Netherlands) formulated a flowchart called the 'IMI Decision Tree' which is an essential tool for users and mediation advocates to be able to find the right mediator. Basically, the Decision Tree asks several questions, all of which lead a user to understand the type of mediator he or she would need (see Figure 17.4).[88]

On the other hand, choosing an advocate may also be an important requisite before entering the mediation.[89] In fact, an advocate's role commences even before the mediation during pre-mediation preparations when parties are exploring their strategies, reviewing their case for mediation, and considering potential agreements. In a court-annexed mediation, the advocate representing a party in mediation is commonly the one who also represented the party in the court proceedings before the case was referred to mediation. However, many advocates or litigation lawyers would not be fully aware and knowledgeable about the process of mediation and some may also not be aware of the process, the pros and cons, and so on. An advocate's advocacy (for example, an aggressive or dominating style), or his specific practice experience, or for that matter his lack of experience in mediation could possibly be an impediment to mediation. Even the advocate's seniority and assertiveness may cause impairment in the dialogue with the counterpart and so also to the parties around the mediation table. This is all simply because mediation advocacy

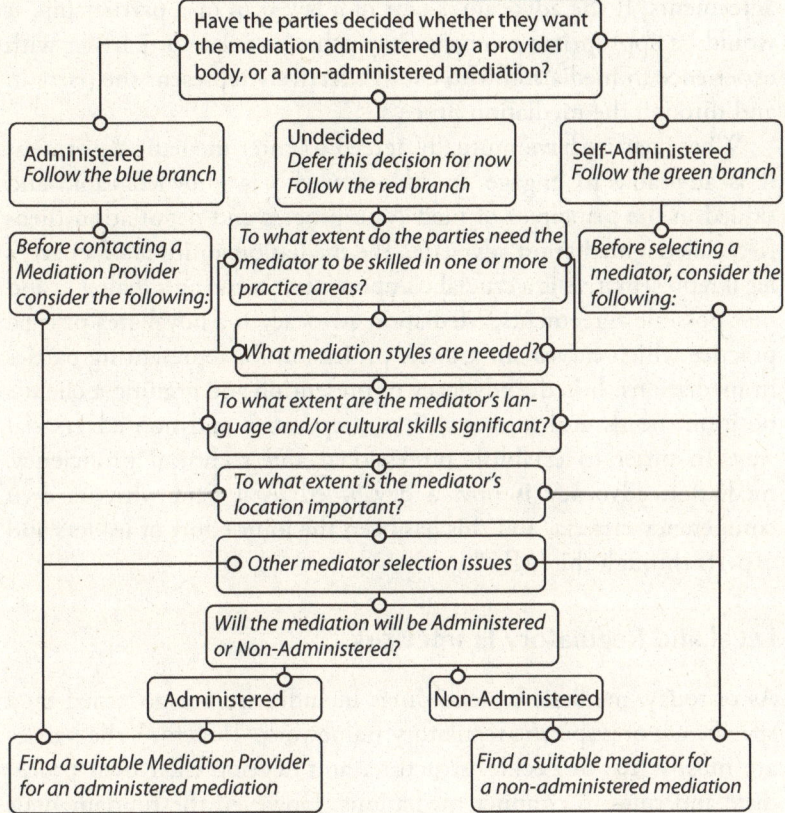

Figure 17.4   The IMI Decision Tree

Source: The International Mediation Institute.

involves a significant paradigm shift for trial lawyers: from an adversarial style to a collaborative style, from past-oriented approach to a future-oriented approach, from a win–lose attitude to a win–win attitude, shifting focus from the lawyers to the parties, from convincing the judge to convincing and reasoning with the opposing party.

Given the situation, with the ultimate decision-making resting with the parties in the mediation, the advocate may be advised to maintain a secondary role. Otherwise, a party may decide to enter mediation on its own, and the advocate may simply advise and educate the party with respect to the case or review any possible agreements. If the advocate is part of a law firm or a partnership, it would be appropriate to engage any other associate or partner with experience in mediation who could effectively represent the party in and through the mediation process.

Where parties have mutually agreed to enter mediation privately, it is advisable to engage an advocate who is knowledgeable and skilled in the principles of mediation process and negotiation theories, called a mediation advocate. The mediation aptitude of a party's legal representative is a crucial component in securing a dialogue and best possible agreements. Mediation advocacy is a novel area of legal practice which carves out a niche profession for representing parties in mediations. It is the advocacy of presenting and arguing a client's position, needs and interests, in a cooperative and non-adversarial way. In order to establish professional and technical proficiency, mediation advocacy is now a developed legal field with its own competency criteria, and this has been the joint effort of leaders and experts through the IMI.[90]

Legal and Regulatory Framework

As of today, mediation proceedings in India are not governed by a specific act or a specific regulatory framework. Therefore, the parties are mostly free to decide, structure, and develop their own procedure and rules to conduct mediations. However, the fundamentals of mediation have been defined and given certainty to by the law, which gives parties the autonomy and liberty to conduct mediations to their specific needs, but within the outline of law. The primary legal framework and regulatory construct that governs mediation in India are the Indian Arbitration and Conciliation Act, 1996, and the Code of Civil Procedure, 1908. These legislative enactments have been overlaid by precedents time and again interpreting the various enactments governing mediation.

Arbitration and Conciliation Act, 1996

The Arbitration and Conciliation Act, 1996 was enacted with three parts consolidating the law relating to domestic arbitration and international commercial arbitration (contained under Part-I),

enforcement of foreign arbitral awards (Part-II), and the law relating
to conciliation (Part-III). The 1996 Act was based on the UNCITRAL
Model Law on International Commercial Arbitration, 1985, and the
UNCITRAL International Commercial Conciliation Rules, 1980.[91]
In 2015, the 1996 Act went through an overhaul that brought extensive amendments completely morphing the 1996 Act.[92] The amendments, however, brought no change with respect to the conciliation
part of the 1996 Act, and the same remains unamended.

Consent Award or an Award on Agreed Terms under the 1996 Act

Part-I, dealing with domestic arbitration and international
commercial arbitration, has a few provisions where arbitration and
mediation converge. Arbitrators are empowered to encourage parties to a settlement. With the consent of parties, arbitrators may
show them the route to consider consensual methods at any time
during the arbitral proceedings, and this is fully compatible with the
arbitration agreement (see Table 17.6).

Conciliation under the 1996 Act

Part-III runs from Sections 61 to 81 of the 1996 Act. Each of these
sections and other provision relevant to conciliation may be observed
in Table 17.7.

Is There a Difference between Conciliation and Mediation?

In the Indian context, the authors are of the view that there is no
such difference, and even if there is any, conciliation and mediation
are only superficially different, but exactly the same in substance.
However, there is some misperception among commentators and
mediation professionals as to whether there is a difference between
conciliation and mediation.[99] The fundamental features, such as the
guidance of a neutral third-party, the voluntary nature of the process,
confidentiality, and the parties' right to self-determination, are shared
by both terminologies. In fact, conciliation may be called one of the
models of mediation where the mediator's intervention is at a peak
with an aim of arriving at a settlement agreement.[100]

Table 17.6 Synopsis of Provisions under Part-I of the 1996 Act Relating to Consent Award or Award on Agreed Terms

Section 30	It provides that with the agreement of the parties, the arbitral tribunal may use mediation, conciliation, or other procedures to encourage a settlement between the disputing parties. It is not clear in law if the arbitrator should stop and refer parties to consensual modes of dispute resolution or can he himself wear the hat of a mediator or a conciliator and get on with the process. In principle, however, the latter would seem more appropriate where if a settlement is arrived upon, the parties have the option to request the arbitrator for an award on agreed terms[93] or retain the agreed terms as simply a settlement agreement or a contract.
Section 34	An arbitral award (including a consent award or award on agreed terms) may be challenged under Section 34 of the 1996 Act. However, this comes with a caveat. Such challenges are difficult considering that the parties entered into a settlement agreement by mutually agreeing to every term.
Sections 35 and 36	An arbitral award (including a consent award or award on agreed terms) shall be final and binding on the parties, and the same shall be endorsed under the CPC in the same manner as if it were a decree of the court.

Source: Authors.

Table 17.7 Synopsis of Provisions under Part-III of the 1996 Act Relating to Conciliation

Section 61	It makes Part-III applicable to conciliation of disputes arising out of a legal relationship, whether contractual or not, and to all proceedings relating thereto. In the same way, Part-III does not apply to any dispute where there exists a specific bar provided by law.
Section 62	Conciliation proceedings commence when one party sends a written invitation of conciliation to the other party. These proceedings are deemed to commence on the acceptance of the invitation.

Sections 63 and 64	It prescribes the number of conciliators and the procedure for appointment. As a general rule, there shall be only one conciliator, unless the parties agree for two or three conciliators. Where parties have decided to appoint three conciliators, where each party appoints one conciliator and the third conciliator is appointed jointly (unlike arbitration where the third arbitrator is appointed by the other two arbitrators). Alternatively, parties may enlist the assistance of an institution.
Section 65	The conciliator has the privilege of requesting each party to submit to him a brief statement of positions and interests, supplemented by documents. The conciliator may even request for additional information at any stage of the conciliation proceedings.
Section 66	The conciliator is not bound by the Code of Civil Procedure, 1908 or the Indian Evidence Act, 1872.[94]
Section 67	The role of the conciliator is to assist the parties in an independent and impartial manner. He must be guided by the principles of fairness and justice, taking into consideration, inter alia, the rights and obligations of the parties, circumstances, business practices. The conciliator may conduct these proceedings in such a manner as he considers appropriate. He may even suggest proposals for the settlement of dispute for the parties to mutually agree upon.
Section 68	The conciliator, with the consent of the parties, may arrange for administrative assistance by a suitable institution or person.
Section 69	The communication between the conciliator and the parties may either be in writing or oral and may be in joint or separate sessions.
Section 70	When the conciliator receives factual information concerning the dispute from a party, he obligated to disclose it to the other party in order that the other party may have the opportunity to present any explanation which he considers appropriate, unless the conciliator received it with a specific condition of confidentiality.

(Cont'd)

Table 17.7 *(Cont'd)*

Section 71	The parties are obligated to cooperate in good faith with the conciliator, in particular.
Section 72	The parties may, on their own initiative or at the invitation of the conciliator, submit a suggestion for the settlement of the dispute.
Section 73	The conciliator is obligated to formulate a possible settlement when it appears to him that there exist elements of a settlement. He may further reformulate the terms of a possible in light of the observations made by parties. Where the parties reach a mutual agreement, a settlement is drawn which is final and binding on the parties.[95]
Section 74	The settlement agreement gets the same status as that of an arbitral award on agreed terms rendered by an arbitral tribunal on the substance of the dispute.[96] Therefore, if a party defaults, not acting in accordance with the award, the said award may be enforced against the defaulting party.[97]
Section 75	It is obligatory that the conciliator and the parties keep all matters, relating to the conciliation proceedings, confidential. This is the second layer of confidentiality protecting conciliation proceedings, after Section 70, and it is notwithstanding anything contained in any other law in force in India.
Section 76	It deals with the termination of conciliation proceedings and lists the conditions under which the proceedings terminate.
Section 77	The provision places a bar on the parties from initiating arbitration or judicial proceedings in the respect of the dispute, that is, the subject matter of the conciliation, except where initiating such proceedings are necessary for preserving the rights of the party. For instance, a party may seek interim orders for the preservation of property or appointment of a receiver as a measure of protection.
Sections 78 and 79	These provisions deal with administrative matters relating to costs and deposits.

Section 80	The conciliator is not to act as an arbitrator or a representative or counsel of a party in any tribunal or judicial proceedings in respect of a dispute that is the subject of the conciliation proceedings. However, parties may agree otherwise.
Section 81	It deals with the admissibility of evidence in other proceedings. It basically provides that may not rely on or introduce as evidence, in arbitral or judicial proceedings, that which relates to the conciliation proceedings.[98] This third layer of confidentiality (after Section 75) has a wide scope and even extends to views expressed or suggestions made.

Source: Authors.

Such divide between conciliation and mediation may be attributed to various reasons. Section 73 is first on the list. The provision can lead to a misunderstanding that a conciliator's formulation and reformulation of possible terms of settlement is a necessary part of the conciliation process. This is a miss by a mile. There is no denying the fact that a conciliator, in many cases, would not have any need to intervene with his suggestions over a settlement agreement, and commercial parties may very well be generating movement towards mutually acceptable resolution.[101] Besides, reiterating the point, the degree of the neutral's intervention is apparent and made redundant by the fact that there are other models of mediation (like evaluative mediation and a settlement mediation) that reflect a high degree of intervention from the mediator.[102] What is regrettable is that India uses the terminologies as distinct from one another, as if there were two difference concepts. For instance, CPC makes the use of terms 'conciliation' and 'mediation' distinctly in Sections 89(1)(b) and 89(1)(d), respectively, implying the existence of a difference when there isn't one. Moreover, Section 30 of the 1996 Act also follows CPC in dividing the two terms as different modes of CDR.

This differentiation can be a potent formula for a serious legal conundrum.[103] However, users need not worry about the controversies. Whether it be a 'conciliation' or 'mediation', a 'mediation' done in private, on the premise of the parties' agreement or under the rules of an institution, it would be treated as 'conciliation' under the Arbitration and Conciliation Act, 1996,[104] making Part-III of the 1996 Act applicable to mediations in India.

Section 89 of the Code of Civil Procedure, 1908

Section 89 of the Code of Civil Procedure, 1908, was inserted by a CPC (Amendment) Act, 1999, and came into force on 1 July 2002. It was an attempt to bring ADR mechanism into the mainstream of the judicial system by encapsulating the model of settlement of disputes outside court.[105] The provision empowers judges to refer matters to ADR when it appears to him that there exist elements of settlement. Section 89, in addition to Rules 1A, 1B, and 1C of Order X of the CPC, imposes a mandatory duty on the court to endeavour for a settlement by referring the parties to any one of the ADR mechanisms, including mediation and conciliation, both having separate protocols of reference.

To keep it succinct, a civil court exercising power under Section 89 cannot refer a suit to arbitration or conciliation unless all the parties to the suit agree to such reference. The court has to record that the reference is by mutual consent. However, if the reference is to any other non-adjudicatory ADR process, such as mediation, consent is no longer a condition. Though the process under Section 89 appears to be lengthy and complicated, in practice the process is simple: know the dispute; exclude 'unfit' cases; ascertain consent for arbitration or conciliation; if there no consent, select Lok Adalat for simple cases and mediation for all other cases, reserving reference to a judge assisted settlement only in exceptional or special cases.

When a dispute in court is referred to conciliation (through parties' consent) or mediation, the dispute does not go beyond the domain of the court's supervision. If there is no settlement in the conciliation or mediation proceedings, the matter is then referred back to the court and it eventually goes through trial. And if parties reach a settlement, the settlement agreement is brought before the court, for it to be examined and recorded as a consent decree, keeping with the principles of Rule 3 of Order XXIII of the CPC. The plain scheme is that the court educates the parties about the choices available regarding ADR processes; it allows them to elect one of the

ADR processes by consensus; and if there is no consensus between the parties, the court proceeds to choose the process (mediation, Lok Adalat, or judicial settlement).

***

With the foundations being laid, and the subsequent support and promotion for the advancement of commercial mediation garnered by India's judiciary and legislative body, the moment to embrace this evolving flagship of ADR is now. In this day and age, national and international communities interact with increased frequency and overlap, exposing the need for high-level cooperation and efficiency at the level of domestic commerce and across the domain of international trade and investment. India's role as an increasingly relevant player on the global stage highlights this need for efficacy even more so.

Conflict is, however, inevitable in commercial dealings as in life more broadly. That mediation offers itself as a robust, efficient, and effective alternative to litigation in matters of commercial dispute is evident. It is unique in its flexible and voluntary nature, and in the way in which it may be utilized by parties at various points on a dispute trajectory. This chapter has, thus, explored the processes and considerations required in deciding how, if and when to mediate. Equally, the selection of the team of professionals serving as advocates and mediators offering their guidance and support to disputing parties has been attended adequately to encourage the use of mediation as a fitting method to resolve disputes. Given India's litigious culture and the paralysis of the judicial system, mediation is the need of the hour.

It is proposed and accepted that mediation is not appropriate for all disputes nor does it guarantee a settlement. However, in the context of lengthy and expensive adjudicatory processes, the possibility for saving time, preserving relationships and commercial reputation, and generating progressive, creative settlement options, far outweighs any alternative observed in the adversarial arena. Having said that, mediation is not a technique to manage the inability of courts but a defined and structured mechanism of CDR and an independent means of providing access to justice. There are a myriad possible rewards a party may receive from a successful mediation, with a very important precept of parties having the opportunity to articulate their case and to be fully heard.

In light of the recent developments in ADR, it has been a view in India that a number of principles pertaining to mediation should now be accepted as forming part of a separate mediation law.[106] In India, the emphasis placed upon mediation has been sharply articulated time and again. It, therefore, remains to be seen how far and wide will the message be received and accepted in the commercial sphere. An important reason for the minimum use of mediation can be narrowed to the fact that ADR users and advocates without any experience or background in mediation are hesitant to use it, while parties and advocates with some exposure to mediation are more amenable in trying it. The challenge now is to break the cycle of no experience, no use.[107] With the increase in awareness of mediation in India, levels of acceptance of the process are certain to increase. At the heart of this chapter, the authors encourage users and practitioners to appraise the potential benefits of mediation beyond the basic prospect of settlement.

Notes and References

1. According to the UNCITRAL Model Law on International Commercial Conciliation with Guide to Enactment and User 2002 (Model Law on International Commercial Conciliation):

   > Commercial ... should be given a wide interpretation so as to cover matters arising from all relationships of a commercial nature, whether contractual or not. Relationships of a commercial nature include, but are not limited to, the following transactions: any trade transaction for the supply or exchange of goods and services; distribution agreement; commercial representation or agency; factoring; license; construction of works; consulting; engineering; licensing; investment; financing; banking; insurance; exploitation agreement or concession; joint venture and other forms of industrial or business cooperation; carriage of goods or passengers by air, sea, rail or road.

2. Negotiation, which is another form of consensual dispute resolution, is not suggested to be replaceable by mediation. Rather, mediation augments the negotiation process in terms of structuring it, bridging trust and communication gaps, eliminating counterproductive elements, and fostering clear and open discussion.

3. Henry J. Brown and Arthur L. Mariot, *ADR Principles and Practice*, 2nd ed. (Sweet & Maxwell, 1997), p. 127 ('Mediation' is a facilitative process in which 'disputing parties engage the assistance of an impartial third party, the mediator, who helps them to try to arrive at an agreed resolution of their dispute. The mediator has no authority to make any decisions that are binding on them, but uses certain procedures, techniques and skills to help them to negotiate an agreed resolution of their dispute without adjudication'); Justice M. Jagannadha Rao, 'Concepts of Conciliation and Mediation and Their Differences', Law Commission of India, available http://lawcommissionofindia.nic.in/adr_conf/nageswara%20rao10.pdf, accessed 5 August 2016; Article 1 of the Model Law on International Commercial Conciliation:

> [A] process, whether referred to by the expression conciliation, mediation or an expression of similar import, whereby parties request a third person or persons ('the conciliator') to assist them in their attempt to reach an amicable settlement of their dispute arising out of or relating to reach a contractual or other legal relationship. The conciliator does not have the authority to impose upon the parties a solution to the dispute.

4. Generally signed at the commencement of the mediation session.
5. Nadja Alexander, 'The Mediation Metamodel: Understanding Practice', *Conflict Resolution Quarterly*, 26 (1, 2008). There are several models of mediation like settlement mediation, facilitative mediation, evaluative mediation, transformative mediation, positional bargaining, interest-based, dialogue, expert advisory mediation, wise counsel mediation, and tradition-based mediation. The most common being facilitative and evaluative mediation. P.H. Gulliver, *Disputes and Negotiation: A Cross-Cultural Perspective* (1979), pp. 200–25; N.N. Antaki, 'Cultural Diversity and ADR Practices in the World', in J.C. Goldsmith and Arnold Ingen-Housz, and Gerald Pointon (eds), *ADR in Business: Practice and Issues Across Countries and Cultures* (2006), p. 5.
6. Nadja (2008).
7. Also known as 'reality checking'. See Julie Barker, 'International Mediation: A Better Alternative for the Resolution of Commercial Disputes', *Loyola of Los Angeles International and Comparative Law Review*, 19 (1, 1996–7): 'Reality checking is a method whereby a mediator serves as an agent of reality by questioning the parties and ascertaining each party's weakness. The mediator then gently and tactfully attempts to help the parties realise the differences between their unrealistic assumptions and the realities of their particular situations.'

8. Sriram Panchu, 'Note on Mediation Process', Law Commission of India, Papers presented in International Conference on ADR and Case Management, 3 and 4 May 2003.

9. The new regime under the Arbitration and Conciliation (Amendment) Act, 2015, requires certain minimum levels of independence and impartiality of the arbitral tribunal, regardless of the parties' apparent agreement. The new regime requires specific disclosures by the arbitrator, at the stage of his possible appointment.

10. An alternative approach to Med-Arb involving parties agreeing to mediate certain issues in the dispute and arbitrate the rest. Yet another approach to Med-Arb is where the mediation process runs simultaneously and independently from the arbitration proceedings, where the mediation process has a specified time frame for completion.

11. In the online mediation world, 'technology' is also referred to as the 'fourth party' suggesting its influence on communication and power dynamics of the mediation process.

12. Prathmesh Popat, 'Online Dispute Resolution in India', Proceedings of the UNECE Forum on ODR, 2003, available http://unpan1.un.org/intradoc/groups/public/documents/apcity/unpan021307.pdf, accessed 5 August 2016.

13. In the case of a court-referred mediation, the referral court applies the principles of Order XXIII Rule 3, of the Code of Civil Procedure, 1908 (CPC), for passing decree/order in terms of the agreement. As for private mediations, the agreement may be enforceable as a decree of the court as per Section 74 of the Arbitration and Conciliation Act, 1996 (1996 Act) by giving a settlement decree the status of a consent award or an arbitral award on agreed terms.

14. These often include those areas which are inherently unsuited for an adversarial adjudicatory process.

15. Lon Fuller, 'The Forms and Limits of Adjudication', *Harvard Law Review*, 92 (353, 1978).

16. Doing Business 2016 data for India (World Bank Group), available http://www.doingbusiness.org/data/exploreeconomies/india/, accessed 9 August 2016.

17. Justice Dhananjaya Y. Chandrachud, 'Mediation: Realising the Potential and Designing Implementation Strategies', Law Commission of India, available http://lawcommissionofindia.nic.in/adr_conf/chandrachud3.pdf, accessed 5 August 2016.

18. National Judicial Data Grid, available http://njdg.ecourts.gov.in/njdg_public/main.php, accessed 5 August 2016.

19. (2005) 6 SCC 344.

20. See also the section titled 'Section 89 of the Code of Civil Procedure, 1908' in this chapter.
21. See also the section titled 'The Role of an In-House Legal Counsel in Mediation' in this chapter.
22. Making an offer for settlement and its response, and the filing of a lawsuit are two separate aspects, where the former should not be merely looked at as a trigger to initiate the latter.
23. Mediation Advisory Centre, 'Industry Sensitization on Mediation in Consumer Disputes', available http://www.mediationadvisory.in/html/press.html, accessed 2 August 2016.
24. Dispute Resolution Overview, available http://pages.ebay.com/services/buyandsell/disputeres.html, accessed 2 August 2016.
25. Protection for Sellers, available https://www.paypal.com/cgi-bin/webscr?-cmd=xpt/cps/general/Protections-outside, accessed 2 August 2016.
26. SquareTrade (eBay's preferred dispute resolution provider) offers two services: a free web-based forum which allows users to attempt to resolve their differences on their own or if necessary, the use of a professional mediator. Modria is yet another platform that companies use to deliver fast and fair resolutions to disputes of any type and volume.
27. Press Trust of India, '295 Infra Projects Delayed: Cost Overrun at over Rs. 1 Lakh Crore', *The Economic Times*, New Delhi, 4 December 2014, available http://articles.economictimes.indiatimes.com/2014-12-04/news/56723426_1_cost-overrun-62-projects-rs-1-lakh-crore, accessed 2 August 2016 ('As per flash report released by Ministry of Statistics in August 2014, as many as 295 infrastructure sector projects worth Rs 150 crore or more were delayed with total cost overrun of over Rs 1 lakh crore'); Press Trust of India, '101 Infra Projects See Rs 1.29 Lakh Crore in Cost Overruns', New Delhi, 31 July 2016, available http://www.financialexpress.com/economy/101-infra-projects-see-rs-1-29-lakh-crore-in-cost-overruns/333956/, accessed 2 August 2016 ('The Statistics Ministry monitored 286 infrastructure projects, each worth Rs 1,000 crore or more across sectors such as power, railways and roads in April 2016').
28. Praveen Sharma, 'Delays Shoot Up Infrastructure Project Costs by Rs. 1.77 Lakh Crore', *DNA India*, New Delhi, 28 January 2015, available http://www.dnaindia.com/india/report-delays-shoot-up-infrastructure-project-costs-by-rs-177-lakh-crore-2056081, accessed 2 August 2016.
29. Alexander, 'The Mediation Metamodel', p. 97. Expert advisory mediators are usually senior lawyers or other professionals selected on the basis of their expertise in the subject matter of the dispute and their seniority, rather than their process skills.

30. Law Commission of India, 126th Report on Government and Public Sector Undertaking Litigation Policy and Strategies, 1988, available http://lawcommissionofindia.nic.in/101-169/report126.pdf, accessed 2 August 2016.

31. Ministry of Law and Justice, 'The National Litigation Policy', available lawmin.nic.in/la/nlp.doc, accessed 2 August 2016; Ministry of Law and Justice, 'Status Note on National Litigation Policy', available http://lawmin.nic.in/la/status%20note%20on%20nlp.pdf, accessed 2 August 2016.

32. *Chief Conservator of Forests v. The Collector*, (2003) 3 SCC 472.

33. The Arbitration and Conciliation Act, 1996, Section 28(2): 'The arbitral tribunal shall decide *ex aequo et bono* or as amiable *compositeur* only if the parties have expressly authorised it to do so.'

34. This is called the continuum of tension. Mediation and Conciliation Project Committee, 'Mediation Training Manual of India', 10.

35. 21st Century Corporate ADR Pledge: 'Our company pledges to commit its resources to manage and resolve disputes through negotiation, mediation and other ADR processes when appropriate, with a view to establishing and practicing global, sustainable dispute management and resolution processes.'

36. Indian Institute of Arbitration and Mediation, 'Pledge to Mediate', available http://www.arbitrationindia.org/pledge.html, accessed 2 August 2016.

37. Roger Fisher, William Ury, and Bruce Patton, *Getting to Yes: Negotiating Agreement without Giving in* (New York: Penguin Books, 1991).

38. 'Better Solutions for Business: Commercial Mediation in the EU' (CPR Institute for Dispute Resolution 2004, available http://www.cpradr.org/Portals/0/Across%20Borders/Why%20Businesses%20Need%20Mediation.pdf, accessed 5 August 2016.

39. K.V.W. Stone, 'Alternative Dispute Resolution', *Encyclopedia of Legal History* (2004), p. 3.

40. Andrew Goodman, *Effective Mediation Advocacy*, 3rd ed. (Kerrypress Ltd, 2009), p. 62.

41. Goodman, *Effective Mediation Advocacy*, p. 62.

42. Normally found in construction contracts. The decision/report of a DRB or an expert determination does not have the force of an arbitral award or a court decree.

43. Sriram Panchu, *Mediation Practice & Law: The Path to Successful Dispute Resolution* (Nagpur: LexisNexis Butterworths Wadhwa, 2011), p. 187.

44. IMI, 'Olé! Online Dispute Analysis', available https://imimediation. org/ole, accessed 2 August 2016.
45. IMI aims to offer a benchmark of high-quality mediation not by requiring uniform standards but through a harmonizing mechanism such as client review, mediator peer, and a code of professional conduct for mediators on the premise of all-embracing principles of trust, transparency, competence, confidentiality, and impartiality.
46. In international scenarios when a dispute resolution clause is omitted, the uncertainties of international commercial litigation in the procedure, substantive law, jurisdiction, and enforcement, can be minimized with a well-drafted dispute resolution clause.
47. *Tulip Hotels (P) Ltd. v. Trade Wings Ltd.* (2009) SCC OnLine Bom 1222.
48. For that reason, the continuing willingness of the parties to participate in the mediation process is essential for its ultimate completion.
49. However, for mediation involving international commercial disputes, the parties may avoid many uncertainties (especially relating procedural and jurisdictional implications) involved in constructing their own rules by agreeing that the mediation would be governed by institutional rules. Institutional mediation is the most preferred in international commercial mediation.
50. Parties would be prudent to adopt an off-the-shelf mediation rule, a flexible system that is already tried and tested by institutions. Once a package is selected, the parties may then consider any special needs which need to be adapted.
51. K. Scanlon, *Mediator's Deskbook* (CPR, 1999); and L. Riskin, *Mediation Training Guide* (1997).
52. The mediator may also request the parties to prepare a 'statement of positions and interests' or a 'position paper' which is planned to orient the parties towards settlement. The mediator may request for information pertaining to a party's factual matrix and the legal issues in dispute; any previous offers and counteroffers; the party's understanding as to what the case needs to achieve a settlement, etc. The content will, therefore, vary.
53. Morton Deutsche and Peter T. Coleman, *The Handbook of Conflict Resolution* (San Francisco: Jossey-Bass Publishers, 2000), p. 534.
54. Mediation and Conciliation Project Committee, 'Mediation Training Manual of India', 36.
55. Deutsche and Coleman, *The Handbook of Conflict Resolution*, pp. 530–1.

56. This is becoming a specialized form of a legal practice known variously as mediation lawyering, mediation advocacy or mediation lawyering or mediation representation.

57. Fisher et al., *Getting to Yes*. In a large number of cases, the law is a relevant external factor. Therefore, in that sense, all mediations and negotiations are done 'in the shadow of the law'.

58. Goodman, *Effective Mediation Advocacy*, p. 47.

59. Also see the section titled 'Arbitration and Conciliation Act, 1996' in this chapter, for more on the legal and regulatory framework.

60. *Moti Ram v. Ashok Kumar* (2011) 1 SCC 466. If the mediation succeeds, then the mediator should send the agreement signed by both parties to the court without mentioning what transpired during the mediation proceedings. If the mediation is unsuccessful, then the mediator should only write one sentence, 'mediation has been unsuccessful'. Beyond that, the mediator should not write anything which was discussed, proposed, or done during the mediation proceedings.

61. Mediation and Conciliation Project Committee, 'Mediation Training Manual of India', 24.

62. Code of Civil Procedure, 1908 s 89 ('Settlement of Disputes outside Court'); Order-X Rules 1A, 1B, and 1C of the CPC ('Direction of the court to opt for any one mode of alternative dispute resolution').

63. Code of Civil Procedure, 1908 Order-XXIII Rule 3 ('Compromise of suit').

64. Code of Civil Procedure, 1908 Order XLIII Rule 1A of the CPC ('Right to Challenge Non-Appealable Orders in Appeal Against Decree').

65. To enforce a consent decree, a party must look to each country where a debtor party has assets and ascertain whether that country has a bilateral arrangement with India or a history of enforcing Indian judgments (although, existence of a precedent would not make it obligatory). India is not a signatory to the 'Convention on the Recognition and Enforcement of Foreign Judgments in Civil and Commercial Matters, 1971'.

66. *O. Konavalov v. Commander, Coast Guard Region*, (2006) 4 SCC 620: 'The comity of nations is a reciprocal courtesy which one member of the family of nations owes to the others.'

67. Abla J. Mayss, *Principles of Conflict of Laws*, 3rd ed. (Cavendish Publishing Ltd., 1999) p. 88; and Adrian Briggs, *Conflict of Law*, 3rd ed. (Oxford University Press, 2014), p. 138.

68. Code of Civil Procedure, 1908 s 44A ('Execution of Decree Passed by Courts in Reciprocating Territory'), or by instituting a suit on a

foreign judgment. For both the cases, Section 13 of the CPC provides for when foreign judgment would not be conclusive.

69. Arbitration & Conciliation (Amendment) Act, 2015, No. 3 of 2015 (Arbitration Amendment Act), s 74.

70. Arbitration & Conciliation (Amendment) Act, 2015, No. 3 of 2015 (Arbitration Amendment Act), s 30.

71. Arbitration & Conciliation (Amendment) Act, 2015, No. 3 of 2015 (Arbitration Amendment Act), s 35 and 36.

72. 'International Commercial Conciliation' has been defined under the Arbitration and Conciliation Act, 1996. The definition has the same wordings as that of 'International Commercial Arbitration' in Section 2(1)(f) of the 1996 Act. International Commercial Conciliation, therefore, basically relates to a dispute arising out of legal relationships (whether contractual or not) considered as commercial under the Indian law and where at least one of the parties is: (a) an individual who is a national of, or habitually resident in, any country other than India; or (b) a body corporate which is incorporated in any country other than India; or (c) a company or an association or a body of individuals whose central management and control is exercised in any country other than India; or (d) the Government of a foreign country.

73. UNCITRAL Conciliation Rules, 1980, available https://www.uncitral.org/pdf/english/texts/arbitration/conc-rules/conc-rules-e.pdf, accessed 8 August 2016.

74. Justice R.S. Bachawat, *Law of Arbitration and Conciliation*, trans Anirudh Wadhwa and Anirudh Krishnan, 5th ed. (Nagpur: LexisNexis Butterworths Wadhwa, 2010).

75. Larry A. Samovar, Richard E. Porter, and Edwin R. McDaniel, *Intercultural Communications: A Reader*, 13th ed. (1992).

76. In situations like these, direct negotiations may tend to further polarize disagreeing parties, expanding the gaps of misunderstanding. And in cases where such negotiations were undertaken and they broke down, outside intervention is required in the form of mediation.

77. Working Group II (Arbitration and Conciliation), available http://www.uncitral.org/uncitral/en/commission/working_groups/2 Arbitration.html, accessed 2 August 2016.

78. Working Group II (Arbitration and Conciliation).

79. United Nations Convention on the Recognition and Enforcement of Foreign Arbitral Awards, 1958, UNDOC/E/CONF.26/8/Rev.1 ('New York Convention').

80. The most celebrated regime, however, has been the Arb-Med-Arb (AMA) Protocol by the Singapore International Mediation Centre

(SIMC) which effectively pays attention to cross-border needs of ADR users. The Arb-Med-Arb Protocol is an ingenious technique of filling the vacuum that exists in enforcing settlement agreements resulting from international commercial mediation.

81. Mediation and Conciliation Project Committee, 'Mediation Training Manual of India':

> The Committee decided 40-Hours Mediation Training and 10 actual mediations as the essential qualification required for a mediator to be able to be entrusted the task of mediating disputes. A Sub-Committee was constituted under the able guidance of Hon'ble Mr Justice Cyriac Joseph (former Judge, Supreme Court of India and Member, MCPC) to lay down a uniform Mediation Training Manual of India.

82. Code of Civil Procedure, 1908 Order-X Rule 1A; See, *Afcons Infrastructure Ltd. v. Cherian Varkey Construction Co. (P) Ltd.*, (2010) 8 SCC 24:

> The only practical way of reading Section 89 and Order-X Rule 1A is that after the pleadings are complete and after seeking admissions/denials wherever required, and before framing issues, the court will have recourse to Section 89. But, once the evidence stage has commenced, the court will be reluctant to refer the matter to an ADR process lest it becomes a tool for protracting the trial.

83. Strengthening Mediation in India: Interim Report on Court-Annexed Mediations (Vidhi Centre for Legal Policy, July 2016); Delhi Mediation Centre, available http://www.delhimediationcentre.gov.in/statistical.htm, accessed 2 August 2016; Bombay High Court Mediation Centre, available http://mediationbhc.gov.in/1068/Court-Wise, accessed 2 August 2016; and Allahabad High Court Mediation Centre, available http://www.allahabadhighcourt.in/mediation/mediation.html, accessed 2 August 2016.

84. Section 89 and Order X Rule 1A of the CPC empowers judges to refer a matter to mediation, conciliation, or arbitration to provide for settlement of disputes outside courts with an attempt to blend the judicial and non-judicial dispute resolution mechanism.

85. The IMI (Hague, Netherlands) provides for an International Directory and a Global Search Centre for Certified Mediators, Young Mediators, and Mediation Advocate/Advisor.

86. Also see the section titled 'What Role Does a Mediator Play?' in this chapter for a discussion that would complement the selection process of a mediator.

87. Nadja (2008).

88. The Decision Tree, IMI, available https://imimediation.org/decision-tree, accessed 9 August 2016.

89. Also see the section titled 'What Role Does an Advocate Play?' in this chapter for a discussion that would complement the selection process of an advocate.

90. IMI, 'Competency Criteria for Mediation Advocates/Advisors', available https://imimediation.org/mediation-advocacy-criteria, accessed 9 August 2016.

91. However, in 2002, the UNCITRAL Model Law on International Commercial Conciliation (2002) was adopted by UNCITRAL on 24 June 2002. The Model Law provides uniform rules in respect of the conciliation process to encourage the use of conciliation and ensure greater predictability and certainty in its use.

92. Arbitration & Conciliation (Amendment) Act, 2015, No. 3 of 2015, (Arbitration Amendment Act).

93. Section 30(2) of the 1996 Act.

94. *Haresh Dayaram Thakur v. State of Maharashtra*, (2000) 6 SCC 179. The conciliator is vested with wide powers to decide the procedure to be followed by him, untrammelled by the procedural law like the Code of Civil Procedure and the Evidence Act.

95. *Mysore Cements Ltd. v. Svedala Barmac Ltd.* (2003) 10 SCC 375: Looking at the memorandum of conciliation and letter of comfort, the conciliator and both parties had agreed to certain terms, however, the same could not be enforced straightaway: the various steps contemplated in Section 73 of the 1996 Act were not adhered to and which is why; the memorandum had no consequences for non-compliance nor did it have any compensation mentioned. Virtually, a letter of comfort was sought to be enforced within the meaning of Section 74. Neither the memorandum nor the letter of comfort can be assigned the status of a settlement agreement under Section 73.

96. *Mysore Cements Ltd. v. Svedala Barmac Ltd.* (2003) 10 SCC 375. A consent agreement is in a sense analogous to a compromise agreement or consent order which enforced by using the machinery of court.

97. IMI, 'Competency Criteria for Mediation Advocates/Advisors'. Settlement agreement is final and binding on the parties and persons under them if it is signed by the parties since only then does it acquire the status, effect, and legal sanctity of an arbitral award.

98. In view of s 81, a conciliator or a mediator cannot be called as a witness.

99. *Salem Advocate Bar Assn. (2) v. Union of India* (2005) 6 SCC 344 (in conciliation there is little more latitude and a conciliator can suggest some terms of settlement too); Law Commission of India,

'Consultation Paper on ADR and Mediation Rules', available http://lawcommissionofindia.nic.in/alt_dis.pdf, accessed 2 August 2016; and Justice R.V. Raveendran, 'Section 89 CPC: Need for an Urgent Relook' (2007) 4 SCC J 23.

100. Alexander, 'The Mediation Metamodel'.
101. Section 72 of the 1996 Act.
102. Section 72 of the 1996 Act.
103. *Ravi Aggarwal v. Anil Jagota*, 2009 SCC OnLine Del 1475.
104. *Afcons Infrastructure Ltd. v. Cherian Varkey Construction Co. (P) Ltd.*, (2010) 8 SCC 24.
105. *Salem Advocate Bar Assn. v. Union of India*, (2003) 1 SCC 49. It is quite obvious that the reason why Section 89 has been inserted is to try and see that all the cases which are filed in court need not necessarily be decided by the court itself. Keeping in mind the law's delays and the limited number of judges which are available, it has now become imperative that resort should be had to ADR mechanism with a view to bringing to an end litigation between the parties at an early date. The ADR mechanism as contemplated by Section 89 is arbitration or conciliation or judicial settlement including settlement through Lok Adalat or mediation.
106. In terms of the UNCITRAL Model Law on International Commercial Conciliation (2002).
107. Harold I. Abramson, 'Time to Try Mediation of International Commercial Disputes', *ILSA Journal of International and Comparative Law*, 4 (323, 1997–8).

18

Mediation in India

Practical Tips and Techniques

Thomas P. Valenti and *Tanima Tandon*

> Darkness cannot drive out darkness; only light can do that. Hate
> cannot drive out hate; only love can do that.
>
> —Martin Luther King Jr.

What Is Mediation?

Defined as an out of court dispute resolution mechanism which
enables parties to negotiate their disputes hardly does justice to
the process of mediation. To be true to the spirit of the process, it
would be fair to say that mediation is a forum provided to parties
in a dispute where they can allege, argue, discuss, vent, brainstorm,
and overcome the root cause of their disputes. It is cognizant of the
fact that human relationships go beyond the written letter of the law
and disputes as such must be met with a space to resolve and preserve
relationships. In sum, mediation is a confidential process facilitated
by a neutral third party which gives the warring parties freedom to

explore creative settlements outside the scope of the written letter of the law without breaking it. The question that begs to be raised at this point is the sanctity of the confidentiality of the process, since a third party is present in the room and why would it not be better to opt for conciliation at this point. It is important to highlight two key points as a response to this oft-repeated dilemma: Firstly, the Supreme Court of India has in the case of *Moti Ram (D) Tr. LRs and Anr. v. Ashok Kumar and Anr*[1] held that mediation proceedings are confidential in nature and the mediator should send only a copy of an executed agreement to the court. This goes to show that even the Apex Court respects the confidentiality of the process and does not expect to be shown the facts and deliberations of the mediation table [refer to 'Case Law and Interpretations' for a more detailed discussion]. Second, the use of a mediator limits the risk of reactive devaluation. It is imperative to remember that both parties are in dispute and convinced that they are right. In this scenario, neither party is willing to listen to the other and therefore likely to tune out any proposed solutions rendering the process redundant. This is where the importance of a neutral mediator is best felt. He/she can accept proposals from one party and put them forth to the other without colouring it as a suggestion from the opponent. When this is done, the vision clouded by an automatic response is cleared and parties become more receptive to discussing proposals.

Following is a summary of benefits:

- Autonomy
- Empowerment
- Speed
- Confidentiality
- Creativity
- Reality testing

Another advantage of mediation is the autonomy it vests in the parties themselves. Parties are free to voice their own opinions and concerns without relying on lawyers to first convert the concern into legalese. The simplicity and sense of understanding gives both parties a sense of ownership of the process thereby instilling in them the confidence that they are indeed empowered to resolve their dispute themselves. This empowerment brings with it a sense of responsibility as they have no one but themselves to blame if the resolution is not in their favour and thus they become more open and creative while thinking of a solution. This is a unique feature of mediation where it allows parties to think out of the box and look for solutions that expand the pie rather than divide it. What this means is that parties are free to create value rather than divide the status quo. Given that it is an informal setting, and mediators delve far deeper into the lives of the parties to identify their real needs and interests, this approach works to the benefit of both parties. An example cited very often is that of splitting the orange. Consider a situation where two women are arguing over the possession of one orange. Assuming that both have equal claim over it, a court of law would ordinarily rule to have it divided in two and be shared equally by both women. What a mediator would do, instead, is to understand from both women why they want the orange. For example, if one of them says she wants to make a fruit cake and needs the rind and the other one says she wanted to drink a glass of orange juice, the court's judgment seems to do justice to neither of them. However, the mediator's recommendation now would be to give the whole rind to one and the whole pulp to the other to meet both their interests to the fullest. This is a classic example of creating value rather than dividing it. It is essential for a good mediator to be able to differentiate between equitable distribution vis-à-vis equal distribution. Keep in mind that a good value proposition takes into consideration the interests of both sides by understanding and developing the real needs of the parties.

This flexible approach to creative solutions in the parties' best interests is a key feature of mediation and one that sets it apart from other forms of judicial settlements.

Historical Evolution of Mediation in Indian Society

Conflict is an omnipresent phenomenon in every society and so is the need to resolve it, to ensure the balance between peace and harmony. In India, dispute resolution has been practised in several formal and informal forums such as courts, lok adalats, tribunals, panchayats, gram panchayats, and community settlements and has grown from the stage to village elders sitting under a banyan tree and resolving disputes to gaining statutory recognition.

392 Thomas P. Valenti and Tanima Tandon

Mediation owes its roots to the methods of dispute resolution devised and utilized by several religious sects before the emergence of formal legal and judicial systems worldwide. The first and most widely known instance is the judgment of King Solomon to 'split the baby' which he passed when two women came before him claiming to be the mother of the same child. From then on, its presence was identified in Islamic law, Roman law as also the ideology of the Christian communities spread over the United Kingdom, the United States, and Europe. It then seeped into the administration of US and UK governments and became the foundation of the judicial setup in these countries. From then on, this mechanism evolved into arbitration and thereafter came the modern-day adversarial system.

Mediation was very popular amongst businessmen during pre-British rule in India when respected members of the business community (Mahajans) resolved disputes between members of the business associations. This informal procedure was a combination of mediation and arbitration, now known in the Western world as Med-Arb. However, it had no legal sanction in spite of its acceptance in the business world. There were different grades of mediators with provisions for appeals in certain cases from the award of a lower grade mediator to one of a higher grade. Apart from the King, who was revered as God's representative on earth, other tribunals were also recognized in the ancient *smritis* and digests. The Yajnavalkya refers to three types of popular courts (Sharan, 1978):[2]

1. Puga: Comprised of persons dwelling in the same place, irrespective of their caste or employment. They were competent to decide cases in which the local public was interested.
2. Sreni: Comprised of persons engaged in similar pursuits professionally. They were competent to decide matters relating to their specialities as traders.
3. Kula: Comprised of members of a particular community who were empowered to adjudicate social matters.

This period gave way to the more popular system of the Panchayati Raj. Panchayats have been following a hybrid model of mediation and arbitration for property disputes, torts, and even criminal offences, such as murder and rape, since time immemorial. A Panchayat is

a representative body of the members of a particular caste or village. One of the most important functions of these Panchayats is
the dispensing of justice. It is a mechanism that is still favoured in
innumerable villages across India primarily because of inaccessibility
to judicial services and expense of the process and, second because of
the need to resolve an internal dispute within the confines of a village
rather than publicize the matter.

In rural areas, not following the judgment of the Panchayat
was considered an insult to the village elders and led to
consequent social ostracism. The observation that the earliest
known judicial tribunals were indeed Panchayats has been acknowledged by the court in *Chambasappa Gurushantappa v. Baslingayya
Gokurnaya Hiremath*.[3]

Legislative Evolution in India: Historical Overview

Mediation, as a dispute resolution procedure was recognized as early
as 1879 and found its place alongside arbitration in the Codes of Civil
Procedure Code 1879, 1882, and 1908. Mediation got legislative recognition for the first time in the Industrial Disputes Act, 1947, where
the conciliators are charged with the duty of mediating in and promoting the settlement of industrial disputes under Section 4 of the Act.
The Indian Legislature made considerable progress in this direction by
enacting the Legal Services Authorities Act, 1987 and constituting the
National Legal Services Authority as a central authority with the Chief
Justice of India as its patron in chief. It has been vested with duties to
perform the following functions:

1. encourage the settlement of disputes by way of negotiations
2. lay down policies and principles for making legal services available in the conduct of any case
3. frame effective and economical schemes
4. optimize utilization of funds
5. undertake research in the field
6. submit recommendations to the government
7. develop legal training and educational programmes and establish
   legal services clinics
8. act in coordination with governmental and non-governmental
   agencies

Confidentiality and Disclosure

Rationale: What Is the Need of Confidentiality?

Confidentiality is a motivating incentive for parties to choose mediation to resolve a dispute. It plays an even more crucial role in enabling parties to reach settlement because of the protection that can be afforded with the results of mediation. The ability to effectively assure confidentiality in the mediation process is essential to its success and integrity. Knowing that everything said or done in mediation will remain confidential allows parties to confide in the mediator more freely. It opens the door to frank and honest discussion. Indeed, candour with, and full disclosure to, the mediator in confidence can be the key to a successful resolution of even the bitterest of controversies. To be able to negotiate freely, parties need to be willing to make their needs and interests known, to make concessions and to make offers that may be risky. They can only do so if they are certain that confidentiality principles will apply and protect all settlement discussions between them. This confidentiality applies to every stage of the process, from the preliminary emails and phone calls, written statements, the negotiating positions of the parties, and follow-up communications, and even to the very fact that a mediation took place.

Terms and Rules

At the outset, all participants in the mediation should enter into a written agreement providing for strict confidentiality. This can be done by inserting confidentiality clauses within the terms of the agreement to mediate, if there is one used.[4]

Parties are free to agree on terms pertaining to confidentiality in their agreement to mediate. A very basic sample is included for reference. In addition, the rules of most institutions that administer mediation cases have their own provisions for confidentiality. For example, the Mediation Rules of the International Chamber of Commerce (ICC) provide that unless otherwise agreed by the parties or required by applicable law, mediation (but not the fact that it is taking place, has taken place, or will take place) is private and confidential. As a result, submissions made by parties or the mediator may not be used in any arbitration, court case, or similar proceeding. The same confidentiality principles apply to views expressed, concessions, offers, or any admissions made by the parties to a mediation.

India enacted the Arbitration and Conciliation Act in 1996. Section 75 of the Act provides that the conciliator and the parties shall keep confidential all matters relating to the conciliation proceedings including the settlement agreement, except where its disclosure is necessary for purposes of implementation and enforcement. In India, the terms 'mediation' and 'conciliation' are, still, often used interchangeably.

Where disputes are referred by a court to arbitration or conciliation under Section 89 of the Code of Civil Procedure, the procedure set out in the Arbitration and Conciliation Act, 1996, will apply. However, where disputes are referred by the court to mediation, the courts are required to follow the procedure that may have prescribed. Unlike arbitration or conciliation, there is no specific statute that deals with mediation in India. Therefore, confidentiality in mediation proceedings is not specifically provided for in any statute in India.

Case Law and Interpretations

The Indian legal system has upheld the important role that confidentiality plays in mediation. On 7 January 2011, in the case of *Moti Ram (D) Tr. LRs and Anr. v. Ashok Kumar and Anr.*,[5] the Supreme Court of India referred the matter for mediation to a mediator. After the conclusion of the sessions, the mediator's report was put before the Court. The report mentioned various settlement proposals made by the parties. As a result, the Supreme Court stressed that mediation proceedings are strictly confidential. The Court went on to clarify the requirement and purpose of the report, namely, that when successful, the mediator should send the settlement agreement signed by the parties to the Court without mentioning what occurred during the mediation proceedings. When unsuccessful, the mediator should simply state that mediation has been unsuccessful. The Supreme Court affirmed that any disclosure of what occurred in a mediation destroys the confidentiality of the mediation process. Prior to this judgment, parties were free to make a contractual agreement to maintain confidentiality of mediation proceedings but no statutory authority provided that mediation proceedings were confidential. The judgment is expected to improve the popularity of mediation as a method of resolving disputes in India, particularly amongst non-Indian parties.

In *Rama Aggarwal v. PIO, Delhi State Legal Service Authority*[6] that came up before the Central Information Commission (CIC), the CIC held that a party cannot seek information pertaining to mediation proceedings under the Right to Information Act. The CIC observed that 'Information regarding negotiation, mediation, conciliation and counselling are exempt from disclosure, being personal and given in fiduciary capacity and, no public interest could be established for disclosure'. The Court recognized that the larger public interest in protecting that information from disclosure so as to help mediation flourish.

Different high courts in India have framed rules applicable to their own jurisdictions. One example is the Mediation and Conciliation Rules, 2004 issued by the Delhi High Court. The rules require parties to maintain confidentiality in respect of events that have transpired during the course of mediation and prohibit parties from relying and/or introducing such information in any other proceedings.

Indian laws are regarded as adequately providing for confidentiality in mediation, in line with international standards. In addition, the Indian Courts have supported the importance of confidentiality in mediation.

Areas for Dispute Resolution

Indian Context

Court-Annexed Mediation

In India, mediation through its courts has its authority under Section 89 of the Code of Civil Procedure, 1908. Mediation Centres have now been established at many courts, and the courts have started referring cases to such mediation centres. This is generally referred to as 'Court-Annexed Mediation'. The terms 'Court-Annexed Mediation' and 'Court-Referred Mediation' are often used interchangeably in common parlance. However, there is an essential distinction between the two concepts. Court-annexed mediation entails mediation services provided by the court as a part and parcel of the same judicial system, while court–referred mediation pertains to disputes which are merely referred by courts to a mediator.

The element that these two concepts have in common is that they are both concerned with disputes in litigation. Many High Courts in India have framed mediation rules so that once a settlement is reached upon during the course of mediation, the settlement should be put in writing, signed by the concerned parties and forwarded to the court in which the suit is pending. The court then records the settlement and passes a decree in accordance with the terms of the settlement. Only on passing of a decree on the basis of the settlement agreement will it be considered final, binding and effective. No revisions or appeals are to be taken from such a decree.

Private Mediation

Private mediation mainly involves pre-litigation disputes. It differs from court-annexed or court-referred mediation insofar as the parties on their own accord approach a mediator with a view to reach an amicable settlement. There is an endless list of cases that are appropriate for mediation, in the area of trade, commerce, land disputes, tortious liability, consumer disputes, estate matters, and family matters, enumerated below.

Suitable Cases

Disputes between:

- Suppliers and customers
- Bankers and customers
- Developers/builders and customers
- Landlords and tenants
- Licensor and licensee
- Insurer and insured
- Husband and wife
- Family members
- Partners

398   Thomas P. Valenti and Tanima Tandon

- Shareholders
- Employees
- Neighbours

Non-suitable Cases

The Indian Supreme Court, in *Afcons Infrastructure Ltd. & Anr v. Cherian Varkey Construction Co. (P) Ltd. & Ors*,[7] as also provided an 'excluded category' where there is no need to refer a matter to an ADR process:

- Representative suits
- Disputes relating to election to public offices
- Suits for grant of probate or letters of administration
- Cases involving fraud, fabrication of documents, forgery, impersonation, coercion, and so on
- Claims against minors
- Claims against the mentally challenged
- Suits for declaration of title against the government
- Cases involving prosecution of criminal offences

Structure and Process of Mediation

Structuring a Mediation Session

Mediation is a voluntary process in which the mediator assists the parties to a dispute to negotiate a settlement. In the process, after the parties agree upon a mediator, they gather together and begin the discussion, under the mediator's guidance. It is generally said that the mediator is in-charge of the process, and the parties are in charge of the problem. Usually the parties first meet together where the mediator explains mediation and the process, and then each party is allowed to make a brief statement summarizing the dispute as they see it. Many mediators follow those statements by creating an agenda which includes a recitation and actual list of the issues that both sides wish to discuss. Following that the mediator decides to have further discussions, either together in what is called a 'Joint Session', 'Conference', (or Caucus) or, privately, in what is called a 'Private Session'. Before the mediation is concluded there is usually a 'Closing' session where either a settlement is confirmed, or the next steps are planned. These steps are used in an informal and flexible manner so that the mediation process builds upon each step.

Stages of a Mediation

More specifically, the mediation process is often described as having these stages:

Convening

Keep in mind that convening the mediation might be challenging. At times it requires the mediator to bring together parties who do not want to mediate, or between whom relations are so strained that they may not want to even see each other, much less negotiate with each other. In India, the parties are not always voluntarily participating. In fact, in the case of court-appointed mediation, the court can order the parties to enter the mediation process under Section 89 of the Code of Civil Procedure.

Also, the parties may not have agreed upon the mediator unanimously. Under the Delhi High Court Mediation Rules, the parties are ordinarily given the freedom to appoint a mediator of their choice. However, the courts have created a panel of mediators from among whom mediators may be chosen to assist the parties.

Introduction of Mediation and Defining the Process of Mediation

At the very beginning of the session, the mediator explains the procedure which will be followed in the rest of the mediation. This helps set the parties expectations and eases them into the process as some of them may be unfamiliar with it. It also aids the mediator in establishing certain ground rules to be followed during the session (see illustration 2 of Annexure I for a sample opening statement).

The parties can even decide upon the rules to be followed in the mediation. The Delhi High Court Mediation Rules state that parties may agree on the procedure to be followed by them as well as the mediator in the conduct of the mediation proceedings. A Sample Mediator's Opening Statement is included. This is one of the principal advantages of mediation and other forms of Alternative Dispute Resolution, namely, that there does not exist rigid and binding rules of procedure which may hamper and delay the process.

Statements by the Parties

In this stage, the mediator will elicit statements from the disputants. This gives each party the opportunity to articulate their positions, so that the other side can clearly understand exactly what they want. This will also help parties to begin to understand the interests of the opponent, which underlie the positions.

Following the statements by the parties/negotiators, the mediator may choose to restate the problem and issues. This is done to build trust and to foster a feeling that the mediator understands the task at hand. When the mediator restates the problem, he attempts to accommodate the differing perspectives presented by all parties. An effective summary can help reduce the parties' perceptions of the differences that exist between them. Often, there is the opportunity to actually find and highlight an area of agreement just from the party's opening statements.

Setting the Agenda for Mediation

This stage involves the setting down of the issues that each party wishes to discuss. The mediator may also set a sequence or order in which the discussion proceeds. This is an important stage because it lets the parties know what to expect, assures them that they will be given the opportunity to discuss what they wish and creates some road map for the mediation. This benefits the mediator in assisting the parties to reach a settlement by having a visual reference for measuring progress. It is beneficial to use a flip chart for this so that the agenda can be seen by the parties and used as a reference as the mediation progresses.

The ultimate goal is to transition from the past conflicts to future resolutions. Have the participants choose topics at a time to discuss and be thorough on the topic before moving on. Label and define the issues clearly. If the participants get stuck, come back to that topic later and move to the next one. Be sure to talk about every concern and idea on the list. A typical agenda is provided as seen in illustration 3 of Annexure I. You can see how the agenda is tailored to suit the dispute.

In family cases, for example, standard issues include the possibility of reconciliation; disclosure in relation to property and finances; the welfare of the children (residence, maintenance, education, and health issues); division of assets; sale of assets and division of proceeds; outstanding debts; future issues; and the associated formalities.

Facilitating the Negotiation, Generating Options, Brainstorming, if Necessary

In this stage, the mediator assists the parties in undertaking the negotiation effectively. It is here that the importance of neutrality and confidentiality on the part of the mediator and in the mediation process, respectively, are crucial.

The generation of options must be undertaken with complete neutrality. The mediator should not evaluate options instead he should facilitate the reaching of a settlement by generating options, one (or a combination of a few or many) which the parties may adopt as the final settlement. Some tips for facilitating the discussion are included as in illustration 4 of Annexure I.

Reaching a Settlement

This stage of the mediation procedure is the final stage and, usually, involves two steps: the reaching of a settlement and summarizing it.

Non-verbal signs

- Smile
- Eye Contact
- Posture
- Mirroring
- Tapping

Verbal signs

- Reflection
- Reframing

- Extending
- Clarifying
- Summarizing

This is practically the most important part of the mediation process and thus care and caution must be exercised in this process by the mediator. There is no fixed procedure which must be followed in all circumstances; there are certain factors to be kept in mind by the parties as well as the mediator. First, the mediator must, through the use of options discussed earlier, direct the parties towards reaching a settlement which he believes will best satisfy their interests. Only then will the mediator succeed in securing the commitment of the parties to the mediation and the settlement reached. Next, once the settlement is reached, the mediator should summarize the settlement and put it down in writing. This procedural requirement is critical because an essential requirement to secure compliance is that the both parties understand and agree on the exact content of the settlement.

The mediator prepares or supervises the preparation of a memorandum of understanding of the settlement which should include all the material terms which the parties agreed upon, making sure that the details are sufficient to make an enforceable settlement agreement. This is important because the mediation settlement agreement has the force of a binding contract and can be enforced by a court of law, as mentioned in other sections of this chapter.

Example of Delhi High Court Process Rules

Some local courts set forth their own procedures by way of an example. The Delhi High Court rules governing the procedure for mediation are:

Rule 10: Procedure of mediation/conciliation.
1.   The parties may agree on the procedure to be followed by the mediator/conciliator in the conduct of the mediation/conciliation proceedings.
2.   Where the parties do not agree on any particular procedure to be followed by the mediator/conciliator, the mediator/conciliator shall follow the procedure hereinafter mentioned, namely:

i.   he shall fix, in consultation with the parties, a time schedule, the dates and the time of each mediation/conciliation session, where all parties have to be present;

ii.   he shall hold the mediation/conciliation at the place prescribed by the High Court or the District & Sessions Judge or the place where the parties and the mediator/conciliator jointly agree;

iii.   he may conduct joint or separate meetings with the parties;

iv.   each party shall, ten days before a session, provide to the mediator/conciliator a brief memorandum setting forth the issues, which according to it, need to be resolved, and its position in respect to those issues and all information reasonably required for the mediator/conciliator to understand the issue; such memoranda shall also be mutually exchanged between the parties. However, in suitable/appropriate cases, the period of ten days may be curtailed in the discretion of the mediator/conciliator; and

v.   each party shall furnish to the mediator/conciliator such other information as may be required by him in connection with the issues to be resolved.

3.   Where there is more than one mediator/conciliator, the mediator/conciliator nominated by each party may first confer with the party that nominated him and thereafter interact with the other mediator/conciliator, with a view to resolve the dispute(s).

No matter where or under whose rules the mediation is conducted, the key features of the mediation process are:

- Flexible and informal procedure
- Voluntary process
- Freedom to negotiate without prejudice to the party's legal position
- Confidentiality

Mediation Styles

Overview of Different Mediation Styles

Early in the ADR movement, mediation was being taught and largely practiced in a form typically labelled 'facilitative mediation'.

This approach to mediation is based on the fundamental belief that disputants can work together constructively if placed in a neutral, safe, and supportive environment. Accordingly, the mediator's role is to facilitate such an opportunity. Proponents of facilitative mediation believe that disputants, with the aid of their own legal counsel, are capable of understanding their situations better than third parties and therefore 'can develop better solutions than any the mediator might create' (Waldman, 1998).[8] Consequently, facilitative mediation emphasizes assisting the disputants in evaluating their own situations rather than evaluating the disputes for them. Thus, the facilitative mediator does not give advice and does not provide opinions on the merits of arguments and the relative value of the case. Nor does the facilitative mediator make predictions about how a suit would likely be decided. Instead, the facilitative mediator assists the parties in reaching a mutually agreeable resolution by enhancing and clarifying communication, by reorienting efforts away from fighting in support of positions and towards identification of true interests, and by helping the disputants to identify and analyse their options. Moreover, facilitative mediation offers a therapeutic approach to dispute resolution because the outcome of facilitative mediation is an agreement based on information and understanding rather than mediator influence or coercion.[9]

During the 1990s, there was an enormous growth in the use of mediation. Much of this growth was the result of court referrals and orders. In this adversarial setting, there arose a practice of 'evaluative mediation' modelled somewhat after judicial settlement conferences. The evaluative mediator is more concerned with the parties' legal rights than with satisfying their interests. Evaluative mediation is based on the fundamental belief that disputants can benefit when a knowledgeable and objective third party provides guidance about substantive issues and the merits of their positions.[10] The evaluative mediator gives advice, makes assessments, renders opinions on issues, and predicts outcomes—including expressing an opinion about how a judge or jury would likely decide the case. As a part of this process, the evaluative mediator usually devotes considerable time in convincing the parties about the weaknesses of their case and the cost of pursuing a litigated resolution. The process is often adversarial throughout, with the mediator pressing the disputants to make new demands and offers more in line with the mediator's evaluations. Given this legal rights focus, it is common for evaluative mediators to be lawyers or retired judges with considerable substantive legal expertise.[11]

Having been conditioned to receive a 'judgment' from a person in authority, mediation in India has gravitated towards a model wherein parties seek advice and direction from the mediator, much like a decision. This solicitation of advice is a classic feature of evaluative mediation. It is commonplace and manifests itself in forms such as women seeking solace by confiding in the mediator about their broken marriage and ruing their kids' futures or businessmen seeking legal advice from the mediator on the options they have to avoid litigation as in Section 138 cases against them for dishonouring cheques. Given the vast expanse of concerns that can be mediated, the range of advice sought is manifold but converges in one clear expectation—that of receiving the solution from someone perceived to be in a position of power, which, in the case of mediation, is the mediator. Recall that a key feature of mediation is its voluntary nature and the ability of parties to customize solutions for themselves. It thus becomes pivotal for the mediator to inculcate this very essence of the process in the minds of both parties since any solution imposed by the mediator is against the fundamental nature of the process and simply does not hold any value.

Barriers to Mediation in India

Seen from a 30,000 feet perspective, mediation seems to be an ideal solution for resolving disputes and if adopted, the future seems promising for a country where the judicial system is notoriously synonymous with delayed deliverance of justice. Then what, one may ask, is the reason for the delay in the implementation of a mechanism that is seemingly the utopian solution for the disputants. The fact that it could greatly relieve the burden of pendency on the courts is also stacked in favour of the process. However, mediation still has a long way to go in terms of gaining widespread acceptance from the Indian audience. We will now examine a few of the barriers obstructing the success of the mediation process in India.

Positions v. Interests

Parties often gauge success of dispute resolution based on the order, if it is in their favour or not. The concept of everyone being a winner does not gain favor with much of the Indian population. One of the most commonly mediated areas in India is matrimonial disputes, wherein there is a very high probability of involvement of high egos and emotions which tend to derail the process of amicable settlement. It becomes a mediator's responsibility to help a party identify their real interest and develop on that and move away from the position of wanting to be proven right at all costs. A simple example of the thin line between positions and interests is given as follows:

Mary and Harry are involved in a custody battle over the custody of their four-year-old daughter Sia. While Mary is a hard-working stay at home mother, Harry is the one who earns more money of the two. In this scenario, both put forth the reasons why they should have the custody of their daughter ranging from stability to secure future to the ability to provide every luxury that money can buy. While indulging in this power struggle, they are demonstrating their positions and justifications for the same; what they neglect is their real interest of providing a safe home for nurturing Sia. It is thus the mediator's role to step in and ask them to pivot from their positions and consider the real interests at stake. This could well dawn the realization on Harry that a young child would require her mother's love more than she would any worldly luxuries or vice versa. The important point is that it opens up a forum for discussion beyond the limited sphere of the individuals' constricted thinking.

Social Conditioning

As a society, Indians are fairly conservative and inordinately conscious of the extent of their dirty linen they want to wash in the public. It makes one conscious while talking about personal matters relating to dowry, abuse, domestic violence, cheating, and so on, which are a few of the most commonly areas of matrimonial disputes that are brought for mediation these days. While it is imperative that both parties voice their thoughts as honestly as possible in order to resolve the dispute to the best of their interests, there is no shying away from the fact that their version may well be watered down and filtered. In a majority of cases, the women are shy to disclose the extent of their suffering which skews the fact matrix and handicaps the mediator from gaining a fair understanding of the case at hand. Being a barrier of expression brought on by social conditioning, mediators are urged to make optimum use of the tools at their disposal to make parties feel comfortable in opening up and sharing the full fact scenario. This can be done by certain ways such as calling for private sessions or even going to the extent of asking the lawyer to remain out of the room, stressing on confidentiality, building a connect by talking about more general topics and then refocusing on the matter at hand, and so on.

Adversarial Judicial System

India, having been burdened with the cross of the adversarial judicial system since the time of the British rule in India, is now seeing the option of mediation. It is a system which places higher value on winning rather than establishing the truth or helping find the best possible solution. In line with this, when litigants sit across each other at the mediation table, more often than not, it is to find faults with the other party and establish a strong case for themselves rather than exploring opportunities to find mutual ground. Words like 'settlement' and 'compromise' are perceived as weak and the concept of dividing the pie substantively hurts the ego of both sides. It takes high level of skill on the part of the mediator to calm each party down and a number of private sessions to help both begin to see eye-to-eye.

Vested Interests

Some lawyers who charge their clients per hearing may be understandably unhappy with the growing popularity of the process. Efficient mediation centers and peaceful clients can impact the number of hours spent by lawyers on a case which can reduce their fee. Unfortunately, many lawyers have this view, even though it is not universally true. Many times the lawyers spend considerable hours preparing for mediation and participating in the mediation. So, it is not always true that the fee is reduced. Keep in mind that it is generally true that client satisfaction is higher with mediated settlements as the client has personally participated and the solution is a joint one, rather than imposed by a court. So clients are usually more pleased with the settlement than with a judicial decision. Having conducted and observed several mediation cases, it is safe to conclude that the chances of parties successfully reaching a resolution were higher in cases where the mediator asked for cross caucuses between the parties with the exclusion of the attorneys. Attorneys, in India, are still getting used to the idea, learned in other jurisdictions that clients appreciate a quicker resolution and will be more prone to refer other matters to counsel when resolution is swift and where the client has had an active role. It is important to understand that these matters are personal for the parties and there is always a light at the end of the tunnel, however steep the path to it may be.

Party Representatives, Third Parties, and Advocacy

Introduction to Mediation Advocacy

Advocacy at every stage has to move disputants from their wants to their needs. Wants are often instinctive, impulsive actions/offers and needs intuitive, innovative actions/offers coupled with willingness to move on. In the dialogue, the mediator assists the disputants to build the bridge to enable trust and rapport. Then the disputants are nudged in the direction that they do not wholly understand at that point, but will get to, once the sequential negotiation happens.

Advocacy: Preparation Stage

Preparing to mediate is in many respects no different from planning for any serious negotiation. Mediation differs from direct bargaining, however, in several important ways. One is in intensity. Ordinary bargaining may occur intermittently over a period of months or years, without any clear structure and often over the telephone or by email. Mediation, by contrast, is usually set up as a 'settlement event': Parties agree to meet on a certain date in the presence of a third party and to bargain continuously to a resolution. In addition, unlike direct negotiation, which is often conducted through telephones or by email, participants in mediation almost always meet in person. As a result, the decision-makers will observe and interact with—and be open to observation by—the opponent and the mediator. The most important difference between mediation and direct negotiation, however, is the mediator. The presence of the neutral means that the process sometimes resembles a two-party facilitated negotiation and at times a three-sided interaction among the parties and the mediator. As a lawyer in mediation, you will bargain with your opponent over settlement terms but may also negotiate with the mediator about how the process will be conducted. In the preparation phase, a party and its counsel should engage in the following steps:

Create a Case Road Map

1. **Identify the issues in dispute**: Each case has its own set of issues. Many times these are not articulated in court documents but are uniquely known to the client. These should be shared with counsel in the preparation stage. Counsel should probe the client concerning what the constraints are relative to settlement, and whether there are any unknown circumstances (for example, authority, timing, cash availability, performance restrictions, and so on) that may impact the negotiation and therefore the settlement. The result should be a list of items to be resolved, which contains the specific constraints that apply to each issue.

2. **Plan your presentation**: Consider what information about your interests and the facts of the case you want to disclose to the mediator and what information you want to disclose to the opposing side. Usually, full disclosure to the mediator helps facilitate a successful settlement. There should be a strategy employed to gradually disclose information to the other side, in exchange for information from the other side. If there is no reciprocity in the exchange, counsel and client should be less inclined to continue sharing with the other side. However, disclosing information to the mediator can still be useful, as it will allow the mediator to look at both side's confidential information and assess whether a solution may still be possible.

3. **Prepare a simple case summary**: Anticipate what story you will
    tell during the opening session of the mediation and rehearse it.
    Often it is useful to have counsel outline the legal arguments and
    the client to outline the facts and the impact of the dispute. Since
    you have already submitted a written statement of the case, the
    oral presentation should be clear and concise. It should outline
    the position of the party relative to settlement. It is best to just
    tell the story you want to and not discuss what you feel the other
    party will be saying. This summary will be delivered as the open-
    ing for your side. It is best not to refer to documents. However,
    in a case that does involve documents, keep copies of documents,
    photos, or other writings available for the mediator and oppos-
    ing counsel.

Develop a Negotiation Strategy

1. Identify the current negotiating position of the parties
2. Determine 'wants' and 'needs'
3. Create favourable perceptions
4. Develop options for mutual gain

Make It Easy to Reach an Agreement

1. **Cultivating a sense of mental detachment**: Take yourself
    out of the negotiations playing field and insert the dispute in
    your place. This allows you to talk about the issues in dispute,
    rather than getting bogged down with personality adversaries.
2. **Meeting the other side's needs**: You can better understand your
    opponent's needs by listening actively, acknowledging and para-
    phrasing their arguments. Express your views without provoca-
    tion. This is an effective tool to 'disarm' your opponent while
    understanding their point of view.
3. **Problem solving**: This is the time to recast what your opponent
    says in a form that directs attention back to the problem of sat-
    isfying both side's interests. Ask 'what' and 'how' questions to
    move towards a solution. Sometimes asking 'why' will cause your
    opponent to be defensive.

4. **Considering the consequences**: Ask reality testing questions such that your opposition will understand what will happen if agreement is not reached.
5. **Bridging the gap**: Reach agreement by helping your opponent save face. Try to satisfy unmet needs and involve your opponent in the process. Don't rush into the agreement, it will fall into place naturally.

Preparing Your Client

The special nature of mediation requires an attorney to cover the following topics with a client, in addition to the issues involved in preparing for an ordinary negotiation.

1. How the format of mediation differs from that of a typical negotiation, including:
   i. The procedure: for example will there be an opening session?
   ii. The confidentiality rules that apply and exceptions if any.
2. How the client should interact with the mediator and the opposing party, including:
   i. The mediator's background, personality, and style. Alert the client that the mediator may change style as the process moves forward, for example, by changing from an empathic listener to legal evaluator.
   ii. The allocation of roles between you and your client. For instance, will the client have a speaking role in the opening session? In private discussions, will you talk while the client listens, waiting to confer until the mediator leaves the room? Will the client play 'polite policeman' while you play a tough one?
   iii. The role you will play in the process. Explain that your overall goal, getting the best possible outcome for the client, remains the same, but that you must adapt your tactics to the fact that you are in a bargaining session involving a neutral facilitator.
   iv. You may act more conciliatory in mediation than you would in a court.
   v. You may not mention favourable evidence, so as not to alert your adversary.

3.   How the client should respond to questions?
    i.   Note that the client is free to decline to answer questions posed by the opponent or even the mediator.
    ii. Warn the client that you may argue politely with the mediator.
    iii. Explain that you can ask the mediator to leave the room so that you and the client can talk privately.
    iv. Explain that the client may be invited to meet privately with the other party and the mediator outside your presence and that she should talk with you before agreeing to this.

Conducting a Mediation

A key aspect of any negotiation is exchanging information, and part of mediation's value is its ability to enhance the flow of data between bargainers. What information is relevant in a case will depend again on your goal in the process. If bargaining turns on a money claim, then legal evidence and arguments are likely to be important. If your goal is to repair a relationship, knowing the 'why' behind a disputed action will be significant. If the objective is to restructure a business arrangement, financial data may be useful. As a rule, negotiations that focus on creative options require a broader range of information than discussions that revolve solely around money. A great deal of information exchange can occur during the process itself.

Let us now examine each stage of the mediation process and look at the issues to be considered at each step of the process.

Conducting a Mediation: Advocate's Opening Statement

1. **The audience**: To give or not to give. Although nominally directed to the mediator, the opening statement is really directed to the opposite side. Therefore, what are you planning to accomplish? Is an attack your most strategic choice or, at least in some cases, is it counterproductive? Do you always want to give an opening statement?
2. **Who gives the opening?** If your client presents well, there may be a benefit to having the client give part or all of the opening. Even if your client is not so great at presenting, does he or she

need to vent? Whatever your choice is, it should be a strategic one, and one your client understands.

3. **Techniques used in some openings**: Mediation is a long communication, and there are many ways to communicate. There are many ways to acknowledge that the other side is upset or has a particular view of the facts or the law without admitting that they are right. It also may be a more effective way to introduce why you and your client see the facts and law differently.

4. **Be prepared**: Without threatening or being theatrical, a lawyer may communicate that the other side will not like litigating by being prepared and thoroughly versed in the law and facts of the case. A prepared lawyer may also gain credibility for him/herself or his/her client by being prepared.

If the case warrants it, the following are techniques that may, if coupled with a well-thought out and effective oral presentation, further the impression of being prepared:

1. Outline key points on easel, leave easel in room when leaving for separate room so other side sees it.

2. Hand out highlighted documents, including excerpts from cases, key exhibits, charts.

3. Very occasionally, you may consider using PowerPoint or overhead projector and transparencies.

Bear in mind, however, that in a small case where the other side is not likely to make such a presentation, using such techniques may be counterproductive.

The Caucus

1. Sharing information with the mediator that you may or may not authorize the mediator to share with the other side. Be clear on what can be shared.

2. Use the mediator: a good mediator's objective is to obtain a settlement not to obtain what, in the mediator's opinion, is the fairest possible judgment.

3. Consider whether or not to tell mediator your true bottom line.

4. Who makes the first offer?
5. How are you using your time when the mediator is not in the room?

The Role of Counsel

1. Be familiar with the specific details of your case. The greater your familiarity with the case and the greater the ease of presentation, the more expeditious and effective the proceeding. Have the basic documents of your case succinctly arranged so that they can be referred to easily to aid your presentation and to educate the mediator.
2. Consider whether there are any objective criteria to measure the appropriate damages and evaluate settlement offers/demands.
3. Consider what realistic alternatives your client has if the parties do not reach agreement. This includes a hard evaluation of the outcome of the case if litigated. It also involves assessing other factors, for example, the cost to litigate the dispute (your fees, expert fees, costs client's time, witnesses' time); effect on the workplace and/or the parties (disruption, emotional impact, and consequence of publicity).
4. Consider how the other party is likely to evaluate the probable outcome if the case is litigated and the other factors suggested above. Consider what you could do in your mediation presentation to change that evaluation.
   i. If questions exist as to liability or damages, be prepared to argue with the most dispositive precedents you have.
   ii. If there are crucial differences in how the parties view what happened, be prepared to buttress your client's view (e.g., witnesses' statements).
   iii. Based on what you know about and from the other party, be prepared to rebut any concerns you suspect they have.
   iv. If information that has not already been shared (for example, about other 'similarly situated' employees or the origin and intent of policies) is at issue or may be helpful, bring it with you. You can always control how it is used.
5. Consider whether there is anything to be learned from the negotiations that have already taken place, if any. What are the barriers in reaching agreement that will need to be overcome

during the mediation? How can you help the mediator overcome those barriers?

6. Consider what you could do during the opening mediation presentation to create the most favorable circumstances for negotiation. Remember, this is not an adversarial or adjudicator forum. Your goal is to persuade the other decision-maker that is in his or her interest to find settlement terms that you will also find agreeable. How can you phrase your argument so that your opponent is all ears and is receptive to your client's viewpoint and interest?

7. Think about items that would appeal to your client as part of a settlement package. Do not limit yourself to the types of damages asserted in the litigation. Think about options that might appeal to the other side and that are not costly to you. Possible options include: ongoing services agreements, continuation of benefits, early retirement options under pension plans, structured settlements, characterizing payments as something other than compensation, agreed upon reference letters and/or public statements, personnel policy changes, training programmes, out placement services, and best effort agreements to influence actions of others.

8. Make certain the person(s) necessary to effect a settlement will be present and that you will be able to reach benefits personnel or others whose input you may need. Do not allow risk manager or insurance company representative to be 'on call' unless they are really available for the whole period of the mediation. Check with your client—is there really someone else who 'calls the shots' such as the spouse of the employee?

9. Support your client's exploration of resolution. Litigiousness may break down relationships. Side bars should be encouraged to help client evaluate options offered. Lawyers can help clients think positively—what if the problem were solved?

10. Be prepared to document any agreement that is reached. What clauses will you need? Do you have them with you in your laptop or in hard copy?

The Role of Clients

The advocate must be sure to know who will really make the decision for the client. It is best to have this person at the mediation, with subdued authority. In its absence, the person with authority should be available by phone. In addition, try to determine who the real decision maker is on the other side.

While, not common, witnesses and other support personnel can be included, but they should sign the confidentiality agreement as well so as to protect all parties and the process. The use of experts in mediation is not common. A better practice is to use and distribute in advance a written report of the expert's findings. Ideally, this is done well in advance of the mediation and should be part of a cross-exchange of each party's respective witness reports.

In especially complex, multi-session cases, the mediator may suggest and assist the parties in selecting a shared or neutral expert who would be invited to a later session to explain his/her findings.

Specific Advocacy Tools

Advocacy: Overall Advocacy at the Mediation

1. **Opening statement**: It is generally most effective to express this in a neutral fashion. This is a settlement discussion, not a trial. It is not wise to create a hostile atmosphere at the outset. Generally, a firm tone expressing the willingness to have your interests considered is ideal. If there are large differences in how the parties view what happened, what will be the most effective way to buttress your client's view? Use the client to personalize the impact of the dispute.

2. **Effective use of the mediator**: If the mediator knows your strategy, he or she may be able to help you achieve your goals. Mediators must keep the confidences of the parties. So, you should be comfortable in doing this. Specifically, make an effort to use the mediator:
   i. As a negotiating 'partner' (How should we respond?)
   ii. To test your position (Are we missing something here?)
   iii. To help generate ideas
   iv. To help break down communication barriers
   v. As a sounding board to help develop offers, counteroffers, and non-monetary remedies
   vi. As a process consultant (Where do we go from here?)

3. **Encouraging resolution**: A good lawyer/advocate keeps a balanced tension between getting the best deal possible and work-

ing towards a settlement that may be less than the best deal, but better than going to trial or arbitration.

4. **Be patient**: Experience shows that several offers and counter-offers are necessary to achieve most settlements. Lawyers should help clients understand that early offers that may not be acceptable are not necessarily final offers, and that they are used merely as a starting point.

5. **Discuss realistic options with client**: In the preparation phase, the advocate should have explored the client's needs and interests. Throughout the mediation, you must keep the client focused on these. What are the client's options if the case does not settle (BATNA/WATNA)? Clients do get frustrated and discouraged and want to 'draw the line in the sand'. The lawyer should continually help the client see advantages of continuing the negotiation, the costs, and benefits of stopping negotiations and should encourage the client to generate offers that meet the needs and interests of the other side.

Dealing with Obstacles to Reaching Agreement

Think about when and how to raise these issues and how you will suggest they are resolved. Sometimes parties get stuck emotionally or get angry or offended by something that happens during the mediation. Consider how your conduct and the communications you authorize the mediator to relay can avoid creating obstacles or can solve them. There are obviously disagreements or you would not be in mediation. Don't waste time on unnecessary disagreements, such as demanding that your terminology be used when adopting the other party's definitions will not hurt your client and will get you what you want in the end.

Given that impasses or deadlocks do occur in mediation, the parties and counsel should be prepared to engage in techniques to break the impasse or deadlock. Brainstorming with the mediator is an effective tool to get the parties to think past whatever is creating an impasse. This can occur in either a private or a joint session. Effective mediators can do this in a joint session, and measure each party's reaction to suggestions, their willingness to respond to their counterpart's ideas, body language in response to ideas, and so on. All of this can result in the parties getting alternative ideas on the table to think about different ways to get to a solution.

Impasse

If you employ the sky-high demand or the lowball response, you may be in for a long day. Even if you don't, there may come a time when negotiations bog you down. How do you close the gap without capitulating? If you spend the time to create a logical and reasoned basis for your offer or demand, detailing how it meets your needs and interests, this often goes a long way towards receiving a response that brings you closer together.

Options include bracketing, hypothetical offers, and mediator's proposals. You and the mediator can talk about which is most useful for you or can create others. Creative ways to transfer value also can be discussed.

Advocacy Settlement Agreements

1. Leave sufficient time to conclude the mediation with a settlement. Don't have any other important commitments on the day of the mediation (or into the evening).
2. Binding Agreement: Any agreement reached between the parties through mediation is as binding as any other contract. You may need to prove that the parties did reach an agreement, though, and you will not be able to call the mediator as a witness.
3. Written Agreement: Ideally, all material points should be negotiated and settlement agreement drafted at the mediation (a further documents clause is beneficial). The mediator can assist the parties with resolving the settlement agreement details. How will you document your agreement—verify in advance if word processing equipment is available and compatible? Consider when to negotiate on language—before or after agreement on economics.

Advocacy: Ending Before Settlement

Although it can be frustrating, sometimes an agreement is not reached by the end of the session. Sometimes there are particular facts that need to be checked or rulings that need to be made. Other times, the parties need to assess their positions.

You still have choices as to how you end the session. Knowing that, like most cases, this one is likely to settle at some point, why burn bridges? Maintain a positive, problem-solving tone. Consider making it clear that you expect the negotiations to continue and to succeed—with a commitment to reconvene on a certain date or after certain information is exchanged, with a commitment for counsel to talk with the mediator by phone on a certain date, with a commitment for counsel to exchange certain information by a certain date, and so on. Momentum has already been lost but specific commitments with specific short-term dates attached may keep communications open and commitment to ultimately settling maintained. You may want to consider Med-Arb on one or more aspects of the case or might consider other dispute resolution options.

Settlement

At the outset, it should be stressed that compliance with settlement agreements is extremely high, often reported to be in excess of 90 per cent. This is because both parties are in mediation as a voluntary undertaking to negotiate an agreement that meets their needs and interests. However, in the rare instance of noncompliance, there are ways a mediation settlement agreement can be enforced. A sample simple settlement agreement is provided as in illustration 5 of Annexure I.

Enforceability of a Private-Mediated Settlement

At the outset, it should be stressed that compliance with settlement agreements is extremely high, often reported to be in excess of 90 per cent. This is because both parties are in mediation as a voluntary undertaking to negotiate an agreement that meets their needs and interests. However, in the rare instance of noncompliance, there are ways a mediation settlement agreement can be enforced.

As a Contract between the Parties

Any mediation settlement agreement, signed by the parties becomes an enforceable contract. The Mediation Training Manual of India published by the Supreme Court of India recognizes the enforceability and binding nature of a settlement reached at a pre-litigation stage as a contract. The agreement is a contract between the disputants which can be enforced by one of the parties alleging a breach. The Delhi High Court has taken the view that in such a case, the remedy of execution is not available and the party alleging breach will have to initiate appropriate legal proceedings in accordance with law for seeking enforcement of the settlement in the form of a private agreement.

As a Conciliator's Award

The parties can agree, in the settlement agreement, to treat it as a conciliation agreement which then will be governed by the provisions of the Arbitration and Conciliation Act, 1996.

In such a case, the written agreement containing terms of settlement reached upon in the course of mediation is required to be signed by the parties and authenticated by the mediator's signature. The agreement will then be treated as a 'conciliation agreement' which will be governed by Sections 73 and 74 of the Arbitration and Conciliation Act, 1996, which provides that the terms of such an agreement will then be final and binding on the parties, and the status and effect of the settlement agreement will be the same as an arbitration award.

Enforceability of a mediated settlement is also possible when such an agreement is reached in a mediation which has been initiated by the arbitral tribunal during arbitral proceedings under Section 30 of the Arbitration and Conciliation Act, 1996. The arbitral tribunal may record the settlement in the form of an arbitral award on such agreed terms. However, it is only when the mediation settlement agreement is recorded in the form of an arbitral award that it is given the same status as an arbitral award.

Filing a Suit under Order 23 Rule 3 of the Code of Civil Procedure, 1908

The Code of Civil Procedure, 1908 recognizes the possibility of compromise of a suit. If during the course of a suit, the parties come to a mutual understanding to reach a settlement, the terms of which are put in writing and signed by the parties, which is then ordered to be recorded by the court and a decree is passed in accordance with the terms of such compromise.

The Supreme Court of India, in *Afcons Infrastructure Ltd. & Another v. Cherian Varkey Construction Company Pvt. Ltd. and*

Others,[12] observed that 'whenever such settlements reached before non-adjudicatory ADR fora are placed before the court, the court should apply the principles of Order 23 Rule 3 of the Code and make a decree or order in terms of the settlement, in regard to the subject matter of the suit or proceeding'.

It is up to the parties to a mediated settlement agreement to file a suit regarding the subject matter of dispute and subsequently, make an application under Order 23 Rule 3 of the Code of Civil Procedure in order to have a decree passed by the court on the basis of such mediated settlement. Once such a decree is passed by the court, the mediated settlement will be final and binding on the parties therein. This is a peculiar but effective approach to ensure enforceability of a mediated settlement, wherein the parties approach the court after resolving their dispute.

Local Context

Local courts can have rules that address enforceability as well. For example, the Delhi High Court, 'Rule 24: Settlement Agreement' states:

Where an agreement is reached between the parties in regard to all the issues in the suit or proceeding or some of the issues, the same shall be reduced to writing and signed by the parties or their constituted attorney. If any counsel has represented the parties, the conciliator/mediator may obtain his signature also on the settlement agreement.

1. The agreement of the parties so signed shall be submitted to the mediator/conciliator who shall, with a covering letter signed by him, forward the same to the court in which the suit or proceeding is pending.
2. Where no agreement is arrived at between the parties, before the time limit stated in Rule 18 or where, the mediator/conciliator is of the view that no settlement is possible, he shall report the same to the court in writing.

***

Settlement agreements in mediation are, thus, enforceable even without specific statutory authority.

Given that a conciliation settlement agreement is enforceable in the same manner as an arbitral award, the possibilities of structuring a mediated settlement as a conciliation settlement agreement strengthens its enforceability. In order to provide the mediation settlement agreement with stronger enforceability, the disputing parties may be encouraged to call the settlement arrived during mediation as a conciliation settlement agreement.

Contemporary arbitration rules seem to be attempting to reconcile different approaches of alternate dispute resolution by trying to bring in mediation within the framework of arbitration. Med-Arb agreements are one of the preferred forms in which mediation tends to present itself. The advantage of such an agreement is that the mediated settlements may be issued in the form of consent arbitral awards and therefore it enjoys the benefits of arbitration's enforceability. If the mediation is unsuccessful, the arbitration can continue and the parties are assured of a final outcome in the form of an arbitral award.

Notes and References

1. [2010] 14 (ADDL.) SCR 809.
2. M.K. Sharan, *Court Procedure in Ancient India.* (Abhinav Publication, 1978).
3. AIR 1927 Bom 565.
4. See illustration I of confidentiality clause. Annexure I for a sample.
5. [2010] 14 (ADDL.) SCR 809.
6. CIC/SA/A/2015/000305.
7. (2010) 8 SCC 24.
8. Ellen A. Waldman, 'The Evaluative-Facilitative Debate in Mediation: Applying the Lens of Therapeutic Jurisprudence', *Marquette Law Review*, 82(1), 1998.
9. James Stark, 'The Ethics of Mediation Evaluation: Some Troublesome Questions and Tentative Proposals, from an Evaluative Lawyer Mediator', *South Texas Law Review*, 1997.
10. Robert A. Baruch Bush and Joseph P. Folger, *The Promise of Mediation: Responding to Conflict through Empowerment and Recognition* (San Francisco Jossey-Bass Publsihers, 1994).
11. Samuel J. Imperati, 'Mediator Practice Models: The Instersection of Ethics and Stylistic Practices in Mediation', *Willamette Law Review*, 33(703), 1997.
12. (2010) 8 SCC 24.

Annexure I

Resources

Illustration 1: Sample Confidentiality Clause

Every person involved in the Mediation will keep confidential and not use for any purpose all information learned in the Mediation, including the resolution and its terms. Information learned in the Mediation will be, without prejudice, privileged and not admissible as evidence or disclosable in any current or subsequent litigation or other proceedings whatsoever. None of the Parties to the Mediation Agreement will call the Mediator as a witness, in any litigation or other proceedings arising from the matters in issue in the Mediation.

Illustration 2: Sample Mediator Opening Statement

Hi, my name is _____

I would like to start off by thanking you for choosing me as your mediator today. You have already taken a big step just by coming here to try out what is probably an unfamiliar process.

Mediation gives you the opportunity to discuss the issues and concerns that have brought you here. We hope that each of you will find mediation helpful for thinking about your goals and identifying your options for dealing with your situation. Just by talking through things here you may find that you are better able to make choices about what is important to you and determine a course of action.

You may also hear and better understand the views and perspective of the other person. Together, you may find that you are able to resolve the issues in a way that is satisfactory to both of you.

My role here is to assist you both to talk about your concerns and to fully understand the issues involved. I will listen and ask questions, and you will also have the opportunity to listen to and ask questions of each other. I will also help you think about possible options that may resolve the situation. I do not make any decisions, however. I am not a judge—I try to stay as neutral as we can in helping you make decisions and talk through the problem. Whatever comes out of this mediation will be something that you have developed and chosen.

I want to emphasize that mediation is entirely voluntary. If at any point you decide that you do not want to continue, just let me know. Please also feel free to raise any questions or concerns you have about the process.

Mediation is also confidential. Whatever you discuss here we will keep in confidence. If we end up meeting with you separately—which we often do—then I will also hold that information in confidence, and won't communicate anything to the other person without your permission. I may take notes to help us keep track of things, but we will destroy them at the end.

Any questions so far?

Let me say a little more about how this will work. We will meet all together to start with, and each of you can discuss what brought you here, what's important to you, and what you hope might come out of this mediation today. After a while, we will take a brief break to meet by ourselves. From there, I will meet with you either separately or together as we discuss the issues further and help you think about possible resolutions. If at any point when we are meeting together you feel that a private meeting would be helpful, let me know.

If we reach the point where you have worked out some agreements that you both want, we will meet all together to finish that agreement up.

Do you have any questions or concerns about that?

Are you both comfortable proceeding at this point?

So we're going to continue meeting together for a while, and we'll start with having each of you talk about the situation and how you hope this mediation might be helpful.

Illustration 3: Sample Agenda for a Partnership Dissolution Dispute

1. What are the assets and liabilities of the partnership?
2. How should the assets be divided among the partners?
3. What needs to be done in relation to the liabilities?
4. How should the clients of the partnership be dealt with?
5. What legal formalities are required for the dissolution?
6. What else is required to finalize the matter?
7. How should post-dissolution problems be dealt with?

Illustration 4: Sample Mediator Questions

Understanding the conflict

- Tell me what has been happening.
- What is your view of the dispute
- Can you tell me more about....?
- What is important to you?
- What documentation or proof do you have to validate your position?
- What else do you think I should know?

Exploring Interests & Needs

- Why is that important?
- What is your biggest concern about the situation?
- Is there something the other side does not understand that you think may help move us forward?
- Would you explain the reasons for your position?
- What part of their proposal gives you the most concern?

Generating Options

- How could you move this forward?
- What do you think would work for you and the other party?
- What can you do to resolve this?
- Is there any reason you can't?
- What can the other party do?
- What would make this idea work better for you?

- Why do you think this is a fair and reasonable term or condition?
- What options do you have if you do not settle?
- What problems may the other side have with this?

Sample questions for clarification

- What I hear from you is ... is that correct?
- I'm not quite sure I understand what you are saying.
- I don't feel clear about the main issue here.
- When you said ... what did you mean?
- Could you repeat...?

Illustration 5: Sample Settlement Agreement

Re: Mediation of *ABC v. XYZ*
Date:

The mediation of the above-referenced matter having concluded by settlement, the undersigned parties hereby evidence that agreement to settle the referenced action on the following terms:

- will pay to the total sum of $.
- All parties will execute a mutual general release of all claims.
- Plaintiff will file a Request for Dismissal with Prejudice.
- The parties intend that this document be binding, enforceable. This agreement shall be binding and final whether or not a further formal agreement is executed.
- Additional terms:

_____   _____
Defendant XYZ   Plaintiff ABC

Annexure II

References

Mediation Process, Skills, Training

- *AGREED! Negotiation/Mediation in the 21st Century*, Thierry Garby (2016)
- *Mediation Practice and Law—The Path to Successful Dispute Resolution*, Sriram Panchu (2015 2nd ed.)
- *How to Master Commercial Mediation*, David Richbell (2014)
- *International Comparative Mediation: Legal Perspectives*, Nadja Alexander (2009).

Negotiation

- *Integrative Negotiations Examples: Negotiating Skills and Negotiation Tactics for Managing Relationships*, Lawrence Susskind (2015)
- *The Art of Negotiation: How to Improvise Agreement in a Chaotic World*, Michael Wheeler (2013)
- *Beyond Winning: Negotiating to Create Value in Deals and Disputes*, Robert H. Mnookin (2004)
- *Good for You, Great for Me: Finding the Trading Zone and Winning at Win-Win negotiation*, Lawrence Susskind (2014)
- *Negotiating Across Cultures: International Communication in an Interdependent World*, Raymond Cohen and Samuel W. Lewis (2013)

- *Negotiating Rationally*, Max H. Bazerman and Margaret Ann Neale (1993)
- *Getting To Yes*, Roger Fisher and William Ury (2012)
- *Getting Past No*, William Ury (2012)
- *Bargaining with the Devil*, Robert H. Mnookin (2010)

Mediation Advocacy

- *Effective Mediation Advocacy—: A Guide for Practitioners*, Andrew Goodman (2016)
- *Mediation Advocacy: Representing Clients in Mediation*, Stephen Walker (2015)
- *Mediation Representation: Advocating in a Problem-Solving Process*, Harold I. Abramson (2010)

Index

Addhar Mercantile Private Limited v. Shree Jagdamba Agrico Exports Pvt Ltd (Addhar), 277–8
ad hoc arbitration, 92–4
  problems with, 94–6
  v. institutional arbitration, 308–9
adversarial judicial system, 407
advocacy at mediation, 408–12, 416–17
  ending before settlement, 418–19
  settlement agreements, 418, 426
Afcons Infrastructure Ltd. & Another v. Cherian Varkey Construction Company Pvt. Ltd. and Others, 421
Afcons Infrastructure Ltd. & Anr. v. Cherian Varkey Construction Co. (P) Ltd. & Ors., 148
Agreement for the Promotion and Protection of Investments (ASEAN), 1987, 207
Albon (T/A NA Carriage Co.) v. Naza Motor Training SDN BHD 2008, 292
alternate dispute resolution (ADR)

confidentiality aspect, 7
  defined, 6
  development of, 8
  in India, 8
  objectives, 7
  process of, 7
  rationale for use of, 8–9
Ambedkar, B.R., 20
anti-arbitration injunctions, 292–4
arbitral authority, 21
  administration of quasi-justice, 31
  appropriate disclosure, 22
  arbitrator's material or financial interest, issue of, 32
  costs, 95
  duty of, 22
  grounds of challenge to independence or partiality, 28–33
  guidelines on independence and impartiality, 24–8
  independence and impartiality of the person, 21–3
  mandatory requirement of disclosure(s), 33–4

matter of principle and
    propriety, 23
oath or affirmation, 21–2
quality and availability of
    arbitrators, 95–6, 98
relationship between arbitrator
    and parties or its counsel,
    29–31
relationship of arbitrator to
    dispute, 31–2
retired judges as arbitrators, 95
arbitral institutions, 209–10
arbitral tribunal, 182
arbitration, 4, 172–3. *See also*
    institutional arbitration
    agreement, drafting of, 174–6
appointment of presiding
    arbitrator, 181–2
as a cheaper option, 179
dispute resolution clause, 181
jurisprudence in India, 179–80
need for infrastructure, 183
practical perspective of, 181–2
process as a miniature form of
    litigation, 177–8
selection of arbitrators, 178–9
spirit of, 176–7
Arbitration Act 1940, 44–6, 66–7,
    259
arbitration agreement, 54, 57–8
Arbitration and Conciliation
    (Amendment) Act, 2015, xxvii,
    13, 25, 28, 99–102, 147, 187,
    240
    Amendment Act 3 of 2016,
    57–8
Arbitration and Conciliation
    (Third) Ordinance, 1996, 147
arbitration fees, 234
arbitration-mediation process, xxv,
    364–5

Arbitration (Protocol and
    Convention) Act, 1937, 67
*Ascot Estates Pvt. Ltd. v. Bon Vivant
    Life Style Ltd.*, 84
ASEAN *Comprehensive Investment
    Agreement* (2009), 227n44
Asia Pacific Economic Cooperation
    (APEC), 207
*Associated Builders v. Delhi
    Development Authority
    (Associated Builders v. DDA)*,
    74–6, 303, 306–7

Bangalore Mediation Centre and
    the Mediation Centres, 148–9
*Bharat Aluminium Company v.
    Kaiser Aluminium Technical
    Service, Inc. (BALCO)*, 15–16,
    180, 188, 196–8, 255, 274–6,
    286, 311n7
*Bhatia International v. Bulk Trading
    S.A.*, 179, 190–1, 194, 261–2
Bilateral Investment Protection
    Agreement (BIPA), 207
Bilateral Investment Treaty (BIT),
    206–7
    India and, 217–18, 220–4
    models, 220–4
    protection against expropriation,
    210–11
    rights under, 216
*The Board of Trustees of the Part
    of Kolkata v. Louis Dreyfus
    Amateurs SAS & Arv*, 299
*Burn Standard Company Ltd. v. Mc
    Dermott International Inc. and
    Ors.*, 244–5

Cairo Regional Centre for
    International Commercial
    Arbitration (CRCICA), 209

Calvo Doctrine, 215
case management, 4
Centre for Advanced Mediation
    Practice (Bangalore), 362
Centre for Advanced Mediation
    Practice (CAMP), 366
challenging arbitration award, law
    for, 64–72
    in British India, 66
    compliance issues, 73
    grounds of 'public policy of
        India', 'fundamental policy of
        Indian law', 76–8
    grounds on, 69–70
    judge-centric approaches, 64,
        72–3
    ONGC case, 69–70
    reasonableness, principle of,
        73–8
    Renusagar case, 68–9
    section 34, 67–8
China International Economic and
    Trade Arbitration Commission
    (CETAC Rules), 236
China–Tunisia BIT 1998, 226n42
Chloro Controls India Private
    Limited v. Severn Trent Water
    Purification Inc. & Arv., 55,
    58–9, 295
Civil Procedure Code
    (Amendment) Act 46 of 1999, 9
Code of Civil Procedure, 1908, 9,
    147, 244, 361, 370, 386n82,
    396, 420–1
    Order 39, Rule 2A of, 14
Code of Compulsory Costs, 240
Coke, Lord, 155
Commercial Arbitration Act of
    2010, 150–1
Commercial Courts, Commercial
    Division, and Commercial

Appellate Division of the High
    Courts Act, 2015, xxiv, 80–1,
    103
    apparent error/mistake in
        Section 10(2) of, 85, 90n2
    discrimination due to drafting
        error, 87–8
    ground of 'patent error', 86
    grounds for review, 85–7
    repeal and savings clause, 88–9
    review application, 84–5
    section 13, 91n8
    section 37, 82–5
    statutory right to appeal, 81–4,
        89
commercial disputes, features of,
    333–5
commercial mediation, 319–21,
    331. See also mediation
    reasoning in, 330–1
'competent court' in India, 285–7
Competition Act, 2002, 164–6
Comprehensive Economic and
    Trade Agreement (CETA),
    207
Comprehensive Economic
    Cooperation Agreements
    (CECA), 207
Comprehensive Economic
    Partnership Agreements
    (CEPA), 207
conciliation, 4, 149, 371
Cook, Ashley, 158
cost allocation in international
    arbitration, 233–4
    agreement between the parties,
        234, 239
    applicable laws, 235
    application of other rules or
        guidelines, 235
    complexity of the case and, 240

conduct and behaviour of the
parties, 238
considerations, 234–5
cultural expectations, 235
general practices followed by
arbitral tribunals, 237–8
in India, 240–6
international aspects, 236–40
Law Commission suggestions,
243
parties written arbitration
agreement, 234
principles of, 239
reasonableness, 240
rules, 235
standard for, 237
terms of reference in relation
to, 235
uncooperative and unacceptable
behaviour of parties, 239
court-annexed mediation, 359,
366–8
Indian context, 396–7
court-referred mediation, 359
Crum, Thomas, xxiii
The Magic of Conflict, xxiii

damages, claims, and quantum
computation filed in
arbitrations, 139
delay in justice, 6
Delhi High Court Mediation
Rules, 399, 402
Dimes v. Grand Junction Canal,
31
direct expropriation, 211–12
dispute resolution mechanisms,
174
Doha Development Agenda, 2001,
207
domestic arbitration, 81, 250

*Dozco India Private Limited v.
Doosan Infracore Company
Limited (Dozco)*, 194–5, 266

*Eitzen Bulk A/S and Ors. v.
Ashapura Minechem Ltd. and
Ors*, 200, 273–4
emergency arbitration, 120–1,
132–4, xxv
arbitral process (curial law),
127–8
attempts at providing urgent
interim relief, 121–2
due process concerns, 129
ICC Rules, 124–5
in India, 130–2
institutional rules, 124
LCIA Rules, 125, 130
legal framework governing,
124–8
role of domestic courts, 121
SIAC Rules, 124–7, 130
standards for granting
emergency interim relief, 132
emergency arbitrator, 122
appointment of, 131
enforcement of the decision of,
128
historical background of, 122–4
mechanism and legal hurdles,
128–30
*Enercon (India) Ltd & Ors v.
Enercon GmbH & Anr (Enercon)*,
198–9, 256
Energy Charter Treaty (ECT),
246n3
English Arbitration Act, 1996, 50
English Courts, application of
arbitration clause, 40–4
equal access to justice, 3
evaluative mediation process, 152

expert testimony services, 141–2
expert witness, xxv
    appointment of, 136–7
    best practices, 137
    business and financial experts,
        140–1
    common forms of disputes and
        crucial role of, 136–7
    in construction disputes and
        claims, 141–2
    evolving role in arbitrations,
        137–9
    in Intellectual Property (IP)
        disputes, 142–3
    in joint venture and shareholder
        disputes, 143–5
    reason for, 135
    role and functions, 135–6
    technical experts, 139–41
expropriation, 223
    direct and indirect, 211–12
    protection against, 210–11

fair and equitable treatment (FET),
    212–14, 222
    exclusion of, 214
    scope of, 213–14, 222
    standards (*Mondev* tribunal and
        Saluka tribunal), 213–14
fast-track arbitration process, 100
Federal Security Act, 1933, 165
financial consequences of disputes,
    6
*Firm Ashok Traders v. Gurumukhdas
    Saluja*, 17–18
*First Options of Chicago, Inc. v.
    Kaplan*, 50
*Food Corporation of India v. Indian
    Council of Arbitration*, 53
Foreign Awards (Recognition and
    Enforcement) Act, 1961, 67, 99

Free Legal Aid, 3
Free Trade Agreements (FTA),
    207
French Code of Civil Procedure,
    Articles 1465 and 1448, 50

*Garikapati Veeraya v. N. Subbiah
    Choudhary*, 83
General Agreement on Trade in
    Services (GATS), 207
Geneva Convention on the
    Execution of Foreign
    Arbitral Awards (the Geneva
    Convention), 259
German Institution of Arbitration
    (1998 DIS Rules), 236
Grynbaum, Joseph, xxiii
*Guru Nanak Foundation v. Rattan
    Singh & Sons*, 146

*Harbour Assurance Co. (UK) Ltd.
    v. Kansa General International
    Assurance Co. Ltd.*, 46–8
Hardwicke, Lord, 155
*Hardy Oil and Gas Limited v.
    Hindustan Oil Exploration
    Company Limited and 3 Ors*,
    262–3
*Haresh Dayaram Thakur v. State of
    Maharashtra*, 387
*Harmony Innovation Shipping Ltd.
    v. Gupta Coal India Ltd. and
    Ors*, 200
Hewart, Lord, 20
Heyman v. Darwins Limited, 41,
    43–4, 46
*Hirji Mulji v. Cheong Yue Steamship
    Company Limited*, 41
Hong Kong International
    Arbitration Centre (HKIAC
    Rules), 237

Hoosein Kasam Dada (India) Limited v. State of Madhya Pradesh, 82
HSBC v. Avitel, 133

IMAX Corporation v. E-City Entertainment (I) Pvt Ltd, 200–1
IMI Decision Tree, 368–9
India, legislative evolution in, 393
Indian Arbitration Act, 1940, 99
Indian Arbitration and Conciliation Act, 1996, 10, 45, 51–7, 147, 180, 243, 247n6, 250, 260–81, 324, 370–1
Addhar Mercantile Private Limited v. Shree Jagdamba Agrico Exports Pvt Ltd (Addhar), 277–8
amendments, 12, 28–9
anti-arbitration injunctions, 292–4
anti-suit injunctions, 290–1
appeals against interim relief, 11
appointment of tribunal, 56
arbitral institutions, role of, 308–10
Article 16, 51–2
Associated Builders v. Delhi Development Authority (Associated Builders v DDA), 303, 306–7
Bharat Aluminium Company v. Kaiser Aluminium Technical Service, Inc. (BALCO), 274–6, 286, 311n7
Bhatia International v. Bulk Trading S.A., 261–2, 285
conciliation under, 371
consent award or an award on agreed terms under, 371

definition of 'public policy', 302–3
distinction between types of issues, 53–4
Dozco India Private Limited v. Doosan Infracore Company Limited (Dozco), 266
Eitzen Bulk A/S v. Ashapura Minechem Ltd & Anr, 273–4
enforcement of a foreign award, 299–301
foreign awards, 253
ground of bias or disqualification, 26–7
Hardy Oil and Gas Limited v. Hindustan Oil Exploration Company Limited and 3 Ors, 262–3
Harmony Innovation Shipping Ltd v Gupta Coal India Ltd (Harmony), 200, 269
interim measures, 11, 14–18, 282–99
interim measures of protection, 12, 14
interim relief in international commercial arbitration, 252–3
Mathura Prasad Bajoo Jaiswal v. Dossibai N.B. Jeejeebhoy, 271
mother agreements, 295–6
nominated, 27
objectives, 10–11
ONGC Limited v. Western Geco International Limited (ONGC v. West Geco), 303, 306
ONGC v. Saw Pipes (Saw Pipes), 115, 304, 307
Phulchand Exports Limited v. OOO Patriot (Phulchand), 304–5

provisions, 372–5
reforms, 251–3, 276–7, 301–2,
  307–8
Reliance Industries Limited &
  Anr v. Union of India 31 *and*
  Union of India v. Reliance
  Industries Limited & Anr,
  266–72
relief after constitution of an
  arbitral tribunal, 284
relief after the making of an
  arbitral award, 284–5
relief before commencement
  of arbitral proceedings,
  283–4
Renusagar Power Plant Ltd
  v General Electric Co.
  (Renusagar), 303–4
Sasan Power Limited v. North
  American Coal Corporation
  India Pvt. Ltd (Sasan Power),
  278–81
seat and venue of arbitration,
  254–8
section 2(2), 15–16, 252, 260–1
section 9, 281–2, 285, 287–8
section 45, 294–5, 298–9
section 48, 299–301
section 16 of, 51–2
sections 9 and 17, 11, 13–14,
  16–18
sections 12 and 13, 24–6
sections 14 and 34, 26–8
sections 73 and 74, 420
Shri Lal Mahal Ltd v. Progetto
  Grano Spa (Shri Lal Mahal),
  305–6
terms inoperative and incapable
  of being performed, 296–8
in UNCITRAL Model Law and
  Rules, 51

Venture Global Engineering v.
  Satyam Computer Services
  Limited (Venture Global),
  263–4
Videocon Industries Limited v.
  Union of India and Anr,
  264–5, 272–3
Yograj Infrastructure Limited v.
  Ssang Yong Engineering and
  Construction Co Ltd (Yograj),
  265–6
Indian Contract Act 1872 (the
  Contract Act), 279, 313n58,
  324
Indian Council of Arbitration
  (ICA), 310
Indian Institution of Arbitration
  and Mediation, 362, 366
indirect expropriation, 211–12
indispensable prerequisites of the
  arbitration process, xxiv
INDTEL Technical Services Pvt. Ltd.
  v. W.S. Atkins PLC, 192–3
Indus Mobile Distribution Pvt. Ltd.
  v. Datawind Innovations Pvt.
  Ltd. and Ors., 201–2
Industrial Disputes Act, 1947,
  149
in-house counsel, xxv, 173–4
institutional arbitration, 103,
  180–1. *See also* arbitration
administrative and
  infrastructural assistance
  from, 97–8
appointment of an arbitrator,
  100
appointment of arbitrator,
  180–1
challenging the award, 102
code of conduct and conflicts of
  interest, 98

fast-track arbitration process,
100
fees chargeable by arbitrators,
102
fee structure, 98
guidelines on conflict of interest,
101
in India, xxv, 93
initiation of proceedings, 101
interim relief, 101
Law Commission's
recommendations on, 98–9,
112n51, 118n68
monitoring and supervision, 97
pre-established rules and
procedures, 96–7
provision for costs, 102
quality and availability of
arbitrators, 98
reputation, 97
scope of public policy challenge,
101
time-bound arbitration, 100
vs ad hoc arbitration, 308–9
institutional mediation, 366–7
Intellectual Property (IP)
early signs of disputes, 142–3
life cycle, 142
role of experts in disputes, 143
interim measures under Indian
arbitration law, xxiv
international arbitration, India-
centric lens, 187–9, xxv
*Bharat Aluminium Company v.
Kaiser Aluminium Technical
Services Inc.*, 196–8, 203
*Bhatia International v. Bulk
Trading S.A.*, 179, 190–1,
194, 203
deciding on curial law, 188–9
domestic arbitration, 250

*Dozco India P. Ltd. v. Doosan
Infracore Co. Ltd*, 194–5, 203
*Eitzen Bulk A/S and Ors. v.
Ashapura Minechem Ltd. and
Ors.*, 200
*Enercon (India) Ltd. and Ors.
v. Enercon GMBH and Anr*,
198–9
*Harmony Innovation Shipping
Ltd. v. Gupta Coal India Ltd.
and Ors*, 200
*IMAX Corporation v. E-City
Entertainment (I) Pvt Ltd*,
200–1
*INDTEL Technical Services Pvt.
Ltd. v. W.S. Atkins PLC*,
192–3
*Indus Mobile Distribution Pvt.
Ltd. v. Datawind Innovations
Pvt. Ltd. and Ors.*, 201–2
*Inventa Fischer GmbH and Co.
v. Polygenta Technologies Ltd.*,
192
Law Commission
recommendations and
Amendment Act, 202
*National Thermal Power
Corporation v. Singer
Company & Anr*, 193
Pricol v. Johnson Controls, 200
*Reliance Industries Limited and
Anr. v. Union of India (UOI)*,
199–200
*Sara International Ltd. v. Arab
Shipping Co. (P) Ltd.*, 193,
203
*Venture Global Engineering Case
v. Satyam Computer Services
Ltd*, 179, 191–2, 203
*Videocon Industries Limited v.
Union of India (UOI)*, 195

Yograj Infrastructure Ltd. v. SSANGYONG Engineering and Construction Company Ltd., 196
International Bar Association (IBA), 24
International Centre for dispute Resolution (ICDR), 236–7
International Centre for Settlement of Investment Disputes (ICSID), 208
Arbitration Rules, 22
International Chamber of Commerce (ICC), 124–5, 137, 209, 236, 309–10, 362
Rules, 30
international commercial arbitration, xxvi, 16, 54, 58, 67, 179–80, 188, 190, 199, 203, 219, 250–1
arbitral institutions, 209–10
interim relief in, 252–3
international commercial mediation, 361–5
International Court of Dispute Resolution (ICDR), 122
International Institute for Conflict Prevention and Resolution (CPR), 340
International Investment Agreement (IIA) network, 207
Inventa Fischer GmbH and Co. v. Polygenta Technologies Ltd., 192
investment arbitration, xxvi
investment treaty arbitration, xxvi
Investor State Dispute Settlement (ISDS), 206, 221
Dabhol case, 219
Devas v. India, 219–20
development of, 210
global backlash against, 216–17

IMFA v. Indonesia, 220, 230n100
regimes, 208–10
White Industries Australia Ltd. v. Republic of India, 218–19

J. Jarvis case, 168–9
James, William, xxiv
Jessel, Lord, 156
Johannesburg Municipal Council v. Stewart, 41
Joseph Constantine S.S. Line Ltd. v. Imperial Smelting Corp. Ltd., 43
Joubert, Joseph, xxvi
judicial settlement, 4
Jules Buck et Louis Dolivet v. Eddie Constantine et Gaston Terminet dit Allain, 60
Jureidini v. National British and Irish Millers Insurance Company Limited, 41

Kaye, Kenneth, xxiv
Kerala State Mediation Centre, 149
Khardah Company Ltd. v. Raymon & Co. (India) Private Ltd., 45
Kill v. Hollister, 155
Kompetenz-Kompetenz doctrine, xxiv, 38–9, 57, 59, 158
arbitration clause, 44–6
arbitrator's jurisdiction, 39–40
existence or validity of arbitration agreement, 49
origin, 40–4
separability principle, 39–40, 46–8
in UNCITRAL Model Law and Rules, 48–50
Konkan Railway Corporation Ltd. v. Rani Construction P. Ltd., 52–3, 61

Law Commission of India, 5, 24,
118n68
Legal Services Act, 1987, 148
limits of arbitrability, xxv, 154–69
allegation of fraud, 158–64
anti-competitive agreements,
164–6
oppression and mismanagement,
166–7
public law remedies, 157–8
logistics of arbitration, 96
London Court of International
Arbitration (LCIA), 125, 130,
137, 209, 236, 310, 362

Madras High Court Arbitration
Centre (MHCAC) (Internal
Management) Rules, 2014, 130
Malynes, Geraud, 156
*Mathura Prasad Bajoo Jaiswal v.
Dossibai N.B. Jeejeebhoy*, 271
*McDonald's India Private Limited
v. Vikram Bakshi and Ors*, 292,
294
meaning of ADR, xxiv
mechanisms of ADR
Lok Adalat and conciliation,
148
section 89 of the Code, 147–8
mediation, xxiii, xxvi, 4, 148–9
advocacy, 368–70, 408–12,
416–17
advocate's role, 352–6
*Afcons Infrastructure Ltd. &
Anr v. Cherian Varkey
Construction Co. (P) Ltd. &
Ors*, 398
agreement, 347–9
appropriateness of, 343–6
aversions of commercial parties
to adopt, 329–31

barriers in India, 405–8
choosing a mediator and
mediation advocate, 367–70
clients, role of, 415–16
commercial, 319–21
comparison between judicial
process and, 326–7
conciliation agreement, 420
conducting a, 412–14
confidentiality in, 356–7, 394
in construction disputes, 336–7
in consumer business, 336
in contractual disputes, 338–9
convening a, 399
counsel, role of, 414–15
court-annexed, 359, 366–8
court-referred, 359
dealing with obstacles, 417
defining the process of, 399–400
definition, 389–91
Delhi High Court rules
governing, 399, 402
difference between conciliation
and, 371
diversity of, 335–6
enforcement of mediated
settlement agreements,
357–9
facilitating the negotiation,
generating options,
brainstorming, 401
facilitative and evaluative, 323–4
factors motivating to adopt,
327–9
frequently asked questions
about, 349
functional stages, 357–8
in India, 331–40, 391–422
infrastructure in India, 365–70
in-house legal counsels, role of,
339–40

institutional, 366–7
mediator's role, 349–52, 379n3
*Moti Ram (D) Tr. LRs and Anr.
   v. Ashok Kumar and Anr.,*
   395–6
non-verbal signs and verbal
   signs, 401–2
perceptions and myths *vs* reality,
   321–31
preparation of a memorandum
   of understanding of the
   settlement, 402
private, 359–61
private-mediated settlement,
   419–21
for public sector undertaking
   (PSU), 337–8
*Rama Aggarwal v. PIO, Delhi
   State Legal Service Authority,*
   396
rationale to choose, 341–3
reaching a settlement, 401–2
sample mediator opening
   statement, 423–4
sample mediator questions,
   425–6
setting an agenda for, 400–1
settlement, 419–22
statements by the parties/
   negotiators, 400
structure of session, 398–9
styles, 403–5
terms and rules, 394–5
universal properties associated
   with, 323
mediation advocate, 370
Mediation and Conciliation Project
   Committee (MCPC), 365
Mediation-Arbitration (Med-Arb),
   150–3, 325, 364–5, 380n10
methods/techniques of ADR

arbitration, 4
case management, 4
conciliation, 4
judicial settlement, 4
mediation, 4
plea bargaining, 4
private mediation, 4
summary trial, 4
Mitsubishi Motors Corporation case,
   165
model arbitration clause, 203–4
Model Arbitration Law, 10, 12
*Modi Entertainment Network and
   Another v. W.S.G. Cricket Pte.
   Ltd,* 290
Moscow Chamber of Commerce
   and Industry (MCCI), 209
most-favoured-nation clause,
   215–16, 222–3
Moti Ram v. Ashok Kumar,
   384n60
*M/s. Sundaram Finance Limited v.
   M/s. NEPC India Limited,* 17
*M/s Addhar Mercantile Private
   Limited v. Shree Jagdamba Agrico
   Exports Private Limited,* 16
multilateral agreement on
   investment (MAI), 207
*Mysore Cements Ltd. v. Svedala
   Barmac Ltd.,* 387n95–6

*National Insurance Co. Ltd. v.
   Boghara Polyfab Pvt.Ltd.,* 53
*National Thermal Power Corporation
   v. Singer Company and Ors,* 193,
   259–60
national treatment clause, 215,
   222–3
*Naviera Amazonica Peruana S.A.
   v. Compania International De
   Seguros Del Pent,* 189, 254–5

negotiation, 378n2
Netherlands Arbitration Institute (NAI), 122
New Model BIT, 220–4
NHAI v. K.K. Sarin & Ors, 27
non-adjudicatory ADR mechanisms, 148

O'Connor, Sandra Day, xxvii
ONGC Limited v. Western Geco International Limited (ONGC v. West Geco), 303, 306
ONGC v. Saw Pipes (Saw Pipes), 304
Online Dispute Resolution (ODR), 325, 346–7
O.P. Gupta case, 167
Organisation for Economic Co-operation and Development (OECD), 206

'panch' (arbitrator), 8
'panchayat' (arbitration), 8
partnership dissolution dispute, 425
party autonomy, 23–4
pending cases in India, 332
Permanent Court of Arbitration (PCA), 209, 236, 246n3
Phulchand Exports Limited v. OOO Patriot (Phulchand), 304–5
plea bargaining, 4
practitioners of ADR, xxvii
precedent, xxv
Pricol v. Johnson Controls, 200
private mediation, 4
  Indian context, 397

Raja Shatrunji v. Mohammad Azmat Azim Khan & Ors., 86

reality checking, 379n7
Redfern and Hunter on International Arbitration, 254–5
Reliance Industries Limited & Anr v. Union of India and Union of India v. Reliance Industries Limited & Anr, 199–200, 266–72
Renusagar Power Plant Ltd v General Electric Co. (Renusagar), 68–9, 303–4
Repley v. Great Northern Rly, 156
resolution of family business conflicts, xxiv
Roger Shashoua & Ors. v. Mukesh Sharma & Ors., 83, 255

SAIL v. Gupta Brother Steel Tubes Ltd., 70–1
Salem Advocated Bar Association v. Union of India, 331, 387n99
Sanjeev Kumar Jain v. Raghubir Singh Charitable Trust, 242
Sara International Ltd. v. Arab Shipping Co. (P) Ltd., 193
Sasan Power Limited v. North American Coal Corporation India Pvt. Ltd (Sasan Power), 278–81
S.B.P. & Co. v. Patel Engineering Ltd., 53, 61
Scott v. Avery, 155
seat and venue of arbitration, 254–8
  ambiguous clauses, 255–8
  Court of Appeal in England observation, 254–5
  vs governing law, 258
separability principle, 39–40, 46–8
Shin-Etsu Chemical Co. Ltd. v. Aksh Optifibre Ltd., 54, 294
Shin-Etsu principle, 61

Shri Lal Mahal Ltd v. Progetto Grano Spa (*Shri Lal Mahal*), 305–6
Siemens v. Argentina, 215
Singapore International Arbitration Centre (SIAC), 93, 124–7, 130, 137, 237, 310
Singapore International Mediation Centre (SIMC), 362
Slovenia–Turkey BIT 2004, 227n43
social conditioning and mediation, 406–7
Sojuznefteexport v. Joc Oil Ltd., 47
Sri Krishan v. Anand, 14
Stabilization Clause, 224, 231n123
statutory appellate jurisdiction, 65
Statutory Embodiment of the Governing Law Approach (the 1937, 1940, and 1961 Acts), 258–60
Stockholm Chamber of Commerce (SCC), 209, 237
Sumitomo Heavy Industries Ltd. v. ONGC Ltd. and Ors., 189
summary trial, 4
Supreme Court of India, 9
Szilard v. Szasz, 23

Thyssen Krupp Werkstoffe GMBH v. Steel Authority of India, 245
time-bound arbitration, 100
Tolaram Nathmull v. Birla Jute Manufacturing Company Ltd., 44
Trade Related Investment Measures (TRIMs), 207
Trans-Pacific Partnership (TPP), 207

Umbrella Clause, 224, 231n122
UNCTAD Investment Report 2015, 207

Union of India v. Competition Commission of India, 165
Union of India v. Dahbol Power Company, 293
Union of India v. Kishorilal Gupta and Bros., 44
Union of India v. M/S Singh Builders Syndicate, 94, 241
Union of India v. Sube Ram, 86
United Nations Commission on International Trade Law (UNCITRAL), 1985, 10, 48–50, 67, 98, 157, 236, 260, 362, 364, 371, 378n1
arbitration agreement, 54, 57–8
arbitration rules, 209
Article 17 of, 12
principle of Article 16(1), 50
regime, 208–9

Venture Global Engineering Case v. Satyam Computer Services Ltd, 179
Venture Global Engineering v. Satyam Computer Services Limited (*Venture Global*), 263–4
'venue' and 'seat' of arbitration, 65
vested interest and mediation, 407–8
Videocon Industries Limited v. Union of India (*UOI*), 195, 264–5, 272–3
Vijay Sekhri case, 166–7
VIP Industries Ltd. v. Commissioner of Central Excise, Nashik, Maharashtra, 86
Vynior case, 155–6

Wednesbury principle, 73
Wellington Associates Ltd. v. Kirit Mehta, 52

Wellington v. Macintosh, 155
Wilco v. Swan, 165
World Sport Group (Mauritius) Limited v. MSM Satellite (Singapore) Pte Ltd 2014, 296

Yahoo! Inc. v. Microsoft Corporation, 129

Yograj Infrastructure Limited v. Ssang Yong Engineering and Construction Co Ltd (Yograj), 196, 265–6

Zuari Cement Ltd. v. Regional Director, ESIC, Hyderabad & Ors., 87

About the Editor and Contributors

Editor

Shashank Garg is a partner at Advani & Co., New Delhi, India. He is a dispute resolution practitioner with diverse experience, and handles commercial litigation and arbitration verticals at the firm. He is the standing counsel for the state of Goa in Supreme Court and Special Counsel for Delhi Development Authority. Being a certified civil and commercial mediator of the ADR group, London, his current appointments include Regional Representative India for the International Chamber of Commerce Young Arbitrators Forum for 2017–19; Reporter for India Jurisdiction by International Bar Association (IBA) Arbitration Sub-committee; Member, Delhi High Court Arbitration Committee; advisor to KIIT Centre of International Arbitration; visiting faculty at Indian Law Institute; and member of the Chartered Institute of Arbitrators, the International Congress and Convention Association, Miami International Arbitration Society (MIAS), IBA, Young International Arbitration Group, Supreme Court Bar Association, and Lawasia.

Contributors

Sheila Ahuja is Of Counsel in Allen & Overy's Global Arbitration group based in the Hong Kong office. She has advised on a wide range of arbitration matters and arbitration-related court matters involving various jurisdictions, such as Hong Kong, Singapore, England and

Wales, the Philippines, Myanmar, the PRC, and, in particular, India. She has particular experience of energy and infrastructure disputes, disputes arising from joint ventures and distributorship arrangements, and disputes relating to complex financial products. She represents clients in both commercial arbitrations and investor-state arbitrations.

Ajay Bhargava is a partner at the Dispute Resolution Group at Khaitan & Co, New Delhi, India. He specializes in civil, criminal, and corporate litigation with 20 years of experience. His fora of experience of practise include Supreme Court, high courts, arbitration (international and domestic), quasi-judicial tribunals (National Company Law Tribunal), National Company Law Appellate Tribunal, and National Green Tribunal. He advises on constitutional matters, civil, and criminal matters, intellectual property rights laws, employment laws, and corporate-commercial disputes. He also advises on matters before the police investigation wings relating to corporate criminal prosecutions (white-collar crimes).

Madhukeshwar Desai is the founder of Mumbai Centre for International Arbitration, India. He studied law at Christ College, Bengaluru, and practised for four years at PXV Law Partners, a leading corporate law firm. He currently acts as the legal advisor to the Maharashtra Basketball Association, the Basketball Federation of India, and the Padukone–Dravid Centre for Sports Excellence. He also works with the Government of Maharashtra on the upcoming International Financial Services Centre at the Bandra Kurla Complex.

Sanjeev Gemawat is executive director with Dalmia Bharat Group, New Delhi, India. He has more than two decades of experience as head of legal, taxation, and secretarial functions of esteemed corporates, multinational corporations, and joint ventures in India. He is a postgraduate in law and holds a doctorate in insider trading from Jai Narain Vyas University, Jodhpur. He is a fellow member of the Institute of Chartered Secretaries and Administrators, UK; the Institute of Chartered Accountants of India, New Delhi; the Institute of Company Secretaries of India, New Delhi; International Corporate Counsel, New Delhi, and the Institute of Cost Accountants of India, New Delhi. He is a member of the International Bar Association and a founder member of the Indian Corporate Counsel Association.

Satyajit Gupta is a principal partner and lead of M&A lawyer at M/s. Advaita Legal, Attorneys & Advocates, New Delhi. He is a graduate of National Law School of India University, Bengaluru, and has over 14 years of experience. He has also authored articles and op-eds on emerging issues in the area of corporate/commercial laws. He is a member of the Young International Arbitrators Group and has served as an officer of both the International Bar Association and the American Bar Association.

Suresh C. Gupte has practised on both original and appellate sides in the Bombay High Court. His areas of practise include civil, constitutional, company, indirect taxation, and arbitration matters. He has regularly appeared before the Supreme Court, various high courts, tribunals, and district courts. He was elevated as a High Court Judge on 21 June 2013. He presided over the first commercial court division (Single Judge) established in the Bombay High Court.

Shreyas Jayasimha is an advocate, arbitrator, and trained mediator based in India, and is the founding partner of Aarna Law, Bengaluru, India, a boutique counsel-led international and domestic dispute resolution practice. His practice areas include intellectual property, technology law, corporate and commercial dispute resolution, investment arbitration, constitutional law, regulatory and fraud investigations, among others. He has been visiting faculty at Indian Institute of Management Bangalore, National Law School India University, Bengaluru, among others, having taught courses on contracts, international trade law, private international law, and international commercial and investment arbitration.

Tejas Karia is partner at Shardul Amarchand Mangaldas & Co, New Delhi. He has wide expertise in international and domestic commercial arbitrations. He has extensive experience in strategically advising and representing public and private corporations in a wide variety of international arbitrations involving complex commercial and technical disputes in various sectors including oil and gas, shareholders' agreements, joint ventures, constructions, insurance, real estate, and private equity. He is fellow of Chartered Institute of Arbitrators, London. He has co-authored a number of publications on arbitration.

R.C. Lahoti was appointed as the Chief Justice of Supreme Court of India in 2004. In 2006, he was presented with National Law Day Award by Manmohan Singh, then prime minister of India, for his unique contribution in the field of administration of justice making it more friendly to the people at large. He has immense interest in legal aid services and alternate dispute resolution systems, holds keen interest in educational reforms, and propagates Indian cultural values and traditions.

Divyakant Lahoti graduated from University School of Law and Legal Studies, Guru Gobind Singh Indraprastha University, Delhi, India. He is an advocate, a dedicated and driven lawyer with an LLM in International Commercial Law from King's College, London. He has also secured a specialization in intellectual property rights from the University of South Africa and WIPO in 2011. He is a Member of Chartered Institute of Arbitrators and Young ICCA Advisory Member 'Buddy'. He has authored several articles which have been published in recognized legal journals.

Manish Lamba is a bachelor of law from the University of Delhi, India, and has more than 20 years of experience in the areas of corporate laws advisory, litigation, commercial matters, capital market, intellectual property, corporate restructuring, and compliances. He has worked for Coca-Cola and Bharti Group, where he worked for their telecom, infrastructure, and real estate retail sectors. He regularly speaks on arbitration, corporate restructuring, compliances, and legal reforms. He has been a part of the Legal Committee of Assocham, PHD Chambers of Commerce, The Federation of Indian Chambers of Commerce and Industry, and Gurgaon Chambers of Commerce.

Allison M. Malkin began her mediation career after completing her postgraduate studies in conflict and dispute resolution from Trinity College, Dublin, Ireland. She has contributed to research and writing in the commercial mediation sector and assisted in the development, and ongoing management, of a global non-profit mediation resource, Mediation World. More recently, her work has focused on project management, mediation, intercultural dialogue, and conflict transformation.

Tushar Mehta is the additional solicitor general of India and represents the government in several crucial cases. He holds several awards and accolades to his name. He was awarded Late Justice Shri N.G. Shelat Memorial Medal, Late Shri G.D. Shah Medal, and Late Shri D.D. Medh Medal by Gujarat University; and Shri Nani Palkhiwala Medal and Shri Dolat Trivedi Medal by Gujarat Law Society.

Atmaram N.S. Nadkarni was appointed advocate general on 29 November 1999 and was the youngest advocate general in India, appointed at the age of 36. Presently, he is practising before the Supreme Court of India and holds experience in constitutional law, service law, administration law, tax law, arbitrations, and criminal law. He is the lead counsel for state of Goa before a unique and rare ongoing interstate water dispute namely the Mahadayi water dispute tribunal, between states of Goa, Karnataka, and Maharashtra.

Arijit Pasayat retired as a Supreme Court judge after delivering more than 2,500 reported judgments which is a world record for all supreme courts in the world. He was awarded doctorate in law by Utkal University, Bhubaneswar, and LLD (Honoris Causa) by Fakir Mohan University, Balasore and Northern Orissa University, Baripada, India. He is the recipient of National Law Day Award, 2009, in recognition of his lifetime contribution to the 'Cause of Administration of Justice'. He is presently vice chairman of Special Investigation Team on black money.

Gagan Puri is the managing director of Navigant and a chartered accountant, and has an honors degree in commerce from the University of Delhi, India. He has over twenty years of work experience across twenty-nine countries on a range of forensic, dispute, risk consulting, and advisory matters. He is a prominent expert witness with multi-country experience in providing testimony on matters related to disputes, investigations, and general contractual matters. He has extensive experience on joint venture disputes, family disputes, protecting interests of minority shareholder, management disputes, significantly high value claims, contract disputes, evaluation and impact of corporate debt restructuring packages, and valuation reports, among others.

Radha Raghavan is an associate of Aarna Law, Bengaluru, India, focusing on commercial and investment treaty arbitration. She holds a bachelors of law degree from University Law College, Bengalore University, India, and a masters of law degree from the New York University School of Law, USA. She is admitted to practise law in India.

Deepto Roy is a corporate lawyer who specializes in projects, project finance, and banking. He has wide expertise in energy, power, renewable power, oil and gas, mining, and infrastructure, and represents project developers, construction contractors, banks, and financial institutions on project finance transactions. He also writes extensively on projects related to dispute resolution and infrastructure.

Vikramjit Sen graduated from St. Stephen's College with a degree history and pursued LLB from the Faculty of Law, both at the University of Delhi, India. He was appointed as an additional judge of the Delhi High Court in 1999 and a permanent judge of Delhi High Court in 2000. In 2011, he was anointed as the acting chief justice of High Court of Karnataka and assumed office as chief justice, High Court of Karnataka in December 2011. He took an oath as judge, Supreme Court of India, in 2012.

Deepankar Sanwalka leads the Advisory practice of PricewaterhouseCoopers Private Limited, India and is also a member of the India Leadership Team of PwC. He is a chartered accountant with three decades of experience as a professional. He specializes in the fields of forensic accounting, dispute resolution, and providing expert witness services to diverse clients. He is also currently a Member of the London Court of International Arbitration (LCIA) India Northern India Users' Council. He was a former president of the board of the India chapter of the Association of Certified Fraud Examiners, Texas, USA.

Geetu Singh works as a partner with forensic and dispute practice of PricewaterhouseCoopers Private Limited, India. She has over 17 years of work experience across practice areas of forensic services, disputes and litigations, and valuation and audit services. She is a chartered accountant and a member of the panel of arbitrators of the Institute of Chartered Accountants of India. She is a member of the London Court of International Arbitration, India, Western India Users' Council. She is also a member of the YSIAC Forum (Young Singapore International Arbitration Centre Forum).

Sonal Kr. Singh spearheads one of the dispute resolution teams at A.K. Singh & Co. New Delhi, India, and advises Indian and multinational clients on several issues pertaining to international arbitration and commercial disputes. He is also a qualified solicitor at England and Wales. He has been appointed on the Regional Committee of Young Arbitrator's Forum, International Chambers of Commerce (Asia), and also as the counsel for Government of National Capital Territory, Delhi High Court, India. He holds a bachelor's degree in law from the University of Delhi and a master's degree in commercial and corporate laws from King's College London, University of London, UK. He has to his credit a postgraduate diploma in cyber law also from the Indian Law Institute, New Delhi, India.

Rajiv Shakdher obtained a bachelor's degree in commerce from the University of Delhi and a degree in law from the Faculty of Law, the University of Delhi, India. He completed chartered accountancy from the Institute of Chartered Accountants of India, New Delhi, India, and pursued an advance course in law at the Institute of Advanced Legal Studies, University of London, UK. He was designated as a senior advocate in 2005 and appointed as an additional judge of the High Court of Delhi in 2008. Subsequently, he was appointed as a permanent judge in 2011. He was appointed as the judge of the High Court of Madras in 2016.

Tanima Tandon is a certified civil and commercial mediator with the ADR Group, London. In addition to her day job as the compliance and regulatory manager with General Electric Company, Gurugram, India, she has been a Consensual Dispute Resolution Competition (CDRC) Young Global Ambassador and part of the Peacekeeping and Conflict Resolution Team, Goa, India. She graduated from National Law University, Delhi, India, and enjoys promoting and spreading awareness of the increasing use of alternative dispute resolution tools as the primary dispute resolution mechanism for both civil and commercial disputes.

Parag P. Tripathi is a senior advocate since January 2000 and has been practising in India since 1983 in the Supreme Court, the High Court of Delhi, and other high courts, judicial tribunals and bodies, Customs, Excise And Service Tax Appellate Tribunal (CEGAT), National Company Law Tribunal (NCLT), National Company Appellate Law Tribunal (NCALT), and commercial arbitrations. He completed his graduation in economics from St. Stephen's College, University of Delhi, and graduated from Campus Law Centre, University of Delhi, India. He pursued his LLM from the prestigious Harvard Law School, Cambridge, USA. His areas of specialization include constitutional law, administrative law, commercial and corporate laws, including both in court litigation and private forum litigation like arbitrations, negotiations, and out of court settlements.

D. Gracious Timothy is an alumnus of the V.M. Salgaocar College of Law, Goa University, from where he graduated with a degree in law in 2015. He is a 2018 LLM candidate at the Straus Institute for Dispute Resolution, School of Law, Pepperdine University, USA, as a JAMS scholar. He is a qualified lawyer in India and has a primary interest in international commercial arbitration and litigation. He is the founding member of the Peacekeeping and Conflict Resolution Team, a group for the promotion of consensual dispute resolution in India.

Thomas P. Valenti is an attorney, mediator, arbitrator, facilitator, and trainer. He has been extensively trained in all aspects of dispute resolution. He is a former board member of Mediators Beyond Borders International, USA. His interest in understanding the issues raised with cross-cultural disputes is also enhanced by his work with the International Academy of Dispute Resolution, Chicago, USA which is a charitable organization set up to further the interest of mediation amongst law students globally. He has judged numerous International legal, negotiation, arbitration, and mediation competitions. He has travelled to the UK, Dubai, India, and Europe to train and teach courses in negotiation, mediation, and arbitration.